LIBRARY OF NEW TESTAMENT STUDIES

524

Formerly Journal of the Study of the New Testament Supplement Series

Editor
Chris Keith

Editorial Board
Dale C. Allison, John M.G. Barclay, Lynn H. Cohick, R. Alan Culpepper,
Craig A. Evans, Robert Fowler, Simon J. Gathercole, Juan Hernandez,
John S. Kloppenborg, Michael Labahn, Love L. Sechrest, Robert Wall,
Steve Walton, Catrin H. Williams

CHRIST REDEEMED 'US' FROM THE CURSE OF THE LAW

A Jewish Martyrological Reading of Galatians 3:13

Jarvis J. Williams

t&tclark
LONDON • NEW YORK • OXFORD • NEW DELHI • SYDNEY

T&T CLARK

Bloomsbury Publishing Plc

50 Bedford Square, London, WC1B 3DP, UK
1385 Broadway, New York, NY 10018, USA
29 Earlsfort Terrace, Dublin 2, Ireland

BLOOMSBURY, T&T CLARK and the T&T Clark logo are trademarks of Bloomsbury Publishing Plc

First published in Great Britain 2019
This paperback edition published in 2021

Copyright © Jarvis J. Williams, 2019

Jarvis J. Williams has asserted his right under the Copyright, Designs and Patents Act, 1988, to be identified as Author of this work.

All rights reserved. No part of this publication may be reproduced or transmitted in any form or by any means, electronic or mechanical, including photocopying, recording, or any information storage or retrieval system, without prior permission in writing from the publishers.

Bloomsbury Publishing Plc does not have any control over, or responsibility for, any third-party websites referred to or in this book. All internet addresses given in this book were correct at the time of going to press. The author and publisher regret any inconvenience caused if addresses have changed or sites have ceased to exist, but can accept no responsibility for any such changes.

A catalogue record for this book is available from the British Library.

A catalog record for this book is available from the Library of Congress.

ISBN: HB: 978-0-5676-5757-2
PB: 978-0-5677-0033-9
ePDF: 978-0-5676-5758-9
ePUB: 978-0-5676-5759-6

Series: Library of New Testament Studies, volume 524

Typeset by Forthcoming Publications (www.forthpub.com)

To find out more about our authors and books visit www.bloomsbury.com and sign up for our newsletters.

For my Grand Daddy (deceased since 1989)

Contents

Acknowledgments	ix
Abbreviations	xi

Chapter 1
INTRODUCTION AND THESIS — 1
  I. Method — 4
  II. Contribution — 4
  III. History of Research — 5
  IV. Chapter Summaries — 48

Chapter 2
DEUTERONOMIC BLESSINGS AND CURSES IN SECOND TEMPLE JEWISH MARTYROLOGICAL TRADITIONS — 52
  I. Blessing, Curse, and the Promises to Abraham — 53
  II. Deuteronomic Blessings and Curses in Second Temple Jewish Martyrological Traditions — 57
  III. Deuteronomic Blessing and Curse through Martyrdom, Military Action, and Effective Prayer — 70
  IV. Conclusion of Deuteronomic Blessings and Curses in 2 Maccabees — 82
  V. Deuteronomic Blessings and Curses in 4 Maccabees — 84
  VI. Summary of Deuteronomic Blessings and Curses in 4 Maccabees — 95
  VII. Conclusion — 96

Chapter 3
DEUTERONOMIC BLESSINGS AND CURSES IN GALATIANS — 97
  I. Deuteronomic Curse and Abrahamic Blessing in Galatians — 98
  II. Conclusion — 130

Chapter 4
REPRESENTATION AND SUBSTITUTION IN SECOND TEMPLE JEWISH MARTYROLOGICAL TRADITIONS AND IN GALATIANS 3:13 — 133
  I. A Definition of Jewish Martyrology — 133
  II. Representation and Substitution in LXX Daniel 3:24–90 — 134

III. Martyrdom and Reconciliation in 2 and 4 Maccabees	138
IV. Jewish Martyrdom, God's Mercy, Satisfaction, and Purification in 4 Maccabees	147
V. Deuteronomy, Jewish Martyrology, Representation, Substitution, and Galatians 3:13	156
VI. Summary	167
VII. Conclusion	168

Chapter 5
LEXICAL, GRAMMATICAL, AND ADDITIONAL CONCEPTUAL SIMILARITIES BETWEEN SECOND TEMPLE JEWISH MARTYROLOGICAL TRADITIONS AND GALATIANS — 169
   I. Lexical and Grammatical Similarities Between the Martyrological Traditions and Galatians — 170
   II. Polemical Similarities Between the Jewish Martyrological Traditions and Galatians — 182
   III. Additional Theological and Conceptual Similarities Between the Jewish Martyrological Traditions and Galatians — 184
   IV. Conclusion — 185

Chapter 6
CONCLUSION:
A JEWISH MARTYROLOGICAL READING OF GALATIANS 3:13 — 186
   I. Deuteronomic Blessings and Curses in Second Temple Jewish Martyrological Traditions — 186
   II. Deuteronomic Blessings and Curses in Galatians — 188
   III. Representation and Substitution in Second Temple Jewish Martyrological Traditions and in Galatians 3:13 — 190
   IV. Lexical, Grammatical, and Additional Conceptual Similarities Between Second Temple Jewish Martyrological Traditions and Galatians — 191
   V. The Contribution of a Jewish Martyrological Background Behind the Death of the Cursed Christ in Galatians 3:13 — 192

Bibliography — 194
Index of References — 203
Index of Authors — 219

Acknowledgments

I wish to express many thanks and appreciation to the many people who helped me complete this monograph. First, I thank my wife of 17 years, Ana, and my son of 10 years, Jaden. They provided much love, support, laughter, prayers, and fun the past five years as I worked on this monograph. Second, I thank the board of trustees at the Southern Baptist Theological Seminary for granting me a sabbatical leave during the spring 2017 academic semester to focus on this monograph. The majority of the secondary research was completed during this sabbatical leave. Third, I thank my colleague and *Doctorvater*, Tom Schreiner, for reading the entire manuscript and making very helpful criticisms and suggestions to help make the argument better. Fourth, I thank my PhD student and assistant, Trey Moss, for his help with formatting the manuscript. Fifth, I thank the many colleagues at the Society of Biblical Literature who commented on and gave me feedback about papers I presented, related to the monograph, in the Pauline Epistles group, in the Cult and Atonement group, and in the Function of the Apocrypha and Pseudepigrapha on Early Christianity group from 2012–14. Sixth, I thank the circulation workers at the James P. Boyce Centennial Library for their very helpful assistance and patience as I was not always quick to return overdue books. Seventh, I thank the many classrooms, students, and churches where I've taught Galatians the past 6 years. Eighth (and certainly not least), I owe many, many thanks to LNTS, to Mark Goodacre (the former editor), and to the current editor Chris Keith for accepting and supporting this project. I especially thank Chris for being a gracious, kind, and precise editor and for his encouragement throughout the writing process. Ninth, I express many thanks to Brill Academic, Wipf & Stock/Pickwick, and the Society of Biblical Literature Press for granting me permission to reprint material in this monograph from publications with them.

Finally, I thank Worthy Williams, my grandfather (deceased since 1989), for taking me in and helping raise me so many years ago when I was a child. He is the only man I have ever called "Daddy." I still remember the deep grief I felt as a young 6th grader when the phone rang on that early weekday morning and my aunt told me that Daddy lost his battle with cancer. If he were alive today, he certainly would not read this book! But he would be proud of me in his own way. In loving memory, I dedicate this book to my Grand Daddy.

Abbreviations

AB	Anchor Bible
BECNT	Baker Exegetical Commentary on the New Testament
BN	*Biblische Notizen*
BZNW	Beihefte zur Zeitschrift für die neutestamentliche Wissenschaft und die Kunde der älteren Kirche
BNTC	Blackwell New Testament Commentaries
CBQ	*Catholic Biblical Quarterly*
CBQMS	Catholic Biblical Quarterly Monograph Series
CBR	*Currents in Biblical Research*
CEJL	Commentaries on Early Jewish Literature
CP	*Classical Philology*
CRINT	Compendia rerum Iudaicarum ad Novum Testamentum
EFN	Estudios de filología Neotestamentaria
ESEC	Emory Studies in Early Christianity
FRLANT	Forschungen zur Religion und Literatur des Alten und Neuen Testaments
HA	Handbuch der Altertumswissenschaft
JBL	*Journal of Biblical Literature*
JSHRZ	Jüdische Schriften aus hellenistisch-römischer Zeit
JSJ	*Journal for the Study of Judaism in the Persian, Hellenistic, and Roman Periods*
JSJSup	Supplements to the Journal for the Study of Judaism
JSNT	*Journal for the Study of the New Testament*
JSNTSup	Journal for the Study New Testament Supplement
JSOTSup	Journal for the Study of the Old Testament Supplement
JTS	*Journal of Theological Studies*
LA	*Liber Annus*
LNTS	Library of New Testament Studies
MBT	Münsterische Beiträge zur Theologie
MNTC	Moffat New Testament Commentary Series
NCCS	New Covenant Commentary Series
NICNT	New International Commentary on the New Testament
NIGTC	The New International Greek Testament Commentary
NIB	New Interpreters Bible
NTL	New Testament Library
NTM	New Testament Monographs
NTS	*New Testament Studies*

PW	*Paulys Real-Encyclopädie der classischen Altertumswissenschaft*
RAC	Reallexikon für Antike und Christentum
SANT	Studien zum Alten und Neuen Testament
SBLDS	Society of Biblical Literature Dissertation Series
SBLSP	Society of Biblical Literature Seminar Papers
SCA	Studies in Christian Antiquity
SCI	*Scripta Classica Israelica*
SCS	Septuagint Commentary Series
SNTSMS	Society of New Testament Studies Monograph Series
STDJ	Studies on the Texts of the Desert of Judah
TSAJ	Texte und Studien zum antiken Judentum
USFSHJ	University of South Florida Studies in the History of Judaism
WBC	Word Biblical Commentary
WMANT	Wissenschaftliche Monographien zum Alten und Neuen Testament
WUNT	Wissenschaftliche Untersuchungen zum Neuen Testament
WUNT 2	Wissenschaftliche Untersuchungen zum Neuen Testament 2 Reihe

1

INTRODUCTION AND THESIS

Galatians 3:10–14 is vexing to many NT scholars because of its many scriptural, exegetical, grammatical, and theological complexities.[1] This monograph is narrow in its scope. It engages in a comparative analysis of Jewish martyrological texts with the intent of answering the question whether the martyrological ideas in those texts are an illuminating background in front of which to understand Paul's remarks about the "cursed Christ" in Gal 3:13.[2]

My thesis is twofold. First, Jewish martyrological ideas,[3] codified in 2 and 4 Maccabees and in selected texts in LXX Dan 3, provide *a* background in front of which to understand Paul's statements about the cursed Christ in Gal 3:13 and the soteriological benefits his death achieves for Jews and Gentiles in Galatians. Second, Paul modifies Jewish martyrological ideas to fit his exegetical, polemical, theological, and conceptual purposes in Galatians in order to persuade the Galatians not to embrace the "other" gospel.

To support my thesis, I provide five arguments throughout the monograph. First, Galatians has scriptural points of contact with Jewish

1. See, for example, N. T. Wright's comments in the early 1990s in *The Climax of the Covenant: Christ and the Law in Pauline Theology*, 1st paperback ed. (Minneapolis: Fortress, 1993), 137; N. H. Young, "Who's Cursed—and Why? (Galatians 3.10–14)," *JBL* 117 (1998): 79–92; Richard B. Hays, "Galatians," *NIB* 12:257.

2. The phrase the "cursed Christ" is conceptually taken from Gal 3:13, but it is also from Bradley H. McLean, *The Cursed Christ: Mediterranean Expulsion Rituals and Pauline Soteriology*, JNTSup 126 (Sheffield: Sheffield Academic, 1996). When the reader sees the phrase "cursed Christ" throughout this monograph, she or he should keep in mind I borrow this phrase from Paul and McLean's monograph. I disagree with McLean about the specifics of the "cursed Christ" in Gal 3:13.

3. Throughout this monograph, I use the words "Jewish martyrological texts," "martyrological narratives," "martyr theology," "Jewish martyrological traditions," or "Jewish martyrological ideas" to refer to the traditions about the deaths of Torah-observant Jews for the benefit of Israel.

martyrological ideas. Second, Galatians has theological and conceptual points of contact with Jewish martyrological ideas. Third, Galatians has lexical and grammatical points of contact with Jewish martyrological ideas. Fourth, Galatians has polemical points of contact with Jewish martyrological ideas. Fifth, Galatians has discontinuities with Jewish martyrological ideas.

This monograph contends the authors of 2 and 4 Maccabees and selected texts in LXX Dan 3 suggest the Jewish martyrs died for the soteriological benefits of fellow Jews out of loyalty to the law (2 Maccabees), for the sake of virtue (4 Maccabees), and for the sins of the people to provide salvation (2 and 4 Maccabees and LXX Dan 3).[4] The analysis of 2 and 4 Maccabees and LXX Dan 3 argues the martyrs' deaths function within the narratives to support the superiority of Judaism over Hellenism as the authors seek to persuade their respective audiences to resist Hellenism and to remain faithful to Torah. Paul offers a different polemical and soteriological argument in Galatians than the authors of these Jewish martyrological traditions, as he seeks to persuade the Galatians to avoid turning toward Judaism and away from his non-Torah-observant, Gentile-inclusive gospel, which delivers them from the curse of the law, and to discourage them from embracing his opponents' Torah-observant, Gentile-exclusive gospel, which places them under the curse of the law (Gal 3:10–14). Death for Israel because of loyalty to the law or virtue to achieve their soteriological benefit is a reason for which the martyrs die in the narratives and the pathway on which the Jewish nation and the martyrs experience life in the current age, experience honor in the present age, and participate in life in the age to come. In Gal 3:13, the death of the one cursed Christ for "us" delivers Jews and Gentiles from Torah's curse, distributes the Spirit to Jews and Gentiles, and grants them life in this age and in the age to come.

Explicit or implicit references to the cross frame Galatians (1:4; 6:17). Paul's remarks in Gal 3:13 are arguably the most explosive reference to the cross in the letter: "Christ delivered us from the curse of the law by becoming a curse for us, as it has been written: 'Cursed is everyone who is hanged upon a tree'." He further asserts Christ died to "deliver us from the present evil age" (1:4); he "was crucified with Christ" (2:19); Christ "gave himself for me" (2:20); Christ did not die "in vain" (2:21), proclaims Christ "as having been publicly betrayed to have been crucified" (3:1), affirms he stopped preaching circumcision so that the "stumbling block

---

4. Numerous scholars have recognized these concepts in 2 and 4 Maccabees and LXX Dan 3.

of the cross" would not be severed (5:11), proclaims Jews and Gentiles in Christ "have crucified the flesh with its passions and lusts" (5:25), boasts in the "cross of our Lord Jesus Christ" (6:14), and boldly declares he "bears in his body the marks of Jesus Christ" (6:17). The latter is a reference to the crucifixion.

In 3:13, Paul contrasts his remarks about the curse of the law and the blessing of faith in 3:10–12 with the climactic statement about the cursed Christ's death on a cross: "Christ redeemed us from the curse of the law by becoming a curse for us, as it has been written: 'Cursed is everyone who is hanged upon a tree'." He states in 1:4 that Christ's death on the cross turned the ages by delivering "us" from the "present evil age." In 3:13–14, he says the Christ's death delivers "us" from the law's curse by becoming a curse for "us," so that he would distribute to Jews and Gentiles the blessing of the Spirit (3:14).[5] The significant point here is deliverance from the present evil age and participation in the blessing of Abraham in the age to come become realized in Galatians not by law-observance, but by means of the death of the cursed Christ.

In the following chapters, I argue for *a* Jewish martyrological background behind Gal 3:13. Jewish martyrological narratives connect soteriological blessing to the death of the martyrs who die for non-Torah-observant Jews to deliver them from the curse of the law and to distribute to them the blessing of life to lead to the realization of the Abrahamic blessing (cf. 2 Macc 7:30–38; 4 Macc 6:28–29; 17:21–22).[6] Paul connects the Abrahamic blessing of life promised in Torah to the cursed Christ apart from works of the law and extends the blessing to Jews and Gentiles (cf. Gal 3:1–14).

---

5. I argue for this reading in the exegesis of Gal 3:13–14.

6. For my analysis of 2 and 4 Maccabees on this specific point, see Chapter 2. This monograph does *not* argue Jewish martyrology is *the* background behind understanding Paul's remarks about Jesus's death in Gal 3:13, but *a* background in front of which to read Paul's remarks in Gal 3:13. Matthew J. Harmon (*She Must and Shall Go Free: Paul's Isaianic Gospel in Galatians*, BZNW 168 [Berlin: de Gruyter, 2010]) has recently made a compelling case that Isaiah is an important background for Paul in Galatians. I argue Jewish martyrological traditions provide *a* background behind Paul's remarks in Gal 3:13 by a comparative analysis of these traditions with Galatians. I argue this comparison illuminates Paul's remarks in Gal 3:13 by providing a Jewish background against which to understand the significance of his argument in Gal 3:10–14 and his specific comments about the cursed Christ in 3:13. This monograph neither argues Paul actually read or had the texts of 2 and 4 Maccabees and LXX Dan 3 in front of him as he composed Galatians nor that he had access to the texts that record the martyrological narratives.

I. Method

I argue the thesis by a grammatical-historical exegesis of the relevant Jewish martyrological texts and texts in Galatians. My exegesis of these texts provides the basis of my comparative analysis of the relevant Jewish martyrological texts and texts in Galatians.[7] The analysis of these texts seeks to illuminate Gal 3:13 in particular and the argument of Gal 3:10–14 in general by reading Paul's remarks about the cursed Christ in Gal 3:13 in front of Jewish martyrological ideas. This method helps highlight the potential Jewish martyrological background behind Gal 3:13 and the continuities and the discontinuities between the martyrological ideas in the martyrological texts and in Galatians to shine a ray of light onto his argument to the Galatians about the significance of the death of the "cursed Christ" for them.

II. Contribution

To my knowledge, no book-length monograph in English-speaking scholarship has been written to compare and contrast Jewish martyrological traditions with Gal 3:13 with the intent of arguing they provide *a* background in front of which to understand Paul's remarks about the cursed Christ in Gal 3:13. This monograph endeavors to argue Jewish martyrological traditions are *a* background behind Gal 3:13, but they are not saying exactly the same thing about the martyrs' deaths for Israel (Jewish martyrological traditions) and Christ's "redemption of us from the curse of the law by becoming a curse for us" (Gal 3:13). This monograph additionally seeks to contribute to the representation versus substitution debate.[8] Finally, the monograph provides a history of research of selected scholarship of Gal 3:13 relevant to my thesis.

---

7. Specifically regarding method, in his monograph on the Isaianic background behind Paul's gospel in Galatians, Harmon offers a helpful methodological guide for detecting an Isaianic background behind Paul's gospel in Galatians. Harmon and I focus on two different potential backgrounds behind Paul, and my focus is narrower than Harmon's in that I focus specifically on Gal 3:13, whereas he focuses on the entire letter of Galatians. I came up with my methodological categories independently of reading Harmon's work. For Harmon's methodological criteria, see his *She Must and Shall Go Free*, 26–43.

8. For a recent discussion of Jesus's death in NT scholarship, see David A. Brondos, *Jesus' Death in New Testament Thought*, 2 vols. (Mexico City: Comunidad Teológica de México, 2018).

III. History of Research[9]

Scholars have commented on the background behind Paul's remarks in Gal 3:13 in chapters on atonement in Paul, in commentaries, in monographs, in essays, or in articles.[10] However, to my knowledge, no scholar has devoted an entire monograph in English-speaking scholarship to a comparative analysis of Jewish martyrology and Gal 3:13 with the intent of arguing the thesis I set forth here. Many scholars have assumed or argued in commentaries, monographs, articles, and essays that Paul's background behind his remarks in Gal 3:13 was the "Jewish Scriptures,"[11] "ancient, pagan expulsion rituals,"[12] a "commercial background,"[13] or (in addition to other views) a "fixed pre-Christian confessional formula" inherited by Paul.[14] These interpreters point out Paul asserts Jesus was

---

9. For a history of interpretation of Galatians, see John Riches, *Galatians, Through the Centuries* (Oxford: Blackwell, 2013).

10. For two examples, see the monographs by Basil S. Davis, *Christ as Devotio: The Argument of Gal 3:1–14* (Lanham, MD: University Press of America, 2002); Stephen Finlan, *The Background and Content behind Paul's Cultic Atonement Metaphors*, Academia Biblica 19 (Atlanta: SBL, 2004).

11. For those who assume an OT background, see John Chrysostom, *Hom. Gal.* 13.27; Augustine's *Commentary on Galatians: Introduction, Texts, Translation, and Notes*, trans. Eric Plumer, Oxford Early Christian Studies 5 (Oxford: Oxford University Press, 2003), 161; J. B. Lightfoot, *The Epistle of St. Paul to the Galatians*, 2nd ed. (London: Macmillan, 1865; repr., Grand Rapids: Zondervan, 1957), 139–40. Riches, *Galatians*, pointed me to the preceding primary sources. For additional scholars assuming an OT background, see also F. F. Bruce, *The Epistle to the Galatians*, NIGTC (Grand Rapids: Eerdmans, 1982), 163–7; Ronald Y. K. Fung, *The Epistle to the Galatians* (Grand Rapids: Eerdmans, 1988), 147–50; Andrew H. Wakefield, *Where to Live: The Hermeneutical Significance of Paul's Citations from Scripture in Galatians 3:1–14*, Academia Biblica 14 (Atlanta: SBL, 2003). For an argument for an OT background, see Kjell Arne Morland, *The Rhetoric of Curse in Galatians*, ESEC 5 (Atlanta: Scholars Press, 1995), 218–24. In a 1986 article, Terrence L. Donaldson argues interpreters should read Gal 3:13–14 against Jewish texts that discuss the eschatological inclusion of the Gentiles. Donaldson, "The 'Curse of the Law' and the Inclusion of the Gentiles: Galatians 3.13–14," *NTS* 32 (1986): 94–112, esp. 99–100, 105–6.

12. Bradley H. McLean, "Christ as Pharmakos in Pauline Soteriology," *SBLSP* (1991): 187–206; idem, "The Absence of Atoning Sacrifice in Paul's Soteriology," *NTS* 38 (1992): 531–53; idem, *The Cursed Christ*.

13. Ben Witherington III, *Grace in Galatia: A Commentary on Paul's Letter to the Galatians* (Grand Rapids: Eerdmans, 1998), 238–9.

14. See discussions in Richard N. Longenecker, *Galatians*, WBC 41 (Nashville: Thomas Nelson, 1990), 122; J. Louis Martyn, *Galatians*, AB 33A (New York:

under the curse of the law, that he delivered those under the curse of the law from the curse "by becoming a curse" for them (Gal 3:13), and that Paul applies Deut 27:26; 28:58; 30:10; Hab 2:4; Lev 18:5 to Jesus in Gal 3:10–14.[15] Other scholars have argued later Jewish traditions, such as the *Akedah*[16] or the Targums,[17] are the background behind Paul's remarks in Gal 3:13. In the history of research below, I discuss some of the major views and selected scholars regarding the potential background behind Paul's remarks in Gal 3:13 about the cursed Christ. The goal of the history of research is to highlight my contribution by summarizing the most important scholarship on Paul's potential background behind his remarks about the cursed Christ in Gal 3:13.

a. Greco-Roman Background Behind Galatians 3:13

1. Noble Death. David Seeley argues the Greco-Roman concept of noble death is the backdrop against which Paul's soteriology should be viewed. Seeley's discussion suggests noble death is the background behind Gal 3:13. Seeley investigates the "temple cult,"[18] the use of "Suffering Servant language,"[19] "the *Akedah*," "the mystery religions,"[20]

Doubleday, 1997), 273. For a discussion of different views, see A. Andrew Das, *Galatians*, Concordia Commentary: A Theological Exposition of Sacred Scripture (St. Louis: Concordia, 2014), 310–36.

15. I discuss additional views in the history of research below.

16. Nils Dahl, "The Atonement—an Adequate Reward for the Akedah? (Rom. 8.32)," in *Neotestamentica et Semitica: Studies in Honour of Matthew Black*, ed. E. Earle Ellis and Max Wilcox (Edinburgh: T. & T. Clark, 1969), 15–29. See also Robert Daly, *Christian Sacrifice*, SCA 18 (Washington, DC: The Catholic University of America Press, 1978); idem, "Soteriological Significance of the Sacrifice of Isaac," *CBQ* 39 (1977): 72. For additional scholarship on the Aqedah in twentieth-century Pauline interpretation, see sources cited in A. Andrew Das, *Paul and the Stories of Israel: Grand Thematic Narratives in Galatians* (Minneapolis: Fortress, 2016), 95–124.

17. Anthony Tyrrell Hanson, *Studies in Paul's Technique and Theology* (Grand Rapids: Eerdmans, 1974), 6; Max Wilcox, "'Upon the Tree'—Deut 21.22–23 in the New Testament," *JBL* 96 (1977): 85–99; R. B. Hamerton-Kelly, "Sacred Violence and the Curse of the Law (Galatians 3.13): The Death of Christ as Sacrificial Travesty," *NTS* 36 (1990): 98–118.

18. David Seeley, *The Noble Death: Graeco-Roman Martyrology and Paul's Conception of Salvation*, JSNTSup 28 (Sheffield: Sheffield Academic, 1990), 19–37, 64–5, 104–5.

19. Ibid., 39–57.

20. Ibid., 67–82.

and "4 Maccabees."²¹ He concludes 4 Maccabees provides Paul with the most important background for his understanding of Jesus's death. With respect to Jesus's death, Seeley states the Jewish martyrs and Paul have the following conceptual commonalities: "obedience, the act of enduring physical vulnerability, a military setting, vicariousness, sacrifice, and the Greco-Roman contest."²²

When discussing 2 Maccabees, Seeley argues the martyrs' deaths are vicarious in a "mimetic" or "imitative" sense and not in an "expiatory" sense.²³ He further argues the concepts of "obedience, a military context, and the overcoming of physical vulnerability" are quite strong in 2 Maccabees.²⁴ Seeley says 4 Maccabees presents the martyrs as atoning sacrifices,²⁵ but this concept (in his view) is not an important feature of the book.²⁶ Rather, he says "The more fundamental, historically conceivable (if not historically accurate) mode of expressing vicariousness is once again the mimetic process."²⁷ Seeley only spends a couple of pages discussing Gal 3:13.²⁸

2. Mediterranean Expulsion Ritual. Bradley H. McLean's work on Jesus's death focused on both the background of Jesus's death in Galatians and on the concept of atoning sacrifice.²⁹ His major contribution to the conversation was his 1996 monograph *The Cursed Christ*. This monograph focuses on "Mediterranean expulsion rituals and Pauline Soteriology."³⁰ Here McLean investigates both the meaning and background behind Gal 3:13. McLean's method compares Paul's soteriology "with the concepts implicit in Mediterranean apotropaeic rituals, that is, rituals used in averting evil, curses, and defilement, the best known example being the Levitical scapegoat ritual."³¹

McLean analyzes both ancient Greek and Jewish texts and compares them with Paul's discussion of the cursed Christ in Galatians "to document, to the extent possible, both continuity and change in the practice

21. Ibid., 83–112.
22. Ibid., 13–41.
23. Ibid., 83, 87–91.
24. Ibid.
25. Ibid.
26. Ibid.
27. Ibid., 92.
28. Ibid., 64–5, 104–5.
29. McLean, *The Cursed Christ*.
30. Ibid.
31. Ibid., 18.

and theory of sacrifice in the time of Paul."[32] McLean's analysis of these texts leads him to conclude that the "Jewish thank offering" is not comparable with Jesus's death in Galatians.[33] He claims the priests in the Jewish community sacrificed animals to God, and they presented these sacrifices to him as part of their cultic act of worship.[34] Furthermore, McLean asserts the priests focused their sacrificial ritual on the act of purification.[35] McLean does not think the concept of atoning sacrifice is present in the uncontested Pauline letters.[36] Based on his reading of ancient Greek and Jewish texts, McLean states, "Finally, nothing is more clearly stated, nor more strongly insisted upon in Gal 3:13 than the fact of Christ's cursedness…"[37] McLean declares Paul identifies Jesus as a curse (Gal 3:13), but the Jewish sources nowhere identify the "purification-offering" as a curse or as a "substitutionary victim."[38] He claims, "there is no text in the Jewish tradition which contains teaching that a righteous man can vicariously atone for the sin of others by becoming accursed and sinful."[39] McLean's analysis of sacrifice in comparison to the "cursed Christ" in Galatians leads him to conclude that Jesus's death was not an atoning sacrifice.[40]

According to McLean, the goat in the Levitical cult functions as an "apotropaeic ritual."[41] Especially important for the "apotropaeic ritual" was the "transference of the curse" from the community by means of the "substitutionary victims" and the victims' "permanent expulsion."[42] McLean argues that in the Greco-Roman world, there are examples of "apotropaeic rituals with humans as victims."[43] He states Athenians named the victim a "*pharmakos*,"[44] others as a "magic man,"[45] while claiming "*pharmakon* means drug or medicine."[46] Thus, McLean

32. Ibid., 27.
33. Ibid., 27–63.
34. Ibid., 27.
35. Ibid., 52–64.
36. Ibid., 41–50.
37. Ibid., 51.
38. Ibid.
39. Ibid.
40. Ibid., 13–145.
41. Ibid., 65–81.
42. Ibid., 87–104, esp. 87.
43. Ibid., 88–104.
44. Ibid.
45. Ibid., 88.
46. Ibid.

claims "*pharmakos*" has "associations with disease, medical cures, and probably has the meaning one who heals people."[47] He also points out the *pharmakos* ritual was not practiced in a monolithic way in the Mediterranean world,[48] and argues both humans and animals were involved in the ritual practice.[49]

McLean argues Paul's explanation of the cursed Christ is connected to the issue of the relationship between sin, Torah, and faith in Christ,[50] because his reference to the "cursed Christ" in Gal 3:13 appears with his emphatic appeal to the Galatians not to subject themselves to Torah.[51] McLean contends one should understand Paul's "under a curse" language to mean that violators of Torah bring upon themselves the curse of death because they are under the curse's power.[52] McLean supports his understanding by pointing out that Paul describes sin in Galatians as a "physical power" that is both attached to human flesh and subjects humans to slavery.[53] According to McLean, sin in Paul should not be understood "merely" as transgressions, but as an "infectious and dangerous" power.[54] Consequently, McLean affirms Paul's terminology of "under a curse" in Gal 3:10 is parallel with "under sin" in Gal 3:22.[55] McLean infers that if Christians could perfectly obey Torah, they would continue to be under the curse of the law since the law belongs to the old age and leads to a curse.[56]

After criticizing "traditional anthropocentric" critiques of the law, McLean offers (what he thinks are) better ways to understand the problem of the law in relation to the death of Christ in Galatians.[57] First, he says, contrary to traditional "anthropocentric" readings of the law, Paul nowhere explicitly states or implies in Galatians the law was given to save Israel (cf. Gal 2:21; 3:21).[58] Instead, McLean claims the law was given because of sin (Gal 3:19), to imprison the world "under sin" (3:22), "in order to

---

47. Ibid.
48. Ibid., 91–104.
49. Ibid.
50. Ibid., 113.
51. Ibid.
52. Ibid., 123.
53. Ibid.
54. Ibid.
55. Ibid.
56. Ibid.
57. Ibid., 113–14.
58. Ibid., 114.

prepare the world to receive Christ's eschatological kingdom."[59] Second, McLean states readings that start with "anthropocentric" critiques of the law or with a human's incapacity to obey perfectly the whole law disagree with Paul's self-perception in texts in which he clearly states he was "blameless" as he lived "under the law" (cf. Phil 3:6).[60] Third, McLean says "anthropocentric" critiques of the law in Paul wrongly begin their analysis of the law in Paul with the intent of highlighting the so-called problem under the law and the so-called provision in Christ.[61] McLean thinks Albert Schweitzer's comments are more helpful.

McLean states Schweitzer argued that Paul's problem with the law was that God in Christ constituted a "new creation in which Torah was no longer valid."[62] McLean declares Paul believed the law was for sinful humans,[63] but in Christ the law becomes "incompatible with the new age created for a redeemed humanity."[64] McLean says Galatians assumes the "antithesis between Christ's *new* creation and the *old* and unredeemed creation of the flesh, sin, and death."[65] According to McLean, "The new creation is the domain of God's Spirit, blessing, faith, and freedom (Gal 2:16; 3:1–5; 5:1–6)," whereas works of law and lawlessness are part of the old age (Gal 5:6; 6:14).[66] McLean continues, "in Galatians Paul employs the term 'law' to designate a reality much broader than simply 'Jewish law' (torah). Law has become a comprehensive symbol for the way of the old world, whether Jewish or non-Jewish."[67] To support the preceding statement, McLean cites Paul's remarks that Jews and Gentiles are under "the elemental cosmic powers (cf. Gal 3:19–25; 4:1–3, 8–10)."[68]

McLean claims in Galatians, the Torah is an agent "of the powers of the old age, the powers of the flesh, sin, and death," and the entire letter emphasizes the "ramifications" of the invasion of the "new age into the old age."[69] When God raised Christ from the dead, he "inaugurated

---

59. Ibid., 114–15.
60. Ibid., 115.
61. Ibid.
62. Ibid., 116–17. Cf. Albert Schweitzer, *The Mysticism of Paul the Apostle* (New York: Seabury, 1931), 192.
63. McLean, *The Cursed Christ*, 116–17.
64. Ibid.
65. Ibid., 117.
66. Ibid.
67. Ibid., 118.
68. Ibid.
69. Ibid.

a new creation in juxtaposition" to the old age.[70] Before God grants one acceptance into the new age, one must renounce "all previous associations" with the old age, associations which include the "renunciation of the Jewish law (Gal 5:1; cf. 1:3–4, 11–17; 4.8–11; 6:14–15)."[71] Therefore, McLean concludes Paul "does not argue that Christians *are not obliged* to follow the law, but rather that they *must not* follow the law."[72] In McLean's view, Paul asserts God must deliver Christians from the old age so that they will experience life in the new age.[73]

McLean says Christians who seek to obey the law continue to pursue allegiance to the "old creation,"[74] and they are "under a curse (Gal 3:10)."[75] However, says McLean, "as a remedy God transferred the curse from humanity" to Christ, who functioned as a "substitutionary victim,"[76] to provide the solution to humanity's predicament of being under the curse.[77] That is, according to McLean, Gal 3:13 suggests Christ voluntarily died as a "payment for" and "in exchange for" Christians enslaved to Torah.[78] McLean identifies Christ's death in Gal 3:13 as a "commercial metaphor."[79] He states Christ's "commercial exchange" is Paul's way of articulating to the Galatians the way in which Christ's death delivers Christians from the curse of the law.[80]

For McLean, the starting place in Gal 3:13 for Christ as substitute is Paul's remarks that Jesus redeemed Christians from the law's curse by "becoming a curse for us."[81] McLean asserts Paul's comments here are his application of Deut 21:23 to the "cursed Christ."[82] With this application of Deut 21:23, McLean says Paul's "grammatical features" of "curse" and "cursed" is his "emphatic way of saying Christ became the object of a curse."[83] Or, as McLean says, relying upon Marie-Joseph

---

70. Ibid., 119.
71. Ibid.
72. Ibid., emphasis in original.
73. Ibid.
74. Ibid.
75. Ibid.
76. Ibid., 123–4, esp. 124.
77. Ibid., 131.
78. Ibid.
79. Ibid.
80. Ibid.
81. Ibid., 124.
82. Ibid.
83. Ibid.

Lagrange, "Christ became a curse personified."[84] McLean continues this curse of the "cursed Christ" is the "same curse" believers carried "before their baptism" and the "same curse" carried both by those preaching another gospel in Galatia and by those who were in danger of accepting their gospel.[85] McLean states that similar to many biblical texts, the Galatian curse is "accompanied by social rejection and divine excommunication (cf. Gen 3:16–19, 23–24; 4:14; Deut 29:18, 25, 27–28; Jer 17:5–6)."[86]

"Likewise," asserts McLean, "the state of cursedness resulting from observance of the law implies expulsion from the Christian community (cf. Gal 1:8; 1 Cor 16:22; 2 Cor 5:4–5) and from Christ's new creation characterized by the reception of God's blessing and Spirit (Gal 3:14; cf. Rom 9:3)."[87] According to McLean, the community's experience of the curse and expulsion "is the same expulsion" that the "cursed Christ" suffered when he bore the curse.[88] McLean says, in Paul's view, the only hope to bridge the chasm "between Christ and the now redeemed Christians" was for Christ to become a curse and "to remove the danger" of the curse by means of his execution, which consequently transferred the curse to Christ and removed it away from the "now redeemed Christians."[89]

McLean does not argue for a genealogical connection between "apotropaeic rituals" and Gal 3:13.[90] Instead, he argues Paul shares a "common paradigm" with these rituals.[91] Therefore, McLean concludes Paul's conception of atonement in Gal 3:13 can be understood in front of the expulsion ritual context that stands behind the letter.[92]

3. *Devotio*. In his 2002 monograph *Christ as Devotio: The Argument of Galatians 3:1–14*, Basil S. Davis argues Paul presents Jesus as a *devotio*

---

84. Ibid., 125. For original citation, see Marie-Joseph Lagrange, *St. Paul, Epître aux Galates*, 2nd ed. (Paris: Librairie Lecoffre, 1925), 172.
85. McLean, *The Cursed Christ*, 125.
86. Ibid., 125 and n. 62.
87. Ibid., 125.
88. Ibid.
89. Ibid.
90. Ibid.
91. Ibid. 13–19.
92. Ibid., 19. For an essay that focuses on the pagan background behind Jesus's death in the NT, see Henk S. Versnel, "Making Sense of Jesus's Death: The Pagan Contribution," in *Deutungen des Todes Jesu im Neuen Testament*, ed. Jörg Frey and Jens Schröter, WUNT 181 (Tübingen: Mohr Siebeck, 2005), 227–53.

sacrifice in Gal 3:13.[93] In his chapter on redemption from the curse of the law (Chapter 5), Davis's thesis is "Paul is describing (a) the Law as a binding force acting in a manner analogous to the curses inscribed on the *defixiones* (curse tablets), and (b) the redeeming act of Jesus's death in terms of the voluntary sacrifice of the *devotio*."[94] Davis uses the term *devotio* in the monograph "as a general term for the redeeming fine to be paid to the deity for the purpose of releasing the thief from the curse."[95] Davis's analysis of numerous ancient texts, curse tablets, and inscriptions claims that in the Greco-Roman world, there were different types of *devotio* sacrifices.[96] One type died in order to save the people from destruction.[97] The *devotio* background, says Davis, "incorporates both the curse and Jesus's redeeming action."[98] He continues the *devotio* has the "merit of being fully consistent with the vocabulary of Gal 3:1–14 as well as with what we know of the Greco-Roman conventions that were familiar to Paul and the Galatians."[99]

Davis sets his thesis in the context of the exegetical issues related to his thesis,[100] discusses "the structure" of the letter,[101] defines the curse in Gal 3:10,[102] discusses the opposing views of his interlocutors,[103] and he criticizes Kjell Arne Morland's research in *The Rhetoric of Curse in Galatians* (I discuss this work below) as having too many overstatements that Paul's background was only Jewish.[104] Davis, then, undertakes efforts to find a potential background for the curse terminology in Gal 3:13 in Greco-Roman sources.[105] Davis argues these sources provide a better potential background for Paul's ἡ κατάρα τοῦ νόμου terminology based on his analysis of numerous ancient texts, curse tablets, and ancient inscriptions.[106]

---

93. Davis, *Christ as Devotio*.
94. Ibid., 120.
95. Ibid., 166.
96. Ibid., 121–200.
97. Ibid., 121–200, esp. 174–5.
98. Ibid., 120.
99. Ibid.
100. Ibid., 1–13.
101. Ibid., 14–45.
102. Ibid., 46–118.
103. Ibid.
104. Ibid., 139–41.
105. Ibid., 139–200.
106. Ibid., 141–200.

Davis carefully qualifies that a similarity with, e.g., Plato, suggests neither Paul nor the Galatians were familiar with Plato.[107] Instead, Davis provides evidence from Plato to correct Morland's search to find "the actual occurrences of composites, synonyms, antonyms, forms, affinities, and associations to the curse" terminology in Galatians only in Jewish sources.[108] Davis asserts the "timeless nature" of curse terminology in ancient Mediterranean texts and culture makes the occurrence in Plato (and in other ancient sources) relevant for identifying a background behind Paul's curse terminology in Gal 3:13 other than a Jewish one.[109]

Davis claims his discussion of the ancient sources demonstrates that curses appeared in important literature of antiquity.[110] In this literature, Davis suggests a curse "could refer to the condition or state of being cursed, or it could refer to the act of placing a curse upon some persons or things."[111] Davis says curse terminology functions in both ways in Galatians.[112] For example, in Gal 1:8–9, Davis notes Paul places an apostolic curse upon those who preach another gospel.[113] In Gal 3:10, Davis asserts those who identify with works of law are "in a state of being cursed."[114] In Gal 3:13, Davis says "Christ delivers" the cursed "believers" from the "state of being cursed" with the same word (κατάρα) as Euripides in *Electra*.[115]

Davis provides evidence of the prominence of curses in "ancient Mediterranean life" from a number of ancient sources (Euripides, *Electra* 1323–24, etc), all of which mention curses.[116] He asserts Virgil's poetry (*Aeneid* 4.607–29) and Homer's *Iliad* (9.456) also mention curses.[117] Additionally, Davis states curses occur in Plato (*Laws* 871b, 931b–c), Pliny (*Natural History* 28.10–21), and Seneca (*Epistulae Morales* 94.53) (cf. also the histories of Livy 30.20.7; Tacitus 2.69; Plutarch, *Crassus* 16).[118]

---

107. Ibid., 143–4.
108. Ibid.
109. Ibid., 144.
110. Ibid., 147.
111. Ibid.
112. Ibid.
113. Ibid.
114. Ibid.
115. Ibid.
116. Ibid.
117. Ibid., 147–8.
118. Ibid., 148.

Davis shows "epigraphic evidence" and "funerary curses inscribed on tombs" support that ancients in the Mediterranean world widely used curses.[119] As a result of this evidence, Davis concludes, "It is these curse tablets that provide the most direct information about the views of the Galatians concerning curses."[120]

Davis claims there are numerous *defixiones* published from the ancient world.[121] He defines the *defixiones* as "curses carved most commonly in lead and sometimes in other materials and generally pierced through by nails."[122] Davis discusses different functions of curse tablets.[123] He states one is especially pertinent for his thesis about Gal 3:13: namely, the "*defixiones* against calumniators and thieves, of which we have an impressive collection from the sanctuary of Demeter at Cnidus..."[124] Davis states this kind of curse is important for his thesis because it explicitly targets "criminals" as "transgressors of laws."[125]

Davis begins his defense of this premise by discussing the so-called "judicial curse tablets,"[126] the kind of curse that Davis finds in Gal 3:13.[127] Davis says this form of curse "provides an insight into a dominant view of the mechanism...in the curse language of Gal 3:10–13."[128] Relying upon the work of John Gager,[129] Davis asserts judicial curses discovered since the 1970s are the "largest single category of all the curse tablets and binding spells."[130] He further notes Henk S. Versnel,[131] in agreement with R. S. O. Tomlin and Gager,[132] has carefully documented that these

---

119. Ibid.
120. Ibid.
121. Ibid., 149–50.
122. Ibid.
123. Ibid., 152–3.
124. Ibid., 153.
125. Ibid., 154–60.
126. Ibid., 154.
127. Ibid.
128. Ibid.
129. Ibid., 155. Original citation in John G. Gager, *Curse Tablets and Binding Spells from the Ancient World* (New York: Oxford University Press, 1992), 177.
130. Davis, *Devotio*, 154.
131. Versnel, "Beyond Cursing: The Appeal to Justice in Judicial Prayers," in *Magika Hiera: Ancient Greek Magic and Religion*, ed. Christopher A. Faraone and Dirk Obbink (Oxford: Oxford University Press, 1997), 60–106.
132. S. O. Tomlin, 'The Curse Tablets," in *The Temple of Sulis Minerva at Bath*, vol. 2: *The Finds from the Sacred Spring*, ed. B. Cunliffe (Oxford: Oxford University Press, 1988), 70–2; Gager, *Curse Tablets and Binding Spells*, 177.

curses occur in different languages and show affinity to diverse places and periods of time.¹³³ With Versnel,¹³⁴ Davis suggests the various widespread similarities are "a conscious imitation and borrowing of styles."¹³⁵

Davis explains judicial prayers in ancient curse tablets contain "a demand" for a "divine action aimed" to remedy either "perceived" or "real injustice" experienced "by the author."¹³⁶ The remedy could be "redress" or "revenge,"¹³⁷ but this depends "on the nature of the divine punishment sought to be applied to the offending party."¹³⁸ He says the petitions could be understood as "prayer" or "curse."¹³⁹ He declares since "the prayer is written down" and since it is understood as efficacious because it was inscribed, the curse tablet is analogous to a "standard *defixio*" or "curse tablet."¹⁴⁰ Davis surveys several curse tablets and funerary curse inscriptions to support this point.¹⁴¹ He states these sources contain examples of prayers invoking some kind of curse or sickness upon the offender,¹⁴² and that the "gods" and "goddesses" curse the offender in these ancient sources.¹⁴³

Davis points out an ancient funerary inscription in Phrygia (Asia Minor) uses the noun "κατάρα for the curse that would light upon the violator."¹⁴⁴ The inscription pronounces a curse upon the one who moves the bones of the deceased from a burial site.¹⁴⁵ Davis concludes the combination of κατάρα and a form of the verb "to be" in this inscription "strengthens the case for using the judicial curse tablets as relevant data for interpreting the curse language of Gal 3:10–13."¹⁴⁶

As noted above, Davis clams that in the ancient curse tablets he surveyed, the gods were the "agents" of the curse.¹⁴⁷ Further, as noted above, Davis also claims the curses became efficacious when they were

---

133. Davis, *Christ as Devotio*, 154.
134. Original citation in Versnel, "Beyond Cursing," 91.
135. Davis, *Christ as Devotio*, 155.
136. Ibid.
137. Ibid.
138. Ibid.
139. Ibid.
140. Ibid.
141. Ibid., 156–63.
142. Ibid.
143. Ibid., 155–63.
144. Ibid., 161–3.
145. Ibid., 163.
146. Ibid., 161–3.
147. Ibid.

inscribed.[148] Likewise, says Davis, the curses of the law of Moses were "potent" because they were inscribed (Gal 3:10).[149] Davis's translation of Gal 3:10, he asserts, supports this premise: "All those upon whom the Law operates is under a curse, for it is written, 'Cursed is everyone who does not remain in everything written in the book of the Law in order to do them'."[150]

According to Davis, "it is quite likely" the teachers in Galatia frightened the Galatians with the curse-pronouncements in Deuteronomy to emphasize the necessity of doing the law to escape the curse.[151] Davis claims the teachers in Galatia likely said to the Galatians the inscribed curse in Deuteronomy was written about them.[152] He continues the Galatians, then, thought "the only way" to be delivered from the curse was to embrace circumcision to receive justification, "but Paul warns them" justification comes not by law observance (Gal 3:11–12).[153] Davis says Paul "assures" the Galatians "they need not fear the curse of the Law because Jesus has delivered them from the curse."[154]

Davis claims "the universal belief in the potency of curses"[155] leads him to ask "what if any were the means of escape available to the human targets" of the curse?[156] Davis claims one "safeguard" from the curse was "the use of amulets," which the cursed used as "phylacteries" to protect the one who wore them from the evil things "inscribed" on them.[157] That is, Davis says these amulets functioned "as a prophylactic against adverse magic."[158] Davis continues that while many ancients believed amulets protected them from "unprovoked and unjustified attacks" of injustice, they could not protect them from "the power of the gods who had been commissioned to redress injustices."[159] He states further once someone was aware "she" or "he" was under a curse, that person would have no choice but to "make restitution."[160] Davis states evidence of restitution

---

148. Ibid.
149. Ibid.
150. Ibid., 163.
151. Ibid., 164.
152. Ibid.
153. Ibid.
154. Ibid.
155. Ibid.
156. Ibid.
157. Ibid.
158. Ibid.
159. Ibid.
160. Ibid.

appears in "so-called confessional inscriptions" from South Galatia "in the second and third centuries CE."[161] The "confessional inscriptions" reveal "the gods…did have the power to execute the curses inscribed on the tablets" and that the "culprit" of the curse had to rectify the curse by paying the specific restitution "exacted either by the deity—i.e. the priest who served at the sanctuary—or by the writer of the curse tablet."[162]

Davis claims that "at least one" curse tablet records the price paid for restitution is identified as the *devotio*.[163]

> Cenacus complains to the god Mercury about Vitalinus and Natalinus, his son, concerning the draught animal that was stolen. He begs the god Mercury that they will not have a good health until they repay me promptly the animal they have stolen and (until they pay) the god the "devotion" (*devotio*) that he himself will demand from them.[164]

Davis says this curse inscription pertains to "the restitution of a stolen animal."[165] Davis points out the author of the inscription calls the "fine" a *devotio*.[166] As a result, Davis "henceforth" in his monograph employs the term *devotio* "as a general term for the redeeming fine to be paid to the deity for the purpose of releasing the thief from the curse."[167]

According to Davis, "the noun *devotio* is related to and derived from the verb *devovere*."[168] He claims "there is an emerging consensus that this verb itself is derived from the root *vovere*."[169] He continues, "the latter verb" relates to the noun "*votum*,"[170] which, Davis says, refers to "a magical rite."[171] He claims the curse tablet functioned as a magical

---

161. Ibid., 164–5. For examples from curse tablets, see E. Lane, *Corpus Monumentorum Religionis Dei Menis*, 4 vols. (Leiden: Brill, 1971), no. 58, 69. Source cited in Davis, *Christ as Devotio*, 165.
162. Davis, *Christ as Devotio*, 166.
163. Ibid.
164. Ibid.
165. Ibid.
166. Ibid.
167. Ibid.
168. Ibid. For original citation, see K. Winkler and K. Stuiber, "Devotio," *RAC* 3 (1972): 849–62, esp. 849.
169. Davis, *Christ as Devotio*, 166. For original citation, see Henk S. Versnel, "Two Types of Roman Devotio," *Mnemosyne* 29 (1976): 365–410; L. H. Janssen, "Some Unexplored Aspects of Devotio Deciana," *Mnemosyne* 34 (1981): 357–81.
170. Davis, *Christ as Devotio*, 166.
171. Ibid.

rite (i.e. "as a *votum*").[172] He says further the provision for canceling the curse is the *devotio*.[173] "This *devotio* is distinct from the actual restitution of the stolen goods."[174] He asserts in the curse tablet cited above, the god demands the *devotio*.[175] The priest, who serves on behalf of the god, "determined the amount of the *devotio*."[176] The priest expected the thief "to return the stolen animal to the owner" and to pay the appropriate restitution (i.e. the *devotio* sacrifice), "determined by the priest, through the brokerage of the temple."[177] Davis concludes both "the restitution of the stolen property" and "the payment of the *devotio*...secured the redemption or release of the culprit from the curse."[178] Thus, "the *devotio* was in a sense the price of the freedom of the victim himself or herself."[179]

According to Davis, "vicarious redemption" (i.e. an innocent victim dying in the place of the other for the benefit of the other) is not present "in the curse tablets."[180] The cursed one either would make "restitution" by making a "monetary" payment or by his own death.[181] Davis says, "It appears that vicarious suffering by an innocent third party would not have been acceptable to the writers of these curse tablets."[182] Davis describes the curse tablets suggest the offended "aims" the curses at the offenders "by identifying them by name or by describing the theft or the damage caused by them."[183]

Yet, argues Davis, acts of "vicarious redemption" occur in both Greek and Roman sources (e.g. Livy, *Histories* 10.28.12–18; 10.29.5; Virgil, *Aeneid* 12.845).[184] In these texts, Davis says the gods extend the curse upon the breakers of the specific law, and the human sacrifice functioned to deliver the violator "from death and destruction."[185] Davis thinks this "public sacrifice—known to the Latin writers as *devotio*—parallels the

172. Ibid.
173. Ibid.
174. Ibid.
175. Ibid.
176. Ibid.
177. Ibid.
178. Ibid., 170.
179. Ibid.
180. Ibid., 173.
181. Ibid.
182. Ibid.
183. Ibid.
184. Ibid., 174–6.
185. Ibid.

devotio of the curse tablets."[186] He argues the *devotio* is the background in front of which to understand Paul's remarks in Gal 3:13.[187]

Davis appeals to evidence from the curse tablets and from Greek and Latin authors who were contemporaries of Paul.[188] Davis thinks one should look beyond the Jewish background when searching for the origins of Paul's cursing language in Gal 3:10–13.[189] According to him, if one finds similar curse language in non-Jewish texts as in Gal 3:10–13, then one should include those texts in the investigation by considering the meaning of the curse language in their literary contexts as a key for interpreting the curse language in Gal 3:13.[190]

Davis offers an impressive analysis of ancient Greek and Latin texts with a *devotio* theme in them with the intent of highlighting the parallels between those traditions and Gal 3:10–13.[191] Davis argues since the *devotio* curse formula was present in Paul's Greco-Roman culture and since Paul states Jesus redeemed the "us" from the curse of the law with language similar to that of ancient *devotio* texts, the latter likely provided Paul with the background for his description of Christ as a redeemer of those under the curse.[192] He is right to point out there are similarities between the *devotio* human sacrifice in Livy and Greco-Roman authors and Paul's presentation of Jesus's death in Gal 3:13 (e.g. both have humans dying for the deliverance of others).

However, Davis's own observation is the strongest piece of evidence against the Greco-Roman *devotio* as *the* background for Paul in Gal 3:13: namely, both the *devotio* human sacrifice died to deliver the army or the country from death and the enemies are handed over to God in death.[193] Jesus, on the other hand, died to "deliver us from the curse of the law by becoming a curse for us" (Gal 3:13). Neither Jesus nor God makes the cursed accursed. Rather, the law places people under a curse. Jesus's death for those under the curse delivers them from the curse without requiring the death of those under the curse. Jesus becomes accursed to help those who are under a curse. Once he dies to deliver them from the curse, they suffer the curse no more. Those who are delivered from the curse through

---

186. Ibid.
187. Ibid., 174–250.
188. Ibid., 119–200.
189. Ibid., 139.
190. Ibid., 141.
191. Ibid., 119–220.
192. Ibid.
193. Ibid., 176–7.

the death of Jesus are crucified with Christ, but they do not die in the same way as the enemy in the *devotio* human sacrificial pattern. Because of Christ, the Galatians die to the present evil age so that they might receive life in their human flesh (Gal 2:17–21).

4. The Imperial Cult. In his doctoral thesis published in 2008, Justin K. Hardin investigates Galatians in light of the imperial cult. His work investigates the "pervasiveness" of emperor worship in the first century CE. His thesis is the imperial cult is the lens through which interpreters should read Galatians and that an imperial lens illuminates Pauline theology.[194]

In her 2010 monograph on Galatians, Brigitte Kahl offers a fascinating study of Galatians in light of Roman Imperial ideology.[195] Kahl employs several critical methods to advance her thesis as she attempts to "re-imagine" the Galatian context for the purpose of understanding Galatians in its own historical context.[196] According to the abstract on the back of the monograph, by discussing "the history of Roman interactions with the Gallic/Galatian people, perceptions of Galatian savagery in the empire, and representations of Gauls/Galatians," Kahl highlights "the Great Altar of Pergamon and its specific codes of cultural conflict."[197] She argues the themes of "imperial propaganda, such as order versus lawlessness, civilization versus barbarity, and harmony versus anarchy" occur in Paul's letter and illuminate the Galatian crisis.[198] She claims Paul is troubled in the letter because of "Galatian anxiety" about social status in a society in which many viewed with suspicion the Galatians' withdrawal from Roman "civic celebrations."[199] Kahl claims Paul's concern in the letter has nothing to do with "Jewish antagonists," but with Roman antagonists.[200]

According to Kahl's own chapter summaries, Chapter 1 "addresses the visual presence of Dying Gauls/Galatians in classical antiquity."[201] Kahl "confronts," as she says, the "Christian construct of Galatia and

---

194. Justin K. Hardin, *Galatians and the Imperial Cult*, WUNT 237 (Tübingen: Mohr Siebeck, 2008). Summary based on the abstract on the back of the book.
195. Brigitte Kahl, *Galatians Re-Imagined: Reading Galatians Through the Eyes of the Vanquished* (Minneapolis: Fortress, 2010).
196. Ibid.
197. Ibid.
198. Paraphrase and quotes from the summary on the back of the book.
199. Ibid.
200. Ibid.
201. Ibid., 25; see also 31–75.

Galatians with historical exploration."[202] Her analysis discusses "the ancient perception of the Gauls/Galatians," and the ancient worldview in front of which to understand that "perception."[203] Chapter 2 "presents a semiotic analysis of the Great Altar of Pergamon as a paradigmatic image of the Dying Galatians/Gauls within the imperial law and religion of Western civilization."[204] Kahl claims the "imperial ideology" of Paul's day highlighted the "superior self" as engaging in "symbolic combat with an antithetical and inferior other."[205] She claims the so-called "superior self" conquered and exploited the barbaric Galatians because of the power the "superior self" gained from the "sacred power of its god-given victory over vanquished barbarians."[206]

Chapter 3 discusses "Roman imperial religion."[207] Kahl argues against the conventional thesis that Roman imperial religion was polytheistic by defending instead a "peculiar Roman monotheism" that highlighted "the emperor and Rome at the center of the civic and religious cosmos."[208] Kahl claims Roman monotheism was evident in the buildings of the day and in both "religious and political ritual."[209] According to Kahl, Paul's letter to the Galatians mainly criticizes "this new type of universal imperial world religion."[210] Kahl thinks Paul primarily critiques in Galatians Roman ideology as idolatry.[211]

Chapter 4 discusses the Roman province of Galatia in Paul's day.[212] Kahl specifically explores the "imperial resurrection of the Dying Gauls/Galatians as Augustan Galatians."[213] She embarks upon this analysis by using a set of devices that she thinks "reinscribed the Galatian body."[214] Kahl claims such devices included the construction of "imperial roads, cities, temples, and dynastic power structures among the vanquished…"[215]

---

202. Ibid.
203. Ibid.
204. Ibid., 25; see also 77–127.
205. Ibid., 25.
206. Ibid., 25–6.
207. Ibid.
208. Ibid., 25–6; see also 129–67.
209. Ibid., 26.
210. Ibid.
211. Ibid.
212. Ibid.
213. Ibid., 26; see also 169–207.
214. Ibid., 26.
215. Ibid.

1. Introduction and Thesis 23

She argues these devices also included the act of inducting the Galatians into both military participation and participation in the religion of the empire.[216]

Chapter 5 discusses circumcision, which Kahl claims was "the specific issue at stake" in Galatians.[217] She argues the practice within Paul's Christ-following communities was a "radical subversion of those Roman principles that governed the ordering of associations among the vanquished nations through relation to Rome."[218] According to Kahl, models of unity non-compliant with strict devotion to the empire "emerge as the two core issues signified by Galatian foreskin."[219] Kahl claims the primary problem in Galatians is the tension between "God-in-Christ and the divine Caesar," not a conflict between "law-free Christianity and law-abiding Judaism."[220] Kahl clearly states "the core conflict of Galatians was between messianic law and imperial law."[221]

Chapter 6 offers a "critical re-imagination" of Galatians "at the foot of the Great Altar of Pergamon."[222] Kahl suggests interpreters should read Paul's comments in Galatians as "visual intertextuality" with "Pergamene imagery" and as "scriptural intertextuality with the biblical root narratives of exodus and exile."[223] Kahl seeks to establish a basic exegetical model by which to "decode Galatians" and Paul's teaching on justification by faith "as an intervention into the imaginary construct of Roman imperial ideology and idolatry."[224] She claims the Torah's first commandment, prohibiting idolatry, is the primary issue behind Paul's attack of the "other gospel."[225] "Imperial monotheism and its combat order appear as the ultimate other rejected by Paul's theology of unity and construction of a new self."[226] Paul's criticism of law relates to "the embodied practice of an alternative community based on love as self-othering, that is, the loss of the self as privileged and dominant, now in solidarity with the other."[227]

---

216. Ibid., 26; see also 209–43.
217. Ibid., 245–89.
218. Ibid., 26.
219. Ibid.
220. Ibid.
221. Ibid.
222. Ibid.
223. Ibid., 26–7.
224. Ibid., 27.
225. Ibid.
226. Ibid.
227. Ibid.

Kahl's work offers a detailed historical analysis of the history of Galatia.[228] She sets Galatians firmly within this historical construct. Yet, despite her detailed historical work and her innovative critical re-imagination of the situation in Galatians, unless I have overlooked comments on Gal 3:13 elsewhere, with the exception of one sentence linking Gal 3:13 with Deut 27–30 and Isa 53,[229] Kahl says little about Gal 3:13.[230]

5. Greek and Jewish Cosmic Drama. In a 2010 monograph, Sang Meyng Lee argued Paul presents salvation as a "divine drama." Lee claims Paul's letters show his Jewish and Greco-Roman background.[231] Lee further claims Paul used the OT as a Hellenistic Jew with Hellenistic sensitivities to appeal to his Gentile context.[232] Paul "creatively" appropriates elements from Jewish and "Hellenistic traditions to narrate his salvific drama."[233] Lee's study suggests "cosmological and anthropological concepts of God as Monad, the cosmic body as a geocentric universe, heroes as half-gods, monism and dualism, body/soul dualism, cosmic powers, *Logos*, *paideia*, natural law, conscience" and "the roles and functions of the Mosaic law within Paul's grand drama of salvation" are important concepts for Paul's presentation of salvation in his undisputed letters.[234] Lee's thesis is "the cosmological, anthropological, and soteriological understanding of how various heavenly powers including two main characters, the law and Christ, play their roles in connection with human salvation in Paul's cosmic drama."[235] He states further, "Paul's view of the law cannot be separated from his cosmology and anthropology, since in his thought the Mosaic law and Christ are directly related to the plight and salvation

---

228. Ibid.

229. "In Gal 3:13, this vicarious messianic self-sacrifice links Isaiah 53 and the curse traditions in Deuteronomy 27–30: Christ redeemed us from the curse of the law by becoming a curse for us (Deut. 21.23 and 27.26)." Ibid., 262.

230. Even when commenting explicitly about the historical function of the cross in Galatia in context of deliverance from Roman ideology and idolatry, her remarks about the background behind Gal 3:13 still seem to lack an explicit connection with her arguments for the anti-Roman imperial context of Galatians. Ibid., 156–60.

231. This paragraph paraphrases the summary given on the back cover of Sang Meyng Lee, *The Cosmic Drama of Salvation: A Study of Paul's Undisputed Writings from Anthropological and Cosmological Perspectives*, WUNT 276 (Tübingen: Mohr Siebeck, 2010). See also, ibid., 2.

232. Ibid.
233. Ibid.
234. Ibid.
235. Ibid.

of human beings in God's salvific drama projected on the grand cosmic canvas."²³⁶

6. Conflation of Galatian Religion and Law with Scapegoat Ritual.
In his 2004 book on the background behind cultic atonement metaphors in Paul, Stephen Finlan suggests Paul converges the "protective curse" in the religion of Galatia and Torah observance with the scapegoat ritual in Gal 3:13.²³⁷ Finlan claims in Gal 3:10, Paul reminds the Galatians they are under the Deuteronomic curse if they disobey the law.²³⁸ However, Finlan claims Paul concludes Gal 3:13 with a short introduction to the act of "someone becoming" a curse and carrying it away, which Finlan claims is not strictly Deuteronomic.²³⁹ Finlan claims Paul "likely refers either to an expulsion victim who purges a community by bearing away its curse or sin, or to the protective legal curses common in Galatian society."²⁴⁰

Finlan states in Deuteronomy, only Jews are under the curse of the law.²⁴¹ Once the Jews participated in "national repentance," then the curse would end.²⁴² Israel did not escape the curse by means of an individual "curse-bearer" on behalf of the people.²⁴³ Gentile salvation was not realized by means of the removal of the Deuteronomic curse, which (Gentile salvation), Finlan says, is the issue of Gal 3:14.²⁴⁴ According to Finlan, "It is likely that Paul meant to allude both to the protective curse in Galatian religion and law, and to the biblical scapegoat" ritual since curse-bearing terminology is present in both Leviticus and in Gentile religion.²⁴⁵

b. Jewish Background Behind Galatians 3:13

1. Jewish Scriptural Background. In his 2000 monograph, C. Marvin Pate affirmed an OT background behind Christ's redemption in Gal 3:13.²⁴⁶ Pate suggests readers should interpret Gal 3:13 against the background of

---

236. Ibid.
237. Finlan, *Background and Content*, 101–11, esp. 110.
238. Ibid., 110.
239. Ibid.
240. Ibid., 110; cf. 105.
241. Ibid.
242. Ibid.
243. Ibid.
244. Ibid.
245. Ibid.
246. C. Marvin Pate, *The Reverse of the Curse: Paul, Wisdom, and the Law*, WUNT 114 (Tübingen: Mohr Siebeck, 2000), 212–31.

his "pre-Christian" Jewish understanding of Deuteronomy.[247] Pate claims Paul's Jewish reading of Deuteronomy affirms the Deuteronomic curses come upon those who either disobey Torah or upon those who attempt to persuade others to be Torah disobedient.[248] Pate says there will be an end-time "reverse of the curse" after one converts to Christ.[249] According to Pate, first Israel receives the blessings of Torah if they obey Torah, following which Gentile nations will be blessed if they do likewise.[250]

However, Pate claims after Paul converts to Christ, he gained a different perception as to how Jews and Gentiles experience the Deuteronomic blessings.[251] Pate suggests that because of Jesus's death and resurrection, Paul argues after his conversion, the Gentiles receive the blessings first and the Jews second when both groups are justified by faith in Christ.[252]

Pate claims Paul's reading reverses a common Jewish interpretation of Deut 27:26.[253] He says both Paul's Jewish contemporaries and Paul agreed Israel's history is one of exile because of disobedience to Torah.[254] Pate continues Paul's converted reading of Deut 27:26 suggests all seeking to obey Torah in the messianic age will not receive the blessings of Torah, but rather the curses of Torah for two reasons: (1) the law demands and expects perfect obedience, but no one can perfectly obey it. (2) Jesus perfectly obeyed Torah, died in perfect obedience to the law, and yet still suffered the curses so that all those justified by faith in Christ would receive the blessings.[255] Pate concludes that Paul's converted reading of Deut 27:26 teaches the pathway for individuals to receive the blessings of Torah is now in this messianic age only by faith in Christ and not by obedience to the law, but the way in which all people experience the curses of Torah is by obedience to Torah.[256]

In his 2006 monograph on Deuteronomy in the Pauline epistles, Guy Waters explores Paul's use of Deut 27–30 and 32 in his Second Temple Jewish context.[257] Waters argues Paul's reading of these chapters was

---

247. Ibid., 145–52.
248. Ibid.
249. Ibid.
250. Ibid.
251. Ibid., 211–31.
252. Ibid., 211–12, 222.
253. Ibid.
254. Ibid.
255. Ibid., 214–24.
256. Ibid.
257. Entire paragraph based on the back cover summary of Guy Waters, *The End of Deuteronomy in the Epistles of Paul*, WUNT 221 (Tübingen: Mohr Siebeck, 2006).

informative for every aspect of his apostolic ministry.[258] After providing a detailed history of research of Paul's reading of Scripture and Second Temple Jewish readings of Deut 27–30 and 32,[259] Waters discusses the function of Deut 27–30 in Galatians.[260] He does not focus on the background of Paul's remarks in Gal 3:13, but rather he investigates the argument of Gal 3:10–14 as he engages Paul's reading of Deuteronomy.[261] Still, his monograph suggests a Deuteronomic background behind Gal 3:13 since Paul quotes multiple texts from Deuteronomy in Gal 3:10 and 3:13 to highlight the law and the curse.[262] Waters too entertains the possibility that this background was part of a pre-Pauline Christian tradition.[263] Waters astutely says the following in relation to his thesis:

> Even if one were to grant that Paul has adapted to his purposes early Christian confessional material at Gal 3:13, one must still concede the language, style, and the content of the whole of the argument of Gal 3:10–13 to be unmistakably Pauline. In other words, one's conclusions respecting the pre-Pauline heritage of the material of Gal 3:13 do not at all militate against considerations of the engagement at Gal 3:13 as Pauline in nature.[264]

I interpret Waters to mean that even if material in Gal 3:13 is part of a pre-Pauline Christian tradition, Paul's remarks about Jesus's death here are Pauline. A point that is at least implicit in Waters's monograph if not explicit is Paul's reading of Deuteronomy shapes his understanding of the death of Jesus as the solution to the curse in 3:13.

In his revised 2015 monograph on Paul's hermeneutics of faith,[265] Francis Watson provides a robust reading of Paul's reading of Scripture. He argues that ancient Jewish readers of Scripture read the same texts in different ways.[266] Watson claims when seeking to understand how Paul reads Scripture, interpreters must keep in mind there is a "three-way conversation" taking place: the citation in its original context, Paul's reading of the citation, and other contemporary Jewish readings of the same

---

258. Ibid.
259. Ibid., 4–77.
260. Ibid., 79–113.
261. Ibid.
262. Ibid., 92–113.
263. Ibid.
264. Ibid., 92–3.
265. Francis Watson, *Paul and the Hermeneutics of Faith*, 2nd ed. (New York: T&T Clark, 2015), 1.
266. Ibid.

citation.[267] Instead of studying these texts in isolation from each other, Watson endeavors "to get these texts talking to each other…to show how they are as they are by virtue of an ongoing conversation in which they already participate."[268]

Watson offers a detailed analysis of key Pauline themes (e.g. promise, justification, etc.) as he reads Paul alongside the ancient scriptural texts and the Second Temple Jewish readings of these texts.[269] Watson's work is primarily concerned with Paul's hermeneutic, but Watson grounds Paul's remarks in Gal 3:13 in the Scripture pertaining to the Abrahamic promise: "The promise that 'in you shall all Gentiles be blessed' is the promise of a future divine action with universal scope. That promised action has, for Paul, now become reality in the death of Christ under the law's curse, which took place 'so that the blessing of Abraham might come to the Gentiles in Christ Jesus…'"[270]

Regarding Gal 3:13–14, Watson asserts, "according to Galatians 3:13–14…the promise of Genesis 12:3 has now been realized in the death and resurrection of Christ, the event in which the curse of the law gives way to the blessing of Abraham."[271] Consequently, Watson affirms Paul can say, "as it could not be said purely on the basis of scripture,"[272] that God's promise to Abraham comes to the Gentiles "in Christ Jesus."[273] Watson states elsewhere, "Deut 21:23 enables Paul to speak of the manner of the redemption achieved by Christ—in particular, that this involves his entering fully into the dire state of those needing to be redeemed."[274] Watson affirms that Jesus's crucifixion demonstrates he suffered the very curse for which he died to liberate others.[275] Paul learns this about Christ from Deuteronomy; he did not use Deuteronomy to support what he already knew to be true.[276]

2. Covenant Renewal. In his 1991 monograph *The Climax of the Covenant*, N. T. Wright argues Paul understands Jesus's "death and resurrection as the climactic moment" in Israel's covenantal history and that

---

267. Ibid., 2–5.
268. Ibid., 2.
269. Ibid.
270. Ibid., 174.
271. Ibid.
272. Ibid.
273. Ibid.
274. Ibid., 387.
275. Ibid.
276. Ibid.

this "climactic moment" led him to change his view of the law.²⁷⁷ As to Christ's death in Gal 3:13, Wright argues Paul's statement must be interpreted in context of covenant and that interpreters must resist reading Paul's remarks as individual explanations of Jesus's death or as Paul's effort to support "justification by faith" with Scripture.²⁷⁸ Rather, Wright says Paul's remarks emphasize "the fact that in the cross of Jesus, the Messiah, the curse of exile itself reached its height, and was dealt with once and for all, so that the blessing of covenant renewal might flow out the other side, as God always intended."²⁷⁹

Wright argues his thesis with an analysis of primary texts from the Second Temple period to support some of Paul's Jewish contemporaries at least understood Israel to be in a continued state of exile (cf. CD I.5–8).²⁸⁰ Wright claims that Rome's dominant rule over Israel was the example of Israel's continued exile.²⁸¹ Wright says Jews would have likely still been awaiting the deliverance from exile during Roman rule because of the prophetic traditions (e.g. Ezekiel, Isaiah) that promised a future restoration.²⁸² Wright says, "As long as Herod and Pilate were in control of Palestine, Israel was still under the curse of Deuteronomy 29."²⁸³ According to Wright, it "is clear" Paul would have had this mindset because of his remarks in Gal 1:4 "where he speaks in regular Jewish language of the present evil age."²⁸⁴

The theme of covenant is crucial to Wright's argument in Galatians.²⁸⁵ He claims that this theme is present in Paul's argument in Gal 3:10–14 where he offers an exposition of Deuteronomy and Genesis.²⁸⁶ Wright argues Gal 3 provides an exposition of Gen 15,²⁸⁷ which, according to Wright, is a significant chapter about covenant in the OT.²⁸⁸ Wright says

---

277. In this monograph, I refer to the first paperback edition published by Fortress in 1993. See Wright, *Climax*. The above summary of Wright's thesis statement is paraphrased from the abstract on the back of the book.
278. Ibid., 141, esp. 137–56 for full argument.
279. Ibid., 141.
280. Ibid.
281. Ibid.
282. Ibid.
283. Ibid.
284. Ibid.
285. Ibid., 140.
286. Ibid.
287. Ibid.
288. Ibid.

Paul's argument in Gal 3 is covenantal from beginning until the end,[289] which, Wright claims, Paul's references to Abraham and the language of curse and blessing support.[290] Deuteronomy 27–30 focus on blessing, curse, and covenantal renewal, and Paul engages Deuteronomy in Gal 3:10.[291]

Wright's "starting point" for his analysis of Gal 3:10–14 is 3:6–9.[292] He claims the γὰρ in 3:10 connects 3:10–14 with 3:9, but he says the connection is not obvious.[293] According to Wright, perhaps Paul offers an additional reason for his conclusion in 3:9: "having demonstrated that the family of Abraham consists of those characterized by faith, he now says 'and this is further proved by the fact that there is no way into this family by works of Torah'."[294] However, Wright asserts the language of covenant and curse links 3:9 and 3:10 (supported by the words blessing and curse).[295]

"Any Jew," says Wright, with a knowledge of Torah would hear an appeal to Deuteronomy when they heard the "covenantal words blessing and curse," for Deuteronomy (especially chs. 27–30) was "the great covenant document" for Jews.[296] Wright continues Deut 27–30 explicitly state "Israel's covenantal obligations to God" and a specific list of blessings for obedience and curses for disobedience.[297] Paul, Wright claims, cites Deut 27:26 in Gal 3:10 to support that works of the law bring a curse instead of providing the blessing.[298] Paul's point is not that Gal 3:10 "further proves" 3:9 by asserting "works of Torah cannot provide" Gentiles' entrance into the family of Abraham.[299] Moses's remarks in Deuteronomy about the certain future disobedience of Israel "set the context" for Paul's remarks in Gal 3:10.[300] However, Wright quickly says, "this is not a matter of counting up individual transgressions, or proving that each individual Israelite is in fact guilty of sin. It is a matter of the life of the nation as a whole."[301]

---

289. Ibid.
290. Ibid.
291. Ibid., 140.
292. Ibid., 141.
293. Ibid.
294. Ibid., 142.
295. Ibid.
296. Ibid.
297. Ibid.
298. Ibid.
299. Ibid.
300. Ibid.
301. Ibid.

Wright continues Paul writes in Gal 3:10–14: (1) God gave promises to Abraham;[302] (2) Jews were under the curse of the law.[303] Paul's thought transcends the ideas of "the plight of the sinner convicted by a holy law" and "the plight of Israel caught in the trap of nationalism."[304] Paul's thought in 3:10–14 is the following:

> God promised Abraham a worldwide family, characterized by faith. The promises were entrusted to Israel, the people whose life was lived ὑπὸ νόμον. The Torah, however, held out over this people, the agents of promise, the curse which had in fact come true, and was still being proved true, in the events of exile and its strange continuance right up to Paul's day and beyond.[305]

The unfulfilled promises to Abraham because of Israel's plight, due to their disobedience to Torah, leads Paul to ask the following question: "How could the promises, the blessings promised to Abraham, now reach their intended destination?"[306] The Torah appears to threaten the promises to Abraham, "and to his worldwide family," by considering them "null and void."[307] Paul combats this wrong conclusion without identifying Torah as evil.[308]

Wright says Paul's argument in Gal 3:10–14 suggests God's promises to Abraham "remain the vital thing."[309] Torah consigns a "valid interdict on these promises."[310] Yet, Wright claims, Paul demonstrates God has rectified the problem by bringing his covenant to a climax in Jesus's death, the death of Israel's Messiah.[311] Jesus's death confers the promises of Abraham to Gentiles in whom these promises are realized in their reception of the Spirit.[312] Jewish Christians are the "we" who receive the Spirit (3:14), and the Jews are the "us" whom Christ redeemed from

---

302. Ibid.
303. Ibid.
304. Ibid.
305. Ibid.
306. Ibid. See also similarly George S. Duncan, *The Epistle of Paul to the Galatians*, MNTC (London: Hodder & Stoughton, 1934); Lagrange, *Saint Paul aux Galates*.
307. Wright, *Climax*, 142.
308. Ibid., 143.
309. Ibid.
310. Ibid.
311. Ibid.
312. Ibid. Contra James D. G. Dunn, *Galatians* (Grand Rapids: Baker, 1993), 225–30; Seyoon Kim, *The Origin of Paul's Gospel*, WUNT 4 (Tübingen: Paul Siebeck, 1981), 309; E. P. Sanders, *Paul, the Law, and the Jewish People* (Minneapolis:

Torah's curse.[313] Torah placed Jews under a curse, whereas "Gentiles are only in that state by a peculiar sort of extension."[314]

According to Wright, it is true that in Gal 4:1–11, Paul identifies both Jews and Gentiles as being under a plight.[315] While Paul asserts Jews were under the τὰ στοιχεῖα, he does not confirm "Gentiles were under Torah" since "they never possessed" it.[316] Paul's argument is as follows: "God promised to Abraham a blessing intended for the whole world; the Torah looked like preventing that blessing getting to its destination; the death of Christ has broken through this problem, and now the blessing can reach its destination securely."[317]

Wright says the questions Paul answers in Gal 3:10–14 pertain "to whom do the promises really belong" and who are Abraham's children?[318] He contends the covenant theology of both Gal 3:10–14 and Deuteronomy provide a satisfactory solution to the problem of interpretation.[319] Wright says, however, Paul's immediate problem in this section in Gal 3 is whether the promises to Abraham will be realized since Torah has brought a curse upon Israel.[320]

Wright asks later, "How then is the blessing of Abraham to come on either Jew (enclosed and threatened by Torah) or Gentile (whose promised blessing will thus never reach him)?"[321] Paul's answer is the death of Jesus is the solution to Torah's threat to the blessing.[322] He further claims Gal 3:13 elaborates Paul's earlier remarks about Jesus's death in 2:19–20.[323] Wright states to understand Paul's argument in Gal 3:13 one must grasp his "corporate Christology."[324] Wright says "because the Messiah represents Israel, he is able to take on himself Israel's curse and exhaust it."[325]

Fortress, 1983), 82; Heikki Räisänen, *Paul and the Law* (Minneapolis: Fortress, 1986), 19; Stephen Westerholm, *Israel's Law and the Church's Faith: Paul and His Recent Interpreters* (Grand Rapids: Eerdmans, 1988), 195.
   313. Wright, *Climax*, 143.
   314. Ibid.
   315. Ibid.
   316. Ibid.
   317. Ibid., 143–4.
   318. Ibid.
   319. Ibid.
   320. Ibid.
   321. Ibid., 151.
   322. Ibid.
   323. Ibid.
   324. Ibid.
   325. Ibid.

1. Introduction and Thesis

The Romans (Gentiles) killed Jesus, who was "the King of the Jews."[326] Roman oppression of the Jews was still the "present and climactic form of the curse of exile itself."[327] Jesus's crucifixion is the *"quintessence of the curse of exile, and its climactic act."*[328]

Wright contends, therefore, Paul's remarks in Gal 3:13 are not "general" statements about "atonement theology applicable equally, and in the same way, to Jew and Gentile alike."[329] Rather, Paul emphasizes Jesus's death in 3:13 applies to Jews since Christ is Israel's Messiah who represents the whole nation.[330] This is why Paul uses the first person plural ἡμᾶς.[331] Christ is Israel's "representative Messiah," who "achieved a specific task" for Israel: namely, he took upon himself the curse of the law.[332] The curse of the law hanging "over Israel" also "prevented" Abraham's blessing from "flowing out to the Gentiles."[333] The Messiah has subjected himself to Israel's curse in order to be Israel's *"redeeming* representative."[334] Because of the curse and blessing pattern in Deuteronomy, Israel needed this representative redeemer.[335] "The pattern of exile and restoration is acted out in his death and resurrection."[336] As Israel, Jesus dies under the curse of the law, resurrects to "new covenant life beyond," puts an end to the curse of exile, and extends the blessings to Jews and Gentiles.[337] Because of the death and resurrection of the Messiah, Gentile Christians become full members with God's covenant community, but Jewish Christians experience covenant renewal.[338]

3. Covenant Theology. In his 2010 monograph on *Paul and the Early Jewish Encounter with Deuteronomy*, David Lincicum argues Paul's remarks in Gal 3:10 and 3:13 operate "under the model of covenant theology, with his citation of Deut. 27 tapping into the broader context of

---

326. Ibid.
327. Ibid.
328. Ibid.
329. Ibid.
330. Ibid.
331. Ibid.
332. Ibid.
333. Ibid.
334. Ibid.
335. Ibid., 151–2.
336. Ibid., 152.
337. Ibid.
338. Ibid., 154–5. Though his concern is not primarily Gal 3:13, for a covenant background behind 3:10, see also David Lincicum, *Paul and the Early Jewish Encounter with Deuteronomy* (Grand Rapids: Baker, 2010), 142–7.

Deut. 27–30."[339] Lincicum argues Deut 27:26 works within Deut 27 both as a summary of and a representation of the previous and more specific curses in Deut 27:15–25.[340] But Paul changes the text from "in all of the words of this law" (LXX Deut 27:26) to "all the things written in the book of the law."[341] Lincicum affirms this alteration seems "minor," but the phrase "book of the law" occurs throughout Deut 28–30 (cf. 28:58 and 30:10).[342] Paul's citation, thus, "emphasizes the representative nature" of Paul's citation even more.[343] "The curse of the law, then, is the curse the law threatens for those who disobey it."[344]

Lincicum claims the curse may address individual and national concerns, but "Paul here stands in the line of those who survey Israel's history retrospectively and find it lacking."[345] Since Israel's history is inseparable from the curse, this proves "that the law does not in fact lead to blessing but to a curse."[346] Quoting James M. Scott, Lincicum says, "The likeliest explanation as to why Paul considers Israel to be under a curse is that the Deuteronomic curse to which Dan 9:11 refers came upon the people."[347] Thus, the Galatian preachers' compulsion of these Gentile Christians to observe Torah is absurd given the historical plight of Israel because of the law.[348] Lincicum continues "because Christ died and righteousness comes to Jew and Gentile by faith, the law must necessarily have failed to—or not have been designed to—achieve justification (cf. Gal 2:21)."[349] Thus, Lincicum infers, one should likely not understand Paul's argument as only "solution to plight" or only as "plight to solution."[350] Rather, "Scripture and gospel are mutually interpretive."[351]

339. Lincicum, *Paul and the Early Jewish Encounter with Deuteronomy*, 143–4.
340. Ibid., 144.
341. Ibid.
342. Ibid.
343. Ibid.
344. Ibid.
345. Ibid.
346. Ibid.
347. Ibid. For original citation, see James M. Scott, "Restoration of Israel," in *Dictionary of Paul and His Letters*, ed. G. F. Hawthorne and R. P. Martin (Downers Grove, IL: Intervarsity, 1993), 796–805, esp. 802; idem, "For As Many As Are of Works of the Law Are Under a Curse (Galatians 3.10)," in *Paul and the Scriptures of Israel*, ed. Craig A. Evans and James A. Sanders, JSNTSup 83 (Sheffield: JSOT, 1993), 187–22; idem, "Paul's Use of Deuteronomistic Tradition," *JBL* 112 (1993): 645–5.
348. Lincicum, *Paul and the Early Jewish Encounter with Deuteronomy*, 145.
349. Ibid.
350. Ibid.
351. Ibid.

If the above analysis is correct, Lincicum claims, "Gal 3:11–12 introduces the tension that will lead to Paul's further explanations in 3:15–25 about the nature and purpose of the law."[352] According to Lincicum, Paul intentionally reads Hab 2:4 against Lev 18:5 to make sense of the difference between the faith "answered by justification in Israel's history (cf. 3:6–9) and the demand for obedience that never actually eventuated in the life promised (cf. 3:10)."[353] When Paul states that "those from works of law are under a curse" and when he implies observance to the law does not remove the curse, "Paul prepares for the Christological punchline of 3:13: Christ redeemed us from the curse of the law by having become a curse on our behalf."[354] Lincicum says if his "covenantal reading of Deut 27:26" is right, ἡμᾶς "specifically refers to Jewish Christians under the curse of the law."[355]

According to Lincicum, the statement in 3:13a is supported by Deut 21:23, a verse connected with curse and crucifixion.[356] Paul "puts this to theological use in Gal 3:13 to suggest only by enduring the curse himself was Christ then able to nullify its power to release the blessing that is the curse's structural opposite."[357] Lincicum claims Christ redeemed Israel from the law's curse to extend the blessing of Abraham to Gentiles upon being justified by faith in Christ (3:6–9), so that all might receive the promised Spirit by faith (3:2).[358] He says Paul's discussion of the solution to the curse via Christ's death occurs as he states "the intention of the covenant with Abraham can be fulfilled."[359] This suggests, says Lincicum, that if Paul and his Jewish contemporaries agree on Israel's plight in light of Deuteronomy, his solution is very different because it is "bound up with the crucifixion (and implicitly the resurrection) of the Son of God, and so naturally rejects the nomistic exhortations that characterize some other Jewish contemporaries."[360] Lincicum concludes that in Gal 3:10–14, Deuteronomy has a twofold function: "it both announces the curse to which Israel in her disobedience is subject, but also hints at the means by which that curse has been overcome, resulting in blessing to the nations."[361]

352. Ibid.
353. Ibid.
354. Ibid., 145.
355. Ibid., 145–6.
356. Ibid.
357. Ibid.
358. Ibid.
359. Ibid.
360. Ibid., 146–7.
361. Ibid., 147.

4. OT Sacrificial System. In a 1983 article, Daniel R. Schwartz argues Paul's background in Gal 3:13 is the Day of Atonement's scapegoat ritual in Lev 16 since both texts use the verb ἐξαγοράζω and a word meaning "to send."[362] In a 1987 essay on the death of Jesus in Paul, Helmut Merklein suggests Paul's presentation of Jesus's death in Gal 3:13 is similar to the sacrificial cult in Lev 4–5 and 16–17. He claims the expression "to become a curse" connects "Christ and the curse."[363]

5. Conflation of Levitical Cultic and Deuteronomic Traditions. In a 1995 monograph on the rhetorical function of curse in Galatians, Kjell Arne Morland argues Paul's use of curse plays a key role in the choice before the Galatians to embrace Paul's gospel or to embrace the law of Moses.[364] As to Gal 3:13, Morland argues Jewish texts are the most notable background behind Paul's remarks in Gal 3:13–14.[365] Morland offers a "semantic field analysis" of Gal 3:10–14 to support the role of the curse rhetoric in Galatians to persuade the Galatians to choose life in the gospel.[366]

Morland claims the curse rhetoric of κατάρα του νόμου and γίνομαι κατάρα in Gal 3:10–14 is similar to the curse rhetoric in Deut 27–30.[367] The focus of his analysis is "to search for a Jewish background for the curses of Gal 3:8–14 by first concentrating on the structure of Gal 3:8–14 and then focusing on the additional elements in the curses of Gal 3:10 and 3:13–14 respectively."[368] Morland suggests Gal 3:8–14 presents "curse" and "blessing" both in "antithesis" and in "sequence," a structure, says Morland, present in multiple Jewish curse texts (e.g. Isa 65; Jer 17; 24;

---

362. Daniel R. Schwartz, "Two Pauline Allusions to the Redemptive Mechanism of the Crucifixion," *JBL* 102 (1983): 429–35.
363. Paraphrased from Morland, *Curse*, 11. Original citation from Helmut Merklein, "Die Bedeutung des Kreuzestodes Christi für die paulinische Gerechtigkeits und Gesetzesthematik," in *Studien zu Jesus und Paulus*, WUNT 43 (Tübingen: Mohr Siebeck, 1987), 1–106, esp. 26–31.
364. Morland, *Curse*, 11.
365. Ibid., 10–11. However, on the curse/blessing antithesis in ancient Near Eastern Literature, see generally Paul A. Keim, "When Sanctions Fail: The Social Function of Curse in Ancient Israel" (PhD diss., Harvard University, 1992). On the curse/blessing antithesis in ancient Near Eastern Literature and in Deuteronomy, see W. Morgan, "The Ancient Near Eastern Background of the Love of God in Deuteronomy," *CBQ* 25 (1963): 77–87.
366. Morland, *Curse*, 218–24.
367. Ibid.
368. Ibid., 28.

Mal 1.20–23; 1 En. 5; 102; T. Levi; T. Naph; Philo, *Praem.* 126–72; 1QS II; CD I; Josephus, *Ant.* 4.302–307).³⁶⁹ Morland claims "thirteen" of these curse texts occur in Deut 27–30 or in other Jewish traditions that correspond to Deuteronomy.³⁷⁰

The exegetical payoff of Morland's analysis is to provide a background in front of which to understand Paul's curse rhetoric in Galatians. Morland claims his semantic field analysis of multiple Jewish texts reveal semantic connections with these texts and Gal 3:8–14.³⁷¹ In Chapter 5 and Chapter 10, Morland focuses on the "sequence of curse and blessing in history" (Chapter 5) and "the curses of Gal 3:10 and 3:13" in Galatians (Chapter 10).³⁷² Regarding "curse and blessing in history," Morland suggests "expressions similar to κατάρα του νόμου" and γίνομαι κατάρα "almost exclusively" occur in Deut 27–30.³⁷³ He infers this confirms Deut 27–30 is vital for Paul's curse rhetoric in Galatians.³⁷⁴ Similar to eight Jewish texts (cf. LXX Deut 29:19–29; 2 Chr 34:24–28; Dan 9:11; Bar 1:20; DSS 1QS II.16; V.12; CD I.17; XV.2–3),³⁷⁵ Morland claims Paul's phrase κατάρα του νόμου in Gal 3:13 demonstrates the law is the source of the curse.³⁷⁶ These connections of curse and law between these Jewish texts and Galatians support the premise that expressions similar to κατάρα του νόμου in Gal 3:10 refer to the covenantal curses of Deut 27–30.³⁷⁷

Morland continues the clause "γίνομαι κατάρα metonymically" posits "Jesus as a curse" in Gal 3:13.³⁷⁸ In the Jewish texts corresponding to Deut 27–30, Morland states Israel becomes a curse because of disobedience to Torah (cf. LXX 2 Kgs 22:19; Jer 24:9; 49:18; 51:8, 12; Zech 8:13).³⁷⁹ Morland sees similar statements in Second Temple Literature (cf. 1 Bar 3:8; Jub. 1:16; T. Levi 10:4; 16:5).³⁸⁰

Morland says in three places "individual lawbreakers are denoted metonymically as a curse" (cf. LXX Num 5:27; Deut 21:23; 1 En. 5:6).³⁸¹

---

369. Ibid., 33–68.
370. Ibid.
371. Ibid.
372. Ibid., 69–80, 181–233.
373. Ibid., 69.
374. Ibid.
375. Ibid.
376. Ibid.
377. Ibid., 70.
378. Ibid.
379. Ibid.
380. Ibid., 70–1.
381. Ibid.

With the exception of Num 5:21–27, Morland infers these texts support Deut 27–30 are "a suitable background for Gal 3."[382] These texts primarily compel Israel toward "covenantal obedience."[383] "They refer to the curse of the law as a constant threat to Israel in their history, and most of them identify the disobedient and punished Israel with the curse."[384]

Morland claims the curse texts from the Abrahamic narratives with the blessing and curse formula are also important for his thesis.[385] He says, "These texts are important not only because of this feature, but also because they contain the antithesis of blessing and curse…, some curses with the form of Gal 3:10…, and even one text with curse and blessing both in antithesis and sequence…"[386] Morland continues Gen 12:3 mentions Gentile blessing, and Paul cites this text with this formula in Gal 3:8.[387] According to Morland, the formula of Gentile blessing occurs in texts where Deut 27–30 converges with the concepts of eschatology and the formulation of "curse and blessing" as "covenantal categories" (cf. Tob 13:9–18; Jub. 25:21–22; 31:20; T. Levi 4:6; Philo, *Mos.* 1.291).[388]

Morland declares, in texts with the promise of Gen 12:3 converging with Deut 27–30, the formula is mostly related "to the future era of blessing (e.g. Jer. 4.2 [cf. Deut. 30.2]; Ps. 72.8, 17 [cf. Deut. 11.24]; Sir. 44.21 [Ps. 72.8]; Philo, *Migr.* 118–26)."[389] Morland acknowledges Gen 12:2 uses the term blessing to speak of the Abrahamic blessing.[390] He further states there are places elsewhere that both speak of individual blessing, because of obedience to Torah (LXX Pss 21:7; 37:26; Prov 10:7),[391] and that speak of both the corporate blessing of Israel and of individual "proselytes" in the age to come (LXX Isa 19:24; Zech 8:13; Ezek 34:26).[392] Morland suggests the promise of Gen 12:3 intersects with "covenantal obedience, even more explicitly than the formula itself."[393] He says God expected Israel to obey to receive the promise (LXX Jer 4:1; Jub. 20:9; Gen 18:19),[394]

---

382. Ibid.
383. Ibid.
384. Ibid.
385. Ibid.
386. Ibid.
387. Ibid., 72.
388. Ibid., 72–3.
389. Ibid., 74.
390. Ibid., 75.
391. Ibid.
392. Ibid.
393. Ibid., 76.
394. Ibid.

and that Abraham's obedience was necessary to receive the promise (LXX Gen 22:18; 26:5; Sir 44:20).[395] Likewise, Morland states "Philo relates the promise to the righteous" (*Migr.* 120–22).[396] Yet, there are other texts, says Morland, that "demand solidarity from the Gentiles."[397] According to him, God will bless the Gentiles only when "they bless the sons of Israel in the name of Abraham, in order to receive the blessing (Jub. 20.10)."[398]

Morland asserts just as the Abrahamic traditions "contain features that converge" with the blessing and curse rhetoric in Deut 27–30, this section has connections with the Abrahamic tradition (cf. LXX Deut 30:20; Jer 11:5; Bar 2:34; CD IV.4, 9).[399] Morland continues the Gen 12:3 formula of blessing and curse has converged with the Deuteronomic history of Israel's punishment for disobedience (Tob 13:3–5),[400] Israel's restoration because of repentance (13:5–10),[401] and a discussion of the "new Jerusalem" in the age to come follows the Gen 12:3 formula (13:11–18; cf. Jub. 20:6–10; 21:21–24; 22:11–23; 23:16–25; 25:15–22; 31:15–20).[402] Thus, in these texts (esp. the texts in Jubilees), Morland says "both the Abraham and the Deut 27–30 traditions are important" to the author and that he connects these traditions in Jubilees.[403]

Morland eventually returns again to Gal 3. According to him, texts that mention the blessing of the Gentiles in connection with the blessing of Abraham was likely a common practice.[404] In Gal 3, Paul brings together texts from Deuteronomy (Gal 3:10, 13) "with a citation from" Gen 12:3 (Gal 3:8).[405] These connections, concludes Morland, make it "quite possible that Paul has combined curse and blessing according to Deut 27–30 with blessing for Gentiles according to Gen 12."[406]

---

395. Ibid.
396. Ibid.
397. Ibid.
398. Ibid.
399. Ibid., 76–8. Morland asserts Jub. 20:10 applies blessing terminology to Gentiles and that additional texts refer to the blessing of the Gentiles in the age to come (LXX Zech 8:20–23; 1 En. 10:21; Philo, *Praem.* 171–72; Jub. 20:6–10; T. Naph. 8:3; T. Levi 18:9–10; T. Jud. 24:3–6; T. Zeb. 9:8; T. Ash. 7:3).
400. Ibid.
401. Ibid.
402. Ibid.
403. See also his discussion of Isa 24–25, Ezek 17, 3 Bar. 4, and LAB 18, in ibid., 76–8.
404. Ibid., 80.
405. Ibid.
406. Ibid.

In Chapter 10, Morland's primary concern "is to interpret Paul's antithesis between the blessed and cursed in 3:8–10 and his sequence of curse and blessing in 3:13–14."[407] Morland explicitly remarks he has found a "deuteronomistic background for the interpretation of the curses of Gal 3:13."[408] Paul, says Morland, supports that the ages have turned in Christ because he refers to Deut 21:23.[409] Morland explains, "This curse has been understood as a curse on criminals, but Paul has now discovered a deeper meaning in it."[410] God presented the deeper meaning in Scripture when he preached Christ beforehand in it (cf. Gal 3:8).[411] According to Morland, "Deut 21:23 is a hidden prophecy in Scripture about the way Christ would redeem from the curse and inaugurate the new era."[412]

Regarding Christ's redemption in Gal 3:13, Morland follows Merklein, who connects Christ's redemption in Gal 3:13 to traditions about expiation.[413] Morland, per Merklein, observes the Deuteronomic sequence of blessing and curse in multiple texts that await God's soteriological intervention in the age to come (cf. Deut 30:1–10 and 1 En. 93).[414] According to Morland, Merklein further notes other Jewish texts highlight the sinfulness of humanity and the need for expiation to function as the solution to humanity's plight (cf. CD III.18).[415]

Morland agrees with Merklein's suggestions for the Levitical cult as a potential background behind Christ's death as an expiation in Gal 3:13 because Paul states Jesus fulfills Scripture,[416] "the ὑπὲρ ἡμῶν formula" in 1:4,[417] which (the formula), Morland asserts, could "be connected with the concept of expiation,"[418] the verb ἐξηγόρασεν in 3:13,[419] the concept

---

407. Ibid., 181–233.
408. Ibid., 220.
409. Ibid.
410. Ibid.
411. Ibid.
412. Ibid.
413. Ibid., 221–2.
414. Ibid.
415. Ibid., 222.
416. Ibid.
417. Ibid., 222–3.
418. Ibid., 223.
419. Ibid. According to Morland, this verb is related to ἀγοράζω. He notes the verb ἐξαγοράζω occurs in the so-called contested letters of Paul (e.g. Col 4:5; Eph 5:16), "but only" in Gal 3:13 and 4:5 in his uncontested letters. According to Morland, redemption in Gal 3:13 may suggest "Christ has paid the proper price when redeeming us from the curse."

of expiation in the Levitical cult in connection with Gal 3:13,[420] and the Galatians' likely knowledge of the Levitical cultic background of expiation because of "Paul's preaching" (cf. 2 Cor 5:21; Rom 3:25–26; 8:3).[421] Moreland concludes since expiation was regarded as "the most appropriate means of eliminating the power of curses in Hellenistic culture," the Levitical cultic background behind Gal 3:13 is strong.[422]

5. Isaianic Background Behind Galatians 3:13. In a 1990 article about Isa 53 and the cross in Paul, Otto Betz suggests Paul in Gal 3:13 alludes to Isa 53:5.[423] According to Betz, the adjective ἐπικατάρατος in Gal 3:13 is similar to the curse language in Jewish literature (cf. 11QTemple 64.12).[424] He claims Paul may connect curse in Gal 3:13 with the concept of curse in Isa 53:5.[425]

In his 2010 monograph on Galatians, Matthew S. Harmon provides an argument for the Isaianic background behind Gal 3:13 as he provides a detailed argument for the Isaianic background behind Galatians.[426] Harmon argues along four lines of thought to support Isa 53 as the background behind Paul's remarks about Christ's redemption in Gal 3:13.[427] First, Gal 1:4 and 2:20 allude to Isa 53.[428] He says Paul may have appropriated traditional material in Gal 1:4 to refer to his gospel.[429] In 2:20, Paul "personalizes" a Christological statement by "replacing the reference to sins with a personal pronoun" ("for me").[430] Thus, given the similarities with Isa 53 in the context of Gal 3, an "echo here in Gal 3:13 must be judged as at least possible."[431]

---

420. Ibid., 223.
421. Ibid.
422. Ibid., 223. For criticisms of Morland, see Waters, *The End of Deuteronomy*, 88–92.
423. Otto Betz, "Die Übersetzungen von Jes 53 (LXX, Targum) und die Theologia Crucis des Paulus," in *Jesus der Herr der Kirche: Aufsätze zur biblischen Theologie II*, WUNT 52 (Tübingen: Mohr Siebeck, 1990), 197–216; see esp. 205–6. I rely upon Morland, *Curse*, 222 n. 138, for a summary of Betz's view.
424. Again, I rely upon Morland, *Curse*, 222 n. 138, for Betz's view. For the original citation, see Betz, "Übersetzungen."
425. Morland, *Curse*, 222 n. 138.
426. Harmon, *She Must and Shall Go Free*.
427. Ibid., 142–6.
428. Ibid., 142.
429. Ibid.
430. Ibid.
431. Ibid.

Harmon claims the parallels between Gal 1:4 and 3:13 further support an echo of Isa 53 in Gal 3:13.[432] He says the genitive Χριστοῦ in 1:3b and the nominative Χριστὸς in 3:13,[433] the clauses ἐξέληται ἡμᾶς in 1:4 and ἡμᾶς ἐξηγόρασεν in 3:13,[434] the phrases ἐκ τοῦ αἰῶνος τοῦ ἐνεστῶτος πονηροῦ in 1:4 and ἐκ τῆς κατάρας τοῦ νόμου in 3:13,[435] and the reflexive clauses τοῦ δόντος ἑαυτὸν ὑπὲρ τῶν ἁμαρτιῶν ἡμῶν in 1:4 and γενόμενος ὑπὲρ ἡμῶν κατάρα in 3:13 are parallel.[436] Paul does not, says Harmon, "explicitly" link the law or the curse "with the present evil age" in 1:4 and 3:13, but στοιχεῖα "strongly suggests" he aligns the law and the curse with "the present evil age."[437] Harmon says, consequently, readers should interpret 1:4 and 3:13 together.[438] "Thus, Christ becoming a curse for us can be understood as explaining how Christ gave himself for us. In his self-sacrificial death Christ became a curse for all who would be identified with him by faith."[439]

Second, Harmon discusses the similarities with Rom 4 and in Gal 3.[440] Harmon notes the differences between these two texts, but he points out Rom 4:25 "concludes with a statement" about Jesus's death (ὃς παρεδόθη διὰ τὰ παραπτώματα ἡμῶν καὶ ἠγέρθη διὰ τὴν δικαίωσιν ἡμῶν), which many Pauline scholars agree alludes to Isa 53.[441] Harmon infers, "given that Paul saw fit to end his discussion of Abraham in Rom 4 with a strong allusion to Isa 53 (albeit loosely connected to the larger context), we should not dismiss the possibility that his description of Christ's death here also has its roots in Isa 53."[442]

Third, Harmon discusses Isa 53 and points out Israel's plight of exile in Isa 53 because of their disobedience to YHWH (cf. Deut 27–29).[443] Harmon states there are both "new exodus themes" in Isa 40–55 and lexical connections between Deut 27–32 and Isa 53.[444] Because of space constraints, Harmon lists only the most significant connections.[445]

432. Ibid.
433. Ibid.
434. Ibid.
435. Ibid.
436. Ibid., 142–3.
437. Ibid., 143.
438. Ibid.
439. Ibid.
440. Ibid.
441. Ibid., 143–4.
442. Ibid., 144.
443. Ibid.
444. Ibid.
445. Ibid.

1. *Introduction and Thesis* 43

Harmon shows that in Isa 54:4, the Servant "bears the sickness (חֳלָיֵנוּ) of the people,"⁴⁴⁶ a consequence of disobeying YHWH (Deut 28:58–61).⁴⁴⁷ He asserts "YHWH promises to strike" (יַכְּכָה) Israel with suffering (Deut 28:22, 27–28, 35).⁴⁴⁸ He claims Isaiah identifies the Servant as "stricken (מֻכֵּה) by God" (Isa 53:4).⁴⁴⁹ He demonstrates YHWH threatens to disperse Israel throughout the earth (הָאָרֶץ) in Deut 28:64; 29:26–27 if the people disobey (Eng. 29:27–28).⁴⁵⁰ He declares that YHWH "will cut off his Servant from the land (הָאָרֶץ) of the living" (Isa 53:8).⁴⁵¹ Harmon continues Deut 29:15, 19 likens "the curse with death," and Isaiah says the Servant would die (Isa 53:8–9).⁴⁵² Harmon says further the Servant's "vicarious suffering" blesses "his seed" (זֶרַע) and turns away "the curse placed on Israel and her seed (Deut 28:46, 59)."⁴⁵³ Harmon suggests this reversal echoes the Deuteronomic promise of both the "future restoration of Israel and her seed" (Deut 30:6).⁴⁵⁴ Harmon declares Moses states "YHWH promises" to be merciful with his people, to vindicate their blood, and to provide atonement (Deut 32:36, 43).⁴⁵⁵ Likewise, Harmon states Isaiah's Servant comforts his people, experiences vindication, and takes upon himself the sins "of many" (Isa 53:4–5, 10–12).⁴⁵⁶ Harmon concludes, "The fact that Paul conflates Deut 27:26 and 28:58 in Gal 3:10 further suggests he has made" connections with Isaiah.⁴⁵⁷

Fourth, Harmon appeals to "evidence in the early church" to support his thesis. This evidence is important for Harmon because he claims it connects Deut 21:23 and Isa 53.⁴⁵⁸ Harmon first discusses Justin Martyr's *Dialogue with Trypho* to find similar connections as he sees in Galatians.⁴⁵⁹ Harmon claims Justin suggests Trypho objects that Jesus is the Christ because the crucifixion cursed Jesus (*Dial*. 89.1–2).⁴⁶⁰ Harmon says Justin

446. Ibid.
447. Ibid.
448. Ibid.
449. Ibid.
450. Ibid.
451. Ibid.
452. Ibid.
453. Ibid.
454. Ibid.
455. Ibid., 144–5.
456. Ibid., 145.
457. Ibid.
458. Ibid.
459. Ibid.
460. Ibid.

replies by alluding to Isa 53's prediction of Jesus's death (*Dial.* 89.3).[461] Harmon continues that Justin argues Christ experienced the law's curse via the process of crucifixion (*Dial.* 95.1–2).[462] Harmon admits some might protest against evidence from Justin since his work post-dates Paul.[463] But he insists "serious consideration must be given to the possibility that Deut 21:23 was used by Jews in the earliest days of the Christian movement as evidence that Jesus was not the Messiah. If so, the solution found in Isaiah 53 as offered by Justin Martyr may have its roots within the earliest period of the church, and may even be presupposed in Gal 3:10–14."[464]

Harmon concludes it is "probable that in Gal 3:13 Paul is alluding to Isa 53."[465] He admits, however, "the verbal connections between Gal 3:13" and Isa 53 are more explicit in 1:4 and 2:20.[466] Yet, Harmon thinks the parallels between 1:4 and 3:13 are sufficient to establish Isa 53's influence on Christ's act of redemption in Gal 3:13.[467] According to Harmon, Paul's use of Isa 53 in Gal 3:14 to discuss the Gentiles' participation in the Abrahamic blessing of the Spirit further supports his thesis.[468]

6. Pre-Pauline Confessional Formula. In his 1979 Galatians commentary, Hans Dieter Betz briefly discusses the origin of Paul's statement about Jesus's death in Gal 3:13. He claims "liberation from the curse of the" law is "a benefit of Christ's death on the cross."[469] Betz describes his remarks about Jesus's death as "christological-soteriological dogma" with the clause Χριστὸς ἡμᾶς ἐξηγόρασεν ἐκ τῆς κατάρας τοῦ νόμου ("Christ redeemed us from the curse of the law") (3:13).[470] He continues "The very concise formulation of this doctrine employs several concepts which were brought together to define what is meant by redemption."[471] Betz claims Paul presupposes an "unredeemed humanity" that is "enslaved

---

461. Ibid.
462. Ibid.
463. Ibid.
464. Ibid.
465. Ibid.
466. Ibid., 145–6.
467. Ibid., 146.
468. Ibid., 146–73.
469. Hans Dieter Betz, *Galatians*, Hermeneia (Minneapolis: Fortress, 1979), 149. See also Barnabas Lindars, *New Testament Apologetic: The Doctrinal Significance of the Old Testament Quotations* (Philadelphia: Westminster, 1961), 232–37.
470. Betz, *Galatians*, 149.
471. Ibid.

by the elements of the world" (4:3).[472] Betz says Jews experienced this enslavement by "being under the curse of Torah."[473] "God sent Jesus Christ, his Son," to earth in the fullness of time "to redeem humanity from its terrible fate."[474] As a Jew living under the law (4:4), "Christ purchases the freedom of those under the law" (4:5a).[475] As a result, says Betz, "Christ purchases adoption" for those enslaved by "the elements of the world" (4:9; cf. 3:26–29; 4:1–7, 21–31).[476] He continues, stating that Christ's redemption purchased adoption is evident "in the gift of the Spirit."[477]

Betz asserts the background behind Paul's "christological and soteriological doctrine" of redemption is "Jewish Christianity."[478] He claims Paul's remarks in Gal 3:13 support this when he says that Christ subjected himself to a curse for us (γενόμενος ὑπὲρ ἡμῶν κατάρα).[479] Betz states further Paul assumes sacrificial ideas with this participial clause without developing them here.[480] Betz acknowledges several questions emerge, however, from Paul's statement. "Does Paul mean that Christ became the object of the curse in place of us or a curse offering as a means of propitiation for us? Is the notion derived from Judaism, from the pre-Pauline tradition in Gal 4:4–5, or is it a formulation *ad hoc*?"[481]

Betz cautiously remarks one cannot answer these questions with certainty.[482] But he contends, "most likely," Paul makes use of traditional material in Gal 3:13 when he refers to "Jesus's death as a self-sacrifice and atonement."[483] Betz cites Gal 1:4 (Christ "gave himself for our sins to deliver us from the present evil age'") and 2:20 (Christ "loved me and gave himself for me") to support his view.[484] He continues that "Christ's incarnation" (4:4–5) enabled him to suffer "as a human being."[485] Because he was without sin (cf. 2 Cor 5:21), "his death was, in Jewish terms,

---

472. Ibid.
473. Ibid.
474. Ibid.
475. Ibid.
476. Ibid.
477. Ibid., 149–50.
478. Ibid.
479. Ibid.
480. Ibid.
481. Ibid., 150–1.
482. Ibid.
483. Ibid., 151.
484. Ibid.
485. Ibid.

uniquely meritorious."[486] As a result of his death, Betz infers, "we" are now free from the law's curse and "indeed from the law itself,"[487] because "Christ is the end of the law (Rom 10:4; Gal 2:19–20; 3:25; 5:6; 6:15)."[488] Betz admits Paul may have been the only one to conclude this last inference.[489] Yet, "one can still see an underlying concept of Jesus's death interpreted by means of the Jewish concept of the meritorious death of the righteous and its atoning benefits."[490]

7. Jewish Martyrological and Adam-Christological Background Behind Galatians 3:13. In his 1993 Galatians commentary, James D. G. Dunn asserts that Paul's remarks about Jesus

> having become a curse for us is a combination of martyr theology (itself using the imagery of the sacrificial cult) and Adam christology. That is to say, the thought is not just of an action which had benefit for others (a man laying down his life for his friends or country). Much more the thought is of Jesus as acting in a representative capacity, so that his death and its consequences were an enactment of human destiny with effects on humanity; the law printing its curse on Jesus, as it were, so that in his death the force of the curse was exhausted, and those held under its power were liberated.[491]

Dunn offers a careful exegesis of Gal 3:10–14 in the argument of Galatians, arguing Jesus's act of becoming a curse extends the blessing to the Jews and Gentiles.[492] He emphasizes the curse of the law was expulsion from the covenant community.[493] With respect to the citation of Deut 27:26 in Gal 3:10 and obedience to the whole law, Dunn asserts it

---

486. Ibid.
487. Ibid.
488. Ibid.
489. Ibid.
490. Ibid. For additional scholars on a pre-Pauline confessional background with different nuances and emphases, see also Longenecker, *Galatians*, 122–3; Martyn, *Galatians*, 217–319; Hays, "Galatians," 261; idem, *The Faith of Jesus Christ: The Narrative Substructure of Galatians 3:1–4:11*, 2nd ed. (Grand Rapids: Eerdmans, 2022), 77–80. Martyn is particularly concerned with an apocalyptic reading of Gal 3:13. Martinus C. de Boer, *Galatians*, NTL (Louisville: Westminster John Knox, 2011), 210–14, esp. 210 seems to assume traditional material too. Contra J. Blank, *Paulus und Jesus*, SANT 18 (Munich: Kösel, 1968), 262–3.
491. Dunn, *Galatians*, 177.
492. Ibid., 168–80.
493. Ibid.

refers to "living within the provisions of the law, including all its provisions for sin, through repentance and atonement."[494]

Dunn asserts as a matter of fact a Jewish martyrological background behind Gal 3:13, yet without providing compelling exegetical support. Unless I have overlooked his discussion, he neither provides an analysis of the pertinent martyrological texts nor shows evidence that in Galatians, martyr theology is a background in front of which to read Paul's remarks about Christ's death in Gal 3:13.

8. Jewish Martyrological Background in Galatians 1–2. In Stephen Anthony Cummins's 2001 monograph, the author analyzes Paul's autobiographical remarks in Gal 1–2 in light of a "Maccabean martyr model of Judaism."[495] His thesis is "the historical and theological significance of the Antioch incident (Gal 2:11–21) gains great clarity and weight when viewed in relation to a Maccabean martyr model of Judaism as now christologically reconfigured and redeployed in the life and (Antiochene) ministry of the Apostle Paul."[496] After Cummins surveys (what he thinks are) the formative texts for Maccabean martyrdom and Second Temple Judaism, he discusses key texts in Galatians to support the ways in which he thinks Paul "christologically" reworks Maccabean martyrdom and applies it to the messianic community because Jesus, who was the Christian community's "martyred Messiah," died.[497]

In his previous life of Judaism, Cummins claims Paul's (Saul's) zeal for his fathers' ancestral traditions was similar to Maccabean zeal for the law.[498] Paul shows this kind of zeal by violently persecuting the church.[499] But, Cummins says, after his Damascus road experience, Paul then suffers similarly as a martyr as he seeks to be faithful to the martyred Messiah.[500] He claims both Paul's opponents in Galatia, who compelled the Galatians to be circumcised, and Peter in Antioch, who compelled the Gentile Christians there to live a Jewish way of life, behave similar to Antiochus Epiphanes IV, who compelled the Jews to live as Gentiles.[501]

---

494. Ibid., 171.
495. Stephen Anthony Cummins, *Paul and the Crucified Christ in Antioch*, SNTSMS 114 (Cambridge: Cambridge University Press, 2001), 19–92.
496. Ibid., 16–92, esp. 16.
497. Ibid., 93–137, 161–230.
498. Ibid.
499. Ibid.
500. Ibid.
501. Ibid.

Cummins specifically points out that Christian Jews and Gentiles in Antioch are God's persecuted covenant-people.[502] He infers that because of the Messiah, Paul reframes the boundary markers for both the people of God and his enemies.[503] Cummins's work is very illuminating. However, he does not appear to apply his thesis for Gal 1–2 and his arguments to the cursed Christ in Gal 3:13 in a comprehensive way.[504]

IV. Chapter Summaries

In the subsequent chapters, I engage in a comparative analysis of Jewish martyrological texts and texts in Galatians to support my twofold thesis. As I stated above, my thesis is as follows: first, the Jewish martyrological ideas, codified in 2 and 4 Maccabees and in LXX Dan 3, provide *a* background in front of which to read Paul's statements about the cursed Christ in Gal 3:13 and about the soteriological benefits his death achieves for Jews and Gentiles in Galatians. Second, Paul modifies these traditions to fit his exegetical, polemical, theological, and conceptual purposes in Galatians in order to persuade the Galatians not to embrace the "other" gospel. The comparison seeks to illuminate the soteriological significance of a Jewish martyrological background behind Paul's remarks about the cursed Christ in Gal 3:13 and in his argument in Gal 3:10–14. To support my thesis, I provide five arguments. First, Galatians has scriptural points of contact with Jewish martyrological ideas. Second, Galatians has theological/conceptual points of contact with Jewish martyrological ideas. Third, Galatians has lexical and grammatical points of contact with Jewish martyrological ideas. Fourth, Galatians has polemical/argumentative points of contact with Jewish martyrological ideas. Fifth, in Galatians, Paul has numerous discontinuities with Jewish martyrological ideas.

The book has six chapters. The opening chapter has introduced the book's thesis, method, contribution, and offered a selective history of research of scholarship on Gal 3:13. This chapter has also defined the meaning of Jewish martyrological traditions in this monograph. Chapter 2, "Deuteronomic Blessings and Curses in Second Temple Jewish Martyrological Traditions," focuses on the Deuteronomic blessings and curses in Second Temple Jewish martyrological traditions. The intent of this chapter is to analyze the Deuteronomic blessings and curses motif in

---

502. Ibid.
503. Ibid.
504. For his comments on Gal 3:13, see ibid., 109, 218–19, 225–6. For a brief comment about martyrology and Gal 3:13, see Eduard Lohse, *Märtyrer und Gottesknecht*, FRLANT 46 (Göttingen: Vandenhoeck & Ruprecht, 1955), 156.

the Jewish martyrological traditions for the purpose of providing data for a comparative reading of the Deuteronomic blessings and curses motif in Galatians. The analysis in Chapters 2–3 serves to highlight continuities and discontinuities in these texts to support the premise that the deaths of Torah-observant Jews in the Jewish martyrological traditions are a background in front of which to read Paul's remarks about the cursed Christ in Gal 3:13, although they similarly and dissimilarly appropriate the Deuteronomic blessings and curses to Torah-observant Jews who voluntarily died for the soteriological benefit of non-Torah observant sinners to deliver them from the curse of the law.

The analysis in Chapter 2 serves to support six arguments. First, the authors of the Jewish martyrological traditions conflate the Abrahamic blessing and Deuteronomic blessings to show the pathway to the Abrahamic blessing and life in this age and in the age to come is obedience to Torah. Second, the authors of the Jewish martyrological traditions appropriate Deuteronomic blessings to Torah-observant Jews. Third, the authors of the Jewish martyrological traditions appropriate the Deuteronomic curses to non-Torah-observant Jews. Fourth, the authors of the Jewish martyrological traditions posit Torah-observant Jewish martyrs as the means by which non-Torah-observant Jews receive the life promised in Torah. Fifth, the authors of the Jewish martyrological traditions interpret the promise of temporal life in the land as eternal life in the age to come. Sixth, the authors of the Jewish martyrological traditions suggest Torah-observant Jews experience eternal life in the age to come by Torah-observance.

Chapter 3, "Deuteronomic Blessings and Curses in Galatians," argues Paul presents both Jews and Gentiles as recipients of the Deuteronomic blessings and curses. Paul contends that Jesus, the Torah-observant Jew, suffered the Deuteronomic curses for others, experienced the blessing of law (i.e. resurrection-life), and delivered those for whom he died from the curse of the law so that Jews and Gentiles would participate in both the Abrahamic blessing of the Spirit and the Deuteronomic blessing of life apart from works of the law and so that they would be delivered from the law's curse. Chapter 3 intends to support the following three assertions.

First, Paul appropriates the Deuteronomic blessings and curses to Jews and Gentiles. Second, Paul appropriates the Abrahamic blessing of the Spirit and the Deuteronomic blessing of life to those who identify with Jesus Christ by faith, the seed of Abraham, apart from works of the law, and he applies the Deuteronomic curses to those who identify with works of Torah *apart from* or *in addition to* faith in Christ. Third, Paul emphasizes both the Abrahamic blessing and the Deuteronomic blessing are for both Jews and Gentiles, but only experienced by faith in Christ via the distribution of the Spirit apart from Torah observance. Jews and

Gentiles who refuse to place faith in the cursed Christ, Jesus, remain under the curse of the law and fall short of the blessing of Abraham, but receive in full the Deuteronomic curses. Fourth, in light of God's revelation of Christ to Paul, Paul understands the promise in Lev 18:5 and Deut 27–30, that Torah-observance leads to long life in the land, signifies eternal life. This eternal life is experienced apart from the works of the law by Jews and Gentiles who place faith in Jesus because Jesus died to deliver them from the present evil age and from the curse of the law. Jesus took the Deuteronomic curse upon himself for Jews and Gentiles so that they would receive both the Abrahamic blessing of the Spirit and the Deuteronomic blessing of life.

Beyond this, I argue in Chapter 3 Paul conflates the Abrahamic and Deuteronomic blessings and curses motif in Galatians to emphasize that both the Abrahamic blessing and the Deuteronomic blessing are extended to Jews and Gentiles by faith in the Messiah and realized in the death (and resurrection) of the Messiah, Jesus, whereas the Jewish martyrological narratives suggest the covenant with Abraham is fulfilled for Jews by means of Torah observance and the noble deaths of the Jewish martyrs for Israel (2 and 4 Maccabees), by means of military action (2 Maccabees), and by means of effective prayer (2 and 4 Maccabees). Likewise, in Galatians, both the Abrahamic curse and the Deuteronomic curse are realized in Torah-observant Jews and Gentiles, who remain under the curse of the law outside of faith in Jesus, the Messiah. Nevertheless, Jesus received the Deuteronomic curse and blessing on behalf of Jews and Gentiles under the Deuteronomic curse so that the Abrahamic blessing, namely, a universal outpouring of the Spirit upon Jewish and Gentile followers of Christ, would be distributed to Jews and Gentiles by faith apart from Torah observance.

Chapter 4, "Representation and Substitution in Second Temple Jewish Martyrological Traditions and in Galatians 3:13," argues the authors of the martyrological narratives present the Torah-observant martyrs as dying as representatives of and as substitutes for non-Torah-observant Jews. In Gal 3:13, Paul suggests the Christ died as a representative of and as a substitute for non-Torah-observant Jews and Gentiles. The martyrs died for the sins of fellow Jews to deliver them from the law's curse, but Jesus died for the sins of Jews and Gentiles to redeem both groups from the curse of the law, to give them the Abrahamic blessing of the Spirit, to make them part of the seed of Abraham, and to give them the Deuteronomic blessing of life.

Chapter 5, "Lexical, Grammatical, and Additional Similarities Between Second Temple Jewish Martyrological Traditions and Galatians," focuses on lexical, grammatical, and additional similarities between Second

Temple Jewish martyrological traditions and Galatians in order to support the thesis of a martyrological background behind Gal 3:13. I discuss two specific kinds of similarities in this chapter. First, building upon Cummins's lexical and grammatical work in his monograph on Gal 1–2, I discuss lexical and grammatical similarities between Second Temple Jewish martyrological traditions and Galatians. I argue Paul's letter to the Galatians has multiple lexical and grammatical points of contact with the Jewish martyrological traditions. This section briefly analyzes and discusses the texts in which these lexical and grammatical connections occur in order to highlight the lexical and grammatical similarities.

Second, I briefly discuss the additional conceptual similarities between the Jewish martyrological traditions and Gal 3:13 that are important for my thesis. These additional similarities do not provide enough material to warrant their own independent chapter. This part of the analysis argues the Jewish martyrological narratives and Galatians are similar in that they are highly polemical in their efforts to defend Judaism (Jewish martyrological narratives) or the gospel (Galatians). Second Maccabees seeks to defend the superiority of Judaism over Hellenism and argues against extreme Hellenization in an effort to dissuade Jews from eradicating a Jewish way of life with a turn from the law. Fourth Maccabees argues religious reasoning (i.e. devotion to Torah) masters the passions, even in the face of extreme suffering. Paul seeks to defend his Torah-free and Gentile-inclusive gospel against the Torah-observant and Gentile-exclusive gospel of his opponents and argues against Judaizing the Gentiles in an effort to dissuade the Galatians from turning away from his gospel to embrace a Jewish way of life.

Chapter 6, "Conclusion: A Jewish Martyrological Reading of Galatians 3:13," applies the analysis from Chapters 2–5 to support a Jewish martyrological reading of Gal 3:13. Based on the analysis, this chapter concludes there are similarities and dissimilarities between the Jewish martyrological traditions and Galatians. A discussion of these similarities and dissimilarities attempts to strengthen the thesis that the Jewish martyrological traditions are *a* background (not *the* background) in front of which we should read Gal 3:13 and that Paul has discontinuities with these traditions to fit his own exegetical, theological, conceptual, and polemical purposes. While acknowledging there are areas of discontinuity between Jewish martyrology and Paul's presentation of the cursed Christ in Gal 3:13, the concluding chapter also discusses the reason a Jewish martyrological reading of Gal 3:13 provides fresh insights into the death of the cursed Christ "for us" in Paul's soteriology in Galatians.

2

DEUTERONOMIC BLESSINGS AND CURSES IN SECOND TEMPLE JEWISH MARTYROLOGICAL TRADITIONS

This chapter focuses on Deuteronomic blessings and curses in Second Temple Jewish martyrological traditions.[1] The intent of this chapter is to analyze the Deuteronomic blessings and curses motif in the Jewish martyrological traditions for the purpose of providing data for a comparative reading of the Deuteronomic blessings and curses motif in Galatians.[2] The analysis in Chapters 2–3 serves to highlight continuities and discontinuities in these texts to support the premise that the deaths of Torah-observant Jews in the Jewish martyrological traditions are a background in front of which to read Paul's remarks about the cursed Christ in Gal 3:13, although they similarly and dissimilarly appropriate the Deuteronomic blessings and curses to Torah-observant Jews who voluntarily died for the soteriological benefit of non-Torah-observant sinners to deliver them from the curse of the law.

---

1. George W. E. Nickelsburg (*Jewish Literature Between the Bible and the Mishnah* [Philadelphia: Fortress, 1981], 118).

2. Scholars have offered several theories regarding the purpose of the body of 2 Maccabees. Joseph Sievers (*The Hasmoneans and Their Supporters: From Mattathias to the Death of John Hyrcanus I*, USFSHJ 6 [Atlanta: Scholars Press, 1990], 8–10) arranged the different theories under four categories. For examples of the "cultic category," see Carl L. W. Grimm, "Das zweite, dritte, und vierte Buch der Maccabäer, vierte Lieferung," in *Kurzgefasstes exegetisches Handbuch zu den Apokryphen des Alten Testaments*, ed. O. F. Fritische (Leipzig: S. Hirzel, 1857), xii; Felix-Marie Abel, *Les Livres des Maccabées* (Paris: J. Gabalda, 1949), xliv; Arnaldo Momigliano, *Prime line di storia della tradizione Maccabaica*, repr. (Amsterdam: Hakkert, 1968 [1930]), 96–7; Harold Attridge, "2 Maccabees," in *The Jewish Writings of the Second Temple Period*, ed. M. E. Stone, CRINT (Philadelphia: Fortress, 1984), 182; Jochen Gabriel Bunge, "Untersuchungen zum zweiten Makkabäerbuch: Quellenkritische, literarische, chronologische und historische Untersuchungen zum zweiten Makkabäerbuch

The analysis in this chapter serves to support six arguments. First, the authors of the Jewish martyrological traditions conflate the Abrahamic blessing and Deuteronomic blessings to show that the pathway to the Abrahamic blessing is obedience to Torah. Second, the authors of the Jewish martyrological traditions appropriate Deuteronomic blessings to Torah-observant Jews. Third, the authors of the Jewish martyrological traditions appropriate the Deuteronomic curses to non-Torah-observant Jews. Fourth, the authors of the Jewish martyrological traditions posit Torah-observant Jewish martyrs as the means by which non-Torah-observant Jews receive the life promised in Torah. Fifth, the authors of the Jewish martyrological traditions interpret the promise of temporal life in the land as eternal life in the age to come. Sixth, the authors of the Jewish martyrological traditions suggest Torah-observant Jews experience eternal life in the age to come by Torah-observance.

I. Blessing, Curse, and the Promises to Abraham[3]

Deuteronomy focuses on three major speeches given by Moses to Israel before his death and before the people entered the promised land. Moses's first speech occurs in Deut 1:6–4:43. Moses recounts the Lord's historical

---

als Quelle syrisch-palästinensischer Geschichte im 2. Jh. v. Chr." (PhD diss., Rheinische Friedrich-Wilhelms-Universität, 1971), 528, 613; Christian Habicht, *2. Makkabäerbuch*, JSHRZ 1 (Gütersloh: Gerd Mohn, 1976), 186. For the "theological category," see Diego Arenhoevel, *Die Theokratie nach dem 1. und 2. Makkabäerbuch*, Walberberger Studien Theologische Reihe 3 (Mainz: Grünewald, 1967), 122. For the "historiographic category," see Jonathan A. Goldstein, *II Maccabees*, AB 41A (Garden City, NY: Doubleday, 1983), 64–9, 82. For the "propagandistic category," see Robert Doran, *Temple Propaganda: The Purpose and Character of 2 Maccabees*, CBQMS 12 (Washington, DC: Catholic Biblical Association, 1981), 114. Summaries and sources cited from David S. Williams, "Recent Research in 2 Maccabees," *CBR* 2 (2003): 74–5.

3. My summary and discussion of OT texts are dependent upon the accepted outlines in the New Revised Standard Version (NRSV) with Apocrypha in the New Interpreter's Study Bible and in the English Standard Version Study Bible and the English Standard Version translation. My discussion of Deuteronomy in this section relies upon Paul Barker's division of the book in the English Standard Version Study Bible, "Deuteronomy" (Wheaton: Crossway, 2008), 321–9. Unless otherwise indicated, paraphrases and explanations of OT texts and 2 and 4 Maccabees are dependent on the NRSV and the ESV with Apocrypha published by Oxford. Translations of specific Hebrew and Greek phrases or sentences in ancient texts are my own unless otherwise indicated.

dealings with Israel, reminding the people that he entered into a covenant with them and they with him. He reminds them that blessing in the land requires obedience to the stipulations of the covenant, but disobedience results in a curse (cf. Deut 27–30). He recalls YHWH "has set forth the land" before the people (Deut 1:8). He exhorts them to "go forth and inherit the land" (Deut 1:8), which he swore to Abraham and his seed after him (Deut 1:8).

1. God Made Covenantal Promises to Abraham apart from Torah. The blessing of inheritance and peace in the land is connected both to YHWH's promise to Abraham and his offspring and Israel's obedience to the Mosaic covenant. YHWH's original promise to Abraham included land, seed, and universal blessing (cf. Gen 12:1–3). This promise was both conditional and unconditional. YHWH unconditionally promised to bless Abraham and to grant him many blessings without any requirements of law-observance. Yet, Abraham's experience of this unconditional blessing required his faithful obedience to YHWH's commands that he revealed to him throughout his life (cf. Gen 12:1–3; 15:6; 22:1–24). For example, Abraham had to leave Ur of the Chaldeans to participate in the blessings that YHWH unconditionally promised to him (Gen 12:1–3). Abraham had to obey YHWH's command to offer his son Isaac on the altar as proof of his belief in the promise (Gen 22:1–24; cf. Gen 15:1–6).

2. God Made Covenantal Promises to Israel Based on Torah because of his Promise to Abraham. In Deuteronomy, the obedience required to inherit the land and to experience blessings therein depended on Israel's obedience to the stipulations of the Mosaic covenant. YHWH specifies at Sinai (Exod 20:1; cf. Horeb in Deut 1:6) the precise way he expected his people to obey him. The people agree to obey YHWH's covenantal stipulations, and Moses ratifies this covenant by sprinkling blood on the people, the altar, and the book of the covenant (Exod 24:1–8). A commitment to obey the stipulations of the covenant was the prerequisite for blessing in the land (cf. Deut 27–30). Thus, prior to Moses's death and prior to Joshua leading the people into the promised land, the former predicates the fulfillment of the land promise given to Abraham and his offspring upon Israel's obedience to the stipulations of the Mosaic covenant given at Sinai (Deut 7:9–26; 30:15–20; cf. Gen 12:1–3).

2. Deuteronomic Blessings and Curses

To be sure, YHWH chose Israel because of his love for her prior to the giving of the law (Deut 7:1–11). He delivered his chosen people out of Egyptian slavery first and then gave them a law in order to set them apart from other nations as his people and to provide a clear way of life for them to live distinctly as his covenant people in a new land (Exod 20:1–Deut 30:20). Still, the blessing of life in the land, promised to Abraham and his offspring, depended in part upon Israel's obedience to the stipulations of the Mosaic covenant given at Sinai. Israel as a people entered into the land promised to Abraham years after YHWH gave Israel his law at Sinai (cf. Gen 12:1–3; 15:6; Exod 20:1; Joshua).

In his first speech, Moses emphatically reminds the people of the conditional nature of covenantal life in the land by stressing life in the land was conditioned upon their obedience to the Sinaitic covenant (Deut 4:1–43). Moses urges Israel to hear the "statutes" and the "judgments" so that they would live and enter the land (4:1), which "the Lord, the God" of their ancestors would give them (4:1). They could neither add to nor take from the law (4:2). He reminds Israel of YHWH's judgment of those who had sexual relations with the women of Moab and worshipped Baal of Peor as an example of the grave consequences of disobedience to the covenant (4:3; cf. Num 25:1–5). YHWH killed those who worshipped Baal of Peor, while those who "were clinging to YHWH" their God remained alive (4:4). Israel must "keep" and "do" (4:6), "guard" themselves, and "keep" their soul so that that they would not forget Moses's words regarding YHWH's law (4:9). He commands them to make these words known to their sons and their sons' sons so that they too may live long in the land from generation to generation (4:9–10).

YHWH urged Moses to assemble the people so that he would cause them to hear his words (4:10). YHWH spoke to Israel his covenant (i.e. the Ten Commandments) and wrote them on tablets of stone (4:13). YHWH commanded Moses to teach Israel "statutes" and "judgments" in the land they would inherit (4:14). But he would not enter the land with them because of YHWH's anger against him on account of his disobedience (4:21–22; cf. Num 20:10–13; Deut 3:27; 31:2; 32:48–52).

Israel had to be careful not to forget YHWH's covenant with them and avoid giving themselves over to idols (4:23), "because the Lord, your God, is a consuming fire, a zealous God" (כִּי יְהוָה אֱלֹהֶיךָ אֵשׁ אֹכְלָה הוּא אֵל קַנָּא) (4:23). Moses calls heaven and earth as his witness that idolatry (a clear violation of the covenant [Exod 20:2–6; 32:1–35]) in the land would lead to Israel's destruction in the land (4:25–26). He assures the people that YHWH would judge their disobedience and that Israel would be sure to disobey (4:27–29). Because YHWH is merciful, he would certainly not forget the covenant he swore to their fathers (4:31–39). Moses again commands Israel to keep the statutes and commandments so that they would remain in the land, which YHWH planned to give to them "all of the days" (4:40).

Moses's second speech generally focuses on the stipulations of the covenant (4:44–11:32). Here Moses recapitulates the Ten Commandments (5:1–21). He reminds them of the covenantal obligations YHWH set forth to them at Sinai (cf. Deut 5:2, 10). Israel asks him to mediate God's law (5:22–33). He discusses the greatest commandment (6:1–25), the conquest and worship (7:1–26), and exhorts the people to learn from the failures of the wanderings in the wilderness (8:1–20). He reminds them of the Golden Calf episode (9:1–10:11), and he offers final exhortations (10:12–11:32). Moses's second speech highlights specific stipulations of the covenant (12:1–26:19). Moses's third and final speech discusses the blessings and curses of the covenant (27:1–28:68). He promises that curses would certainly come upon Israel in the land if they should disobey the covenant (Deut 27:9–26). YHWH expected Israel to keep "every commandment" that he commanded them before entering into the promised land (27:1; 28:15, 58) so that the people would avoid these curses, which would certainly come upon them in the land if they disobeyed (27:9–26; 28:15–68). The blessings of the covenant would come upon Israel only if the people obeyed all of YHWH's commandments (28:1).

Moses, then, offers Israel final exhortations (29:1–30:20). In Deut 29, Moses reminds the people of the covenant at Moab (29:1). He also reminds Israel of YHWH's previous work on their behalf in the land of Egypt (29:2–3). He shockingly informs them that YHWH had not given Israel "a heart to understand, ears to hear, and eyes to see" what the Lord had done on behalf of them (29:4). Yet, he urges Israel "to keep the words of the covenant" and "do them" so that they would live prosperously (29:9).

Moses's review of Israel's past journeys with YHWH leads to his instructive speech in Deut 30. The speech focuses on Israel's future. YHWH promised to restore the fortunes of Israel by leading them to the land of their fathers if they obey his voice and return to him (30:1–5). YHWH promised to enable Israel to obey his commandments with a promise to circumcise their heart (וּמָל יְהוָה אֱלֹהֶיךָ אֶת־לְבָבְךָ) and the heart of their seed (וְאֶת־לְבַב זַרְעֶךָ), so that they would love YHWH and live (לְאַהֲבָה אֶת־יְהוָה אֱלֹהֶיךָ בְּכָל־לְבָבְךָ וּבְכָל־נַפְשְׁךָ לְמַעַן חַיֶּיךָ) (30:6–8). Their heart-circumcision would lead to Israel's prosperity in the land when they obeyed all of his commandments in the book of Torah and turn to him with all of their heart (30:9–10), because his commandments are not too difficult for them (30:11). Because of YHWH's action, the commandments were near Israel, in their mouths, and in their hearts (30:11, 14). Israel, therefore, would hear the law so that they would do it (וְנַעֲשֶׂנָּה אֹתָהּ וַיִּשְׁמָעֵנוּ) because of YHWH's action within their heart (30:14). Israel's past situation was one of suffering, but YHWH promises he would create a new heart and cause them to walk in a triumphant future. Deuteronomy 31:1–34:12 concludes by focusing on the succession of leadership from Moses to Joshua.

The Jewish martyrological traditions appropriate the blessings and curses of Deuteronomy against Israel and against the Torah-observant martyrs because of the non-Torah observance of some within the nation. Deuteronomy 27–28 asserts that the curses of disobedience come against those who disobey the Torah-covenant (Deut 27) and the blessings of obedience come upon those who obey the Torah-covenant (Deut 28). Moses and the elders of Israel urged the people to obey all of Torah's stipulations (אֶת־כָּל־הַמִּצְוָה), so that the people would experience the blessing of long life in the promised land. References to the law throughout Deuteronomy suggest Moses's remarks in Deut 27–28 pertain to the entire law, not only to the stipulations in Deut 27.[4] The importance of heeding to the stipulations of the covenant emerge in numerous texts throughout the Hebrew Bible and throughout Second Temple Judaism.[5] In the rest of this chapter, I discuss the Deuteronomic blessings and curses motif in the Jewish martyrological traditions.

II. Deuteronomic Blessings and Curses in Second Temple Jewish Martyrological Traditions

Martha Himmelfarb states 2 Maccabees "is the first text to present Judaism and Hellenism as opposing categories."[6] Daniel R. Schwartz

---

4. For examples, see Deut 1:5; 4:1, 5–6, 8, 14, 40, 45; 5:1, 31; 6:1, 17, 20, 24; 7:11; 8:11; 11:32; 12:1, 16; 17:11, 18–19; 27:3, 8, 26; 28:58, 61; 29:20, 28; 30:10; 31:9, 11–12, 24, 26; 32:46.

5. For a discussion of the reception of Deuteronomy in early Judaism, see Lincicum, *Paul and the Early Jewish Encounter with Deuteronomy*.

6. Martha Himmelfarb, *Between Temple and Torah: Essays on Priests, Scribes, and Visionaries in the Second Temple Period and Beyond*, TSAJ 151 (Tübingen: Mohr Siebeck, 2013), 191. According to Himmelfarb, the author of 2 Maccabees created "the term Ἰουδαϊσμός and used the term Hellenismos in a fresh [way]." So also Christian Habicht, "Hellenismus und Judentum in der Zeit des Judaas Makkabäus," in *Jahrbuch Der Heidelberger Akademie der Wissenschaften für das Jahr 1974* (Heidelberg: Carl Winter, 1975), 98. Preceding information paraphrased from Himmelfarb, *Between Temple and Torah*, 191 n. 1.

asserts "the subject" of 2 Maccabees "is clear": "the history of the city of Jerusalem from the beginning of institutionalized Hellenization under the high priest Jason around 175 BCE and until Judas Maccabeus's victory over the Seleucid general Nicanor in the spring of 161 BCE."[7] In 1:7, the author of the first letter mentions that after Demetrius reigned in the 169th year (= 143 BCE), "we Jews wrote to" the Jews in Egypt in the critical moment that overtook "us" when Jason and his companions rebelled "from the holy land and the kingdom."[8] More than one scholar recognizes 2 Maccabees contains information relevant to 1 Macc 1–7.[9] Many scholars suggest the time span of the events covered in 2 Maccabees ranges from 180 to 161 BCE.[10] From the outset of 2 Maccabees, Onias III is the Judean high priest.[11] The book records examples of the importance of the high priesthood in Judea and times of contentions with Gentile rulers. The author records Judas's victory over the Greek general, Nicanor, at the end of the book. 2 Maccabees 2:19–32 is the compiler's preface.[12] He briefly summarizes the story he plans to unfold, the source of his information, and his method. The body of 2 Maccabees (2:19–15:37) claims to be a summary of Jason of Cyrene's lost five-volume work (2:23).[13] 2 Maccabees 1:1–2:18 begins with two letters attached to the body of the book.[14]

---

7. Daniel R. Schwartz, *2 Maccabees*, CEJL (Berlin: de Gruyter, 2008), 3.
8. Ibid., 4.
9. For recent research in 2 Maccabees up to 2003 and earlier scholarship, see Williams, "Recent Research in 2 Maccabees." Williams discusses 2 Maccabees' scholarship that developed over 25 years leading up to 2003. He begins the discussion about "commentaries and translations." He, then, turns his attention to selective scholarly topics of interest during the time period of 2003 and earlier. These topics are "chronological issues related to 1 and 2 Maccabees, the prefixed letters, date and provenance, sources, the purpose of 2 Maccabees, and the structure of the body."
10. Ibid.
11. Ibid.
12. 2 Maccabees is likely a composite text. I refer to the author or compiler throughout the monograph for simplicity.
13. For an example of scholars who argue that Jason was a "fictitious author," see W. Richnow, "Untersuchungen zu Sprache und Stil des 2. Makkabäerbuches: Ein Beitrag zur hellenistischen Historiographie" (PhD diss., Georg-August-Universität zu Göttingen, 1967), 41–2. Contra Doran, *Temple Propaganda*, 81–3. Sources cited in Williams, "Recent Research," 71.
14. For critical discussions of the festal letters attached to the epitome, see Benedikt Niese, "Kritik der beiden Makkabäerbücher nebst Beiträgen zur Geschichte

The first letter claims Jews in Jerusalem address the Jews in Egypt to encourage them to celebrate Hanukkah (1:1–9).[15] The second letter reports that the Jews of Jerusalem,[16] Judea, the senate, and Judas wrote to Aristobulus and to the Jews in Egypt (1:10–2:18). 2 Maccabees 3:1–15:37 is the body of the epitome of Jason's history, in which the composer(s) summarize(s) Jason's five-volume history. The book ends with a short epilogue (15:38–39).[17] It begins with a discussion of the importance of Hanukkah (1:9) and ends with a comment about Nicanor's Day (15:36).[18]

1. The narrative of 2 Maccabees communicates the blessing of Torah-observance and the curse of non-Torah observance in terms of piety and impiety. Jews experienced peace in the land when they obeyed Torah but unrest in the land because of disobedience to Torah. The Deuteronomic

---

der makkabäischen Erhebung," *Hermes* 35 (1900): 268–307; Elias Bickermann, "Ein jüdischer Festbrief vom Jahre 124 v. Chr. (II Macc. 1:1-9)," *ZNW* 32 (1933): 233–53; Bunge, "Untersuchungen zum zweiten Makkabäerbuch," 34 n. 7; Arnaldo Momigliano, "The Second Book of Maccabees," *CP* 70 (1975): 81–8; Habicht, *2. Makkabäerbuch*, 174–5; Goldstein, *II Maccabees*, 167. See these and additional sources cited in Robert Doran, *2 Maccabees: A Critical Commentary*, Hermeneia (Minneapolis: Fortress, 2012), 1–2.

15. For a discussion, see J. W. van Henten, *The Maccabean Martyrs as Saviours of the Jewish People: A Study of 2 and 4 Maccabees*, JSJSup 57 (Leiden: Brill, 1997), 40.

16. Whether Ἰουδαῖοι means "Jew" or "Judean" is a point of debate (cf. 2 Macc 1:1). The debate in part pertains to whether the term makes a specific ethnic designation or refers to an "occupational-status designation." According to the latter position, Ἰουδαῖος could have several ethnic designations. In agreement with Doran, I translate Ἰουδαῖος as "Jew" since "Judean" too narrowly limits Ἰουδαῖος to geography. Discussion in this note paraphrased from Doran, *2 Maccabees*, 24. See also Daniel R. Schwartz, "Judean or Jew? How Should We Translate Ἰουδαῖος in Josephus?," in *Jewish Identity in the Greco-Roman World/Jüdische Identität in der griechisch-römische Welt*, ed. Jörg Frey, Daniel R. Schwartz, and S. Gripentrog, AJEC 71 (Leiden: Brill, 2007), 3–27.

17. For a concise discussion of introductory issues in 2 Maccabees and for a bibliography, see Daniel R. Schwartz, "Maccabees, Second Book of," in *The Eerdmans Dictionary of Early Judaism* (Grand Rapids: Eerdmans, 2010), 905–7; idem, *2 Maccabees*, 1–96; Doran, *2 Maccabees*, 1–19. The authorship of 2 Maccabees is complex. It is outside of the purview of this monograph to engage critical scholars on the topic of authorship of 2 Maccabees. For the sake of convenience, I simply refer to the composer of the book as the "author" of 2 Maccabees throughout the monograph.

18. Schwartz argues Hanukkah is a secondary concern in 2 Maccabees. Schwartz, *2 Maccabees*, 9–10.

principle of blessing and curse appears throughout 2 Maccabees.[19] Peace dwelt in the land (τῆς ἁγίας πόλεως κατοικουμένης μετὰ πάσης εἰρήνης), and laws were strictly observed (καὶ τῶν νόμων ὅτι κάλλιστα συντηρουμένων), because of Onias's piety and his hatred of wickedness (διὰ τὴν Ονιου τοῦ ἀρχιερέως εὐσέβειάν τε καὶ μισοπονηρίαν) (3:1). "Laws" (τῶν νόμων) refer to the stipulations outlined in Torah. Wickedness refers to things contrary to the laws. Laws and commandments occur together in Jewish sources (cf. LXX Exod 18:16, 20; 2 Chr 31:21; Isa 24:5; Amos 2:4; Bar 4:1; Tob. 14:9 [AB]).[20]

In the first letter, the Jews in Jerusalem and in Judea pray the Egyptian Jews would remember God's covenant with Abraham, Isaac, and Jacob (1:2).[21] They also prayed he would give them a heart to worship God and to do his will (1:3), that he would open their hearts to his law and commandments,[22] and that he would bring them peace (1:4). Peace in 1:4 is a covenantal peace since 1:2 begins with the prayer that God would help the Jews in Egypt remember his covenant with Abraham, Isaac, and Jacob. This covenantal peace is also connected to Torah since the author prays that God would open the hearts of the Jews in Egypt to his law and commandments (καὶ διανοίξαι τὴν καρδίαν ὑμῶν ἐν τῷ νόμῳ αὐτοῦ καὶ ἐν τοῖς προστάγμασιν) and that he would grant them peace (καὶ εἰρήνην ποιῆσαι) (1:4).[23]

The second letter claims to address Aristobulus and the Jews in Egypt (1:10–2:18).[24] The author references God's salvation of the Jews from the king when he drove out those who fought against the holy city (1:11–17; esp. 1:11–12). After a short discussion of Nehemiah's sacrifice in exile (1:18–36),[25] the letter speaks of Jeremiah the prophet's remarks to Israel

---

19. The above comments do not suggest that the book should be outlined with a Deuteronomic blessing and curse structure. Rather, the Deuteronomic blessing and curse motif is present in 2 Maccabees. For a Deuteronomic structural understanding of 2 Maccabees, see Nickelsburg, *Jewish Literature*, 118. I agree with Williams, "Recent Research," 76, and his criticisms of Nickelsburg.

20. Observation from Doran, *2 Maccabees*, 27.

21. This part of the first letter is similar to biblical texts where God promises to remember his covenant with Abraham, Isaac, and Jacob if the people repented after God punished them because of their sin (cf. Lev 26:42; Deut 4:31; Ps 105:8–10). So Doran, *2 Maccabees*, 25–6.

22. Cf. LXX 1 Chr 28:9; 1QH 11:15–16; 13:32–33; 22 [frg. 4]:12.

23. Similarly Doran, *2 Maccabees*, 26–7.

24. Most scholars have argued the second letter is a forgery. So Williams, "Recent Research," 72–3. E.g., see Robert Doran, "The Second Book of Maccabees: Introduction, Commentary, and Reflections," *NIB* 4:62–3.

25. Cf. Ezra 2:2; Neh 1:1; 2:1–7:3; 12:27–43.

as they were being deported into exile because of disobedience to Torah (2:1). Jeremiah gave them the law (δοὺς αὐτοῖς τὸν νόμον) so that they would not forget the Lord's commandments (ἵνα μὴ ἐπιλάθωνται τῶν προσταγμάτων τοῦ κυρίου) (2:2). He further exhorted them "so that the law would not turn from their heart" (μὴ ἀποστῆναι τὸν νόμον ἀπὸ τῆς καρδίας αὐτῶν) (2:3).

The author of the second letter connects the law with the Deuteronomic principle of blessing and curse. He asserts Jeremiah went to the mountain Moses had travelled up and that he saw the inheritance of God (2:4). The mountain refers to Mt. Nebo, not Sinai (Deut 32:49; 34:1–4). The inheritance refers to the promised land and relates to the original promise to Abraham (Deut 32:49; 34:1–4; cf. Gen 12:1–3 with 2 Macc 1:2; 4 Macc 6:15–27; 7:7–19; 9:1–25, esp. 9, 1, 21; 13:13, 15, 17; 14:20; 15:28; 16:20, 25; 17:6–22; 18:1, 23). Moses looked from Mt. Nebo into the promised land (cf. Deut 32:49; 34:1–4) before he died (cf. Deut 34:5). God saved his people, gave them their inheritance, the kingship, the priesthood, and the consecration just as he promised through his "law" (2 Macc 2:17–18). In the preface of the epitome (2:19–32), the author speaks of the purification of the temple, the dedication of the altar, and about Judas and his brothers, who bravely fought for Ιουδαϊσμος (a Jewish way of life),[26] regained the temple, liberated the city, and reestablished the laws because the Lord was merciful and patient (2:19–22). As the narrative suggests in the body of 2 Maccabees, the Lord was merciful and patient in part because of the martyrs' Torah-observant deaths, Judas's military zeal for the law, and the effective prayers of Torah-observant Jews (cf. 7:30–8:5).

The author begins summarizing Jason's history, reporting the holy city dwelt in peace and the laws (Torah) were followed. This peace was Deuteronomic blessing. Moses promised rest in the land and peace from Israel's enemies if the people obeyed his Torah (cf. Deut 27–30). In 2 Maccabees, the city experienced God's blessing of peace because Onias, the high priest, hated wickedness and because he was pious (3:1). His piety can also be described as Torah-observance in 2 Maccabees since the letters attached to the epitome urged Egyptian Jews to remember the covenant to Abraham and his descendants (1:2) and since they offered the prayer that God would help them obey his law and commandments

---

26. As John J. Collins points out, in 2 Maccabees, Ιουδαϊσμος "refers to a culture and a way of life" just as Hellenismos refers to a culture and a way of life. So John J. Collins, *Jewish Cult and Hellenistic Culture: Essays on the Jewish Encounter with Hellenism and Roman Rule* (Leiden: Brill, 2005), 1, 22–3. See also Shaye J. D. Cohen, *The Beginnings of Jewishness* (Berkeley: University of California Press, 1999), 132–5.

(1:4).²⁷ The author of 2 Maccabees merges God's covenant with Abraham and his offspring with the Deuteronomic principle of blessing and curse (1:2–15:37; cf. Gen 12:1–3; 15:1–5; Deut 27–30; Gal 3:1–4:31). In the second letter, the Jews from Jerusalem and Judea reminded the Jews in Egypt of God's salvation (1:11). He saved them from the great king who urged Israel to disobey Torah (2:11; cf. 1 Macc 1). However, according to the second letter, God drove out those who fought against the holy city and cut them to pieces in the temple of Nanea (2 Macc 1:11–16).²⁸ As a result, the authors assert "blessed in every way be our God, who has brought judgment on those who act impiously" (1:17; NRSV).²⁹ Blessing in the narrative comes to those who obey Torah (i.e. to those who act piously), but God's judgment (i.e. a curse) comes upon those who disobey Torah (i.e. to those who act impiously). Because of Onias's piety, the Lord spared Heliodorus's life (3:29–33).³⁰

*2. 2 Maccabees 3:1 links the peace of the holy city with the piety (Torah-observance) of Onias III, the high priest.*³¹ Schwartz points out that 2 Maccabees is primarily about Jerusalem (cf. 4:9–11, 48; 5:6; 6:1; 8:2–3, 17, 36; 9:4, 4–15; 10:27; 11:2–3; 12:31, 43; 13:13–14; 14:33, 37; 15:17, 33, 37).³² The author links the peace of Jerusalem with Torah-observance. He states Jerusalem (the holy city) experienced all peace since the laws were being kept because of Onias's piety (τῆς ἁγίας πόλεως κατοικουμένης μετὰ πάσης εἰρήνης καὶ τῶν νόμων ὅτι κάλλιστα συντηρουμένων διὰ τὴν Ονιου τοῦ ἀρχιερέως εὐσέβειάν τε καὶ μισοπονηρίαν) (3:1; cf. 1:12; 9:14;

---

27. For a discussion on the politics of prayer in 2 Maccabees, see Chris L. de Wet, "Between Power and Priestcraft: The Politics of Prayer in 2 Maccabees," *Religion & Theology* 16 (2009): 150–61.

28. Contra 1 Macc 6:1–16; 2 Macc 9:1–29; Polybius, *History* 31.9; Appian, *The Syrian Wars* 11.66.

29. Unless otherwise indicated, all translations of ancient texts are mine.

30. Beate Ego ("God's Justice: The 'Measure for Measure' Principle in 2 Maccabees," in *The Books of the Maccabees: History, Theology, Ideology—Papers of the Second International Conference on the Deuterocanonical Books, Pápa, Hungary, 9–11 June, 2005*, ed. Géza G. Xeravits and József Zsengellér [Leiden: Brill, 2007], 141–54, esp. 141) notes that scholarship on 2 Maccabees has hinted that the "measure for measure principle" is an important characteristic of the book. For examples from scholarship, see Ego, "God's Justice," 141. However, the latter essay does not connect this principle to Deuteronomy, but to God's retributive justice.

31. For more info on Onias III, see Doran, *2 Maccabees*, 78 n. 78. See also Erich S. Gruen, "The Origins and Objectives of Onias' Temple," *SCI* 16 (1997): 48–57.

32. Schwartz, *2 Maccabees*, 6.

15:14). The author also connects Jerusalem's "sanctity" and peace with the purity of the temple (cf. CD XII:1; 11QTemple 45:11–12, 16–17; 4Q248).[33]

A curse came upon the land when Simon (a Jew and member of Judean society [Σιμων δέ τις ἐκ τῆς Βενιαμιν φυλῆς]), an administrator of the temple (προστάτης τοῦ ἱεροῦ) (3:4), attempted to conquer Onias's high priesthood (νικῆσαι τὸν Ονιαν) because of a dispute about the clerk of the city market (3:4). The specific reason for the tension between Simon and Onias is unclear. However, the finances of the market could have contributed to the conflict (cf. Aristotle, *Ath. Pol.* 51.1; Plato, *Laws* 6.764B).[34] Doran continues since Jerusalem was a temple city, market regulation "would have been extremely important," especially during the major festivals that required sacrifices in compliance with Torah (cf. Josephus, *Ant.* 12:146 with 11QT 47:7–18).[35] Doran further states the market contributed to the financial stability of a city.[36]

Simon incited Apollonius, the governor of Coelesyria and Phoenicia, and lied to him about untold sums of money in the temple treasury in Jerusalem (3:5–6). Simon insisted the king could control these funds (3:6). The funds included monies either designated for orphans and widows or included monies deposited by orphans and widows (3:10). The Jews cried out to God, who had given the law of deposits, for help (οἱ δὲ ἱερεῖς πρὸ τοῦ θυσιαστηρίου ἐν ταῖς ἱερατικαῖς στολαῖς ῥίψαντες ἑαυτοὺς ἐπεκαλοῦντο εἰς οὐρανὸν τὸν περὶ παρακαταθήκης νομοθετήσαντα τοῖς παρακαταθεμένοις ταῦτα σῶα διαφυλάξαι) (3:15). Van Henten rightly states, "the Pentateuch is silent about financial deposits in the temple."[37] Simon's act violated parts of Torah related to the proper way to care for orphans and widows

---

33. Ibid., 186.
34. Doran, *2 Maccabees*, 80. Doran also cites Hans Julius Wolff, *Das Recht der griechischen Papyri Ägyptens in der Zeit der Ptolemäer und des Prinzipats*, 2 vols., HA 10/5 (Munich: Beck, 1978), 2:8–27.
35. Doran, *2 Maccabees*, 80.
36. Ibid.
37. Van Henten, *Maccabean Martyrs*, 133. However, he notes that "it is possible that this unwritten provision was based upon a passage of the Pentateuch, for example, upon Exod. 22:7–9 (6–7 LXX): 'When someone delivers to a neighbor money or goods for safekeeping, and they are stolen from the neighbor's house, then the thief, if caught, shall pay double. If the thief is not caught, the owner of the house shall be brought before God, to determine whether or not the owner had laid hands on the neighbor's goods'; LXX: '…he shall swear that he verily has not acted knavishly with the whole deposit (ἐφ' ὅλης τῆς παρακαταθήκης) of his neighbor…'" See also van Henten, *Maccabean Martyrs*, 133 n. 31.

(3:15; cf. MT Exod 22:22–24; Deut 10:18),[38] not stipulations related to the temple. The king sent Heliodorus to retain this revenue. However, two angels of the Lord stopped and beat him when he attempted to rob the temple in the holy city (2 Macc 3:7–28). He escaped death only because of Onias's piety (3:29–34).

Simon's initial plot against Onias and the holy city failed. Still, he did not relent. Instead, he slandered Onias, saying he caused evil to fall upon Heliodorus (4:1). The author anticipates the great doom that is certain to fall upon the holy city in 4:7 with his remarks in 4:1–6 that Simon dared to speak evil of the benefactor of the city (καὶ τὸν εὐεργέτην τῆς πόλεως), the protector of those from the same race (καὶ τὸν κηδεμόνα τῶν ὁμοεθνῶν), and against a zealous devotee to the laws (ζηλωτὴν τῶν νόμων) (4:2; cf. 3:1). By this time in the narrative, Simon appears to be leading a rebellious "faction" (τῆς δὲ ἔχθρας ἐπὶ τοσοῦτον προβαινούσης ὥστε καὶ διά τινος τῶν ὑπὸ τοῦ Σιμωνος δεδοκιμασμένων φόνους συντελεῖσθαι) (4:3; cf. with 3:4–6).[39] Recognizing his dispute with Simon was serious, Onias sought help from King Seleucus IV (cf. 4:5–7).

3. After Seleucus's death, his brother, Antiochus Epiphanes IV,[40] assumed the throne (4:7). During the latter's reign, Jason, the brother of Onias, obtained the high priesthood by corruption (4:7).[41] Jason introduced a comprehensive Hellenistic program to Jerusalem. Because of his actions, the Deuteronomic curse became even more severe against Jerusalem. The author of 2 Maccabees states Jason promised the new king 360 talents of silver and 80 talents from another source of revenue (4:8). He additionally promised to pay the king 150 talents upon the condition that the king would give him permission to establish a gymnasium, a number of youths for it, and to enlist those in Jerusalem as "citizens of Antioch" (4:9).[42]

---

38. Contra van Henten, *Maccabean Martyrs*, 133.

39. Doran, *2 Maccabees*, 92.

40. For a discussion of the name Antiochus Epiphanes, see Otto Morkholm, "The Accession of Antiochus IV of Syria: A Numismatic Comment," *American Numismatic Society Museum Notes* 11 (1964): 63–76.

41. Schwartz argues that the real story of 2 Maccabees begins in 4:7. Schwartz, *2 Maccabees*, 3–6, esp. 6.

42. Himmelfarb points out that the meaning of this statement has received a lot of attention in scholarship. For a discussion of the meaning of this verse, see Schwartz, *2 Maccabees*, 530–2. Agreeing with Himmelfarb, I do not think discerning the nature of this new situation in Jerusalem affects the specific argument I am making in this chapter. The basic point is the "Torah was no longer the constitution of the city" (Himmelfarb, *Between Temple and Torah*, 195). Jason was given the privilege

The king consented. After Jason assumed office, he immediately "turned those from the same race to the Greek likeness" (ἐπινεύσαντος δὲ τοῦ βασιλέως καὶ τῆς ἀρχῆς κρατήσας εὐθέως πρὸς τὸν Ἑλληνικὸν χαρακτῆρα τοὺς ὁμοφύλους μετέστησε) (4:10).

Jason's efforts to establish a Greek way of life in Jerusalem was a direct move to turn the holy city from a Jewish way of life as outlined in Torah. Agreeing with Victor A. Tcherikover, Himmelfarb argues Jason's efforts to establish a polis in Jerusalem put an end to a Jewish way of life as the legal foundation for Jerusalem's municipal powers.[43] Himmelfarb also points out that prior to Antiochus's persecution, neither 4:11–15 nor any other passage in the book says anything "about the introduction of the cult of Greek gods to Jerusalem" (i.e. idolatry).[44] She states the "law" or "laws" in 2 Maccabees refer to a "Jewish way of life" (i.e. to Judaism) in contrast with Hellenism.[45] She rightly observes the author of 2 Maccabees applies the terms law or laws only to the Jewish law (e.g. 2:22; 3:1; 4:2, 17; 5:8, 15; 6:1, 5, 28; 7:2, 9, 11, 23, 37; 8:21, 36; 11:31; 13:14).[46] According to the author of 2 Maccabees, the threat of a comprehensive Hellenistic program in Jerusalem would lead Jews away from living a Jewish manner of life in accordance with Torah.[47]

Jason, a Jew and the new high priest, set aside royal benevolences for the Jews (4:11). These benevolences probably pertained both to allowing Jews to live a Jewish manner of life (Josephus, *Ant.* 12.138–46), and to alliances with Gentile nations (cf. 1 Macc 8:17).[48] Jason also acted contrary to Torah by destroying the lawful citizenship (2 Macc 4:11). He introduced idolatry into the Jewish way of life when he established a gymnasium under the citadel (4:12).[49] The gymnasium was an important

---

to transform Jerusalem into a "new legal entity" known as a polis like Antioch and other cities in the Seleucid Empire. So ibid., 195. See also Susan Sherwin-White and Amélie Kuhrt, *From Samarkhand to Sardis: A New Approach to the Seleucid Empire* (Berkeley: University of California Press, 1993), 180–4.

43. Victor A. Tcherikover, *Hellenistic Civilization and the Jews* (Philadelphia: Jewish Publication Society, 1959), 161–9, 404–9; Himmelfarb, *Between Temple and Torah*, 195.

44. Himmelfarb, *Between Temple and Torah*, 196.

45. Ibid.

46. Ibid., 196–7 n. 23.

47. Ibid., 199.

48. For the benevolences as privileges to live in a Jewish manner of life, see Schwartz, *2 Maccabees*, 220.

49. For a comment about the priority of the gymnasium in Greek culture, see Strabo 5.4.7. Source in and statement paraphrased from Collins, *Jewish Cult*, 27 n. 24.

public building in Greek culture.[50] The author of 2 Maccabees is silent as to what took place at Jason's gymnasium,[51] but scholars have shown that education, "military training," physical exercise, and athletic games were a few things that normally took place in Greek gymnasia.[52] Jason enticed the young men to wear a Greek hat. This hat was closely associated with the Greek god Hermes (4:12).[53] As a result, Jason's Hellenistic program included idolatry.

The author of 2 Maccabees asserts that the program of Jason, who is described by the author as "not a high priest" (καὶ οὐκ ἀρχιερέως), increased Hellenization and an excess of undesirable foreign customs because of his ungodliness and wickedness (ἦν δ' οὕτως ἀκμή τις Ἑλληνισμοῦ καὶ πρόσβασις ἀλλοφυλισμοῦ διὰ τὴν τοῦ ἀσεβοῦς Ἰάσωνος ὑπερβάλλουσαν ἀναγνείαν) (4:13). Jason turned the priests against their service at the altar (4:14). The priests even despised the sanctuary, neglected the sacrifices, and participated in the lawless activities in the gymnasium (4:14). They dishonored the honors prized by their ancestors and placed value in the highest Greek forms of honor (4:15). As a result, "a difficult set of circumstances seized them" (4:16). The Greeks, whose way of life they imitated, became their enemies and punished them (4:16), because "to act in an impious way toward the divine laws is no easy thing" (ἀσεβεῖν γὰρ εἰς τοὺς θείους νόμους οὐ ῥᾴδιον) (4:16; cf. 4:13). Jason's Hellenistic agenda provoked the author to tell the readers that God's curse is sure to follow these actions (4:17a). The ensuing narrative elucidates this point (4:17b–15:37).[54] The author's remarks prepare the way for the Deuteronomic curses to come upon the nation in 5:11–6:17 because of the Torah disobedience of some within the nation.

Jason sent money through ambassadors for the sacrifice of Hercules (4:19). Jason failed to live a Jewish way of life by committing idolatry (cf. Exod 20:3–6; Deut 4:1–40; 5:7–10; 6:5, 13–15; 12:1–31).[55] The ambassadors used the money to pay for the construction of Greek ships

---

50. For a discussion of the gymnasium in the service of Hellenism, see János Bolyki, "As Soon as the Signal Was Given (2 Macc. 4:14): Gymnasia in the Service of Hellenism," in Xeravits and Zsengellér, eds., *The Books of the Maccabees*, 131–9.

51. Ibid.

52. This observation comes from Doran, *2 Maccabees*, 102. See also ibid. for secondary literature on the Greek gymnasium.

53. For a discussion of the Greek hat, see E. Schuppe, "Petasos," *PW* (1938): 1119–24.

54. The author explicitly asserts this in 4:17b: ἀλλὰ ταῦτα ὁ ἀκόλουθος καιρὸς δηλώσει.

55. Similarly, Doran, *2 Maccabees*, 108.

(4:19-20). Jason sent Menelaus to carry money to the king (4:21-23). Menelaus, Simon's brother (the captain of the temple [3:4]), stole the high priesthood from Jason (Onias's brother) with a bribe in a similar manner as Jason stole it from Onias (4:24; cf. 3:4-6). Menelaus outbid Jason for the high priesthood by three hundred talents (4:24), but he stopped making the payments (4:27). Jason was from the high priestly family, whereas Menelaus was not (4:25). Menelaus returned to Jerusalem with the "wrath of a raw tyrant" (φέρων θυμοὺς ὠμοῦ τυράννου) and the "anger of a barbarous beast" (καὶ θηρὸς βαρβάρου ὀργὰς ἔχων) (4:25). Jason, who sacked his own brother's high priesthood, was likewise sacked and banished from the land as a fugitive into the Transjordan region (4:26). The author suggests God gave Jason his just desserts because of the curse of disobedience to Torah (cf. 4:16-17).

The people of Tarsus and Mallos revolted because their cities had been given as a gift to Antiochus's concubine (4:30). As the king attempted to settle the problem, Menelaus considered this uprising to be a convenient time for him to steal some gold vessels from them to give to Andronicus (4:32). Onias publicly exposed these acts once he became aware of them (4:33). Menelaus urged Andronicus, a Jewish man of high rank (4:31), to kill Onias (4:34), and Andronicus obliged Menelaus. Andronicus urged Onias to leave his place of sanctuary in Daphne near Antioch by treacherously persuading him with the right hand of fellowship and "sworn pledges" (4:33-34). Andronicus "shut out" (παρέκλεισεν) Onias, "because he had no regard for the righteous thing" (οὐκ αἰδεσθεὶς τὸ δίκαιον) (4:34). The "righteous thing" would have been to spare Onias's life. Rather, Menelaus participated in an "unjust murder of the man" (ἐπὶ τῷ τοῦ ἀνδρὸς ἀδίκῳ φόνῳ) (4:35).

Both Jews and Greeks were outraged by the murder of Onias (4:35). They expressed their outrage to Antiochus so that even he mourned (4:37). God blessed the people and brought judgment upon Andronicus through Antiochus because of the piety of Onias (cf. 3:1, 29-34). In 4:38, Antiochus burned with anger (πυρωθεὶς τοῖς θυμοῖς) similar to Judas Maccabeus's anger when the latter responded to Gentile blasphemies (πυρωθέντες τοῖς θυμοῖς διὰ τὰς βλασφημίας) against the God of the Hebrews (10:35) and with zeal similar to Razis's zeal for the law (πεπυρωμένος τοῖς θυμοῖς) when he committed "noble suicide" instead of allowing the Gentiles to kill him (14:45).[56] God through Antiochus brought retribution against Andronicus by killing him in the same place where he committed injustice against Onias (4:38). "The Lord gave a worthy punishment to him" (τοῦ κυρίου τὴν ἀξίαν αὐτῷ κόλασιν

56. Ibid., 118.

ἀποδόντος). Divine justice (i.e. a curse) came upon, and eventually took the lives of, Lysimachus, Menelaus, and Jason because of their treachery (cf. 4:39–5:10; 13:3–8). They were traitors to their laws and to their country (cf. 5:15; 13:3–8). Their disloyalty to the ancestral laws incited the Lord's curse upon them through Antiochus (5:17–19; 13:3–8). The author clarifies that God again brought blessing upon the temple and restored its glory when he was reconciled (5:20). As the martyrological narratives show, this reconciliation came upon the Jews in part because of the Torah-observant martyrs (cf. 7:30–38).

Antiochus's goodwill toward the Jews and their way of life was short lived. Led by Menelaus, he dared to enter the Jerusalem temple (5:15; cf. 3:24), pilfered 1800 talents from it, and carried them to Antioch (5:15–21; esp. 5:21). He commissioned commanders to harm the people in Jerusalem and at Gerizim (5:22–23). He commanded Apollonius, the captain of the Mysians, to kill Jewish men and to sell the women and boys as slaves (5:23b–24). Arriving in Jerusalem with an army of 22,000, Apollonius pretended to bring peace. Instead, he rushed into the city on the Sabbath with his armed warriors and "overthrew a multitude" (κατέστρωσεν πλήθη) (5:25–26, esp. 5:26).

Shortly afterward (μετ' οὐ πολὺν δὲ χρόνον), Antiochus aggressively oppressed Judaism (6:1). He sent an old[57] Athenian to compel the Jews to forsake their ancestral laws (ἐξαπέστειλεν ὁ βασιλεὺς γέροντα Ἀθηναῖον ἀναγκάζειν τοὺς Ιουδαίους μεταβαίνειν ἀπὸ τῶν πατρίων νόμων), to stop living by the laws of God (καὶ τοῖς τοῦ θεοῦ νόμοις μὴ πολιτεύεσθαι), and to defile their temple in Jerusalem by naming it Olympian Zeus (μολῦναι δὲ καὶ τὸν ἐν Ιεροσολύμοις νεὼ καὶ προσονομάσαι [6:1–2]).[58] As Doran states, "The polity of Judea is stated to be the Torah, so that to change the polity is to attack the Torah."[59] Evil pervaded the temple and the holy city (6:3). Gentiles engaged in prostitution and sexual intercourse within the temple's precincts (6:4; cf. Ezek 23:36–49).[60] Unfit sacrifices condemned

---

57. Relying upon Adolf Wilhelm ("Zu einigen Stellen der Bücher der Makkabäer," *Akademie der Wissenschaften in Wien, Philosophisch-historische Klasse: Anzeiger* 74 [1937]: 15–30, esp. 20–2), Doran (*2 Maccabees*, 133) asserts the term γέροντα should be understood as a "proper name" (Geron) instead of as an adjective (old).

58. Compulsion occurs again in 6:7, 18; and 7:1. The verb ἀναγκάζειν links the later martyrdoms with the Athenians' mission. This thought comes from Doran, *2 Maccabees*, 133.

59. Ibid.

60. For doubts of sacral prostitution, see JoAnn Scurlock, "167 BCE: Hellenism or Reform?" *JSJ* 31 (2000): 125–61, esp. 150 n. 103. In support of her view, Scurlock also cites Hengel, *Judaism and Gentiles*, 192–3.

by the law lay on the altar (6:3-4). Sabbath-keeping and observance of Jewish festivals were forbidden (6:6). Opting to live a Jewish way of life as prescribed in Torah was not permissible (οὔτε ἁπλῶς Ιουδαῖον ὁμολογεῖν εἶναι) (6:6).[61]

During the celebration of the king's birthday,[62] the Greeks compelled Jews to participate in sacrifices contrary to the law (6:7). They compelled the Jews to show patronage to the Greek god Dionysius during a festival honoring him (6:7). The people of Ptolemais suggested a decree should be issued "to the neighboring Greek cities" to adopt the same policy toward the Jews and to compel them to participate in the sacrifices (6:8). This decree threatened Jews with death if they refused to comply with the Greek customs (6:9). The king murdered women who circumcised their kids because they disobeyed his stipulations (6:10). He burned other Jews for their defiance (6:11).

4. As in 4:16-17 and 5:17-20, the author interjects authorial comments into the narrative in 6:12-17 to explain the purpose of Jewish suffering. LXX Deuteronomy 8:5 states the Lord disciplines his people as a parent disciplines a child (καὶ γνώσῃ τῇ καρδίᾳ σου ὅτι ὡς εἴ τις παιδεύσαι ἄνθρωπος τὸν υἱὸν αὐτοῦ οὕτως κύριος ὁ θεός σου παιδεύσει σε) (cf. LXX Pss 93:12-13; 118:18).[63] The author of 2 Macc 6:12-17 urges his readers not to be discouraged by the narrative (6:12), for the God of the Jews designed the punishments of his people to discipline them (πρὸς παιδείαν τοῦ γένους ἡμῶν), not to destroy them (6:12; cf. 7:32-33). He asserts God distributes justice to the impious (i.e. transgressors of Torah) in the appropriate time "when they reach the full measure of their sins" at the end of the age (6:13-14; cf. LXX Gen 15:16; Dan 8:23; LAB 26:13). But the Lord deals mercifully with his people in the present age through their suffering so that they will not be judged for the full measure of their sins at the end of the age (6:15). His mercy causes him to execute his vengeance against Israel through the Gentiles because of the disobedience of some within Israel in order to save his people from suffering for the full measure of their sins in the age to come (6:15-16). The author also reminds the Jews in Egypt that disobedience to Torah has brought this (Deuteronomic!) curse of Gentile affliction against the Jewish people (cf. Deut 27-30).

---

61. So Van Henten, *Maccabean Martyrs*, 91.
62. For documentation of monthly celebration of Greek kings, see the discussion in Christian Habicht, *Gottmenschentum und griechische Städte* (Munich: Beck, 1956), 152 n. 60, 156.
63. Doran, *2 Maccabees*, 150.

Curse and blessing are in tension with each other. The author shockingly suggests God's disciplinary action through Gentile affliction is an act of divine mercy toward his people (6:16). In the ensuing narrative, this act of divine mercy will result in divine blessing when the Jewish martyrs, Judas Maccabeus, and his army resist the king's Greek policies and remain faithful to Torah through military action (Judas and his army), through the death of the martyrs, and through effective prayer in order to reconcile God to the people once again (6:18–8:5).

III. Deuteronomic Blessing and Curse through Martyrdom, Military Action, and Effective Prayer

In 2 Macc 6:18–8:5, the author discusses the blessing of covenantal obedience through martyrdom, organized military action, and effective prayer. The author first narrates the martyrdom of Eleazar (6:18–31). He functions as a model figure in the narrative. The author describes him as a noble and virtuous scribe (Ἐλεάζαρός τις τῶν πρωτευόντων γραμματέων), as an old and wise man (ἀνὴρ ἤδη προβεβηκὼς τὴν ἡλικίαν καὶ τὴν πρόσοψιν τοῦ προσώπου), and as a "good man" (κάλλιστος) (6:18).[64] The martyrdoms of Eleazar, the seven sons, and the unknown mother are part of a Jewish history that begins with the "reign of Seleucid IV (187–175 BCE) and ends with the Jews' defeat of Nicanor (Adar 13 161 BCE) during the reign of Demetrius I (162–150 BCE)."[65]

1. Antiochus compelled Eleazar to eat unclean food (i.e. swine) (6:19). However, Eleazar refused and instead obeyed Torah by willingly approaching the instrument of torture reserved for those who disobeyed the king's decree (ὁ δὲ τὸν μετ' εὐκλείας θάνατον μᾶλλον ἢ τὸν μετὰ μύσους βίον ἀναδεξάμενος αὐθαιρέτως ἐπὶ τὸ τύμπανον προσῆγεν) (6:19). Eating swine's flesh was a clear Mosaic dietary violation (cf. Lev 11:7–8). Disobeying food restrictions brought the covenantal curses of disobedience upon God's covenant-people (cf. Lev 17:10–16; Deut 14:1–21; Isa 65:4; 66:17; 2 Macc 11:30–31; Jdt 11:11–15). Eleazar courageously refused to eat the meat and suffered death,[66] even when presented with an opportunity to

---

64. On Eleazar as a scribe, see Christine Schams, *Jewish Scribes in the Second-Temple Period*, JSOTSup 291 (Sheffield: Sheffield Academic, 1998), 314.
65. Van Henten, *Maccabean Martyrs*, 17.
66. Two different traditions exist of the events beginning the narrative of Eleazar's martyrdom. One tradition suggests Gentiles forced Eleazar "to open his mouth" to eat swine, which he "spat out" (6:18, 20). The other tradition omits the participle "opening his mouth" (ἀναχανών), but still highlights that he was compelled to eat

deceive the people and to eat his own meat under the guise that he acceded the king's request (2 Macc 4:20; 6:21–22). Eleazar resisted this request and resolved to do nothing to dishonor his old age, his God, and his nation, lest he would be a bad example for the youth (6:23–31). He refused to give in to false pretence (6:24; cf. 5:25; 6:21). He wanted to leave the youth a noble example of dying happily, bravely, and honorably for the "venerable" and "holy laws" (τοῖς δὲ νέοις ὑπόδειγμα γενναῖον καταλελοιπὼς εἰς τὸ προθύμως καὶ γενναίως ὑπὲρ τῶν σεμνῶν καὶ ἁγίων νόμων ἀπευθανατίζειν τοσαῦτα δὲ εἰπὼν ἐπὶ τὸ τύμπανον εὐθέως ἦλθεν) (6:28).

After Eleazar's death, the king likewise compelled with torture a mother and her seven sons to eat swine (7:1).[67] One of the sons stated on behalf of his family that "we are ready to die rather than to transgress the ancestral laws" (7:2).[68] These words infuriated Antiochus (7:3). He ordered pans to be heated and the spokesman's tongue to be cut out (cf. 4 Macc 10:19; 12:3), he ordered his head to be scalped in a Scythian way (7:7; 4 Macc 10:7; cf. Herodotus 4.64–65), and that his hands and feet would be cut off (7:3–4; cf. 4 Macc 10:20).[69] The king ordered his people to take the son to the fire while breathing and to burn him in a pan (7:5). His mother and six brothers encouraged him to die nobly (7:5–6). With an appeal to Deut 32:36, the author asserts the reason for the exhortation: "the Lord God gazes over us and in truth he comforts us, as Moses declared in his song, which bore witness against the people with respect to their face, when he said, 'And he will have compassion on his servants'" (7:5–6; cf. Deut 32:36). After Antiochus murdered the

unclean meat. A choice between the two options does not affect my argument. For a discussion of the two traditions, see Doran, *2 Maccabees* (2012), 151; van Henten, *Maccabean Martyrs*, 96.

67. For an argument that ch. 7 was an interpolation into 2 Maccabees, see Niese, *Kritik*, 37–8; Habicht, *2. Makkabäerbuch*, 171–7, 233; G. W. Bowersock, *Martyrdom and Rome* (Cambridge: Cambridge University Press, 1995), 10–13. For scholarship that argues ch. 7 is fully integrated within 2 Maccabees as a whole, see Himmelfarb, *Between Temple and Torah*, 203; Ulrich Kellerman, *Auferstanden in den Himmel: 2 Makkabäer 7 und die Auferstehung der Märtyrer* (Stuttgart: Verlag Katholisches Bibelwerk, 1979), 54–60; J. W. van Henten, "Das jüdische Selbstverständnis in den ältesten Martyrien," in *Die Entstehung der jüdischen Martyrologie*, ed. J. W. van Henten, Boudewijn Dehandschutter, and H. J. W. van der Klaauw, Studia Post-Biblica 38 (Leiden: Brill, 1989), 132–3.

68. For similar statements about transgressing the laws, see LXX Deut 17:20; 28:14; Sir 10:19; 19:24; Tob. 4:5; 1 Esd 1:46; 4 Macc 13:15; Josephus, *Ant.* 3.218; 8.229. Van Henten, *Maccabean Martyrs*, 108 n. 83, pointed me to these texts.

69. So van Henten, *Maccabean Martyrs*, 109 n. 91.

first brother, he killed the other six and the mother in like fashion because they remained faithful to the Jewish laws and refused to eat the unlawful (non-Torah permitted) meat (2 Macc 7:7–42).

The sixth and the seventh sons, however, conspicuously asserted before their deaths that they suffered because they sinned against their God (δι' ἑαυτοὺς ταῦτα πάσχομεν ἁμαρτόντες εἰς τὸν ἑαυτῶν θεόν ἄξια θαυμασμοῦ γέγονεν [7:18]; ἡμεῖς γὰρ διὰ τὰς ἑαυτῶν ἁμαρτίας πάσχομεν [7:32]). In the narrative, no evidence is given to show that the seven sons or their mother disobeyed God's law (7:9–10, 23). Their remarks are a statement of corporate and covenantal solidarity. The martyrs suffered not for their own individual sins, but for the sins of the people.[70] As van Henten says, "the wicked deeds of some Jewish leaders have led the whole people including the martyrs into a state of sin. This explains why the youngest brother can say at 2 Macc 7:38 that the wrath of the Lord has justly fallen on our whole nation."[71] Further, van Henten astutely observes "the godless actions of Simon, Jason, Menelaus, Lysimachus, Alcimus and the unfaithful soldiers of Judas are the only sins of Jews reported in 2 Maccabees. Nowhere are the sins of the martyrs themselves mentioned."[72] Yet, in the narrative of 2 Maccabees, God's people as a whole suffer the curses of the covenant when a few in the community violate the stipulations of the covenant (cf. Deut 27–28).[73]

The seventh son's mother demanded him to die nobly for the sake of God's law so that he would participate in the resurrection. The promise of resurrection personifies the blessing of life promised in the law (7:20–29; cf. Lev 18:5; Deut 27–28). The seventh son appealed to Torah as his motivation for resisting the king: "I will not obey the king's command, but I will obey the command of the law that was given to our fathers through Moses" (οὐχ ὑπακούω τοῦ προστάγματος τοῦ βασιλέως τοῦ δὲ προστάγματος ἀκούω τοῦ νόμου τοῦ δοθέντος τοῖς πατράσιν ἡμῶν διὰ Μωυσέως (7:30). Their devotion to the law is the reason they refused to eat unlawful meat (cf. Lev 11:1–47). However, their membership within the Jewish nation caused them to suffer along with those who disobeyed Torah, because only obedience to the law leads to life/blessing in the land (cf. Lev 18:5; Deut 11:26–28) and disobedience to the law leads to a curse/suffering/death (Deut 11:26–28; 27:26). Therefore, the seven sons and their mother suffered and died to end the wrath of the Almighty

---

70. Ibid., 137. Cf. also 2 Macc 7:18 and 10:4.
71. Ibid.
72. Ibid.
73. For biblical examples of this, see 2 Kgs 16:1–17:23; 21:1–18; 23:31–24:17.

that justly fell upon them and their entire race because of the sin of some within the Jewish community (2 Macc 7:32–38). The author's appeal to Deut 32 in 2 Macc 7 supports this.

Deuteronomy 32 is Moses's song of praise to the Lord for his faithful provision to Israel. The chapter promises the certainty of judgment if the nation disobeys Torah. In LXX Deut 32:36, the text states the Lord will vindicate his people, and he will show compassion to his servants. 2 Maccabees 7:33–38 applies this text to martyrdom. The seventh son asserted the living Lord is temporarily angry with his people, but he would again be reconciled to his servants (εἰ δὲ χάριν ἐπιπλήξεως καὶ παιδείας ὁ ζῶν κύριος ἡμῶν βραχέως ἐπώργισται καὶ πάλιν καταλλαγήσεται τοῖς ἑαυτοῦ δούλοις) (7:33). The servants refer to both the non-Torah-observant Hebrews and the martyrs since the seventh son has already asserted "we suffer because of our own sins" (ἡμεῖς γὰρ διὰ τὰς ἑαυτῶν ἁμαρτίας πάσχομεν) (7:33) and since there is no evidence in the narrative that the martyrs suffered because they personally disobeyed Torah. 2 Maccabees 7, thus "seems to imply that God's compassion only concerns those members of the people who remain faithful to his law."[74] These people are his own servants (τοῖς ἑαυτοῦ δούλοις).[75]

The seventh son insults Antiochus, as he reminded him that his brothers participated in immortal life because of their steadfast Torah-observance in the face of suffering (οἱ μὲν γὰρ νῦν ἡμέτεροι ἀδελφοὶ βραχὺν ὑπενέγκαντες πόνον ἀενάου ζωῆς ὑπὸ διαθήκην θεοῦ πεπτώκασιν) (7:36). He associates the martyrs' participation in eternal life (ἀενάου ζωῆς) with God's covenant (ὑπὸ διαθήκην θεοῦ) (7:36). Since the martyrs suffer in the narrative because of the nation's disobedience to Torah, ὑπὸ διαθήκην θεοῦ likely refers to the Mosaic covenant as the pathway to receiving the fulfillment of the Abrahamic blessing. The seventh son confirms the connection with the Mosaic covenant in 7:37 when he says his brothers gave their body and life and that he would give his body and life for the "fathers' laws" (περὶ τῶν πατρίων νόμων) (7:37), when he asks God to be merciful to the nation (τῷ ἔθνει), and when he says God's wrath through Antiochus against "our race" was just (τὴν τοῦ παντοκράτορος ὀργὴν τὴν ἐπὶ τὸ σύμπαν ἡμῶν γένος δικαίως ἐπηγμένην).

Then, the seventh son concluded his discourse with a prayer in 7:37–38 that God would "be merciful quickly to the nation" (ἐπικαλούμενος τὸν θεὸν ἵλεως ταχὺ τῷ ἔθνει γενέσθαι) (7:37), that Antiochus would confess that the Hebrews' God is the only God as he receives from him his just

---

74. Van Henten, *Maccabean Martyrs*, 111.
75. So ibid., 111 n. 99.

desserts (καὶ σὲ μετὰ ἐτασμῶν καὶ μαστίγων ἐξομολογήσασθαι διότι μόνος αὐτὸς θεός ἐστιν) (7:37), and that God would bring his just wrath against the nation to a fixed end in/by means of the martyrs (ἐν ἐμοὶ δὲ καὶ τοῖς ἀδελφοῖς μου στῆσαι τὴν τοῦ παντοκράτορος ὀργὴν τὴν ἐπὶ τὸ σύμπαν ἡμῶν γένος δικαίως ἐπηγμένην) (7:38).[76] The seventh son's prayer emphasizes the means by which God will show mercy (namely, through his servants, the faithful martyrs). The narrative suggests that one means by which this prayer is answered is through the Torah-observant martyrs. The martyrs brought the blessing of reconciliation (peace and blessing) to the land by means of their deaths (1:5; 7:33; 8:29). The curses came upon the nation because of non-Torah observance; curses came upon the martyrs because of the nation's non-Torah observance; and blessings came upon the nation and the martyrs because of the martyrs' faithful deaths through Judas's military action and effective prayer. I discuss the latter in more detail below.

2. Martyrdom, military action, and effective prayer are a soteriological turning point in the narrative (cf. 8:1–10:9).[77] Following the stories of martyrdom (6:18–7:42), Judas Maccabeus reappears in the narrative. Until 8:1, Judas had been in the mountains hiding from the Gentiles (cf. 5:27). Through martyrdom (6:18–7:41), Judas's organized military action (8:1, 5–36), prayer (8:2–4), and zeal for the law (12:40–44; 13:10; 15:8–10), the Lord's wrath against Israel turned to mercy (γενόμενος δὲ ὁ Μακκαβαῖος ἐν συστέματι ἀνυπόστατος ἤδη τοῖς ἔθνεσιν ἐγίνετο τῆς ὀργῆς τοῦ κυρίου εἰς ἔλεον τραπείσης) (8:5). God reversed Israel's fortunes. The Jewish community experienced the Lord's covenantal blessings. He punished Antiochus for his actions against the Jews with a painful and prolonged death (9:1–29), and the Jews reclaimed and purified the temple from Gentile invaders (10:1–8).

Judas secretly entered the villages and enlisted thousands of their kindred into his military fight for Judaism (8:1). Judaism was the antithesis to Jason's and Antiochus's Hellenism (4:13–6:31). The Jewish resistance prayed and fought (8:2–4). Echoing the seventh son's prayer (7:37), Judas and his companions asked God "to see, to hear, and to remember."[78] This same refrain is present in Exod 2:24–25 when the text asserts God "heard Israel's groaning, remembered his covenant with Abraham, Isaac, and

---

76. I discuss the meaning of the verse in more detail in later chapters.
77. I say more about the soteriological function of the martyrs' deaths in subsequent chapters.
78. Doran, *2 Maccabees*, 170.

Jacob, saw his people Israel, and knew them."[79] In 2 Macc 7:6, the martyrs assert God sees them from heaven.[80] In 15:2, the author describes Israel's God as one who sees everything.[81]

Scholars have pointed out that prayer in 2 Maccabees has "more in common with the Greek drama than with biblical prayers."[82] Regardless of one's view of this, prayer turns the Lord's anger to mercy in the narrative (8:5). Judas burned towns and villages and caused the enemy to flee (8:6). His bravery and honor quickly spread throughout the land (8:7). Philip, the governor appointed by Antiochus to oppress the Jews in Jerusalem (cf. 5:22), requested help from Ptolemy (the governor of Coelesyria and Phoenicia) (8:9). Ptolemy sent Nicanor, son of Patroclus and one of the "first friends" of the king, with approximately 20,000 Gentiles from mingled nations to "drive away the entire race of Judea" (τὸ σύμπαν τῆς Ιουδαίας ἐξᾶραι γένος [8:9]). Nicanor also appointed Gorgias, an experienced general, to fight against the Jews (8:9). Nicanor had an ulterior motive. He wanted to make up the 2,000 talents the king owed the Romans (8:10). His intent was to sell the captured bodies of Jews into slavery (8:10–11). Thus, he urged the towns on the sea coast to buy Jewish slaves, and he promised to sell 90 slaves for one talent, because he did not know the Lord's judgment would soon come against him (8:11).

When Judas eventually heard about Nicanor's invasion, he informed his companions. Some acted cowardly and fled because they were "distrustful of God's justice" (8:12–13). Others sold their property. Because of God's covenant with their ancestors and with them, they asked God to deliver those "sold by the ungodly" (8:14–15). Judas urged his kinsmen to be brave, to fight nobly, and to remember the lawless outrage of the Gentiles against the city and against those who lived a Jewish way of life (8:16–17). Judas also reminded the Jews of the time God helped their ancestors against Sennacherib (8:19; cf. 2 Kgs 19:35–36), when 185,000 perished, and of the time he helped them in a battle against the Galatians, when 8,000 Jews fought along with 4,000 Macedonians (8:20). The author says the Galatians pressed against the Macedonians, but God helped the 8,000 Jews destroy 120,000 Galatians (8:20).

Judas's words inspired his countrymen, filled them with courage, and made them ready to die nobly for their laws and their country (8:21). He divided his army into various parts (8:21–22). He appointed a man named

---

79. Ibid.
80. Ibid.
81. Ibid.
82. See sources cited in M. Z. Simkovich, "Greek Influence on the Composition of 2 Maccabees," *JSJ* 42 (2011): 293–310.

Eleazar to read publicly the holy book and gave the signal with the words "the help of God" (8:23). With God as their ally because of their zeal for Torah, Judas and his army killed over 9,000 Gentiles and disarmed most of their opponents' army (8:24). Once they took the army's weapons and distributed the spoils amongst the Jewish people, they begged the merciful Lord to be "reconciled to his servants until the end" (ταῦτα δὲ διαπραξάμενοι καὶ κοινὴν ἱκετείαν ποιησάμενοι τὸν ἐλεήμονα κύριον ἠξίουν εἰς τέλος καταλλαγῆναι τοῖς αὐτοῦ δούλοις (8:29; cf. Deut 32:6). Judas and his army killed Timothy because he was a wicked man who greatly troubled the Jewish people (8:30–33). They forced Nicanor to flee like a runaway slave as he proclaimed that Israel's God defended the Jews because of their devotion to his laws (8:34–36, esp. 8:36). Judas's strict Torah-observance was a means by which he and his army experienced military victory over the Gentiles. Their zeal to preserve Torah led to life (i.e. peace) in the land (cf. Lev 18:5; Deut 27–30; 32).

Around this time, Antiochus retreated from places around Persia (9:1). He entered the city of Persepolis to rob temples and to oppress the city (9:2), but a multitude put Antiochus and his army to a shameful flight from the land (9:2). While in Ecbatana, Antiochus heard about the defeat of Nicanor and Timothy (9:3). Becoming infuriated, he plotted to do injury to the Jews who put him to flight (9:4). He arrogantly commanded his charioteer to carry him straight to Jerusalem because he hoped to make Jerusalem "a common burial place of the Jews" (πολυάνδριον Ιουδαίων Ιεροσόλυμα ποιήσω) (9:4). But the Lord, who sees all things, afflicted Antiochus with an incurable and unexpected affliction (9:5). God justly judged Antiochus with insatiable pain in his bowels and with internal torments (9:5), because previously he tortured the bowels of others (9:5–6).

His afflictions increased his rage against the Jews (9:7). The God of the Jews humbled Antiochus with even more afflictions, torturing him every moment as he became fixated on bringing harm against the Jews in Jerusalem (9:7–11). The Lord was not merciful to Antiochus. Antiochus vowed to let the Jews peacefully live a Jewish way of life and then he died (9:13–28).

Meanwhile, the Lord led Judas and his followers to recover the temple and the city from the Gentiles (10:1–3).[83] They destroyed the vestiges of Gentile worship and built altars and worshipped in compliance with a Jewish way of life (10:3–8). They prostrated themselves before the Lord and urged him not again to let them experience these misfortunes (10:4).

---

83. Schwartz, *2 Maccabees*, 6–10, argues ch. 10 is an interpolation.

They prayed he would discipline them with forbearance, if they should ever sin, instead of handing them over to blasphemous and barbarous Gentiles (10:4).

2 Maccabees 10:10–13:26 begins the third major section of the book. The events in this section occur during the reign of Antiochus V Eupator. The author offers a brief summary of the principal calamities that took place during his reign (10:10). Gorgias, after becoming governor of the region, and his mercenaries kept attacking the Jewish community along with the Idumeans (10:14). Judas and his army successfully attacked the strongholds of Idumeans, killing at least 20,000 (10:15–16). Judas also killed more than 20,000 in the two strongholds (10:18–23). Timothy gathered his forces in large numbers, intending to take Judea by force (10:24; cf. 8:30–33). After mourning and prayers of supplication for God's mercy, Judas and his army took up arms and fought against Timothy and his forces. They were victorious over their enemies because of the Lord's help (10:25–38).

Lysias, the king's guardian and relative, gathered nearly 80,000 men and all his cavalry to fight against the Jews (11:1–2). His intent was to make their city a dwelling for Greeks, to levy tribute on the temple, and to sell the high priesthood annually for money (11:2–3). He was disinterested in God's power, but was arrogant with his thousands of forces and cavalry (11:4). He invaded Judea (11:5). Once Judas and his army heard Lysias was sacking the strongholds, they asked the Lord to send an angel to save the nation (11:6).

After praying, Judas took up arms and urged his army to fight (11:7). They fought and won (11:8–12). Judas advanced in the battle because the Lord was merciful to him and his kinsmen (11:10). Lysias pondered his defeat and realized he lost because he thought the Jews were invincible since God fought for them (11:13). Lysias, the Jews' enemy, agreed to make peace with the Jews because of the Lord's mercy, and Antiochus and Rome agreed to maintain this friendly relationship with them (11:13–37). This military peace was divine blessing, which came to the Jews through prayer and military action.

A few leaders in various regions prevented the Jews from living in peace (12:2). The people from Joppa likewise committed evil against the Jews who lived among them, extending to them invitations of friendship to embark on boats in the sea only to drown them and their families (12:3–4). When Judas heard this, he ordered his men to attack those who killed his relatives. Judas prayed and called upon God, the righteous judge (12:5–6). Judas and his men destroyed their enemies (12:5–6). Hearing that those in Jamnia desired to harm the Jews living amongst them in the same way, Judas attacked them and burned their harbor and fleet at night so that the light could be seen 30 miles away in Jerusalem (12:7–9). God helped Judas and his army defeat 5,000 Arabs with 500 cavalry in their march against Timothy (12:10–11). "The defeated begged Judas" to grant them friendship (12:11–12).

Judas attacked Caspin, a fortified city with many Gentile residents (12:13). The residents of Caspin provoked Judas and his men with blasphemous words (12:14). Judas and his men implored "the great sovereign of the world," who singlehandedly overturned Jericho in the days of Joshua, to help them slaughter many in the city (12:15). They sacked the town "by the will of God" and slaughtered the people to the point that the town appeared to be running over with blood (12:16). Judas slaughtered many nations as the Jewish people called upon the power of the Sovereign God (12:26–28).

While asking God for help, Judas assembled his army and entered another city (12:38). Once there, they gathered the dead bodies of fellow Jews to bury them with their ancestors (12:39). Under the dead bodies, Judas and his army "found tokens of the idols of Jamnia" (12:40). Judas was keenly aware the law forbade them from serving idols (12:40). This discovery clarified to the Jews that their kinsmen died because of idolatry (12:40). Judas and his army prayed that God would blot out this sin (12:41–42). Judas urged the people to keep themselves free from sin because of the sin of those who had fallen (12:42). He took up an offering and sent it to Jerusalem for a sin-offering (12:43). He took into account the resurrection and made atonement for the dead so that they would receive forgiveness for their sins (12:43).

The Lord's anger, then, turned against Menelaus in the narrative because of his disobedience to Torah. He turned Antiochus Eupator against Menelaus. Antiochus killed Menelaus, because, as the author says, he was a "lawbreaker" (13:1–7) and "committed many sins" (13:8).

Antiochus Eupator endeavored to treat the Jews more harshly than his father (13:9). After Judas heard about his plot, "he ordered the people" to pray "day and night" to their God that they would not "fall into the hands of the blasphemous Gentiles" (13:9–12). Judas consulted with the elders and determined with the help of God to stand ready to fight against the king's army as they entered Judea (13:13). He committed his decision to Israel's God, "the creator of the world," and exhorted his troops to fight valiantly for the laws, the city, and the country (13:14). Judas and his troops attacked the king's pavilion, killing thousands and filling the camp with much terror and chaos (13:15–16). Because the Lord's help protected Judas (a Torah-observant Jew), he and his troops withdrew from this battle in triumph (13:16–17). The king surrendered to Judas and his men, gave honors to the temple, to their sanctuary, and made an oath to observe their rights (13:18–26).

Alcimus, a Jew from the priestly line of Aaron (cf. 1 Macc 7:14) and who had formerly served as high priest, approached King Demetrius (the son of Seleucus IV) with gifts (14:3–4). Alcimus's intent was to kill Judas and to become high priest again (2 Macc 14:1–13). He angered Demetrius and his friends against Judas by claiming he was a hindrance to peace (14:6–14). Demetrius appointed Nicanor governor over Judea and sent him away to kill Judas, his troops, and to establish Alcimus as high priest (14:12–13). Many Gentiles throughout Judea partnered with Nicanor, thinking Judas's possible misfortune would result in their prosperity (14:14).

The Jews heard about Nicanor's imminent entrance into their city with the Gentiles (14:15). They prayed to their God, "who established his own people forever and always upholds his own heritage by manifesting himself" (14:15). The author of 2 Maccabees describes Nicanor as extending friendship to the Jews because he heard of their honor as they fought for their country (14:18–25).[84]

Alcimus became angry about the friendship between Nicanor and Judas. He deceived the king into thinking Nicanor had been disloyal to the king, claiming he appointed Judas to be his successor as high priest (14:26). Because of Alcimus's deception, the king angrily broke the covenant of friendship that he had established with Judas (14:27). He wrote to Nicanor and immediately urged him to have Judas taken to Antioch as a prisoner (14:27).

Nicanor, though disappointed, responded in compliance with the king's orders (14:28–29). His disposition soon changed towards Judas. After noticing Nicanor's sudden unfriendliness toward him (14:30), Judas gathered several of his men and hid from Nicanor (14:30). After realizing Judas outwitted him, Nicanor approached the temple while the priests were offering sacrifices and demanded the people to hand over Judas (14:31). When the priests swore that they did not know the location of Judas (14:32), Nicanor made an oath promising to destroy their "shrine of God," their "altar," and to build a temple to Dionysius (14:33). The priests asked Israel's God ("the defender of our nation") to keep their recently purified temple from being defiled (14:35–36). God defended Israel when and only when the people lived in compliance with Torah.

---

84. The author of 1 Maccabees describes Nicanor as hating Israel and as being sent by the king to destroy Israel (1 Macc 7:26–30).

3. The author introduces a Jew named Razis into the narrative of 2 Maccabees for the first time (14:37). Razis was accused of Judaism and exposed himself to danger on account of the cause of Judaism during the time of political war (14:38). By referring to Judaism, the author means Razis was accused of living a Jewish way of life since Ιουδαϊσμος in 2:21 and 14:38 occur in context of the author's story about Jews zealously living a Jewish way of life in accordance with Torah (4:2, 17), fighting to preserve a Jewish way of life (2:22; 8:2), or bravely dying to preserve a Jewish way of life devoted to the law (6:1–7:42). Razis's Ιουδαϊσμος and zeal for the law link his narrative with the martyrs and Judas who resisted the Gentiles. Van Henten helpfully points out that during a different era of Seleucid tyranny, Razis may have been prosecuted and convicted for this Judaism but his execution was not immediate.[85]

Similar to the martyrs' deaths in 6:1–7:42 and Judas's prayer in 8:5 immediately after the author records the martyrs' deaths, the Torah-observance of both groups (the martyrs and Judas) turns the Deuteronomic curse to the Deuteronomic blessing of peace in the land. As a result, the people experience the promise of life in Lev 18:5 and Deut 27–30. The seven sons and their mother suffered and died for God's law because of the sins of the people, whose sins resulted in the Deuteronomic curse of suffering, death, unrest, and affliction in the land at the hands of the Gentiles (2 Macc 6:1–7:42). They maintained obedience to Torah as they suffered because of a belief in the resurrection (7:9). Judas fought valiantly to preserve God's law and offered atonement for those who died on account of the sin of idolatry because he believed in the resurrection of life for those who complied with Torah and died in godliness (12:39–45). When Nicanor chose to exhibit enmity against the Jews, he sent to his soldiers to arrest Razis because he thought it would injure the Jews (14:39–40).

When the soldiers arrived, Razis chose to die nobly and fall on his own sword instead of falling "into the hands of sinners" (i.e. Gentiles) (14:41–42). However, the sword missed the necessary mark to ensure his death (14:43). Razis courageously jumped off a wall into a crowd of Gentiles hoping the fall would help him die nobly (14:44–45). After his second effort at noble suicide failed, Razis became infuriated as he walked through the crowd of Gentiles with his blood "flowing like a gushing spring" (φερομένων κρουνηδὸν τῶν αἱμάτων) (14:45). Having become completely bloodless (14:46), Razis pulled out his intestines, threw them at the crowd of Gentiles, and prayed that God would give them back

---

85. Van Henten, *Maccabean Martyrs*, 93–4.

to him again (παντελῶς ἔξαιμος ἤδη γινόμενος προβαλὼν τὰ ἔντερα καὶ λαβὼν ἑκατέραις ταῖς χερσὶν ἐνέσεισε τοῖς ὄχλοις καὶ ἐπικαλεσάμενος τὸν δεσπόζοντα τῆς ζωῆς καὶ τοῦ πνεύματος ταῦτα αὐτῷ πάλιν ἀποδοῦναι τόνδε τὸν τρόπον μετήλλαξεν). The clause ταῦτα αὐτῷ πάλιν ἀποδοῦναι refers to the Deuteronomic promise of life, because the statement is similar to Judas's earlier remarks about the resurrection (12:44–46; cf. 7:9, 23, 29; Lev 18:5; Deut 27–30). Judas's remarks and the author's comments about Razis's relentless efforts to die nobly support the view that 2 Maccabees appropriates a temporal promise of life in Lev 18:5 and Deuteronomy, promised to those who obey Torah, to refer to participation in the resurrection because of Torah observance.

4. After Razis's death, Judas prays for God to help him defeat Nicanor, and God gives him victory (15:20–37). Judas urged his troops not to fear Gentile threats, but to remember God's faithfulness to them in previous times (15:6–8). He read the law and the prophets to his troops as he reminded them of the previous battles they won (15:9). Judas reminded them of Gentile vices, and he motivated them by relaying how Onias and Jeremiah the prophet appeared to them to give Judas a golden sword and to commission him to strike the Gentiles (15:6–16). As Judas and his troops prepared for battle after his inspiring speech (15:17–20), they asked God for help, and he gave them victory (15:21–27). When they noticed Nicanor was dead (15:28), they praised God in their Hebrew language (15:29). They celebrated by cutting off Nicanor's head, his arms, and his boastful tongue (15:30–33). They put them on display in Jerusalem as a sign to everyone that the Lord helps his people when they obey his law (15:28–34). This display also signaled to the people that life had come to those in the land because of the martyrological and military loyalty to Torah.

Prayer in 14:35–36, the death of a Torah-observant Jew for Judaism (14:37–46), and the prayer of Torah-observant Jews for God's protection (15:22–24) are the means by which God brings victory against Nicanor and his army in the narrative of 14:26–37. Disobedience to Torah results in the Deuteronomic curse of divine suffering and death at the hands of the Gentiles. Faithfully living a Jewish way of life through martyrdom, self-inflicted noble death, prayer, and military resistance against the Gentiles leads to the Deuteronomic blessing of life. In 2 Maccabees, apart from the law, there is no life in this age or in the age to come.

IV. Conclusion of Deuteronomic Blessings and Curses in 2 Maccabees

I conclude the following from my analysis of the Deuteronomic blessings and curses motif in 2 Maccabees. First, the Abrahamic covenant is connected to the law. The author of the first letter attached to the epitome urges the Jews in Egypt to remember God's covenant with Abraham (land, seed, and universal blessing) and with Isaac and Jacob (Gen 12:1–50:26), his faithful servants (2 Macc 1:2). Immediately thereafter, the author connects the Abrahamic covenant with the law and with a prayer that God would enable the Egyptian Jews to obey his will (2 Macc 1:3). The author clarifies this prayer by identifying God's will as his law when he prays that God would open their hearts to obey his law and his commandments (1:4).

Second, peace in the land (i.e. blessing) and war in the land (i.e. curse) are connected to Torah-observance (peace) or non-Torah-observance (war). The first attached letter to the epitome emphasizes this point. In 1:4, the author connects obedience to the commandments with peace. This prayer of peace is for Egyptian Jews in the land of Egypt to experience peace (i.e. not war or calamity) in a time of evil. The author prays that God would hear the prayers of his people and be reconciled to the Egyptian Jews and not forsake them in a time of evil. As the letter continues, the author reminds the Egyptian Jews of the distress that came to the land of Jerusalem when Jason and his followers revolted from the holy land (1:7), and he urges the Egyptian Jews to celebrate Jewish festivals (1:8–9). These festivals link the Egyptian Jews with the Jews in Jerusalem and serve as the means of peace in Egypt. By reflecting on Israel's past suffering because of disobedience to the law and on Jeremiah's prophetic appeal to Jews going into exile to be faithful to Torah even while living in a foreign land, the second letter connects the peace of the Egyptian Jews with obedience to the law (1:10–2:18). The letter again urges them to be faithful to Torah in order to receive the blessing that it promises. The ensuing narrative that follows the two attached letters demonstrates the blessings and curses of the people in the land are dependent upon their law observance.

Third, the martyrological narratives in 2 Macc 6:18–7:42 personify the Deuteronomic blessings and curses. After killing Eleazar, Antiochus compelled seven sons with murderous threats to eat unlawful foods (7:1). The mother encouraged her seventh son to trust God as he endured torture and death (7:28–29). As the seventh son faced the threat of torture and death (7:2–42), he asserts "we suffer because of our own sins" (7:32; cf. 5:17; LXX Dan 3:28–29, 37). The confession is similar to the sixth son's confession earlier in the narrative when he claims the martyrs suffered because the nation sinned against their God (ἡμεῖς γὰρ δι' ἑαυτοὺς ταῦτα πάσχομεν ἁμαρτόντες εἰς τὸν ἑαυτῶν θεόν) (7:18). As the evidence above suggests, the martyrs are Torah-observant. Nevertheless, they are complicit in the suffering and sin of the nation because of God's covenant with the nation.

In Deut 27:1–28:68, the author states curses come from disobeying Torah and blessings from obeying Torah. In Deut 27:1, Moses begins his speech by commanding Israel to observe every commandment of the Lord. Deuteronomy reiterates this point throughout the chapter (27:9–10). The commandments to which Deut 27 refers include the stipulations given at Sinai and to other commandments in Torah. Deuteronomy overtly states often that Israel must obey "all" of the statutes that the Lord gave Israel when he led them out of Egypt (e.g. 4:1–26:19). These commandments include more than the commandments mentioned in Deut 27. The reference to the commandments in 27:1 pertains especially to the stipulations in 27:15–26, because the command to obey God's law in 27:1 and the blessings of obedience to God's law in 28:1–14 surround the curses of disobedience to the law in 27:9–26 and because 28:15–68 continues to discuss the curses of disobedience to the stipulations mentioned in 27:9–26.

Deuteronomy 27–28 states that if Israel disobeyed the stipulations in the land, the nation would be cursed in the land, and that if they obeyed, they would be blessed in the land. Deuteronomy 27:26 summarizes the curse pronouncements of 27:9–25 and reiterates to Israel the importance of their obedience in the land by stating, "cursed is the one who will not uphold the words of this Torah to do them" (27:26). According to 27:15–26 and 28:15–62, these curses would overcome Israel while they *lived in the land*. According to 28:64–68, these curses would enslave them to Gentile nations and drive them *out of the land*, which the Lord promised to give them if they obeyed his law. Deuteronomy supports this latter point with earlier statements about obedience to the stipulations results in *long life in the land* (5:33; 8:1; 11:8, 26–32) and by asserting the Lord's curses will stick to Israel "until he destroys" them from *entering the land to inherit it* (28:21). The curses would come against the entire nation even if some within the community obeyed, which Israel's exiles support (cf. Judges, Kings, and Chronicles). The Jewish martyrs in 2 Maccabees (and 4 Maccabees) personify this reality.

2 Maccabees' presentation of martyrdom supports conceptual connections with the Deuteronomic blessings and curses. (1) The Torah-observant martyrs suffered with non-Torah-Jews (7:32). The martyrs represent the nation (7:32). They were members of YHWH's covenant-community for

which they suffered (7:16, 30, 30–32, 38). The author of 2 Maccabees calls Antiochus the adversary of the Hebrews, not simply the adversary of the martyrs (7:31). (2) The martyrological narratives follow statements about the positive role of suffering in the lives of God's covenant-people (6:12–17). The author suggests Antiochus believed the deaths of the seven sons proved the Lord had forsaken his people (7:16). But blessing comes to the nation because of the martyrs' Torah-observant and faithful deaths (7:28–32), while suffering comes because of non-Torah observance (6:18–8:5).

The martyrs suffered and died with and for the nation, although they were Torah-observant. 2 Maccabees' presentation of the martyrs' suffering and death echoes Israel's antecedent Deuteronomic history, thereby personifying the Deuteronomic blessings and curses set forth in Deut 27–28 in a new context in the deaths of the martyrs. The author's appeal to Deut 32 supports this conclusion.

Deuteronomy 32 is Moses's song of praise to the Lord for his faithful provision to Israel. The chapter also promises the certainty of judgment if the nation disobeys Torah. In LXX Deut 32:36, the text states the Lord will vindicate his people, and he will show compassion to his servants. 2 Maccabees 7:33 applies this text to martyrdom by stating the Lord will be reconciled again to his servants. The martyrs brought reconciliation (peace and blessing) to the land by means of their deaths (1:5; 7:33; 8:29). Curse comes to the nation because of non-Torah observance; curse comes upon the martyrs because of the nation's non-Torah observance; and Deuteronomic blessing comes upon the nation because of the martyrs' faithful deaths, Judas's military action, and effective prayer.

V. Deuteronomic Blessings and Curses in 4 Maccabees

The primary purpose of 4 Maccabees is to challenge Hellenistic Jews to remain faithful to Torah (18:1). According to the author, faithfulness to Torah is the truest display of philosophical reason. The author presents the Maccabean martyrs as the personification of resilient Torah-observance. Their steadfastness to Torah in the face of suffering and death for the law proves the author's thesis that "devout" or "pious" reason masters the passions (1:1).[86]

---

86. For introductory matters, see van Henten, *Maccabean Martyrs*, 58–82; David A. deSilva, *4 Maccabees: Introduction and Commentary on the Greek Text in Codex Sinaiticus*, SCS (Leiden: Brill, 2006), xi–xliv.

2. Deuteronomic Blessings and Curses

Scholars generally date 4 Maccabees as late as the first century CE to 100 CE or later.[87] Recent scholarship rejects an early date and instead has offered arguments favoring a second-century CE date.[88] Though named 4 Maccabees, the book has virtually nothing to do with the Maccabean revolt against the Seleucids. Rather, the author glamorizes the stories of martyrdom from 2 Macc 6:18–7:42 in order to defend his thesis: religious reason masters the passions (cf. 4 Macc 1:1).[89]

Van Henten divides the book into six sections. First, the author states his "philosophical thesis, the autonomy of devout reason (1:1–3:18)." Second, he sets the historical context of the martyrdoms (3:19–4:26). Third, he highlights Eleazar's martyrdom and praises him (5:1–7:23). Fourth, he highlights "the martyrdom and praise of the seven brothers" (8:1–14:10). Fifth, he highlights "the self-killing and praise of the mother" (14:11–17:1). Sixth, he concludes the book with a summary and seeks to console the survivors of martyrdom (17:2–18:2).[90]

In 18:3–24, the author infers from the martyrological narratives that the martyrs received mortal honor in this age and secured an eternal inheritance in the age to come (18:3). The author presents the martyrs as establishing peace in the land by their devotion to Torah (18:4). He hails them as victorious over the tyrant Antiochus, who suffered punishment in both life and death, since he failed to compel the Israelites to abandon their ancestral customs (18:5). The author concludes the book with a mother's noble address of her martyred children after their deaths (18:6–24).

1. The author states his philosophical thesis about the autonomy of reason by prioritizing devotion to Torah as the means to virtue. The author urges his (likely) Jewish audience to pay careful attention to the argument about devout reason as the "absolute master over the passions" (αὐτοδέσποτός ἐστιν τῶν παθῶν ὁ εὐσεβὴς λογισμός) (4 Macc 1:1). David A. deSilva asserts that although the author promises to explain what he means by passions (cf. 1:14), he "never even actually defines what he understands the passions to be, as had, for example, Zeno ('a violent movement or assault upon the soul, which is irrational and contrary to nature,' Diogenes

---

87. J. W. van Henten, "Maccabees, Fourth Book of," in Collins and Harlow, eds., *The Eerdmans Dictionary of Early Judaism*, 909.

88. For a discussion of dating, see Jarvis J. Williams, *Maccabean Martyr Traditions in Paul's Theology of Atonement: Did Martyr Theology Shape Paul's Conception of Jesus's Death?* (Eugene, OR: Wipf & Stock, 2010), 29–33.

89. Van Henten, "Maccabees, Fourth Book of," 909.

90. Paraphrased with modifications from ibid.

Laertius, *Vit.* 7.110]).''[91] In the context of 4 Maccabees, these passions could refer to strong emotions, which would result in living in accordance with either virtue or vice (1:2–4; cf. 4 Macc 1:1, 3–7, 9, 13–14, 19–21, 25, 29–30; 2:3, 6–7, 9, 15, 18, 24; 3:1, 5, 17–18; 6:31; 7:1, 5, 10, 16–18, 22–23; 8:28; 13:1, 3, 7; 14:1; 15:1, 4, 32; 16:1–2; 18:2). The author refers to his discourse as philosophy and speaks of the highest virtue, which he identifies as the "praise of understanding" (φρονήσεως περιέχει ἔπαινον) (1:2). The author summarizes the veracity of his assertion in the philosophical discourse on devout reason by praising the martyrs who died for the sake of virtue and nobility because they are the proof that devout reason masters the passions (1:1–12).

After this short introduction, the author associates the law with reason and "rational judgment, justice, courage, and self-control" (1:13–18). Insight or right thinking (ἡ φρόνησις), the author says, is the most sovereign over all things (κυριωτάτη δὲ πάντων ἡ φρόνησις) (1:19). By means of intelligence, devout reason rules over the passions (ἐξ ἧς δὴ τῶν παθῶν ὁ λογισμὸς ἐπικρατεῖ) (1:19). Wisdom comes by instruction in the law, by which one learns both divine and human matters (αὕτη δὴ τοίνυν ἐστὶν ἡ τοῦ νόμου παιδεία δι' ἧς τὰ θεῖα σεμνῶς καὶ τὰ ἀνθρώπινα συμφερόντως μανθάνομεν) (1:17).

The author again appeals to the law as he continues his philosophical discourse. The power of devout reason enables Jews to overcome the passions to eat unlawful food. The law is the source of self-control when one desires foods forbidden in Torah (1:30–35). The law keeps one from coveting since it forbids covetousness (2:5–6). When one adopts a way of life in compliance with Torah, one becomes able to act contrary to his natural inclinations (2:7–9). If one is a lover of money, he lends without interest and cancels debts during the year of Jubilee (2:8). The one devoted to the way of Torah has devout reason so that he performs justice toward the needy in the time of harvest and avoids greed (2:9).

"The law prevails" over one's affections to the parents (2:10). The law rules over one's love for a wife (2:11) and rebukes her because of lawlessness (2:11). The law rules over one's love for children and punishes them because of evil (2:12). The law is master over the custom of friends and rebukes them because of evil (2:13). Reason is even able to rule over one's enmity because of the law (2:14). Reason informed by the law rules over lust, arrogance, boasting, and malice (2:15). God gave the mind the law (2:23). If the mind lives in subjection to the law, it will rule a "sensible, righteous, good, and manly kingdom" (καὶ τούτῳ νόμον

---

91. deSilva, *4 Maccabees*, 69.

ἔδωκεν καθ' ὃν πολιτευόμενος βασιλεύσει βασιλείαν σώφρονά τε καὶ δικαίαν καὶ ἀγαθὴν καὶ ἀνδρείαν) (2:23; cf. 3:1–16).⁹²

2. *The Jewish people experienced peace in the land because of obedience to Torah.* After his philosophical thesis that "devout," "pious," or "sensible" reason masters the passions (1:1–3:18), the author begins to illustrate the premise with a narrative of resilient Jews who remained steadfast to Torah in suffering and martyrdom (5:1–17:24). The author first sets the historical context of this resilience. As he personifies his thesis with the Torah-observant martyrs, the author frames the narrative with the language of Deuteronomic blessing and curse. He states that the fathers enjoyed "deep peace" (βαθεῖαν εἰρήνην) and were "doing well" (ἔπραττον καλῶς) in the land "because of devotion to the law" (διὰ τὴν εὐνομίαν) (3:20). This peace relates both to a Gentile king's (Seleucid Nicanor, the king of Asia) financial provision for Jewish priestly worship at the temple (οἱ πατέρες ἡμῶν εἶχον καὶ ἔπραττον καλῶς ὥστε καὶ τὸν τῆς Ἀσίας βασιλέα Σέλευκον τὸν Νικάνορα καὶ χρήματα εἰς τὴν ἱερουργίαν αὐτοῖς ἀφορίσαι) and to his acceptance of their citizenship (καὶ τὴν πολιτείαν αὐτῶν ἀποδέχεσθαι) (3:20).⁹³ In 3:20, the author uses εὐνομία ("way of life which conforms to the law") instead of νόμος ("law/Torah") to refer to the law-observance of the fathers. However, in 4 Maccabees εὐνομία is in close association with νόμος and Ἰουδαϊσμός ("a Jewish manner of life") (2:5–6, 10; 5:18–21; 8:25; cf. 2 Macc 2:21; 14:38).

Paul L. Redditt says, for example, that in 1:34 the author refers to forbidden foods in accordance with the law (cf. Lev 11:1–31).⁹⁴ In his philosophical discourse, the author refers to coveting (a specific commandment in the Torah [MT Exod 20:17]) (4 Macc 2:5–6).⁹⁵ Redditt continues that in 2:9, the author refers to the appropriate way to harvest by appealing to Lev 19:9–10; 23:22, and Deut 24:19–21.⁹⁶ In 4 Macc 9:2, the author connects law with Moses.⁹⁷ In 4 Macc 2:10–23, the

---

92. Cf. also Philo, *Migr.* 197.
93. As many scholars have pointed out, the author mistakenly confuses Seleucus IV Philopater (187–175 BCE) with Seleucus I Nicanor (305–281 BCE). E.g. Joseph L. Trafton, "4 Maccabees," in the *New Revised Standard Study Bible with Apocrypha*, ed. Walter J. Harrelson (Nashville: Abingdon, 2003), 1728. The former preceded Antiochus Epiphanes IV (4 Macc 4:15).
94. Paul Redditt, "The Concept of Nomos in Fourth Maccabees," *CBQ* 45 (1983): 249–50.
95. Ibid.
96. Ibid.
97. Ibid.

author asserts the law (νόμος) rules over human relationships and over violent emotions. When Antiochus compels Eleazar to eat unlawful meat contrary to Torah, Eleazar informs him that no form of violence would compel him to disobey the law (νόμος) because he and his fellow Jews conducted their lives by living in compliance with the divine law (νόμος) (5:16; cf. 5:17–21).[98] The martyrs refused to eat defiling food in violation of the law and continued to obey the law (νόμος) because they believed God established the law (νόμος) (5:25, 29). The martyrs died for the sake of God's law (νόμος) (6:27, 30); they administered the law (νόμος) (7:8); they lived in accordance with God's "virtuous law" (νόμος) (11:5); and they endured the Tyrant's afflictions because of respect for their law (νόμος) (11:12).

The author praises Eleazar for his faithfulness to the law (νόμος) and his refusal to eat defiling foods (7:6–7). His suffering for the sake of piety (= obedience to Torah) strengthened the Jews' devotion to a way of life conforming to the law (εὐνομία) (7:9). Antiochus was unable to abolish the people's obedience to the nation's law (εὐνομία) by his strict decrees (4:24). Instead, the martyrs' obedience to their nation's law (εὐνομία) abolished all of "his threats and punishments" (4:24). The narrative of 4 Maccabees supports this with the martyrs' refusal to forfeit living in compliance with Torah. Elsewhere, the author says the martyrs obeyed Torah and that Antiochus compelled the people to renounce Judaism (Ἰουδαϊσμός) by putting pressure on them to eat unlawful foods (4:26). In the book's conclusion, the author reasserts the martyrs' piety (= Torah-observance) in the face of suffering for Torah (εὐνομία) made them both honorable in the presence of men and worthy of a "divine portion" (18:3). The Jewish nation experienced peace because the Torah-observant martyrs revived a way of life that conforms to the law through their endurance of suffering for the sake of piety (18:4). Thus, a Jewish way of life lived in compliance with Torah and marked off by Torah-observance provided Israel with blessing in the land and enabled them to avoid the curse. When Torah-observance stopped, God's peace (blessing) in the land ceased.

---

98. deSilva (*4 Maccabees*, 92) observes "Providing a philosophically defensible interpretation of these laws was an order of the first importance for Hellenistic Jews, for the peculiar food laws of Torah tended to bring ridicule rather than respect from Gentile observers (cf. Tacitus, *Hist.* 5.4.3; Juvenal, *Sat.* 14.98–99; Josephus, *Ap.* 2.137)."

3. Jews experienced unrest in the land in the narrative of 4 Maccabees when some within the nation began to disobey Torah for political gain. As the author continues to set the historical context of the martyrdoms (3:19–4:26), he discusses the unrest (curse) and the reason for it in 3:20–4:26. Unrest in the land is the curse of non-Torah-observance. Unrest happened because of Torah-disobedience at the time the fathers were otherwise experiencing peace (blessing) in the land because of Torah-observance (3:20–21). Some Jews used many circumstances to participate in a political rebellion against the common unity of the nation (τότε δή τινες πρὸς τὴν κοινὴν νεωτερίσαντες ὁμόνοιαν πολυτρόποις ἐχρήσαντο συμφοραῖς) (3:21).

Simon (a Jew) was a political antagonist of the virtuous high priest Onias (a Jew) (4:1). Onias served as high priest at a time when it was a lifetime office (4:1).[99] Simon attempted to injure Onias with false accusations (4:1), but failed. As a result, he fled the nation with the intent of betraying the homeland (4:1). Simon formed a political alliance with Apollonius (a Gentile governor of Syria, Phoenicia, and Cilicia) (4:2–3). Simon professed loyalty to a Gentile nation (4:1–2). He showed this loyalty by informing the governor that the Jerusalem temple had significant funds in its treasury and that these funds were suitable for the king (4:3). This news pleased the governor, and he honored Simon for this report (4:4). Apollonius quickly informed the king of these temple funds (4:4). Immediately thereafter, Jerusalem's fortunes changed from blessing to curse because of Simon's political alliance with the Gentiles and his rebellion against the high priest and the nation (3:20–4:5).

The author identifies Simon as "accursed Simon" (καταράτου Σίμωνος) because of his alliance with the Gentiles (4:5; cf. 3:20–4:5; Deut 27–28; Gal 3:10, 13). Simon is also accursed because of his non-Torah-observance. He made injurious accusations against the high priest, Onias, a violation of a stipulation of the law (4:1; cf. Exod 22:28; Acts 23:5). In his article on high priests, James C. VanderKam points out the high priest was the primary officer of the cult in Second Temple Judaism (cf. Sir 50:1–21),[100] and other high priests acted as the primary civil leaders of Judea (possibly Jdt 4:6, 8, 14; 15:8; 1 Macc 12:20–23; *Letter of Aristeas*; Josephus, *Ant.* 11.317–19).[101] Simon's injurious charges against Onias challenged a Jewish manner of life in accordance with Torah. Simon also

---

99. Cf. Josephus, *Ant.* 17.339; 18.34–35; 20.224–51.
100. James C. VanderKam, "High Priests," in Collins and Harlow, eds., *The Eerdmans Dictionary of Early Judaism*, 739–42, esp. 739.
101. Ibid.

violated Torah. The narrative of 4 Maccabees gives no evidence that he brought charges against Onias on the basis of two or three witnesses in compliance with Torah (4:1; cf. Deut 19:15–21). Simon likewise violated laws with respect to the temple in that he informed the Gentiles about the monies set aside for God's holy place and in that he was complicit in Gentile efforts to defile the temple (4:1–7). Identifying Simon as "accursed Simon" indicts him as subject to the curse of Deuteronomy because of non-Torah-observance. The appellation of "accursed Simon" anticipates the Deuteronomic curses that will soon fall on the entire nation in the narrative. The author personifies these curses via the deaths of the martyrs because of Simon's disobedience and eventually the nation's failure to comply with Torah (cf. 4:6–26).

Apollonius journeyed to the Jewish homeland with the accursed Simon, a strong army, and with the authority of the king to take the money from the temple treasury (4:5–6). The Jews strongly protested the governor's words (4:7). They considered his remarks to be terrible (4:7). Apollonius ignored the nation's resistance, threatened the Jews, and continued to endeavor to enter the temple to pilfer the treasury (4:8). The priests, women, and children asked God to protect the temple from the governor's contempt (4:9). God heard the prayers of the priests, the women, and the children in the holy place in the temple. He sent angels from heaven to assault Apollonius as he attempted to pilfer the money from the temple (4:10).

Apollonius fell to the ground with the appearance of a dead man in the court of the temple, stretched out his hands to heaven, and with tears begged the Hebrews to propitiate the heavenly army by praying for him (καταπεσών γέ τοι ἡμιθανὴς ὁ Ἀπολλώνιος ἐπὶ τὸν πάμφυλον τοῦ ἱεροῦ περίβολον τὰς χεῖρας ἐξέτεινεν εἰς τὸν οὐρανὸν καὶ μετὰ δακρύων τοὺς Εβραίους παρεκάλει ὅπως περὶ αὐτοῦ προσευξάμενοι τὸν οὐράνιον ἐξευμενίσωνται στρατόν) (4:11). Apollonius admitted he "committed a sin deserving of death" (ἔλεγεν γὰρ ἡμαρτηκὼς ὥστε καὶ ἀποθανεῖν ἄξιος ὑπάρχειν) (4:12). He promised to honor the holy place if the God of the Hebrews would save him (πᾶσίν τε ἀνθρώποις ὑμνήσειν σωθεὶς τὴν τοῦ ἱεροῦ τόπου μακαριότητα) (4:12). Onias prayed for the governor, and divine justice spared him (4:13–14). Disobedience to Torah brought a curse upon both the Jewish nation via the threat of Apollonius and upon Apollonius via God's heavenly assault of him. But the prayers of the people and the devout and honorable high priest, Onias, brought peace upon the Jewish nation by means of stopping Apollonius's pillaging of the temple treasury and by means of sparing Apollonius from divine justice.

4. Jason's (a Jew) act of non-Torah-observance led to God distributing the Deuteronomic curses upon Jerusalem through Antiochus Epiphanes IV. Antiochus Epiphanes IV ("the glorious" or "the splendid" one) replaced King Seleucus IV after he died (4:15).[102] The author identifies him as an "arrogant" and a "terribly vehement man" (ἀνὴρ ὑπερήφανος καὶ δεινός) (4:15). He removed Onias from the high priesthood and appointed Jason (his brother) (4:16), who financially bribed his way into this important office (4:17–18). As the high priest, Jason was a political leader of the Jewish nation (ὁ δὲ ἐπέτρεψεν αὐτῷ καὶ ἀρχιερᾶσθαι καὶ τοῦ ἔθνους ἀφηγεῖσθαι) (4:18). Yet, although he was Jewish, Jason's manner of life was more compliant with Antiochus's Greek culture than with important aspects of Jewish identity.[103]

Jason altered Jewish customs (4:19). He departed from the nation's Torah-observant life, and he changed the nation's constitution from Torah-observance to lawlessness (καὶ ἐξεδιήτησεν τὸ ἔθνος καὶ ἐξεπολίτευσεν ἐπὶ πᾶσαν παρανομίαν) (4:19). Examples of Jason's lawless government included both the construction of a gymnasium (a Greek symbol that prioritized Greek worship and Greek culture) at the citadel of the temple and the destruction of the temple service (a Jewish symbol that prioritized the Jewish cult) (ὥστε μὴ μόνον ἐπ' αὐτῇ τῇ ἄκρᾳ τῆς πατρίδος ἡμῶν γυμνάσιον κατασκευάσαι ἀλλὰ καὶ καταλῦσαι τὴν τοῦ ἱεροῦ κηδεμονίαν) (4:20). Jason's lawless acts elicited God's divine anger (4:21). Consequently, God brought the curses of Deuteronomy upon the Jewish nation by means of the Greek tyrant Antiochus (4:21–26).[104]

Antiochus ravaged Jerusalem and issued decrees forbidding the Jews in Jerusalem from living in compliance with Torah (4:22–23). He warned that if any Jews disobeyed his decree and lived in compliance with the Jewish law, they would die (καὶ ὡς ἐπόρθησεν αὐτοὺς δόγμα ἔθετο ὅπως εἴ τινες αὐτῶν φάνοιεν τῷ πατρίῳ πολιτευόμενοι νόμῳ θάνοιεν) (4:23). His threats emboldened Torah-observant Jews to remain Torah-observant (4:24–25). Hence, Antiochus introduced torture as a means of compelling the Jews to live as Gentiles and not as Jews (4:26).

---

102. The text wrongly identifies the king as Antiochus's father (4:15), but he was his brother. Among many scholars, so also deSilva, *4 Maccabees*, 112.

103. By this time, Judaism and Hellenism were merged together. For example, see Martin Hengel, *Judaism and Hellenism*, trans. John Bowden (London: SPCK, 1974).

104. deSilva (*4 Maccabees*, 113) makes this general point about the events of blessing and curse in 4 Maccabees. "In keeping with Deut. 28:1–14, Torah observance brings the blessings of political stability and freedom from defeat by one's enemies."

5. *Suffering, endurance, and martyrdom illustrate the Deuteronomic blessings of Torah-observance and the Deuteronomic curses of non-Torah-observance.* The author first highlights the Deuteronomic curses of martyrdom through Antiochus's encounter with and martyrdom of Eleazar (5:1–7:23). Antiochus ordered the spearmen to un-circumcise each Hebrew and to compel the Jews to eat unclean foods contrary to Torah (παρεκέλευεν τοῖς δορυφόροις ἕνα ἕκαστον Εβραῖον ἐπισπᾶσθαι καὶ κρεῶν ὑείων καὶ εἰδωλοθύτων ἀναγκάζειν ἀπογεύεσθαι) (5:2; cf. Lev 11:1–47; 17:10–16; Deut 14:1–2). Antiochus threatened to subject those unwilling to eat foods contrary to Torah to torture and death (4 Macc 5:3).

The king's counselors rounded up a wise, priestly, and learned man in the Torah named Eleazar (5:4). Antiochus urged Eleazar not to disgrace his old age by refusing to eat foods contrary to Torah (5:5–13), as he claimed that perhaps his God would forgive him for transgressing Torah because of compulsion (5:13). Eleazar responds in the narrative by giving a defense of Torah (5:14–38). He asks the king's permission to respond to his compulsory exhortation to eat unlawful food (5:14). He informs Antiochus that he and his fellow Jews govern their lives by Torah and "that there is no compulsion" strong enough to convince them otherwise (ἡμεῖς Ἀντίοχε θείῳ πεπεισμένοι νόμῳ πολιτεύεσθαι οὐδεμίαν ἀνάγκην βιαιοτέραν εἶναι νομίζομεν τῆς πρὸς τὸν νόμον ἡμῶν εὐπειθείας) (5:16).

Eleazar reinforces that neither he nor other Torah-observant Jews would transgress Torah by eating unlawful foods (διὸ δὴ κατ' οὐδένα τρόπον παρανομεῖν ἀξιοῦμεν) (5:17). He claims that transgressing the law by eating from an unclean menu is no little sin even if the law was not divine (καίτοι εἰ κατὰ ἀλήθειαν μὴ ἦν ὁ νόμος ἡμῶν ὡς ὑπολαμβάνεις θεῖος ἄλλως δὲ ἐνομίζομεν αὐτὸν εἶναι θεῖον οὐδὲ οὕτως ἐξὸν ἦν ἡμῖν τὴν ἐπὶ τῇ εὐσεβείᾳ δόξαν ἀκυρῶσαι μὴ μικρὰν οὖν εἶναι νομίσῃς ταύτην εἰ μιαροφαγήσαιμεν ἁμαρτίαν) (5:18–19). To transgress the law in small or great matters is of equal value (τὸ γὰρ ἐπὶ μικροῖς καὶ μεγάλοις παρανομεῖν ἰσοδύναμόν ἐστιν) (5:20). To transgress the law even in small matters dishonors Torah (δι' ἑκατέρου γὰρ ὡς ὁμοίως ὁ νόμος ὑπερηφανεῖται) (5:21). Though Antiochus scoffs at the Jewish law (5:22), it teaches self-control, courage, righteousness, and piety (5:23–24), so that the Jewish nation would "worship, through all the customs, the only true God" (ὥστε διὰ πάντων τῶν ἠθῶν ἰσονομεῖν καὶ εὐσέβειαν ἐκδιδάσκει ὥστε μόνον τὸν ὄντα θεὸν σέβειν μεγαλοπρεπῶς) (5:24). Since God established the law (5:25), Eleazar declares Torah-observant Jews refuse to transgress the laws of the ancestors to eat unclean food (5:25–29). Eleazar, thus, gives Antiochus no occasion to mock him or other Torah-observant Jews for eating unclean foods in disobedience to Torah (5:27–38).

2. Deuteronomic Blessings and Curses   93

After Eleazar's speech, Antiochus's spearman violently "dragged him to the instruments of torture" (6:1). They stripped him naked (6:3), tied his hands behind his back (6:3), and "began to wound him severely with whips" (ἔπειτα περιαγκωνίσαντες ἑκατέρωθεν μάστιξιν κατῄκιζον) (6:3). Though compelled by a bystander to obey the king and disobey Torah, after dropping to the ground as he gushed with blood since his body was unable to endure the wounds in his flesh (6:4–8), Eleazar continued to endure the tortures and remained faithful to Torah (6:8–11). Eleazar says he suffers "for the sake of the law" (6:27); he resisted the king's compulsion for the sake of the law (6:30); and he asserted in his prayer that his suffering was for the sake of the sins of the people (6:28). He conflates suffering for the law with suffering for the people's sins. Eleazar's suffering was a direct result of the nation's transgression of Torah. He prays God would take his life as a recompense for the nation (ἀντίψυχον αὐτῶν λαβὲ τὴν ἐμὴν ψυχήν) (6:29). Deuteronomic curses for violating Torah fall upon Israel and the Deuteronomic curses and blessings are personified in the martyrdom of Eleazar.

6. Deuteronomic curses fall upon an unknown mother and her seven sons.
After proving his thesis that religious reason masters the passions through the aged Eleazar's death for the law, the author supports the argument through the martyrdoms of seven youths and their mother (a widow) (8:1). As the mother is forced to watch her sons suffer martyrdom for the sake of God's law (8:1–15:13), she exhorts them to die well (15:14–32). Along with her seven sons, the mother's own martyrdom is an example of the curses of Torah falling upon the nation because of the non-Torah-observance of some in the nation.

Antiochus urged the youth to renounce their Jewish way of life (ἀρνησάμενοι τὸν πάτριον ὑμῶν τῆς πολιτείας θεσμόν) (8:7) and to embrace "a Greek way of life" (καὶ μεταλαβόντες Ἑλληνικοῦ βίου) (8:8). Antiochus threatened the youth with tortures if they refused to comply (8:9–14). As Antiochus spoke, his spearmen brought forth the instruments of both "the wheels and the instruments of torture applied to limbs" (τροχούς τε καὶ ἀρθρέμβολα), "both racks used as instruments of torture and bone-crushers" (στρεβλωτήριά τε καὶ τροχαντῆρας), "catapults and cooking utensils" (καὶ καταπέλτας καὶ λέβητας), "both frying pans and thumbscrews" (τήγανά τε καὶ δακτυλήθρας), "iron hands" (χεῖρας σιδηρᾶς), and "wedges and bellows of fire" (σφῆνας καὶ τὰ ζώπυρα τοῦ πυρός) to use as instruments of torture for the purpose of persuading the youths to disobey Torah (8:12–13). However, the youths responded in a similar fashion as the aged and wise Eleazar (8:15–9:9). They asserted they were "ready to die" rather than to transgress the ancestral laws (ἕτοιμοι γάρ ἐσμεν ἀποθνῄσκειν ἢ παραβαίνειν τὰς πατρίους ἡμῶν ἐντολάς) (9:1). They affirmed to transgress the law of Moses was to shame their Jewish ancestors (αἰσχυνόμεθα γὰρ τοὺς προγόνους ἡμῶν εἰκότως εἰ μὴ τῇ τοῦ νόμου εὐπειθείᾳ καὶ συμβούλῳ Μωυσεῖ χρησαίμεθα) (9:2).[105] Instead, they shamed Antiochus by their steadfastness in Torah (9:3–9). Thus, Antiochus severely beat, tortured, and executed each youth in front of their mother (9:10–17:24). The important point for my thesis is the following: in the narrative, the martyrs' suffering and death are the result of the Deuteronomic curses upon the nation through a non-Torah-observant Gentile king and nation. Eleazar affirms this when he asks God to use his death to be "their" purification (6:29).

7. Eleazar prays that God would receive his Torah-observance and his death for the sake of God's law as the end of the curses against the nation to give them blessing (6:28–29). The author concludes his narrative of martyrdom with a short commentary by affirming the martyrs' deaths brought national purification (17:21–22). This national purification should be understood as Deuteronomic blessing, which the author interprets as life in this age and in the age to come as a result of martyrdom. The terms "blessing" and "curse" do not occur in Eleazar's prayer. Nevertheless, the concepts are there. Eleazar wants the Jews to experience mercy and purification (i.e. blessing) through the martyrs' deaths (i.e. a curse) (6:28–29).

Torah-observant Eleazar is the antithesis to the non-Torah-observant and cursed Simon and the apostate Jason, who brought the Deuteronomic curse upon the nation. Eleazar's faithfulness and the Torah-observance of the martyrs brought Deuteronomic blessing upon the nation. As the author praises the mother, he honors her love for piety that "saves for eternal life in accordance with God's promise" (τὴν εὐσέβειαν μᾶλλον ἠγάπησεν τὴν σῴζουσαν εἰς αἰωνίαν ζωὴν κατὰ θεόν) (15:3). Piety is connected with virtue (4 Macc 1:2, 8, 30; 2:10; 6:30; 7:22; 9:8, 18, 31; 10:10; 11:2, 4; 12:14; 17:12, 23) and Torah-observance (4 Macc 1:17, 34).[106] The mother's love for godliness/piety because of obedience to Torah is associated with "eternal life" in accordance with God's promise (15:3).

105. Some LXX manuscripts say "knowledge" instead of "Moses." See the Rahlfs-Hanhart textual apparatus on 4 Macc 9:2.
106. 4 Maccabees 2:5–6, 8–11, 14, 23; 3:20; 4:19, 23–24; 5:4, 16, 18, 20–21, 25, 27, 29, 33–35; 6:18, 21, 27, 30; 7:7–9; 8:25; 9:2, 4, 15; 11:5, 12, 27; 13:9, 13, 22, 24; 15:9, 29, 32; 16:16; 18:1, 4, 10.

The mother and her sons assert that dying for the sake of God's law would lead to eternal life with the patriarchs Abraham, Isaac, and Jacob (16:25). This promise is connected with the promise that obedience to Torah leads to life (blessing) and disobedience leads to a curse (Deut 27–30; cf. Lev 18:5). The author states that the martyrs brought national purification to the nation and defeated the tyrant because of their Torah-observant deaths (17:21–22). They vindicated the nation (17:10). Their endurance of suffering and death for the sake of God's law brought them "immortality in endless life" (17:12). This endless life is likely a reference to honor in this age and in the age to come.

The author has already asserted their deaths for the sake of God results in their living to/with God just as the patriarchs (16:25). They live with the patriarchs as they stand before God's throne and live through blessed eternity (17:18). The martyrs were honored by humans and received a divine inheritance (18:3). And, because of the martyrs' Torah-obedience, the nation experienced peace (blessing), revived the law, and defeated the Tyrant (καὶ δι' αὐτοὺς εἰρήνευσεν τὸ ἔθνος καὶ τὴν εὐνομίαν τὴν ἐπὶ τῆς πατρίδος ἀνανεωσάμενοι ἐκπεπόρθηκαν τοὺς πολεμίους) (18:4). The author concludes the book by asserting that the mother and her sons "gather around with respect to a chorus with the fathers because they received from God pure and immortal souls" (οἱ δὲ Ἀβραμιαῖοι παῖδες σὺν τῇ ἀθλοφόρῳ μητρὶ εἰς πατέρων χορὸν συναγελάζονται ψυχὰς ἁγνὰς καὶ ἀθανάτους ἀπειληφότες παρὰ τοῦ θεοῦ) (18:23),[107] and the author then praises them for eternal honor (18:23–24). These references likely refer to eternal life in the age to come (blessing) because the author asserts Antiochus will receive eternal torment (a curse) in the age to come (9:9, 29, 32; 10:11, 15; 11:3, 23; 12:18; 18:5).

VI. Summary of Deuteronomic Blessings and Curses in 4 Maccabees

4 Maccabees 4:19–21 states that after Jason, the high priest, led the nation astray from Torah, the Lord became angry and used Antiochus to wage war against Israel. The elaborate discussions of the martyrdoms of Eleazar, the mother, and her seven sons in 5:1–12:19, and the narrator's comments regarding the efficacy of the martyrs' deaths in 17:21–22 suggest the Lord displayed the curses of Deuteronomy by means of both Jewish exile from the land and death in the land, both of which Deuteronomy connects to

---

107. 4 Maccabees commonly refers to the immortality of the soul and not the resurrection of the body and soul (10:4; 14:5–6; 18:23).

Torah-observance and non-Torah-observance (Deut 21:22, 26; 28:21; 30:15–20). The Lord also distributes the Deuteronomic blessing of peace in the land through the martyrs' deaths (6:28–29; 17:21–22). The author of 4 Maccabees emphasizes "the martyrs' loyalty to the law by asserting more than once they were eager to die for it" (5:16, 33–34; 6:21, 27, 30; 7:7–8; 9:2, 15; 11:12, 27; 13:9, 13; 15:9, 29; 16:16; 17:16).[108] He also alludes to commandments in Torah (1:34; 2:5–6, 8–10, 14).[109] Thus, since death in the land was in fact one of those curses pronounced in Deuteronomy against those who disobey Torah (e.g. 8:1), 4 Maccabees applies the Deuteronomic curses to the non-Torah-observant nation and to the Torah-observant martyrs. Blessings came to the nation in the narrative through the deaths of the Torah-observant martyrs for the law, but disobedience brought a curse.

VII. Conclusion

In this chapter, I analyzed the Deuteronomic blessings and curses motif in the Jewish martyrological traditions for the purpose of providing data for a comparative reading of the Deuteronomic blessing and curse motif in Galatians in Chapter 3. I made six specific arguments in this chapter. First, the Jewish martyrological traditions conflate the Abrahamic blessing and Deuteronomic blessings to show the pathway to the Abrahamic blessing is obedience to Torah. Second, the Jewish martyrological traditions appropriate Deuteronomic blessings to Torah-observant Jews. Third, the Jewish martyrological traditions appropriate the Deuteronomic curses to non-Torah-observant Jews. Fourth, the Jewish martyrological traditions posit Torah-observant Jewish martyrs as the means by which non-Torah-observant Jews would receive the life promised in Torah. Fifth, the Jewish martyrological traditions interpret the promise of temporal life in the land as eternal life in the age to come through faithful Torah-observance. Sixth, the Jewish martyrological traditions suggest Torah-observant Jews would experience eternal life in the age to come by Torah-observance.

---

108. Van Henten, *Maccabean Martyrs*, 132.
109. Ibid., 133.

3

DEUTERONOMIC BLESSINGS AND CURSES IN GALATIANS

In this chapter, I argue that Paul, in ways similar to but different from the Jewish martyrological traditions, presents both Jews and Gentiles as recipients of the Deuteronomic blessings and curses in Galatians. He contends Jesus, the Torah-observant Jew, suffered the Deuteronomic curses for others, experienced the blessing of life (i.e. resurrection), and delivered those for whom he died from the curse of the law. Those without faith in Christ are currently under the Deuteronomic curses and are devoted to destruction if they believe or preach another gospel contrary to the one preached by Paul. The purpose of the analysis in this chapter is to support that Galatians has both continuities with and discontinuities with the blessing and curse motif in the Jewish martyrological traditions in order to add further support that the Jewish martyrological traditions are *a* background behind Paul's remarks about the cursed Christ in Gal 3:13. However, the discontinuities highlight Paul modifies these traditions to fit his exegetical and polemical purposes in Galatians. The chapter makes the following arguments about blessings and curses in Galatians.

First, Paul appropriates the Deuteronomic blessings and curses to Jews and Gentiles without ethnic restriction. Second, Paul appropriates Deuteronomic blessings to those who identify with Jesus Christ, the seed of Abraham, apart from works of the law, and he applies the Deuteronomic curses to those who identify with works of Torah apart from or in addition to faith in Christ without ethnic restriction. Third, Paul conflates the Abrahamic and Deuteronomic blessings and curses in Galatians to emphasize both the Abrahamic blessing and the Deuteronomic blessing are extended to Jews and Gentiles by faith in the Messiah and realized in the death (and resurrection) of the Messiah, Jesus, apart from Torah, while the curses come to those under law. Fourth, Paul understands the promise in Lev 18:5 and Deut 27–30, that Torah-observance leads to long life in the land, as eternal life. This eternal life is experienced in this age and in the age to come apart from the works of the law by Jews and

Gentiles who place faith in Jesus because he died to deliver them from the present evil age and from the curse of the law. Fifth, Jesus received the Deuteronomic curse so that Jews and Gentiles would receive both the Abrahamic blessing of the Spirit and the Deuteronomic blessing of life.

Similar to 2 and 4 Maccabees, Paul applies the Deuteronomic curse to a Torah-observant Jew who suffered the curse of Torah for those under Torah to redeem them from its curse. The Jewish martyrological narratives suggest the covenant with Abraham and Deuteronomic promise of life are fulfilled for Jews by means of their Torah-observance and the noble deaths of the Jewish martyrs for Israel (2 and 4 Maccabees), by means of military action (2 Maccabees), and by means of effective prayer (2 and 4 Maccabees). Paul, however, suggests the Deuteronomic curses are realized in Torah-observant Jews and Gentiles who remain under the curse of the law outside of faith in Jesus, the Messiah, in Galatians. But Jesus, the Jewish Messiah, both personified the Deuteronomic curse (death) by becoming a curse for those under the curse and the blessing (resurrection/life) on behalf of Jews and Gentiles under the Deuteronomic curse so that the Abrahamic blessing of the Spirit would come upon Jewish and Gentile followers of Christ and so that the Deuteronomic blessing of life would be realized by Jews and Gentiles by faith in Christ apart from Torah-observance.

I. Deuteronomic Curse and Abrahamic Blessing in Galatians

Scholars generally agree Galatians is Paul's most rhetorically charged letter, written to dissuade the Galatians from turning away from his non-Torah-observant, Gentile-inclusive gospel to the other Torah-observant, Gentile-exclusive gospel of the rival teachers in Galatia. His fundamental concern is the authority of his gospel, which leads to life, and that the Galatians are in grave danger of turning away from it to embrace Torah, which leads to a curse (1:6–3:14). He warns the Galatians throughout the letter that a turn from his gospel is a turn toward a curse because his gospel centers on the cross (1:4; 2:20–21; 3:1, 13; 6:14) and resurrection (1:1) of Jesus Christ, whereas Torah curses as many who identify with it because it is under the present evil age (cf. 1:4; 3:10; 4:8–11).

Because of the teachers in Galatia, the Galatians think they must become circumcised and do works of law to have full admission into Abraham's offspring as Gentiles. The teachers duped the Galatians to believe the cross of the Jewish Messiah is insufficient to grant them familial ties with Abraham's offspring, but rather they thought they needed circumcision and the law to become full members within Abraham's family (cf. 2:16;

3:1–4:31). Paul argues his gospel of the cross and resurrection of Jesus universally manifests the outpouring of the Spirit upon Jewish and Gentile Christ-followers (3:14; 5:16). If the Galatians give into this false gospel, they would be cursed (3:10) and severed from Christ (5:4) at the end of the age because Christ will not profit them in the judgment (5:2) and because a turn from Paul's gospel about Christ is a fall from the grace of the gospel (5:4).

Paul's burden throughout the letter is to win those who have fallen from his gospel and to warn those who contemplate a turn from it (cf. 1:6). He argues with a scriptural exegesis of texts, likely used by the teachers in the churches of Galatia, against the need for Gentile Christians to become Torah-observant as a pre-requisite for membership into Abraham's family. One of Paul's sharpest arguments against the alternative, Torah-observant gospel, preached by the teachers in Galatia, is that their message only leads to a curse (3:10; cf. 1:8–9), not a blessing/life (3:21). On the contrary, Paul argues his gospel only leads to life/blessing and not to a curse (cf. 3:1–14) because Christ delivered "us" from the curse of the law. Paul emphasizes both the Abrahamic blessing and the Deuteronomic blessing are for both Jews and Gentiles (3:1–4:31), but only experienced by faith in the crucified Christ via the distribution of the Spirit apart from Torah-observance because of the Christ's curse-bearing death (3:13–14). Jews and Gentiles who refuse to place faith in the cursed Christ, Jesus, remain under the curse of the law and fall short of the blessing of Abraham, but receive in full the Deuteronomic curses.

1. Paul begins the letter with two curse-pronouncements in 1:8–9. With these two curse-pronouncements, he connects the apostolic curse in 1:8–9 with Deuteronomic blessing and curse and Abrahamic blessing in 3:1–29. He wishes an ἀνάθεμα upon anyone who preaches a different gospel to the Galatians in contrast to the one he preached to them (Gal 1:8–9).[1] In the LXX, ἀνάθεμα occurs numerous times in the context of divine judgment (cf. LXX Lev 27:28; Num 21:3; Josh 6:17–18; 7:12–13; Judg 1:17; 1 Chr 2:7; Zech 14:11).[2] YHWH sets apart things (LXX Lev 27:28), people (LXX Num 21:3), and cities (Josh 6:17–18) for destruction because of their disobedience to him. The term ἀνάθεμα in Gal 1:8–9 is different from the words translated as curse in Galatians (ἐπικατάρατος [Gal 3:10, 13; cf. Deut 27:15–26; 28:16, 19] and κατάρας [Gal 3:10, 13; cf. LXX Deut

---

1. For a discussion of ἀνάθεμα, see Moisés Silva, "Ἀνάθεμα," in *New International Dictionary of New Testament Theology and Exegesis*, rev. ed. (Grand Rapids: Zondervan, 2014), 1:281–4.

2. See also LXX Deut 13:18; Josh 6:18; 7:1, 11; 22:20.

11:28; 23:6; 27:13; 28:15, 45; 29:26; 30:1]). Still, YHWH's ἀνάθεμα is a divine curse in those LXX contexts, because ἀνάθεμα and the concept of curse are the antithesis of Deuteronomic blessing (cf. LXX Deut 11:26–29 with LXX Deut 27:15–26; 28:16).

In LXX Deut 13:18, Deuteronomy specifically connects ἀνάθεμα (τοῦ ἀναθέματος) with Deuteronomic blessing (οὐ προσκολληθήσεται ἐν τῇ χειρί σου οὐδὲν ἀπὸ τοῦ ἀναθέματος ἵνα ἀποστραφῇ κύριος ἀπὸ θυμοῦ τῆς ὀργῆς αὐτοῦ καὶ δώσει σοι ἔλεος καὶ ἐλεήσει σε καὶ πληθυνεῖ σε ὃν τρόπον ὤμοσεν κύριος τοῖς πατράσιν) and in LXX Deut 13:19 with the necessity of keeping all of YHWH's commandments in order to receive Deuteronomic blessing and to avoid the curse (ἐὰν ἀκούσῃς τῆς φωνῆς κυρίου τοῦ θεοῦ σου φυλάσσειν πάσας τὰς ἐντολὰς αὐτοῦ ὅσας ἐγὼ ἐντέλλομαί σοι σήμερον ποιεῖν τὸ καλὸν καὶ τὸ ἀρεστὸν ἐναντίον κυρίου τοῦ θεοῦ σου). LXX Deuteronomy 13:18–19 promises that Israel would avoid the Deuteronomic curse and receive the Deuteronomic blessing if the people avoided the ἀνάθεμα and that they would receive the blessing of mercy if they obeyed all of YHWH's commandments (see also LXX Deut 13:1–19).

Paul's remarks in Gal 1:8–9 appear to echo LXX Deut 13:12–16.[3] There Moses warns Israel that YHWH would curse the people with a curse if they attempted to lead the people into apostasy.[4] That curse would include exclusion from the community.[5] In Galatians, Paul conflates the concepts of ἀνάθεμα (a thing devoted to destruction by YHWH) (1:10) and the Deuteronomic curse in 3:10 with the prepositional phrase ὑπὸ κατάραν and the adjective ἐπικατάρατος, and in Gal 3:13 with the phrase ἐκ τῆς κατάρας τοῦ νόμου, the participial clause γενόμενος ὑπὲρ ἡμῶν κατάρα, and the adjective ἐπικατάρατος. According to Paul, an angel, or anyone else who preaches a different gospel from the one he preaches, is ἀνάθεμα, i.e., under the Deuteronomic curse (cf. 1:8–9; 3:10–13). Galatians 3:10–13 is important for this argument.

It is beyond the scope of this section to engage every exegetical issue in Gal 3. I say more below about some of the exegetical issues in the chapter. Sufficient for my thesis here is to highlight the way Paul deftly moves from his apostolic ἀνάθεμα in 1:8–9, against anyone who preaches another gospel, to a discussion about the blessing of Abraham, given to those who have faith (3:6–9, 14), and to the curse of the law, under which everyone who relies upon works of law exists (3:10).

3. Roy E. Ciampa, *The Presence and Function of Scripture in Galatians 1 and 2*, WUNT 2/102 (Tübingen: Mohr Siebeck, 1998), 83–8.
4. Ibid.
5. Ibid.

Paul mentions Abraham for the first time in 3:6.⁶ He emerges as an important figure in Paul's argument in Gal 3–4. In 3:2–5, Paul asks a series of questions pertaining to whether the Galatians have supernatural experiences of the Spirit by works of the law or by faith. He explicitly answers the question in 3:6 when he presents Abraham as an example as to how Gentiles receive the blessing of Abraham. Abraham's faith resulted in God counting him as righteous (καθὼς Ἀβραὰμ ἐπίστευσεν τῷ θεῷ, καὶ ἐλογίσθη αὐτῷ εἰς δικαιοσύνην). Gentiles with a faith similar to Abraham's are his sons (γινώσκετε ἄρα ὅτι οἱ ἐκ πίστεως, οὗτοι υἱοί εἰσιν Ἀβραάμ) (3:7). The Scriptures announced in advance to Abraham that God would justify the Gentiles by faith, promising that all the Gentiles will be blessed in/by means of him (προϊδοῦσα δὲ ἡ γραφὴ ὅτι ἐκ πίστεως δικαιοῖ τὰ ἔθνη ὁ θεός, προευηγγελίσατο τῷ Ἀβραὰμ ὅτι ἐνευλογηθήσονται ἐν σοὶ πάντα τὰ ἔθνη) (3:8). Those with faith receive the Abrahamic blessing with faithful Abraham (ὥστε οἱ ἐκ πίστεως εὐλογοῦνται σὺν τῷ πιστῷ Ἀβραάμ) (3:9).

In 3:10, Paul mentions the curse of the law for the first time in Galatians in the same context as the blessing of Abraham (3:10, 14).⁷ In 3:10–14, he conflates the curse of the law (3:10) with the blessing of Abraham (3:14). On the one hand, he identifies those outside of Christ and under the law as accursed (3:10–12). On the other hand, he describes those in Christ apart from the law as the recipients of both Abrahamic and Deuteronomic blessing (3:9–14; cf. also 3:16, 29; 5:25). In my view, the law refers to the entire Mosaic covenant in Galatians (5:3).

There is evidence some Jews in the Second Temple period believed the law required perfect obedience, that certain Jews were honored "for their perfection" (Pr. Man. 8; 1 En. 81:4; 82:4; Jub. 5:10; 10:3; 23:10; 27:17),⁸ and more than one Jewish author emphasizes the intersection of obeying

---

6. For a work on Abraham in Paul's letters, see Bruce W. Longenecker, *The Triumph of Abraham's God: Transformation of Identity in Galatians* (Nashville: Abingdon, 1998).

7. Below I offer a discussion of the passage.

8. Michael F. Bird, *An Anomalous Jew: Paul among Jews, Greeks, and Romans* (Grand Rapids: Eerdmans, 2016), 156 n. 164. Bird rightly comments NT scholars have argued for some time now the law did not require the Jews to obey perfectly the law. He remarks that scholarship by E. P. Sanders, *Paul and Palestinian Judaism: A Comparison of Patterns of Religion* (Philadelphia: Fortress, 1977) and others have argued this with force. But Bird, agreeing with A. Andrew Das (*Paul, the Law, and the Covenant* [Peabody, MA: Hendrickson, 2001], 12–44; idem, *Paul and the Jews*, LPS [Peabody, MA: Hendrickson, 2003], 142–8), says there is evidence that strongly challenges those who question the law's requirement of and expectation for perfect obedience to receive the life that it promises. For primary sources in support of Bird's view, see Bird, *An Anomalous Jew*, 156 n. 164; Simon J. Gathercole, *Where*

"the law and receiving life" (Bar 3:9; Pss Sol. 14:2–3; LAB 23:10).[9] In light of E. P. Sanders's work on Judaism,[10] in which he argued Judaism was based on covenantal nomism, scholars have strongly contested the preceding notion. Though much NT scholarship is sympathetic to Sanders's reading, scholars like James D. G. Dunn and N. T. Wright basically agree with Sanders's understanding of Judaism, but depart from his reading of Paul.[11] Contrary to Sanders, Dunn thought Paul's problem with the law was more complex than simply that Judaism was not Christianity. For Dunn, Paul thought the law and Judaism restricted the grace of God to Jews by focusing on "Jewish particularism."[12] Wright, on the other hand, agreed with Sanders's critique of the so-called old perspective's reading of Judaism, as a legalistic religion, and Paul's understanding of works of law as legalistic works-righteousness. However, Wright has argued in numerous works that Paul's problem with the law is that it focuses on Israel's national identity,[13] which is under the Deuteronomic curses because of disobedience to Torah as a way of life.[14]

In Gal 3:10, however, the phrase ἐξ ἔργων νόμου ("by means of works of the law") refers to those who attempt to do the deeds prescribed in the Mosaic covenant or the Torah and the attempt to meet its demands by doing the stipulations set forth in Torah. Paul neither simply refers to a few select stipulations within Torah nor simply to those who identify with Judaism. This seems correct because Paul uses the phrase "works of law" (3:10) and speaks of "abiding" in the law (3:10) and "doing" the law (3:12) in a parallel way in 3:10–12.[15] He also states one must keep "the whole

Is Boasting? Early Jewish Soteriology and Paul's Response in Romans 1–5 (Grand Rapids: Eerdmans, 2001). For a discussion of different views, see Douglas J. Moo, *Galatians*, BECNT (Grand Rapids: Baker, 2013), 201–5.

9. Ibid.

10. Sanders, *Paul and Palestinian Judaism*.

11. The rest of this paragraph is influenced by John J. Collins, *The Invention of Judaism: Torah and Jewish Identity from Deuteronomy to Paul* (Oakland: University of California Press, 2017), 160–1.

12. James D. G. Dunn, *Jesus, Paul, and the Law: Studies in Mark and Galatians* (Louisville: Westminster John Knox, 1990), 211.

13. N. T. Wright, *What Saint Paul Really Said: Was Paul of Tarsus the Real Founder of Christianity?* (Grand Rapids: Eerdmans, 1997), 84–7.

14. Wright, *Climax*.

15. For a similar point, see Moo, *Galatians*, 203–5. I do not think the term "legalism" is helpful in the current conversation about "works of law" because of the anachronisms attached to the word. For a further representation of my view of works of law, see Thomas R. Schreiner, "'Works of the Law' in Paul," *NovT* 33 (1991): 217–44.

law" (5:3).[16] Furthermore, in Galatians, Paul refers to Judaism (1:13–14), to table-fellowship (2:11–14), and to living a Jewish way of life (2:14), which refers to a life lived in compliance with the Mosaic covenant versus living a Gentile manner of life, which would be a life lived contrary to the law of Moses (2:14). He also mentions circumcision (2:3, 7; 5:3; 6:12–13) and the need to do "the whole law" (5:3). Deliverance from the law's curse, which comes from violating any stipulation of the covenant (cf. Deut 27–30), and the experience of the Abrahamic blessing and the law's blessing come to Jews and Gentiles by faith because of the cursed Christ (3:13), not by Torah-observance.

Galatians 3:10–14 provides the reason for Paul's assertions in 3:6–9. Paul explains how the blessing of Abraham comes to Jews and (especially) Gentiles by faith. The blessing comes to Gentiles by faith (3:6–9), not by law, because the law only brings a curse (3:10–12). But Christ delivered Jews and Gentiles from the curse by suffering a curse "for us" (3:13), so that both groups would receive by faith Abraham's blessing, namely, the Spirit (3:14).[17]

In 3:15–29, Paul continues, explaining that the blessing of Abraham comes to Gentiles by faith apart from works of the law. Here he conflates the covenantal language (διαθήκη) (3:15, 17) from Gen 12–50 and Deuteronomy with other key terminology from the Abrahamic narrative in Gen 12–50 and from Deuteronomy.[18] In this section, Paul refers to the promises (ἐπαγγελίαι) (3:16, 21), promise (ἐπαγγελία) (3:17–18), seed (σπέρμα) (3:16, 29), inheritance (κληρονομία) (3:18), heirs (κληρονόμοι) (3:29), law (νόμος) (3:17–18, 21, 23–24), the giving of life (ζωοποιῆσαι) (3:21), and faith/believing (πίστις/πιστεύω) (3:22) to emphasize God's promise to Abraham regarding land, seed, and universal blessing and the blessing of life in Torah are both realized in the justification of the Gentiles (and Jews) by faith via the death of the cursed Christ (3:8, 13; 4:5). According to Paul, Torah-observance is neither the pathway leading to the Abrahamic blessing nor the pathway leading to the life promised in Torah. Instead, faith in the cursed Christ bestows the blessing of Abraham and the blessing of Torah upon Jews and Gentiles (3:12; cf. 3:21). And, contrary to the law's promise of life (cf. Lev 18:5 with Gal 3:10–12), Paul

---

16. Moo, *Galatians*, 203–5.

17. I understand the second purpose clause in 3:14b (ἵνα τὴν ἐπαγγελίαν τοῦ πνεύματος λάβωμεν διὰ τῆς πίστεως) to be epexegetical to the first purpose clause in 3:14a (ἵνα εἰς τὰ ἔθνη ἡ εὐλογία τοῦ Ἀβραὰμ γένηται ἐν Χριστῷ Ἰησοῦ). I understand the genitive τοῦ πνεύματος in 3:14b to be in apposition to τὴν ἐπαγγελίαν.

18. Some argue for a Greco-Roman testamentary background. For a discussion of this, see Betz, *Galatians*, 154–6.

argues it only leads to a curse (3:10). The law was given as a temporary guardian and warden over those under its jurisdiction until the seed should come because of transgressions (3:19–4:7).

The cursed Christ is the promised seed of Abraham (3:16). He (Christ) leads to life those with faith apart from works of the law because his death delivers them from the present evil age and from the curse of the law (1:4; 2:16, 19–21; 3:12–13; 5:25). The life given to Jews and Gentiles through the cursed Christ includes, but should not be limited to, the internal dwelling of the Spirit (3:14; 4:6; 5:16), who opens up the pathway for those who walk in the Spirit to enter the kingdom of God (5:16–21). The Spirit, who fills all Jewish and Gentile Christ-followers, gives Gentiles everything they need to live a life pleasing to God, to escape the curse, and to inherit the blessing of the kingdom of God/eternal life and new creation (5:16–21; 6:8, 15). Because of the death of the cursed Christ, the Spirit is the blessing bestowed upon Jews and Gentiles who have been liberated from the enslaving curse of the law and who have been granted membership into Abraham's family by faith (cf. 3:10, 13–14; 4:21–5:1). The blessing of the Spirit enables those justified by faith to await the hope of righteousness through Spirit-empowered love (5:5–6, 13–16, 22). The blessing of the Spirit also inaugurates Isaiah's promise of new creation (6:15; cf. Isa 65:17–25). The two curse-pronouncements in 1:8–9 are Deuteronomic in that they apply to those who preach a Torah-observant gospel, which only leads to a curse (3:10), instead of faith in Christ, who delivers those under the curse from the curse to give them the Abrahamic blessing of the Spirit (3:13–14).

2. The Abrahamic blessing of the Spirit and the Deuteronomic blessing of life are conferred upon Jews and Gentiles by faith because of the death of the cursed Christ. Jesus's resurrection and death frame Galatians. Paul begins the letter by appealing to the authority of his apostleship, asserting that it comes from Jesus Christ and God, the Father, "who raised him from the dead" (Παῦλος ἀπόστολος οὐκ ἀπ' ἀνθρώπων οὐδὲ δι' ἀνθρώπου ἀλλὰ διὰ Ἰησοῦ Χριστοῦ καὶ θεοῦ πατρὸς τοῦ ἐγείραντος αὐτὸν ἐκ νεκρῶν) (1:1). After conferring a blessing of grace and peace upon the Galatians (1:3), Paul quickly refers to Jesus's death as the giving up of himself for others (τοῦ δόντος ἑαυτὸν ὑπὲρ τῶν ἁμαρτιῶν ἡμῶν) to deliver them from the present evil age (ὅπως ἐξέληται ἡμᾶς ἐκ τοῦ αἰῶνος τοῦ ἐνεστῶτος πονηροῦ) (1:4). He concludes the letter with a boast in the cross of the Lord Jesus Christ (Ἐμοὶ δὲ μὴ γένοιτο καυχᾶσθαι εἰ μὴ ἐν τῷ σταυρῷ τοῦ κυρίου ἡμῶν Ἰησοῦ Χριστοῦ), affirming that Christ's cross crucified the world to him and him to the world (δι' οὗ ἐμοὶ κόσμος ἐσταύρωται κἀγὼ κόσμῳ)

(6:14). Within the frame of 1:4 and 6:14, Paul either explicitly mentions (2:19–21; 3:1, 13; 5:25; 6:12, 14) or implicitly refers to Jesus's death (4:5; 5:2; 6:17) throughout the letter.

The death and resurrection of Jesus are foundational to Paul's gospel (1 Cor 15). But, in Galatians, apart from his explicit remark in 1:1, Paul often assumes the resurrection or implies it throughout the letter without explicitly mentioning it. For example, whenever he mentions eternal life, he implicitly refers to the resurrection of Jesus since his resurrection/life extends the life-giving power of the Spirit to Jews and Gentile via the cross (cf. 1:15–16; 2:19–21; 3:13–14, 21; 5:16).

To the contrary, Paul accentuates the cross of the cursed Christ as a disruptive turning point in the present evil age (1:4) within salvation-history (4:4–6). The cross is the place from which both the Abrahamic blessing and the Deuteronomic blessing flow, the reason for which they are conferred to Jews and Gentiles by faith, and the moment when God's salvation-historical promises are realized (4:4–6). According to Paul, the blessing of life that comes to Jews and Gentiles by faith apart from works of the law is resurrection/eternal life, which flows from the resurrection and exaltation of the cursed Christ (cf. 1:1, 15–16). Paul affirms in Galatians that the Christ's death ushers in the age of the Spirit and gives life because God raised him from the dead (1:1, 4, 15; 2:19–20; 3:13, 21). Paul explicitly emphasizes in Galatians that the Christ's death was the turning point of the ages for those under a curse to experience the blessing of the life-giving power of the Spirit. That is, the old age met its end in the cross of Jesus (6:14). This end is realized by a universal and unifying distribution of the Spirit by faith upon Jews and Gentiles (3:14, 28; 5:16, 22–23). A rejection of circumcision and the law as marks of identity for the people of God and Jewish and Gentile unity in the Spirit attest to God's cosmological work of new creation and the turning of the ages in Christ (5:2–6:15).

Galatians 1:4 explicitly refers to the cross as providing deliverance from the present evil age. The present evil age is the antithesis of the new age inaugurated by the Spirit, whom God confers upon Jews and Gentiles by faith in Galatians because the Christ/God's son redeemed them from the law's curse (3:13–14; 4:4–6). The present evil age represents the age dominated by sin (3:19, 22), the flesh (5:16–26), the elemental principles of the world (4:3, 9), and a curse (3:10). The present evil age is also a time of slavery to the law (4:3, 21–31; 5:1).

The law is submitted to and dominated by the present evil age because of transgression (3:19). Because of the present evil age, the law only leads to a curse (3:10); it cannot lead to life (3:21). The present evil age is the cursed age (cf. 3:10). Jews and Gentiles without ethnic restriction (3:22; 4:3, 21–27) and the entire creation are underneath the curse because they are enslaved to the present evil age and need to be delivered from it (3:1–5:1). Cosmological bondage to the present evil age is implied when Paul refers to the crucifixion of the world (6:14) and to new creation (6:15). Just as the human agent living within and enslaved to the present evil age needs to be crucified with Christ in order to live (i.e. inherit the blessing of eternal life) (2:19–20), so also the flesh (a power within the present evil age) must be crucified via Jesus's cross (5:24; 6:12, 14), which delivers "us" from the present evil age (1:4) and which begins the process of the cosmological renewal of new creation (6:15). This cosmological renewal is the full realization of the Abrahamic blessing of the Spirit and the Deuteronomic blessing of life in the new age flowing out of the cross of Jesus, from his deliverance of others from the present evil age, and out of the distribution of the Spirit (1:4; 3:13–14; 4:5).

The new creation is dominated by the arrival of the indwelling presence of the Spirit within Jews and Gentiles (4:4–5). The blessing of cosmological renewal is personified through the pursuit of Jewish and Gentile unity in the gospel (2:11–14). The blessing of this unity is possible only because of the blessing of justification by faith conferred to Jews and Gentiles via the cross and the Spirit. This new age of the Spirit liberates Jews and Gentiles from the curse of the law and grants them the freedom to fulfill the entire law by loving one another (5:1, 13–14, 22; 6:2). To be of works of law is to be in compliance with the present evil age and to be opposed to the new age inaugurated by the Spirit (3:14; 5:16–26; 6:15). To be of the present evil age is to be under the Deuteronomic curse (3:10), and to fall short of inheriting both the Abrahamic blessing of the Spirit and Deuteronomic life (cf. 3:1–29). The blessing of Abraham and Deuteronomic blessing merge together in Paul's argument in Gal 3 and are conferred to Jews and Gentiles because of Jesus who died to deliver them from the present evil age (1:4) and to redeem them so that they would receive the blessing of Abraham (3:13; 4:5–6), which is the indwelling presence of the Spirit (3:14). Paul confirms this point in his discussion in Gal 3:10–14.

Galatians 3:10–14 is one of the most difficult texts in the letter.[19] Paul shockingly asserts Torah-observers are under a curse, not a blessing (3:10).

---

19. My comments here only focus on the issues relevant to my thesis. Here I make no effort to discuss the many exegetical complexities in the text. For further discussion, see Jarvis J. Williams, *A Commentary on Galatians*, ed. Michael F. Bird and Craig Keener, NCCS (Eugene, OR: Wipf & Stock, forthcoming).

N. T. Wright's exegesis of this section argues Paul understands the death and resurrection of Jesus as the "climactic moment in Israel's covenantal history."[20]

David Lincicum's recent monograph argues Paul's remarks in Gal 3:10 and 3:13 "operate under the model of covenant theology, with his citation of Deut. 27 tapping into the broader context of Deut. 27–30."[21] Lincicum argues Deut 27:26 works within Deut 27 both as a summary of and a representation of the previous and more specific curses in Deut 27:15–25.[22] But Paul changes the text from "in all of the words of this law" (LXX Deut 27:26) to "all the things written in the book of the law."[23] Lincicum affirms this alteration seems "minor," but the phrase "book of the law" occurs throughout Deut 28–30 (cf. 28:58 and 30:10).[24] Paul's citation thus "emphasizes the representative nature" of Paul's citation even more.[25] "The curse of the law, then, is the curse the law threatens for those who disobey it."[26]

About Gal 3:10–14, Lincicum concludes, Deuteronomy has a twofold function: "it both announces the curse to which Israel in her disobedience is subject, but also hints at the means by which that curse has been overcome, resulting in blessing to the nations."[27]

My analysis of Gal 3:10–14 has points of contact with both Wright and Lincicum. But there are also some differences. In agreement with them, Paul's argument in Gal 3:10–14 needs to be understood in the context of God's covenant with Abraham and Israel,[28] for Abraham and the concepts of covenant, promise, blessing, and inheritance appear throughout chs. 3–4 (e.g. 3:6–4:7, 21–31). However, contrary to Wright's thesis, although Paul presumably was aware of Israel's history of exile, he says nothing explicitly about the curse of exile in Galatians.[29] As I argued earlier, the phrase "works of law" (ἐξ ἔργων νόμου) refers to the stipulations

---

20. Wright, *Climax*, 140–56.
21. Lincicum, *Paul and the Early Jewish Encounter with Deuteronomy*, 143–4.
22. Ibid., 144.
23. Ibid.
24. Ibid.
25. Ibid.
26. Ibid.
27. Ibid., 147.
28. Ibid., 143–44; Wright, *Climax*, 140–55.
29. Contra also Scott, "For as Many as Are of Works of the Law Are under a Curse (Galatians 3:10)," 187–221. Original citation in Moisés Silva, "Galatians," in *A Commentary on the New Testament Use of the Old Testament*, ed. G. K. Beale and D. A. Carson (Grand Rapids: Baker, 2007), 800.

and deeds demanded in the Mosaic covenant. At least one reason the preceding observation seems right is Paul later refers to the deficiency of circumcision unless one obeys the "whole law" (5:3). Deuteronomy 27:26 provides Paul with the scriptural proof for his proposition in Gal 3:10. However, the latter text asserts those who fail to observe Torah are accursed. Paul seems to suggest those who obey works of law in this age are under a curse since Christ died to deliver us from the present evil age (1:4).

In agreement with Lev 18:5, a verse Paul cites in Gal 3:12, Deut 27–30 emphatically promulgates that obedience to Torah leads to life (= blessing), whereas disobedience to Torah leads to a curse.[30] Several scholars have argued that Paul's assertion in 3:10 assumes an implicit premise that his original audience would need to supply.[31] If this is correct, Paul's logic would be something along the following lines:

Premise 1: The law brings a curse to everyone who disobeys it (3:10c).

Implicit Premise: No one can obey (or has obeyed) the law to the degree that it demands and expects (3:10).

Conclusion: Therefore, all people who identify with the law are cursed (3:10a).

Arguments for the implicit premise are compelling. Scholars who argue for this position may be correct.[32] However, the implicit premise argument does not by itself seem to capture Paul's argument against the law in Galatians: namely, the law is part of the present evil age. Norman H. Young has argued for a modified version of the implicit premise.

---

30. Kjell Arne Morland argues the "curse form" found in Gal 3:10 "is similar" to the curse form in many other Second Temple Jewish texts. However, Morland's argument does not interact with the Jewish martyrological narratives. For example, see Morland, *The Rhetoric of Curse*, 51–64. Todd A. Wilson has rightly argued the theme of cursing has a prominent place in the letter. For example, see Todd A. Wilson, *The Curse of the Law and the Crisis in Galatia: Reassessing the Purpose of Galatians*, WUNT 2/225 (Tübingen: Mohr Siebeck, 2007), 23–45. Betz (*Galatians*, 320–1) thinks the entire letter is framed in terms of curse (1:6–9) and blessing (6:16). Morland (*The Rhetoric of Curse*) thinks Paul intends the threat of a curse to serve as a means by which he dissuades the Galatians from embracing circumcision.

31. For examples of scholars and primary literature supporting the implied premise position, see Das, *Galatians*, 311–16.

32. I agree with Frank Thielman's observation that Paul reminds "the Galatians and his Judaizing opponents that membership in the people of God, as it is defined by the Mosaic covenant, is membership in a people with a plight—they are cursed by the

He proposes making the implicit premise an implicit condition—"if those from works of law do not do all the requirements of the law."[33] This modification, says Young, is not subject to the criticisms levelled against the traditional implicit premise view.[34] According to Young's modification, Paul would be saying all who fall under the Mosaic covenant would incur the curse upon themselves "if they abandon any of the covenant's requirements."[35]

Still, regardless of which version of the implicit premise one accepts, Paul seems to argue the law is a dead end, because it does not (and indeed cannot!) lead to life (3:10, 21). Rather, it only leads to a curse because it is part of the present evil age (cf. 2:11–14; 3:10),[36] and because the present evil age enslaves all under the law's curse due to sin (3:22) and the cosmological/elemental powers of evil (4:3, 9, 21–31).[37] The law expects and invites humans to do what they are incapable of doing: namely, obey to inherit life (Lev 18:5). But Paul invites humans to participate in what God has done for them in Christ by faith (3:13–14; cf. 1:4, 15–16). Paul suggests throughout the letter that God has disrupted the cosmos by means of the incarnation (4:4), the death (1:4; 2:20–21; 3:1, 13; 4:5), the resurrection (1:1), and the exaltation of Jesus (1:15–16). Given Paul's remarks about law, slavery, and freedom later in the letter (cf. 3:15–5:1; 5:3–4, 13), interpreters can assume that in 3:10, Paul presupposes no one can obey the law to the fullest. However, even those who hold to an implicit premise position must admit Paul does not explicitly say this, while he does explicitly connect the law with the present evil age when he equates being under the law with being under a curse (3:10), under slavery (3:22–4:7; 4:21–31), under sin (3:22), and under the elements of the world (4:3). He also asserts the law prioritizes human action (3:11–12). Therefore, those who seek to observe Torah (Jews or Gentiles) are accursed because

---

very law that defines them as God's people, because they, as a people and as individuals, have not kept the law." See Frank Thielman, *Paul and The Law: A Contextual Approach* (Downers Grove, IL: InterVarsity, 1994), 127. However, I think Paul is saying more than this when he warns the law curses those under its jurisdiction.

33. Norman H. Young, "Who's Cursed — and Why (Galatians 3:10–14)," *JBL* 117 (1998): 79–92, esp. 86.

34. For arguments, see ibid., 79–86.

35. Ibid.

36. Similarly Wakefield, *Where to Live*, 180–4. I disagree with Wakefield's understanding of life in Galatians. Paul is not simply talking about how one conducts his life. But he is talking about soteriological life.

37. Lee's work, *The Cosmic Drama of Salvation*, argues Paul's soteriology has both "anthropological" and "cosmological" components.

the ages have turned in Christ via his cross (and resurrection) and because the law promises humans what they must do to achieve the life it promises without giving them the ability to do it.

Paul's negative statements about the law in the letter support my above arguments. He says the law does not justify (2:16). By becoming crucified with Christ, he destroyed the law and refused to rebuild it (2:18). He died to the law through the law so that he would experience (eternal) life (2:19–20). He says allegiance to the law nullifies God's grace (2:21). The law is not the pathway to the Abrahamic blessing since it came 430 years later (3:17). The law was given "on account of transgressions" (3:19). The law came through the mediation of angels (3:19). The law does not lead to life (3:21). The law/Scripture imprisons all people and all things under sin and holds those under its jurisdiction in bondage until the promised seed (Christ) would come in the fullness of time to provide redemption for those under the law and to give the life-giving Spirit to sons of God and heirs of Abraham's promises (3:22–4:7).

Paul further states Gentile appropriation of the law is a return to slavery, idolatry, and the fundamental elements of the world (4:3–10). He says that the law and those under its jurisdiction are analogous to the illegitimate slave-woman and her offspring (4:21–5:1). He states the law renders obsolete the Christ (5:2). He declares the law cuts the Galatians off from Christ and severs them from grace (5:4). He contends that the Spirit, not the law, provides the Galatians everything they need to live a life pleasing to God (5:16–26). He asserts the law of circumcision does not matter (6:15), but rather new creation matters (6:15). He concludes the letter by saying the blessing of peace and mercy will be extended only to those who live in accordance with the standard of new creation, not those who live in accordance with the standard of the law (6:16). The law only gives a curse to those who identify with it apart from faith in Christ. Thus, in 3:10, Paul highlights the law's inability to provide life, but only a curse, because it has been taken hold of by the present evil age, which enslaves all under its jurisdiction to sin and the cosmological powers of evil. Galatians 3:10–12 further supports this analysis.

3. In Gal 3:10–12, Paul conflates LXX Deut 27:26 (Gal 3:10), LXX Deut 28:58 (Gal 3:10), LXX Hab 2:4 (Gal 3:11), and LXX Lev 18:5 (Gal 3:12) to emphasize both the Abrahamic blessing of the Spirit and the Deuteronomic promise of life are realized by faith apart from Torah-observance.[38] As I

---

38. For a work on scriptural echoes in Paul, see Richard B. Hays, *Echoes of Scripture in the Letters of Paul* (New Haven: Yale University Press, 1989).

stated in Chapter 2, Deut 27:1–28:68 states that curses come to those who disobey Torah and blessings to those who obey Torah. In Deut 27:1, Moses begins his speech by commanding Israel to observe every commandment of the Lord. Deuteronomy reiterates this point throughout the chapter (27:9–10). The commandments in Deut 27:1 pertain especially to the stipulations in 27:15–26, because the command to obey God's law in 27:1 and the blessings of obedience to God's law in 28:1–14 surround the curses of disobedience to the law in 27:9–26 and because 28:15–68 continues to discuss the curses of disobedience to the stipulations mentioned in 27:9–26. Still, the commandments to which Deut 27 refers include the stipulations given at Sinai and to other commandments in Torah, for Deuteronomy states often that Israel must obey "all" of the statutes the Lord gave to the people when he led them out of Egypt (e.g. 4:1–26:19).

Deuteronomy 27–28 states that if Israel disobeyed the stipulations in the land, the nation would be cursed in the land, and that if they obeyed, they would be blessed in the land. Deuteronomy 27:26 summarizes the curse pronouncements of 27:9–25 and reiterates to Israel the importance of their obedience in the land by stating "cursed is the one who will not uphold the words of this Torah to do them" (27:26). According to 27:15–26 and 28:15–62, these curses would overcome Israel while they *lived in the land*. According to 28:64–68, these curses would enslave them to Gentile nations and drive them *out of the land*, which the Lord promised to give them if they obeyed his law. Deuteronomy supports this latter point with earlier statements that obedience to the stipulations results in *long life in the land* (5:33; 8:1; 11:8, 26–32) and by asserting the Lord's curses will stick to Israel "until he destroys" them from *entering the land to inherit it* (28:21). The curses would come against the entire nation even if some within the community obeyed, which Israel's experiences of exile support (cf. Judges, Kings, and Chronicles).

In Gal 3:11, Paul refers to LXX Hab 2:4. In Gal 3:10, Paul refers to LXX Deut 27:26, and 28:58. Paul mentions these LXX texts prior to his appeal to LXX Lev 18:5 in Gal 3:12, a text about obedience leading to life for those who obey. Paul appeals to these texts to accentuate the importance of God's "divine action" realized by faith in Christ, not obedience to Torah, to experience the life promised in Torah. In other words, Paul begins his argument with texts about the Deuteronomic curse coming to those who subscribe to Torah in order to say that identifying with Torah only leads to a curse in Gal 3:10. Next, he turns in Gal 3:11 to the concept of the Deuteronomic blessing of life in LXX Hab 2:4 to assert that life comes to the one who is righteous by faith, because no one is justified by the law. Finally, in Gal 3:12, he cites LXX Lev 18:5 to say the promise of life in the law is opposed to the promise of life by faith. This line of argument provides the reason those of faith are blessed with faithful Abraham (3:9), because the law only leads to a curse, not to life. I further support this below.

Paul cites LXX Hab 2:4 in Gal 3:11 after his references to LXX Deut 27:26 and before his citation of LXX Lev 18:5 and his reference to LXX Deut 21:23. LXX Habakkuk 2:4 occurs in a context of lament. Habakkuk laments the Lord's people are suffering. He asks the Lord how long he intended to allow Israel to continue to suffer at the hands of her enemies because of the disobedience of the people and when he would deliver his people (LXX Hab 1:1–4). The Lord informs Habakkuk he intends to raise up the powerful Chaldeans to conquer dwellings not their own (LXX Hab 1:6). The Lord's answer provokes a second complaint from Habakkuk (LXX Hab 1:12–2:1). He accuses the Lord of being silent about the suffering of his people at the hands of their enemies (LXX Hab 1:13). But the Lord exhorts Habakkuk to wait patiently for the fulfillment of his promise of deliverance (LXX Hab 2:3). Then, in LXX Hab 2:4, the Lord contrasts the arrogance and unrighteousness of the one who fails to trust in the Lord with the righteous one who lives by faith.

As many scholars have observed, MT Hab 2:4 is ambiguous as to the reference of "his faithfulness" (אֱמוּנָתוֹ). The MT could mean the righteous one lives by "his faithfulness," that is, by YHWH's faithfulness. Or it could mean the righteous one lives by "his faithfulness," that is, by his own faithfulness to YHWH. LXX Habakkuk 2:4 inserts the pronoun "my" (μου) in the statement "the righteous one by my faith shall live" (ὁ δὲ δίκαιος ἐκ πίστεώς μου ζήσεται). Furthermore, the verb ζήσεται links LXX Hab 2:4 with the promise of life in LXX Lev 18:5, but these texts hold forth different means by which one receives life. This life seems to be, however, in both cases a reference to enjoying the covenantal blessings of temporal life in this age in the land since both Lev 18 and LXX Hab 1:12 contrast living with dying. The former mentions life in the context of death, pestilences, and diseases due to covenantal disobedience (Lev 18:1–26:46). The latter mentions life in the context of judgment through the violence of Gentile wickedness (LXX Hab 1:1–11).

With slight differences, Paul's citation of Hab 2:4 in Gal 3:11 comes from LXX Hab 2:4. One striking difference is that the phrase "by faith" is not modified by any pronoun. Some scholars have argued this phrase refers to "Christ's faith/faithfulness"[39] or to both his faith/faithfulness and

---

39. G. Howard, *Paul: Crisis in Galatia: A Study in Early Christian Theology*, SNTMS 35 (Cambridge: Cambridge University Press, 1979), 63–4; Frank J. Matera, *Galatians*, SP 9 (Collegeville, MN: Liturgical Press, 1992), 119; de Boer, *Galatians*, 202–4.

"human faith."[40] Jesus's faithfulness is present in Galatians (cf. 1:4; 2:20; 3:13). However, the phrase ἐκ πίστεώς in Paul's reading refers to one's personal faith, which Paul suggests lies in the realm of both divine and human action, because he has argued in Gal 1 that his apostleship comes from God instead of man (1:1) and that God revealed his son in him so that Paul would preach him as good news to the Gentiles (1:15–16). He further argues in Gal 2–3 that personal faith/believing is necessary to receive soteriological blessings (e.g. justification [2:16] and the Spirit [3:2–5]).[41] Once more, Paul argues in 3:1–29 that faith in Christ is the pathway to the Abrahamic blessing instead of Torah-observance, and he emphasizes in 2:16 that one is justified by faith in Christ apart from works of the law.[42]

Another important point about Paul's use of LXX Hab 2:4 is his conflation of this verse with LXX Lev 18:5 in Gal 3:12. He substitutes the participle ὁ ποιήσας in 3:12 for the noun ἄνθρωπος in LXX Lev 18:5. Paul could have simply used the participle and dropped the noun to parallel what he says in Gal 3:10 ("as many as are from works of law are under a curse") and in 3:11 ("the righteous one by faith shall live").[43] "The one who does" (ὁ ποιήσας) the things in the law refers to the "man" (Jew or foreigner) mentioned in LXX Lev 17:15.[44]

Paul's appeal to LXX Lev 18:5 speaks to the comprehensive nature of the obedience required by the law in Deut 27–28 to inherit the life it promises. The larger context of LXX Lev 18:5 is "the holiness code of Lev 17–26." As Preston M. Sprinkle points out in his detailed study of Lev 18:5, Lev 17–26 concerns "the holiness of the people of Israel as summarized in 20:26: 'Thus you are to be holy to me, for I YHWH am holy; and I have set you apart from the peoples to be mine'."[45] Sprinkle

40. Hays, *The Faith of Jesus Christ*, 138–41; Martyn, *Galatians*, 314; J. C. R. Roo, *Works of the Law at Qumran and in Paul*, NTM 13 (Sheffield: Sheffield Phoenix, 2007), 206–7. Summary in and sources cited in Moo, *Galatians*, 206.

41. Similarly Moo, *Galatians*, 206–10.

42. I take the phrase διὰ πίστεως Ἰησοῦ Χριστοῦ as an objective genitival phrase ("through faith in Jesus Christ"). For essays on both sides of the debate, see Michael F. Bird and Preston M. Sprinkle, eds., *The Pistis Christou Debate, The Faith of Jesus Christ: Exegetical, Biblical, and Theological Studies* (Peabody, MA: Hendrickson, 2009).

43. My view in this paragraph is similar to Moo, *Galatians*, 207–10. Or it is also possible Paul's version of the LXX simply had the words he cites in it.

44. For another possibility, see Preston M. Sprinkle, *Law and Life: The Interpretation of Leviticus 18:5 in Early Judaism and in Paul*, WUNT 2/241 (Tübingen: Mohr Siebeck, 2008), 136.

45. Ibid., 27.

continues that Lev 17 gives "regulations concerning blood," after which ch. 18 focuses on "sexual prohibitions" (18:6–23).[46] Sprinkle asserts Leviticus 20 restates the content of Lev 18.[47] He claims Lev 19 repeats this line of thought.[48] Leviticus 20:22–24 repeats the commands in 18:1–5 and 18:24–30.[49] Sprinkle rightly concludes, therefore, Lev 18–20 is a unit, whose "theme may be summarised as the necessary conditions of Israel's remaining in the land."[50] If Israel disobeys any of the laws in the above unit, YHWH would subject the people to execution (cf. 20:10–20) or to the "termination of one's line."[51] If the entire community violated one of these commands, then the land would "vomit them out" (18:28).[52]

LXX Leviticus 18:5 specifically occurs in a context where Moses instructs Israel to live sexually pure. LXX Leviticus 18:1–4 begins with a reminder that the Lord is Israel's God (LXX Lev 18:2). Moses urges Israel not to live as the Egyptians or the Canaanites (LXX Lev 18:3), but instead to obey all of his statutes (Lev 18:4). LXX Leviticus 18:6–30 commands Israel to live in compliance with Torah in their sexual relations. LXX Leviticus 18:5 reminds Israel that the people must obey Torah to the fullest (καὶ φυλάξεσθε πάντα τὰ προστάγματά μου καὶ πάντα τὰ κρίματά μου). The result of their obedience would be the blessing of covenantal life in the land (καὶ ποιήσετε αὐτά ἃ ποιήσας ἄνθρωπος ζήσεται ἐν αὐτοῖς). Deuteronomy reiterates the importance of obedience to the Torah in order to experience long life in the land (cf. Deut 27–28). Thus, Paul conflates LXX Deut 27:26; 28:58; Hab 2:4, and Lev 18:5 to emphasize the following: although long life in the land in Torah is conditioned by Israel's obedience to all of the Lord's statutes and judgments in both Leviticus and Deuteronomy, the revelation of God in Christ to Paul causes him to recalibrate his conception of the law and life. Because of God's revelation to him about the Christ (Gal 1:15), Paul now understands that the law only leads to a curse (Gal 3:10), while only the cursed Christ leads to blessing/life for those who have faith (cf. Gal 3:13).

The verb ζήσεται links both LXX Hab 2:4 and LXX Lev 18:5 and both Gal 3:11 and 3:12. With his citation of LXX Hab 2:4 in Gal 3:11 and LXX Lev 18:5 in Gal 3:12, and with his reference to life in Gal 3:12, Paul reads the life promised in LXX Hab 2:4 and LXX Lev 18:5 soteriologically

46. Ibid.
47. Ibid.
48. Ibid.
49. Ibid., 27–8.
50. Ibid., 28. For sources relied on by Sprinkle, see, ibid., 28 n. 4.
51. Ibid., 28.
52. Ibid.

(i.e. as a reference to eternal life). But he reads the latter text against his earlier comments about soteriological life in Gal 3:11 when he cites LXX Hab 2:4. His reading of LXX Lev 18:5 suggests the life promised in this text is realized by means of justification by faith in Christ, to which Paul refers in Gal 2:16 and in 3:11 with his citation of LXX Hab 2:4, instead of by obedience to the law. Because no one can be justified by law (cf. Gal 2:16), it is clear that "the righteous one by faith will live" (3:11) since he has already established the law only brings a curse (3:10, 11) and that one is justified by faith (2:16).[53] In Gal 3:11–12, Paul opposes the promise of life in LXX Lev 18:5 can be realized by Torah-observance because the text prioritizes "human action as a condition for attaining eschatological blessing"[54] and because, as I argued above, he thinks the law is part of the present evil age (cf. 1:4) and that no one can obey the law to the degree that it demands (cf. Gal 3:10; 5:4). Human inability to do all the law (5:4) is underneath the powers of the present evil age (1:4; 3:23–4:31).

Scholars have pointed out that Dunn argues LXX Lev 18:5 does not refer to eternal life.[55] Dunn says the verse refers to a "description of how God's covenant people are to regulate their lives."[56] However, against Dunn, Paul understands the promise of life in Lev 18:5 and Deut 27–30 as soteriological (eternal) life, and he suggests the curse of the law in Deut 27:26 (cf. Gal 3:10) nullifies any possibility of achieving soteriological life by obedience to Torah, which he thinks LXX Lev 18:5 promised.[57] That Paul understands life in LXX Lev 18:5 refers to eternal life is supported when he connects this life to justification by faith apart from works of the law (2:16; 3:12; 5:5), to the justification of the Gentiles as the fulfillment of God's Abrahamic promise (3:8), and when he states no one is justified by the law before God (ἐν νόμῳ οὐδεὶς δικαιοῦται παρὰ τῷ θεῷ) (3:11). Paul's latter remarks in 3:11 are the opposite of what LXX Lev 18:5 states with the phrase ἐν αὐτοῖς, when it promises life comes only to those who obey the law since the person will live "by means of

---

53. I agree with the interpreters who take the first ὅτι as causally modifying δὲ ἐν νόμῳ οὐδεὶς δικαιοῦται παρὰ τῷ θεῷ, and δῆλον and the second ὅτι with ὁ δίκαιος ἐκ πίστεως ζήσεται. My translation of the verse is "Now, because no one is justified by the law [since the law only brings a curse], it is clear that the righteous one by faith will live."

54. Sprinkle, *Law and Life*, 134.

55. Ibid., 140–2, esp. n. 32. For primary references, see James D. G. Dunn, *The Theology of Paul the Apostle* (Grand Rapids: Eerdmans, 1998), 152–4, 374–5.

56. Sprinkle, *Law and Life*, 141. The above quotes are from Sprinkle's helpful summary of Dunn's view.

57. Ibid., 134.

them" (ἐν αὐτοῖς) if he obeys them. Paul also connects the promise of life to the crucifixion (1:4; 2:21; 3:1, 13), the Spirit (3:2–14; 5:5, 16),[58] the kingdom of God (5:21), and new creation (6:15). He asserts the law only brings a curse (3:10), and he confirms that neither life nor righteousness (= justification) comes by means of law (3:21). Each of the preceding observations support the view that Paul understands life in the above LXX texts in a soteriological sense as eternal life.

Paul also understands that the curse of the law in Deut 27:26 (cf. Gal 3:10) nullifies the possibility of achieving the life promised in Lev 18:5 because of God's revelation of himself in Christ, a revelation that inaugurates the new age of the Spirit, freedom, and new creation (1:4, 15–16; 2:19–21; 3:1–29; 4:21–5:1, 13–26; 6:14–15). Galatians 3:1–9 that affirms faith in Christ, not works of the law, granted the Galatians supernatural experiences in the Spirit and was the means by which they received the blessing of Abraham. Galatians 3:10–12 specifically contrasts doing works of law with faith, providing the reason those with faith are blessed with faithful Abraham: namely, because the law only brings a curse. Although the law served as a guardian until Christ would come so that Jews and Gentiles would be justified by faith (3:24), Paul argues that law and faith are two different paths leading to two different destinies (the law only leads to a curse [3:10], while faith in Christ leads to justification and life in the Spirit [3:11–14]), and that these paths rely upon two different agents (the law = human agency and faith = divine agency). Law and faith are vastly different, not mutually interpretive (contra Lincicum). As Sprinkle has shown, the law and faith present two "antithetical soteriologies,"[59] but

---

58. The experience of the Spirit in 3:2–14 supports that Paul interprets life from Lev 18:5 as eternal life in Gal 3:12. For example, the means of life is faith in Christ but this life is realized by the Spirit (3:14; 5:25), not by doing the law (3:21). The acquisition of life is possible only because Christ died to deliver us from the present evil age (1:4) and to distribute the Spirit to those with faith (3:13–14). That life in Gal 3:12 refers to eternal life is further realized by associating it with justification by faith (3:6–8, 11–12) and new creation (6:15). Paul connects life to Jesus's resurrection (1:1, 15–16) and to his death (2:19–3:1, 13–14). This life is experienced in this age and in the age to come apart from the works of the law by Jews and Gentiles who place faith in Jesus because he died to deliver them from the present evil age and from the curse of the law, because of the cross of the cursed Christ. This eternal life in Christ is the realization of the Abrahamic blessing of the Spirit (3:14) and the Deuteronomic blessing of life, which Paul interprets as eternal life (5:5) given by the Spirit and justification by faith (2:16; 3:8, 14). Those who walk in the Spirit (i.e. those who have been given the blessing of life) will enter into the kingdom of God (5:16–26; esp. 5:16, 21). Similarly Sprinkle, *Law and Life*, 140.

59. Ibid., 138–40.

only one emphasizes "divine action," namely, faith in Christ. One leads to the Abrahamic and Deuteronomic blessing, and the other leads to the Deuteronomic curse.[60]

4. The Christ took the Deuteronomic curse upon himself for Jews and Gentiles by means of his death so that they would receive by faith both the Abrahamic blessing of the Spirit and the Deuteronomic blessing of life. Galatians 3:13 is the turning point in Paul's argument in 3:10–14. As I stated above, there are numerous exegetical issues in this text.[61] Sufficient for my argument is to highlight the portions of the text relevant for my thesis in this chapter: namely, in a way similar to, while different from, the Jewish martyrological traditions, Paul presents both Jews and Gentiles as recipients of the Deuteronomic curses. However, in Galatians, the death of the Torah-observant Christ who suffered under the curse of the law for non-Torah-observant people confers to both Jews and Gentiles the Abrahamic blessing of the Spirit and the Deuteronomic blessing of life. Specifically, he states that the curse falls upon the cursed Christ so that he would redeem those under the curse of the law to confer to them the Abrahamic blessing of the Spirit and so that the Deuteronomic blessing of life would extend to Jews and Gentiles by faith (3:13–14; 4:5–6).[62]

In 3:13, Paul proclaims Christ redeemed "us" from the law's curse by participating in the curse himself with the intended result of extending the Abrahamic blessing of the Spirit to Jews and Gentiles "through faith" (διὰ πίστεως). Paul fronts 3:13 with the term Christ (Χριστὸς) without a connecting or transitional particle. He also places the direct object (ἡμᾶς) of the verb (ἐξηγόρασεν) beside Χριστὸς and before ἐξηγόρασεν to emphasize the recipients of the Christ's redemption. "Christ," Paul says, "redeemed us from the curse of the law" (ἐκ τῆς κατάρας τοῦ νόμου). Since Paul conflates LXX Deut 27:26 and 28:58 in Gal 3:10 and cites LXX Deut 21:23 in Gal 3:13, the curse likely refers to the Deuteronomic curse/curses that Deut 27–30 held out for those who did not obey Torah. Contrary to scholars who argue the first person pronouns in Gal 3:13 only

---

60. Ibid., 153–64.
61. For a detailed discussion of the various exegetical issues in this text, see the critical commentaries on the Greek text of Galatians. A few examples are Betz, *Galatians*; de Boer, *Galatians*; Das, *Galatians*; Moo, *Galatians*; David A. deSilva, *The Letter to the Galatians*, NICNT (Grand Rapids: Eerdmans, 2018).
62. For an analysis of Messiah language in early Judaism and key texts in Paul's undisputed letters, see Matthew V. Novenson, *Christ Among the Messiahs: Christ Language in Paul and Messiah Language in Ancient Judaism* (Oxford: Oxford University Press, 2015).

refer to Jewish Christians,[63] the "us" for whom Christ died refers to both Jews and Gentiles since Paul asserts in 3:9 that "those from faith" (οἱ ἐκ πίστεως) (Jews and Gentiles) receive the blessing with faithful Abraham and since he states in 3:10 that "as many as" (ὅσοι) are from works of law experience the curse.[64]

The occurrence of ὅσοι in 6:16 further supports taking the ἡμᾶς to refer to both Jews and Gentiles. In 6:16, Paul says peace and mercy would come upon those (ὅσοι) who live by the rule of the gospel instead of the rule of Torah. He additionally adds this peace would even come upon the Israel of God. There is much debate as to the identity of the Israel of God (6:16).[65] Paul seems to redefine Israel here as Jews and Gentiles in Christ since he refers to the rival teachers' efforts in Galatia to compel the Galatians to be circumcised (6:12–13) in order to boast in their flesh, and since he says, in 6:15, neither circumcision nor un-circumcision matters, but new creation. References to circumcision and un-circumcision are explicit references to Jews and Gentiles. However, Paul's remarks about the irrelevance of the circumcised and un-circumcised flesh but the importance of new creation in 6:15 support the view that he understands Israel of God to refer to Jews and Gentiles in Christ.

In 3:10, Paul asserts that the law curses those who identify with it by appealing to Deut 27:26 and 28:58, which say the cursed ones are those who disobey Torah. He contends that the law neither leads to the life it promises nor toward a path away from the curse (Gal 3:11–12). He already established in 3:6–9 the path to the Abrahamic blessing is faith, not works of law. In 3:10–12, he explains the reason is because the law only leads to a curse and gives life only to those who obey.[66] Instead, Christ redeems "us" from the law's curse by entering into the curse "for us" via his death on a tree (3:13).

---

63. For this view, see Wright, *Climax*, 151; Donaldson, "The 'Curse of the Law,'" 94–112.

64. Contra Wright, *Climax*, 151–5. Wright argues Jesus's death in 3:13 applies only to the Jews since he is Israel's representative on the cross.

65. For different views, see Martyn, *Galatians*, 574–7; Witherington, *Grace in Galatia*, 452; Dunn, *The Epistle to the Galatians*, 344–5; Peter Richardson, *Israel in the Apostolic Church*, SNTSMS 10 (Cambridge: Cambridge University Press, 1969), 81–3. For a discussion of and interaction with different views, see Das, *Galatians*, 647–52.

66. For an argument that Paul highlights in 3:10 the ongoing threat of the curse held out by the law, see Christopher D. Stanley, "Under a Curse: A Fresh Reading of Galatians 3:10–14," *NTS* 36 (1990): 481–511.

As I observed earlier, that no one can keep the law to the degree it demands could be implicit in the argument of Gal 3:10–14. Moreover, Paul also asserts that those under the law are slaves under sin (3:22). In agreement with Pate, Jesus perfectly obeyed the law to the degree that it demands. Yet, he still suffered the curse. His curse-bearing death makes sense in Galatians only if he became a curse because the law and he were both under the present evil age (cf. 1:4; 3:10). The law is under the present evil age (1:4), and those under the law are under a curse (3:10).[67]

Galatians 4:4–5 explicitly states Christ was born under the law to redeem those under the law from it. To be born under the law is a birth under the present evil age (1:4) and under all of its enslaving powers (3:23–4:31). While Jesus remained free from violating any aspect of Torah, he identified with sinners (those who disobey Torah) by being born under the law. Redemption from the law in 4:5 is redemption from the present evil age in 1:4 and from the curse of the law in 3:13, especially since 1:4 refers to deliverance "from the present evil age," since 3:13 and 4:5 refer to redemption from the curse of the law (3:13) and redemption from being "under the law" (4:5), and since 3:14 and 4:5–6 suggest Christ's redemption of those enslaved to the present evil age and its enslaving powers distributes to them the Spirit and freedom (5:1, 13). Thus, Christ became a curse first by being born into the present evil age, the proof of which is his execution on the cross. Against the position taken by Pate, there are two reasons those under the law are under a curse: (1) the law is part of the present evil age (explicit) and (2) humans are incapable of doing the law to inherit the life it promises (implicit in 3:10 and explicit in 3:12).

Kjell Arne Morland suggests the expression γενόμενος κατάρα presents "Jesus as a curse" in Gal 3:13.[68] He argues Jewish sources influenced by Deut 27–30 identify Israel as becoming a curse because of disobedience to the law (LXX 2 Kgs 22:19; Jer 24:9; 49:18; 51:8, 12; Zech 8:13).[69] He argues further that Jewish sources also present individual transgressors of the law as cursed (1 En. 5:6; LXX Num 5:27; Deut 21:23).[70] Although Morland uses these connections as evidence to limit Paul's background in Gal 3:13 to Deut 27–30 without any appeal to a martyrological appropriation of these texts by Paul, he helpfully points out those who are cursed according to Deuteronomy are those who individually

---

67. For Pate's view, see *Reverse of the Curse*, 214–18.
68. Morland, *Rhetoric of Curse*, 70–1.
69. Ibid., 71. Cf. also Bar 3:8; Jub. 1:16; T. Levi 10:4; 16:5.
70. Ibid., 70–1.

or corporately violate Torah and consequently reap the Deuteronomic curses therein.[71] In these sources, the curse or curses are associated with suffering and death.[72]

Paul, however, in Gal 3:10 does not explicitly identify law breakers as cursed, but those who identify with Torah as cursed. In 3:12, to be sure, he appeals to LXX Lev 18:5 and states the law promises life only to those who obey it. But that was a promise within the old age prior to God's invasion of the world in Christ and prior to the turning of the ages in Christ (cf. Gal 1:4, 15–16; 2:11–14). As Bradley H. McLean suggests, Galatians teaches the law is part of the present evil age. Jesus created a new age by means of his death and resurrection. As a result, Christian Jews and Gentiles must now show their allegiance to the new age, one example of this being rejecting the law of Moses as a sign of Christian identity (cf. 1:3-4, 11-17; 4:1-11; 5:1; 6:14-15).[73] To clarify, Christian Jews can and should still live a Jewish way of life since their Jewish identifies are transformed and not erased (cf. 3:28; Rom 11:1).[74] However, in Christ, a Jewish way of life in compliance with the law of Moses neither any longer functions as the identifying mark of the offspring of Abraham nor should be a pre-requisite for Gentile Christians to become part of the offspring of Abraham (Gal 3:1–5:1; 6:15–16).

Because the Christ invaded history in the fullness of God's appointed time to disrupt the present evil age and to bring to pass the faith to be revealed, the law no longer operates now in the new age of the Spirit as it once did in the old age (3:23–4:5). Galatians 3:10 and 3:12 together support the law and the promise set forth two entirely different paths and destinies for those under the respective jurisdictions: death and life. Of course, the law was given as a temporary guardian until Christ would come so that those under the law would be justified by faith (3:23–25; esp. 3:24). However, Gal 1:4, 15–16 suggests the law and the promise represent two entirely different ages (cf. 2:16; 3:1–5:1, 16–26; 6:15; an old age dominated by enslaving powers and a new age dominated by the

---

71. Basil Davis sharply criticizes Morland's work for making statistical overstatements and for neglecting to discuss a potential Greco-Roman background behind Paul's remarks about the cursed Christ in Gal 3:13. He understands Paul's remarks about the cursed Christ in light of a voluntary sacrifice of devotion that died to save the community from an imminent disaster. See Davis, *Christ as Devotio*.

72. Ibid.

73. Ibid., 118–19.

74. For an argument that Paul was no longer an ethnic Jew in Christ, see Love L. Sechrest, *A Former Jew: Paul and the Dialectics of Race*, LNTS 410 (New York: T&T Clark International, 2009).

Spirit) and two entirely different paths (one leading to a curse [3:10, 21] and one leading to life [3:12]). In the new age of the Spirit inaugurated by Christ, Torah only brings a curse (3:10). Those who remain under the law or choose to embrace it as a way of life are under a curse (3:10),[75] because, now that God has invaded the current evil age in Christ, the law in this present age is transformed into an enslaving power (3:23–4:31).[76]

With an appeal to LXX Hab 2:4, Paul in Gal 3:11 provides the reason Torah does not justify anyone: namely, the righteous one by faith shall live, not the righteous one by Torah. In 3:13, Paul does not suggest that Jesus became a curse because he broke Torah. Rather, he simply affirms Jesus is cursed. Contrary to the LXX (LXX Lev 18:5) and certain Second Temple texts (e.g. 1 Baruch), Paul claims those from works of the law are already under a curse (Gal 3:10) both because of their disobedience (3:12 and implicitly in 3:10) and because the law is part of the present evil age (1:4). Those from works of law are also under slavery to the elemental principles of the world (4:3). Their obedience will not deliver them from the curse, because no one is justified before God by law (3:11–12). Deliverance from the curse comes only through the cursed Christ (3:13; 4:5–6). Christ participated in the curse with the "us" for whom he died by becoming a curse and dying for them. Christ became a curse not by disobeying the law to receive the curse, but rather by being born under the law in the present evil age in order to become a curse "for us" (γενόμενος ὑπὲρ ἡμῶν κατάρα) "to redeem us from the curse of the law" (Χριστὸς ἡμᾶς ἐξηγόρασεν ἐκ τῆς κατάρας τοῦ νόμου) (3:13). That is, Christ entered into the present evil age as a Jewish man under the law and its curse (4:4–6). Proof of his participation in the curse of the law is personified in his crucifixion (3:13; cf. LXX Deut 21:23).

Paul's remarks in 4:4–6 support this analysis. He says "in the fullness of time, God sent forth his son to be born from a woman, to be born under the law, so that he would redeem those under the law, so that we would receive the adoption" (ὅτε δὲ ἦλθεν τὸ πλήρωμα τοῦ χρόνου, ἐξαπέστειλεν ὁ θεὸς τὸν υἱὸν αὐτοῦ, γενόμενον ἐκ γυναικός, γενόμενον ὑπὸ νόμον ἵνα τοὺς ὑπὸ νόμον ἐξαγοράσῃ, ἵνα τὴν υἱοθεσίαν ἀπολάβωμεν). With these comments, Paul illuminates his statement about Christ's death in 3:13. In God's appointed time in salvation-history (ὅτε δὲ ἦλθεν τὸ πλήρωμα τοῦ χρόνου, ἐξαπέστειλεν ὁ θεὸς τὸν υἱὸν αὐτοῦ), he sent his son into the world to become a Jewish man (γενόμενον ἐκ γυναικός) (4:4).[77] God's son was born a Jewish man

75. McLean, *The Cursed Christ*, 119.
76. Ibid., 118–19.
77. For an argument that seeks to hold in balance "the apocalyptic Paul" with the "salvation-historical Paul" in Galatians, see Bird, *An Anomalous Jew*, 108–69.

under the Jewish law (γενόμενον ὑπὸ νόμον) (4:4) to invade the cosmos and to disrupt the present evil age by dying for "our sins" to deliver "us" from the present evil age (1:4). As a Jewish man who lived (perfectly) under the Jewish law, God's son also lived under the present evil age (1:4), under the power of sin (3:22), under slavery (3:22–23; 4:3), under a pedagogue and under stewards and managers (3:24–4:2), under the elemental principles of the world (4:3, 9), and, therefore, under a curse (3:10).

Paul suggests Christ's human existence under the law resulted in experiencing the same fate as those living under the curse of the law in the present evil age: namely, suffering,[78] exclusion from the community, and death. His death (and resurrection) opens up the pathway for Jews and Gentiles enslaved to the present evil age to participate in the new age/new creation (6:15) by means of justification by faith in Christ (2:16) and the indwelling presence of the Spirit (4:4–6), as they live by the power of the Spirit as those for whom Christ died to deliver them from the present evil age (1:4) and from the curse of the law (3:13; 4:4–6), while he lived and they live in the present evil age. However, Paul nowhere suggests the Christ suffered the curse of death on a cross because of his disobedience to Torah. Rather, because Torah is part of the present evil age, it consequently only leads all under it to a curse, not to the blessing of life. Jesus identified with the curse of the law for those under the law by becoming the cursed substitute on the cross "for us" (3:13), as one who fully identified with those under the law's curse because he too was under the law's curse (cf. 3:10). In Paul's view, then, the law represents the old age, is enslaved to it,[79] and is inherently impotent to give life to the point that it even curses the Christ, who obeyed every aspect of the law.

---

78. John Anthony Dunne recently argues that Paul argues in Galatians that suffering, instead of circumcision, is a mark of distinction for the people of God. This mark sets them apart in Christ to inherit "future blessing and vindication." See John Anthony Dunne, *Persecution and Participation in Galatians*, WUNT 2/454 (Tübingen: Mohr Siebeck, 2017). The preceding summary is paraphrased from the back of the monograph. In his own words, "in Galatians, Paul is informed by the Christ-event and the full implications of participation with Christ in such a way that he sees suffering for the sake of the cross not as incidental, but as one of the alternative marks to circumcision, which demarcates the true people of God and sets them apart for future blessing. In other words, this study will demonstrate that suffering has both ecclesiological and eschatological implications in Galatians, which are rooted in a theology of union with Christ" (ibid., 4).

79. For this specific argument, see Wakefield, *Where to Live*, 180–4.

In 3:13, Paul conspicuously asserts Christ became a curse with a reference to his crucifixion. He appeals to LXX Deut 21:23 to support his premise in Gal 3:13a: "just as it has been written: cursed is everyone who is hanged on a tree."[80] LXX Deuteronomy 21:23 refers to a person who is hanged on a tree because of disobedience to Torah and failure to meet the stipulations of the covenant.[81] As a result, those who disobey Torah suffer the curse of death (cf. LXX Deut 21:22–23).[82] In the context of LXX Deut 21:23, the one hanged on the tree appears to be already dead. He is hanged after he dies so that the community would see what happens to those in their midst who disobey Torah,[83] for LXX Deut 21:22 speaks of the one who potentially commits a crime worthy of death and then is hanged upon the tree. Just like a contemporary Qumran text, 11QT 64.6–13, Paul interprets LXX Deut 21:23 to refer to execution via crucifixion in Gal 3:13.[84] That is, according to these texts, the execution occurs in the act of crucifixion. Both 11QT 64.6–13 and Gal 3:13 suggest crucifixion is the execution. Although 4QpNah frgs. 3–4, col. 1, lines 7–8 and 11QT 64.6–13 refer to live men being hanged/crucified, the latter scroll and Gal 3:13 are the only two extant sources that identify crucifixion with a curse.[85] However, contrary to 11QT 64.6–13, Paul specifically uses

---

80. For a discussion of the differences in the different versions of Deut 21:23 in Jewish and Christian sources, see David W. Chapman, *Ancient Jewish and Christian Perceptions of Crucifixion* (Grand Rapids: Baker, 2010), 117–54.

81. For a discussion of Deut 21:23 in the context of ancient Jewish and Christian perceptions of crucifixion, see ibid., 117–54.

82. Chapman (ibid., 118) astutely points out that although it is "most probable" that the clausal sequence suggests execution precedes the hanging, it is "nonetheless conceivable" that the two clauses appositionally relate to one another.

83. Kelli O'Brien, "The Curse of the Law (Galatians 3:13): Crucifixion, Persecution, and Deuteronomy 21:22–23," *JSNT* 29 (2006): 55–76, esp. 64.

84. Chapman (*Crucifixion*, 243 n. 72) points out certain analyses of Paul's argument in Gal 3:13 discuss the importance of the interpretations of Deut 21:23 in Qumran. For example, see Heinz-Wolfgang Kuhn, "Die Bedeutung der Qumrantexte für das Verständnis des Galaterbriefs aus dem Münchener Projekt: Qumran und das Neue Testament," in *New Qumran Texts and Studies: Proceedings of the First Meeting of the International Organization for Qumran Studies, Paris 1992*, ed. George J. Brooke and Florentino García Martínez, STDJ 15 (Leiden: E. J. Brill, 1994), 178–82.

85. O'Brien, "The Curse of the Law (Galatians 3:13)," 65–70. Martin Hengel and Anna Maria Schwemer suggest Paul's remarks reflect his pre-conversion experience. For example, see Martin Hengel and Anna Maria Schwemer, *Paul Between Damascus and Antioch*, trans. John Bowden (London: SCM, 1997), 99–100; idem, *Paulus*

LXX Deut 21:23 to support his claim that "Christ redeemed us from the law's curse by becoming a curse for us" by means of crucifixion (Gal 3:13).

In an article on the curse of the law and crucifixion in Gal 3:13, Kelli S. O'Brien argues against the prevailing view that "Jews understood crucifixion to be a death cursed by God, with necessary consequences for a crucified messiah."[86] According to O'Brien, Deut 21:22–23 commands the community immediately to bury the person hanged on a tree at the very moment of death.[87] "An executed, hanged and unburied corpse is the 'curse of God' that pollutes the land."[88] She suggests the Temple Scroll (11QT 64.7–8) and the Peshitta change the order of words, which communicates that hanging is an act of execution.[89] Similar to Joseph Fitzmyer,[90] O'Brien notes 4QpNah frgs. 3–4, col. 1, lines 7–8 seems to allude to the act of "hanging men alive on a tree,"[91] but she suggests that "11QTemple 64:10–11 is the only Jewish text to interpret Deut. 21:22–23 to mean that the one crucified is also accursed."[92] She points out that Joseph M. Baumgarten has argued "Jewish texts never consider crucifixion to be a Jewish punishment; however, he admits that the [*Aramaic*] words are used for both hanging and crucifixion."[93] Ultimately, Baumgarten does not think 11QT refers to crucifixion, but rather to "one of the four classic modes of capital punishment in Jewish law (stoning, burning, decapitation, and strangulation)."[94]

---

zwischen Damaskus und Antiochien: Die unbekannten Jahre des Apostels, WUNT 108 (Tübingen: Mohr Siebeck, 1998), 164–5. Chapman, *Crucifixion*, 243 n. 71, pointed me to these references. For a recent study of crucifixion, see John Granger Cook, *Crucifixion in the Mediterranean World*, WUNT 327 (Tübingen: Mohr Siebeck, 2014).

86. O'Brien, "The Curse of the Law (Galatians 3:13)," 55–76, esp. 58. For the Jewish sources where crucifixion is mentioned, see ibid., 68 n. 39. She contends that "not one" of these texts associates crucifixion with a curse and that those crucified are to be pitied and represent those who are honorable (ibid., 68–9).

87. Ibid., 72.

88. Ibid.

89. Ibid., 64.

90. Joseph Fitzmyer, "Crucifixion in Ancient Palestine, Qumran Literature, and the New Testament," *CBQ* 40 (1978): 493–513.

91. O'Brien, "The Curse of the Law (Galatians 3:13)," 64.

92. Ibid., 66.

93. Citation from ibid., 64 n. 28 (emphasis in brackets mine). Original comments from Joseph M. Baumgarten, "Hanging and Treason in Qumran and Roman Law," *Erets-Yisrael* 16 (1982): 7–8.

94. Fitzmyer, "Crucifixion," 505. Original reference in Joseph M. Baumgarten, "Does *TLH* in the Temple Scroll Refer to Crucifixion?" *JBL* 91 (1972): 472–81.

O'Brien says later Jewish Christians may have used this text as a *testimonium* about Jesus's burial so as not to pollute the land.[95] If this text was a *testimonium*, says O'Brien, then "Paul's use of it in Gal. 3:13 may have had little or nothing to do with its use by his opponents. Instead, he was in all probability picking up a prominent text in his larger argument against the Galatians' submitting to the law—which clearly *was* the position argued by Paul's opponents."[96] According to O'Brien, early Jewish objections to Jesus as the Messiah were because he was crucified, not because his crucifixion made him cursed.[97]

By analyzing primary texts, O'Brien offers a helpful corrective against the prevailing view that Jews persecuted Christians and rejected Jesus as the Messiah because his crucifixion made him cursed. However, in my view, regardless of the reason Jews generally rejected Jesus as the Messiah, Paul explicitly connects his crucifixion with a curse in Gal 3:10 and 3:13. He cites LXX Deut 21:23 to make explicit the proof of the curse of Christ in the event of his crucifixion. His citation of LXX Deut 21:23 seems, then, to provide him proof that Jesus was a cursed Messiah, which was not the same Messianic expectation of Paul's Jewish contemporaries. If I correctly understand O'Brien's basic thesis, that Jews would not have necessarily identified a crucified man as a cursed man, then the question becomes why does Paul identify Christ as a cursed man hanged on a tree in Gal 3:13 by citing LXX Deut 21:23 to confirm this? The answer appears to be that the crucifixion proves the Christ participated in the same cursed fate as those under the curse, and LXX Deut 21:23 places the Christ within the realm of the cursed. Not all of those cursed under the law suffered crucifixion. Rather, some suffered stoning (cf. Acts 7:58). However, the crucifixion of the Christ proves the Christ became a curse for those under the curse of the law (Gal 1:4; 3:10, 13), because LXX Deut 21:23 states the hanged person on the tree is cursed (cf. Gal 3:13).

As other scholars have pointed out, when 4QpNahum appeals to Deut 21:23, it seems to suggest the one who is crucified was accursed prior to the crucifixion since the fragment talks about the penalty of his curse was a hanging on the tree of crucifixion. Likewise, when Paul suggests in Gal 3:10 that those from works of law are under a curse and in 4:4–5 that Jesus was born of a woman and born under the law to redeem those under the law, he seems to suggest also Jesus had already placed himself under the curse of the law when he entered into the present evil age. This

---

95. O'Brien, "The Curse of the Law (Galatians 3:13)," 72.
96. Ibid., 72–3.
97. Ibid., 73.

seems right because his birth under the law placed him within the present evil age (1:4), from which he came to deliver us (1:4), under a curse (3:10, 13), under sin (3:22), under slavery (3:23–4:7), under a guardian (3:23; 4:1–2), under the law (4:4), and under the elemental principles of the world (4:3, 9). But, more than that, Paul specifically asserts in 3:13 that Jesus delivered "us" from the law's curse by entering into that curse "for us," to deliver "us" from the law's curse by becoming the personified curse "for us."[98] The curse Christ bore for those under the curse is the same curse to be experienced by all under the law's jurisdiction, by the rival teachers in Galatia for rejecting Paul's gospel,[99] and by those Galatians who had already begun to turn away and sever themselves from Christ by falling from grace (1:6; 5:4).

Similar to McLean's thoughts about curses in Scripture, Christ's curse in Gal 3:13 is accompanied by "social rejection and divine excommunication (cf. Gen. 3:16–19, 23–24; 4:14; Deut. 29:18, 25, 27–28; Jer. 17:5–6), and death. The curse results in expulsion from the Christian community (Gal. 1:8; 4:30; cf. 1 Cor. 16:22; 2 Cor. 5:4–5),"[100] and from "Christ's new creation characterized by the reception of God's blessing and Spirit" (Gal 3:14; cf. Rom 9:3).[101] The cursed Christ is the only means by which the curse is removed from those under it.[102] The crucifixion of the cursed Christ is both the evidence that the Christ became a curse for those under its curse and the means by which God redeems those from the curse of the law (cf. 3:1, 13; 4:5). McLean rightly concludes Christ functions as the substitutionary victim to whom the curse is transferred.[103] LXX Deuteronomy 21:23 gives Paul the proof that Christ, the hanged man on a tree, is cursed. Paul wants the Galatians to know "the law is a cursing force, not one that mediates the blessing promised to Abraham"

---

98. McLean, *The Cursed Christ*, 125.
99. Ibid.
100. Ibid., 125 n. 62.
101. Ibid., 125.
102. Ibid.
103. Ibid., 131. McLean says, "Christ offered his own life as payment for (in exchange for) the lives of Christians who were slaves to the law. This commercial exchange explains how Christians are freed from the curse at the cost of Christ's life which was given in exchange." But McLean does not think Paul presents Christ's substitutionary death as an atoning sacrifice in Gal 3:13. The sacrificial nature of his death in Galatians can be reasonably argued since Paul asserts Jesus died "for our sins" (Gal 1:4) and that he died to "redeem" those under the curse of the law (3:13; 4:5). The combination of death for sins, law, and redemption seem to evoke a sacrificial background.

(or the life promised in LXX Hab 2:4, LXX Lev 18:5, or Deuteronomy).[104] If the law even cursed the Christ, leading to his death instead of providing him with life, if Christ redeemed those under the curse from the curse of the law by becoming a curse for them, and if a verse from the law (namely, LXX Deut 21:23) provides scriptural proof that the crucified Christ became a curse for those under the law's curse by virtue of his being born into the present evil age under the law and by his being hanged on a tree, then, Paul suggests, the Galatians will by no means escape the law's curse or receive the blessing of life by means of the law (cf. Gal 1:4; 3:10–14; 4:5–6; 5:2–4).

Paul's citation of LXX Deut 21:23 provides scriptural proof the Deuteronomic curse is conferred upon the Christ in both life and death to accomplish the blessing of redemption for those under the curse, for the one who is hanged on the tree is cursed. The important point for my thesis is that Gal 3:13–14 and 4:4–7 show that the Abrahamic blessing of the Spirit and the Deuteronomic blessing of life are conferred upon those whom the cursed Christ redeemed from the curse of the law because he died for them after having become what they are: namely, cursed under the law by virtue of being born under the law in the present evil age. Christ's death for them delivers them from the present evil age (1:4) and its enslaving, cosmological powers (4:3, 9) and grants them justification by faith (2:16; 3:6, 8), and deliverance from the curse of the law (3:10, 14). The cursed Christ's death for the cursed also provides Spirit-empowered, supernatural experiences (3:2–4, 14; 4:6),[105] including, but not limited to, enabling the Galatians to conquer the desires of the flesh (5:16–26), emancipation from slavery to sin (3:22) and from bondage to the law (4:3, 21–31), and participation in new creation as the rightful heirs of Abraham in Christ (the Israel of God), heirs who await by the Spirit the hope of righteousness by faith (3:1–6:15).

5. Similar to and different from the way 2 and 4 Maccabees present blessings and curses are conferred upon Jews because of the deaths of the martyrs for disobedience to Torah, Paul argues blessings are conferred

---

104. Quote from de Boer, *Galatians*, 214.

105. Charles H. Cosgrove argues that Paul begins his debate with the Galatians with the argument of Gal 3:1–5. His primary concern is to show the Galatians the Spirit gives them everything they need to live a life pleasing to God. For this argument, see *The Cross and the Spirit: A Study in the Argument and Theology of Galatians* (Macon: Mercer University Press, 1988). Regarding the cursed Christ, Cosgrove argues "for Paul participation in the crucifixion of Christ is the sole condition for ongoing life in the Spirit." Ibid., 172. For the entire argument, see ibid., 172–94.

upon Jews and Gentiles because the Deuteronomic curse was conferred upon Christ. I say more about the substitutionary function of the Christ's death in Chapter 4. Now, I simply discuss that similar to how the Jewish martyrological narratives present the martyrs as bearing the Deuteronomic curse of the law for the people by their suffering and death at the hands of a Gentile tyrant so that they could receive the Deuteronomic blessing of life (cf. 2 Macc 7:28–32; 4 Macc 6:28–30; 17:21–22), Paul asserts Christ became a curse "for us" by becoming accursed, just as those for whom he died were under the curse. The point of comparison and contrast is the way Paul presents the suffering of the cursed Christ as dying for those under the law's curse (cf. Gal 1:4; 2:20; 3:13) so that they would receive the Abrahamic blessing of the Spirit and the Deuteronomic blessing of life, both of which Paul asserts are realized in soteriological blessings in this age in anticipation of the age to come.

Jesus entered into the curse of the law by being born of a woman and being born under the law within the present evil age to redeem those under the law (1:4; 3:13; 4:4–5). In Gal 3:13, Paul cites LXX Deut 21:23 to support that Christ suffered the same fate as those who were under the Deuteronomic curse of the law by bearing the curse of the law upon himself for Jews and Gentiles in his death, which just so happened to be crucifixion at the hands of Gentiles. The cursed Christ was put on public display in his crucifixion so that Paul can say his crucifixion provides the proof that Christ suffered the curse "for us" so that "we" would experience the Abrahamic blessing of the Spirit (3:1, 14), because he became one of us by entering into the present evil age under the law's curse with us (3:13; 4:4–5).

Paul concludes Gal 3:6–9 with a discussion of the Abrahamic blessing. He asserts those of faith receive the blessing of Abraham with faithful Abraham (3:9). He likely conflates multiple texts from the Abrahamic narrative in Genesis (e.g. LXX Gen 12:1–3; 15:6; 18:18). God promised Abraham land, seed, and a universal blessing. Since he mentions the blessing of the families of the earth in/by means of Abraham and righteousness by faith, Paul explicitly conflates at least LXX Gen 12:3 and 18:18 in Gal 3:8 to demonstrate God's universal promise of blessing to Abraham is realized by means of the justification of the Gentiles by faith. According to Gal 3:2–5, the Galatians received the blessing of the Spirit in the same way Abraham received the blessing of righteousness: namely, by faith (3:6). Paul concludes that those from faith are blessed with Abraham (3:7). He elaborates upon the blessing of Abraham, stating it includes the justification of the Gentiles, which the Scripture announced beforehand to Abraham when it says "in you [Abraham] all the Gentiles of the earth will be blessed" (3:8). "Therefore," Paul concludes that those with faith comparable to Abraham's receive the Abrahamic blessing with Abraham (3:9). The Abrahamic blessing likely refers to the righteousness and justification mentioned in Gal 3:6 and 3:8, which are realized by faith by means of the distribution of the Abrahamic blessing of the Spirit because of the death of the Christ (3:13–14; 4:5–6). He offers support for the previous series of premises in 3:10–14.

As I stated earlier, Paul appeals to LXX Deut 27:26 in Gal 3:10 to affirm everyone of works of law is under a curse. But, as other scholars have pointed out, Paul likely has the broader context of LXX Deut 27:1–28:59 and 30:10–20 in mind since these sections talk about the blessings of obedience to Torah and the curses of disobedience to Torah.[106] According to Deut 27–30, those who obey Torah receive its blessings, but those who disobey receive its curses. According to Paul, those with a faith comparable to Abraham's faith are blessed with the Spirit and with accompanying experiences of the Spirit, and they experience the blessing of justification by faith apart from works of the law (Gal 3:6–9). He concludes the argument with a reference to the Deuteronomic curse (3:13) and Abrahamic blessing (3:13–14).

Paul's references to the blessing of Abraham, the Deuteronomic curse, and the Deuteronomic blessing in 3:2–14 suggest Paul sees both the Abrahamic blessing of the Spirit and the Deuteronomic blessing of life as being realized by justification by faith because of the death of the cursed Christ.[107] His comments in 3:16 and 3:29 support this. He says Christ is the seed of Abraham (3:16) and those with faith in Christ are the seed of Abraham and heirs according to the promise (3:29).[108]

Similarly, 2 and 4 Maccabees state that the martyrs suffered the Deuteronomic curses because of the nation's sin, while the Jewish martyrological narratives state nowhere that the martyrs disobeyed Torah. To the contrary, the authors of the narratives underline the martyrs' faithfulness to Torah even unto death (cf. 2 Macc 5:1–8:5; 4 Macc 6:1–17:22). Their suffering was Deuteronomic. They were under the law's curse as Torah-observers by

---

106. E.g. Das, *Galatians*, 311–16.

107. Watson (*Paul and the Hermeneutics of Faith*, 2nd ed., 174) asserts "according to Galatians 3:13–14, in contrast, the promise of Genesis 12:3 has now been realized in the death and resurrection of Christ, the event in which the curse of the law gives way to the blessing of Abraham." Watson's concern is primarily focused on Paul's reading of Deuteronomy.

108. Although I disagree with N. T. Wright's analysis of 3:10–14 at certain points, he is correct to affirm that Paul suggests in 3:10 Torah is not the pathway to the Abrahamic blessing, but Christ is. Wright, *Climax*, 147. Wright perhaps would go a step further and see the above as the emphasis in 3:10.

association with the non-Torah-observant people (2 Macc 7:32–38). The sins of some within the community brought the curse of the law against the martyrs. Nevertheless, the martyrs' steadfast devotion to Torah and their faithful endurance of the evil tyrant Antiochus delivered the nation from the curse of the law and brought both Abrahamic and Deuteronomic blessing to the nation via peace in the land, salvation from their enemies, and the reconciliation between God and the nation (2 Macc 5:1–8:5; 4 Macc 6:28–29; 17:21–22).

Focusing on the mechanism of Christ's death in 3:13, Daniel R. Schwartz in a provocative article argues Paul likely had in mind Yom Kippur's scapegoat ritual from Lev 16 in Gal 3:13 when he identifies Jesus as a curse, because of the references to redemption and being sent.[109] He appeals especially to 4:5, where Paul says God sent his son to be born of a woman under the law to redeem those under the law. Schwartz suggests that the language of sending his son to redeem those cursed by the law links Paul with the scapegoat ritual because of these verbal parallels.[110]

Even if Paul alludes to the scapegoat ritual, such an allusion would not disprove a martyrological point of comparison as a potential background behind Paul's remarks in Gal 3:13; 4:5 since he similarly states in Gal 3:10 that Torah brings a curse upon those who disobey its demands and since 3:13 identifies Jesus as becoming a curse (cf. 2 Macc 7:28–32; 4 Macc 6:28–29; 17:21–22). The martyrs obeyed Torah, but bore the curse of the law for Israel to distribute soteriological benefits to them and to provide salvation from the curse (2 Macc 7:28–32; 4 Macc 6:28–29; 17:21–22). In Gal 3:13, Jesus (a singular Torah-observant Jew) suffered the curse of Torah once for Jews and Gentiles under its curse. The Christ was born under the law (4:4), but he was not a minister of sin (2:17), but died "for our sins" to deliver those under the law's curse from the present evil age (1:4; 3:13; 4:5; cf. 2 Macc 7:28–32; 4 Macc 6:28–29; 17:21–22).

II. Conclusion

In this chapter, I have argued that in a way similar to, while different from, the Jewish martyrological traditions, Paul presents both Jews and Gentiles as recipients of the Deuteronomic blessings and curses in Galatians. He contends that Jesus, the Torah-observant Jew, suffered the Deuteronomic curses for others, experienced the blessing of life (i.e. resurrection), and delivered those for whom he died from the curse of the law. Jesus's death for Jews and Gentiles delivers them from the present evil age so

---

109. Schwartz, "Two Pauline Allusions," 429–35.
110. Ibid.

that they would participate by faith in the Deuteronomic blessing of life in this age and in the age to come and so that they would be delivered from the law's curse. But those without faith in Christ are currently under the Deuteronomic curses and are devoted to destruction if they preach another gospel contrary to the one preached by Paul. The purpose of the analysis in this chapter is to support that Galatians has both continuities with and discontinuities with the blessing and curse motif in the Jewish martyrological traditions in order to add further support that the Jewish martyrological traditions are a background behind Paul's remarks about the cursed Christ in Gal 3:13. However, Paul modifies these traditions to fit his purposes in Galatians. The chapter endeavored to support the following arguments about the Deuteronomic blessings and curses in Galatians.

First, Paul appropriates the Deuteronomic blessings and curses to Jews and Gentiles without ethnic restriction. Second, Paul appropriates Deuteronomic blessings to those who identify with Jesus Christ, the seed of Abraham, apart from works of the law, and he applies the Deuteronomic curses to those who identify with works of Torah apart from or in addition to faith in Christ without ethnic restriction. Third, Paul conflates the Abrahamic and Deuteronomic blessings and curses in Galatians to emphasize that both the Abrahamic blessing and the Deuteronomic blessing pertain to the distribution of the Spirit and justification by faith, extended to Jews and Gentiles by faith in the Messiah, and realized in the death (and resurrection) of the Messiah, Jesus, apart from Torah. The Deuteronomic curses come to those under works of law.

In the Jewish martyrological traditions, the Deuteronomic blessings are conferred to the Jewish martyrs in order to deliver the nation from the curse of the Torah because of the nation's disobedience to it. The Jewish martyrological narratives suggest the covenant with Abraham is fulfilled for Jews by means of their Torah-observance and the noble deaths of the Jewish martyrs for Israel (2 and 4 Maccabees), by means of military action (2 Maccabees), and by means of effective prayer (2 and 4 Maccabees). Paul, however, suggests the Deuteronomic curses are realized in Torah-observant Jews and Gentiles who remain under the curse of the law outside of faith in Jesus, the Messiah, in Galatians. But Jesus, the Jewish Messiah, personified the Deuteronomic curse (death) and blessing (resurrection/life) on behalf of Jews and Gentiles under the Deuteronomic curse to confer the Abrahamic blessing, namely, a universal outpouring of the Spirit (and all of the Spirit's benefits) upon Jewish and Gentile followers of Christ, so that the life, promised in the law, would be realized by Jews and Gentiles by faith in Christ apart from Torah-observance. Fourth, Paul understands the promise in Lev 18:5 and

Deut 27–30, that Torah-observance leads to long life in the land, as eternal life. This eternal life is experienced in this age and in the age to come apart from the works of the law by Jews and Gentiles who place faith in Jesus because he died to deliver them from the present evil age and from the curse of the law. Fifth, Jesus received the Deuteronomic curse so that Jews and Gentiles would receive both the Abrahamic blessing of the Spirit and the Deuteronomic blessing of life.

Sixth, the Abrahamic blessing of the Spirit and the Deuteronomic blessing of life are realized in the universal distribution of the Spirit to Jews and Gentiles by faith because of the death of the Christ who delivers Jews and Gentiles from the curse of the law. Paul conflates the Abrahamic and Deuteronomic blessings and curses in Galatians to emphasize both the Abrahamic blessing and the Deuteronomic blessing are extended to Jews and Gentiles by faith in the Messiah and realized in the death (and resurrection) of the Messiah, Jesus, apart from Torah, whereas the Jewish martyrological narratives suggest the covenant with Abraham is fulfilled for Jews by means of Torah-observance and the noble deaths of the Jewish martyrs for Israel (2 and 4 Maccabees), by means of military action (2 Maccabees), and by means of effective prayer (2 and 4 Maccabees).

Likewise, according to Paul, both the Abrahamic curse and the Deuteronomic curse are realized in Torah-observant Jews and Gentiles who remain under the curse of the law outside of faith in Jesus, the Messiah, in Galatians. But Jesus, the Jewish Messiah, received the Deuteronomic curse on behalf of Jews and Gentiles under the Deuteronomic curse so that the Abrahamic blessing, namely, a universal outpouring of the Spirit upon Jewish and Gentile followers of Christ, would be distributed to Jews and Gentiles by faith in Christ apart from Torah-observance. In Chapter 4, I focus more specifically on the soteriological significance of the deaths of the martyrs in 2 and 4 Maccabees, the soteriological significance of the death of the cursed Christ in Galatians, and the similarities and dissimilarities between Jewish martyrology and Paul's soteriology in Gal 3:13.

4

REPRESENTATION AND SUBSTITUTION
IN SECOND TEMPLE JEWISH MARTYROLOGICAL
TRADITIONS AND IN GALATIANS 3:13

In this chapter, I argue a twofold thesis. First, the authors present the Torah-observant Jewish martyrs as dying as Israel's representatives of and substitutes for non-Torah-observant Jews. Second, in Gal 3:13, Paul presents Jesus as dying as a representative of and a substitute for non-Torah-observant Jews and Gentiles. The martyrs died for the sins of fellow Jews to deliver them from the law's curse, but Jesus died for the sins of Jews and Gentiles to redeem both groups from the law's curse, to give them the Abrahamic blessing of the Spirit, to make them part of the family of Abraham, and to give both groups the Deuteronomic blessing of life in this age and in the age to come.

I. A Definition of Jewish Martyrology

A Jewish martyrology is a story about a Torah-observant Jew who dies as a martyr at the hands of an antagonist Gentile tyrant instead of yielding to the threat of the pagan authorities, when the Tyrant presents the Torah-observant Jew with the choice of renouncing obedience to Torah or suffering death as a result of his obedience to Torah.[1] The Jewish martyr dies to accomplish soteriological benefits for those in the covenant community whose disobedience to Torah provides the reason

1. For a definition of Jewish martyrology, see Tessa Rajak, *The Jewish Dialogue with Greece and Rome: Studies in Cultural and Social Interaction* (Leiden: Brill, 2001), 99–103; van Henten, *Maccabean Martyrs*. In this chapter, agreeing with van Henten (*Maccabean Martyrs*, 7–13, esp. 8), I define Jewish martyrdom in LXX Dan 3 and in 2 and 4 Maccabees as "a person who in an extremely hostile situation prefers violent death to compliance with a demand of the (usually) pagan authorities. This definition implies that the death of such a person is a structural element in the writing about this martyr. The execution should at least be mentioned." See also Williams, *Maccabean Martyr Traditions*, 3–4 n. 10.

in the narrative as to why those Torah-observant in the community suffer martyrdom at the hands of a Gentile tyrant. The Second Temple texts discussed in this chapter fit within this definition. The first text for investigation is LXX Dan 3 since it presents similar Jewish martyrological ideas found in 2 and 4 Maccabees.

II. Representation and Substitution in LXX Daniel 3:24–90[2]

LXX Daniel 3 contains approximately 64 more verses than MT Dan 3.[3] The Greek version contains stories and prayers that are absent from the tradition preserved in the Masoretic text.[4] The additional verses in the Greek version of Dan 3 are to be found in LXX Dan 3:24–97. The additions resemble the traditional stories about Daniel in MT Dan 1–6. Similar to MT Dan 6, the additional stories in LXX Dan 3 are in the context of exile, and there Daniel's enemies throw him into the lion's den.[5]

As Matthias Henze summarizes LXX Daniel 3:24–90 inserts the prayer of Azariah and the Song of the Three Jews.[6] LXX Daniel 3:24–40 highlights Daniel's three friends, who are identified in the LXX version as Ananias (Shadrach), Azarias (Meshach), and Misael (Abednego),

---

2. With slight modifications and fresher insights, the material on LXX Dan 3 and 2 and 4 Maccabees in this chapter was published in my essay, "Martyr Theology in Hellenistic Judaism," in *Christian Origins and Hellenistic Judaism Social and Literary Contexts for the New Testament*, ed. Stanley E. Porter and Andrew W. Pitts (Leiden: Brill, 2012), 493–521, esp. 497, my book *Christ Died for Our Sins: Representation and Substitution in Romans and Their Jewish Martyrological Background* (Eugene, OR: Pickwick, 2015), and my essay, 'Cultic Action and Cultic Function in Second Temple Jewish Martyrologies: The Jewish Martyrs as Israel's Yom Kippur', in *Sacrifice, Cult, and Atonement in Early Judaism and Christianity: Constituents and Critique*, ed. Henrietta L. Wiley and Christian A. Eberhart (Atlanta: SBL, 2017), 233–63. I have borrowed all overlapping material from the publishers with permission. I thank Wipf & Stock/Pickwick, the original publisher of some of the material use in this chapter, for granting permission.

3. Unless otherwise indicated, I use Rahlfs-Hanhart's most recent critical edition of the LXX.

4. Scholars have given these stories and prayers the apocryphal names of The Story of Susanna, the Prayer of Azariah and the Song of the Three Jews, and Bel and the Dragon.

5. This information is from Matthias Henze, "Additions to Daniel," in *Outside the Bible: Ancient Jewish Writings Related to Scripture*, ed. Louis H. Feldman, James L. Kugel, and Lawrence H. Schiffman (New York: Jewish Publication Society, 2013), 122.

6. Matthias Henze, "The Prayer of Azariah and the Song of the Three Jews," Feldman, Kugel, and Schiffman, eds., *Outside the Bible*, 129.

4. *Representation and Substitution* 135

while they prayed as they suffered in Nebuchadnezzar's fiery furnace. They refused "to worship a golden statue" erected by Nebuchadnezzar in Babylon and instead remained faithful to their God. LXX Daniel 3:23 states that Nebuchadnezzar seized the three young men with fetters and had them thrown into the fiery furnace.[7] LXX Daniel 3:24–25 asserts that the Babylonian king expresses shock when he sees four men (Daniel's three friends and an angel) freely walking unharmed in the fiery furnace.[8] The Greek insertions connect the swift transition from the king's anger and his shock with what happens in the fiery furnace to underscore "the miraculous nature" of the story.[9]

While Daniel's three friends were in the fiery furnace, they prayed to God because of the sins of the people. Their prayer acknowledges that Israel suffered the Lord's judgment in exile "because of their sins" (LXX Dan 3:28–37). Azariah blessed the Lord's name and confessed that he was righteous "in all the things" that the Lord had done to them and that the Lord's ways and works were right (LXX Dan 3:27). In LXX Dan 3:28, Azariah continues confessing to the Lord that all of his judgments that he brought upon the holy city were right "because in truth and in judgment you have brought all of these things [upon us] because of our sins" (ὅτι ἐν ἀληθείᾳ καὶ κρίσει ἐπήγαγες πάντα ταῦτα διὰ τὰς ἁμαρτίας ἡμῶν).

To emphasize that the Lord's judgment of exile came upon his people because of their sins, his prayer continues in LXX Dan 3:29 with the words "we have sinned and we have acted lawlessly so that we turned from you and we missed the mark in all things and we did not hear your commandments" (ὅτι ἡμάρτομεν καὶ ἠνομήσαμεν ἀποστῆναι ἀπὸ σοῦ καὶ ἐξημάρτομεν ἐν πᾶσιν καὶ τῶν ἐντολῶν σου οὐκ ἠκούσαμεν). In LXX Dan 3:30–31, Azariah further prays that "we neither treasured up nor did as you commanded to us so that it would be well with us, and all things that you have brought upon us and all things that you have done to us you have done by means of true judgment" (οὐδὲ συνετηρήσαμεν οὐδὲ ἐποιήσαμεν καθὼς ἐνετείλω ἡμῖν ἵνα εὖ ἡμῖν γένηται πάντα ὅσα ἡμῖν ἐπήγαγες καὶ πάντα ὅσα ἐποίησας ἡμῖν ἐν ἀληθινῇ κρίσει ἐποίησας). In LXX Dan 3:32, Azariah confesses "you have given us over into the hands of lawless enemies, who are the greatest of our enemies and to an unrighteous and most evil king in all of the earth" (καὶ παρέδωκας ἡμᾶς εἰς χεῖρας ἐχθρῶν ἀνόμων ἐχθίστων ἀποστατῶν καὶ βασιλεῖ ἀδίκῳ καὶ πονηροτάτῳ παρὰ πᾶσαν τὴν γῆν).

7. καὶ οἱ τρεῖς οὗτοι Σεδραχ Μισαχ καὶ Αβδεναγω ἔπεσον εἰς μέσον τῆς καμίνου τοῦ πυρὸς τῆς καιομένης πεπεδημένοι.
8. Henze, "The Prayer of Azariah and the Song of the Three Jews," 129.
9. Ibid.

In LXX Dan 3:34–35, Azariah begins to pray that God would not break his covenant with his people or withdraw his mercy from them on account of his promise to Abraham, Isaac, and Jacob (μὴ δὴ παραδῷς ἡμᾶς εἰς τέλος διὰ τὸ ὄνομά σου καὶ μὴ διασκεδάσῃς τὴν διαθήκην σου καὶ μὴ ἀποστήσῃς τὸ ἔλεός σου ἀφ' ἡμῶν δι' Αβρααμ τὸν ἠγαπημένον ὑπὸ σοῦ καὶ διὰ Ισαακ τὸν δοῦλόν σου καὶ Ισραηλ τὸν ἅγιόν σου) (cf. also LXX Dan 3:36). In LXX Dan 3:37, Azariah offers a reason for his people in LXX Dan 3:36: "because, O' master, we were reduced in the presence of all the Gentiles, and we are humble today in all the earth because of our sins" (ὅτι δέσποτα ἐσμικρύνθημεν παρὰ πάντα τὰ ἔθνη καί ἐσμεν ταπεινοὶ ἐν πάσῃ τῇ γῇ σήμερον διὰ τὰς ἁμαρτίας ἡμῶν). Azariah's reference to the humility of "today" refers to the Lord's judgment in exile because of sin, the former of which LXX Dan 1:1–2:49 makes abundantly clear and the latter of which Azariah's prayer crystalizes (LXX Dan 3:28, 36–37).

In LXX Dan 3, Azariah and his friends represent the people because he associates them with the sinful nation in exile when he declares that they suffer "because of our sins," even though the text states nowhere that either he or his friends violated Torah. He confesses throughout this prayer that "we" have sinned (ἡμάρτομεν) "because of our sins" (διὰ τὰς ἁμαρτίας ἡμῶν) (LXX Dan 3:27–28, 37), that "we" have broken the law (ἠνομήσαμεν ἀποστῆναι ἀπὸ σοῦ) (LXX Dan 3:29), that "we" have missed the mark (ἐξημάρτομεν) (LXX Dan 3:29), that "we" have not listened to the Lord's commands (τῶν ἐντολῶν σου οὐκ ἠκούσαμεν) (LXX Dan 3:29), that the Lord has handed "us" over into the hands of wicked people (παρέδωκας ἡμᾶς εἰς χεῖρας ἐχθρῶν ἀνόμων ἐχθίστων ἀποστατῶν καὶ βασιλεῖ ἀδίκῳ καὶ πονηροτάτῳ παρὰ πᾶσαν τὴν γῆν) (LXX Dan 3:32), and he prays that the Lord would not destroy him and his people by breaking his covenant with them (καὶ νῦν οὐκ ἔστιν ἡμῖν ἀνοῖξαι τὸ στόμα αἰσχύνη καὶ ὄνειδος ἐγενήθη τοῖς δούλοις σου καὶ τοῖς σεβομένοις σε μὴ δὴ παραδῷς ἡμᾶς εἰς τέλος διὰ τὸ ὄνομά σου καὶ μὴ διασκεδάσῃς τὴν διαθήκην σου) (LXX Dan 3:33–36). Yet, Daniel and his three friends were "young ones without blemish" (νεανίσκους οἷς οὐκ ἔστιν ἐν αὐτοῖς μῶμος) since they were compliant with Torah both prior to and in exile (LXX Dan 1:4). Therefore, they were not individually to blame for exile since they were "without blemish" (LXX Dan 1:4).

LXX Daniel 1:8–19 confirms the faithfulness of Daniel and his three friends to Torah in exile when it states that Daniel refused to eat the king's unclean food and to drink his unclean wine. Instead, they complied with Torah and refused to defile themselves. Consequently, God gave favor to Daniel (LXX Dan 1:8–9). LXX Daniel 1:12–19 suggests that Daniel's three friends complied with Daniel's Torah-observance, because Daniel includes them in his plot to deceive the king regarding their refusal to eat the unclean food and to drink the unclean wine (cf. MT Lev 11:1–47; Jub. 22:16–18).[10] Azariah associates himself and his friends with the sinful nation due to the Deuteronomic principle expressed by Moses in Lev 18:5 and repeated in Deuteronomy: obedience to Torah brings corporate life to Israel in the land (Deut 5:32–33; 8:1; 11:8–9, 18–25, 28; 28:1–14; 30:15–16), but disobedience to Torah results in the Lord's corporate judgment of the people by means of expulsion from the land (Deut 4:25–28; 11:28; 28:15–68; 30:17–20). Both the MT and LXX traditions suggest that Daniel and his three friends were faithful to Torah, but their association with the covenant community meant that they suffered exile along with the people, so that they (Torah-observers) could identify themselves with the sins of the nation.[11] Thus, Azariah's prayer for the nation in exile represents the corporate cry of the Lord's covenant people in exile.

As Azariah continues his prayer, he urges God to deliver Israel from their national suffering in exile (LXX Dan 3:38–40). He laments that the Davidic monarchy has been abolished and that the temple cult had been eradicated (καὶ οὐκ ἔστιν ἐν τῷ καιρῷ τούτῳ ἄρχων καὶ προφήτης καὶ ἡγούμενος οὐδὲ ὁλοκαύτωσις οὐδὲ θυσία οὐδὲ προσφορὰ οὐδὲ θυμίαμα οὐ τόπος τοῦ καρπῶσαι ἐναντίον σου καὶ εὑρεῖν ἔλεος) (LXX Dan 3:38; cf. 2 Kgs 17:22–23; 23:26–25:11; 2 Chr 36:19–20). The eradication of the temple cult meant the abolishment of a sacrificial means by which to attain God's mercy for the nation since YHWH provided cultic sacrifices of atonement in the Levitical cult to be performed at the temple in order to provide atonement for sin and since Azariah's prayer connects God's mercy with Levitical cultic language (e.g. ὁλοκαύτωσις ["burnt-offering"], θυσία ["sacrifice"], προσφορὰ ["offering"], θυμίαμα ["incense"], and καρπῶσαι ["to bear fruit"]).[12] Furthermore, without access to the temple cult, Israel could neither celebrate daily cultic sacrifices of atonement or the traditional Yom Kippur ritual (Lev 1–6; 16). As a result, the absence of the temple cult in exile in LXX Dan 3 meant that there was not a means by which or a place at which the Lord's people could perform cultic

---

10. See also 1 Macc 1:11–15, 41–45; 3:58–59; 4:54–60; 2 Macc 5:15–20; Pss Sol. 2:2; Josephus, *Ant.* 15.5.417; Acts 21:27.

11. Contra Tobit. The setting of Tobit is likewise exile, but Tobit overtly states that he (a Torah-observant Jew) was not to blame either for Israel's or for his exile. To defend this, Tobit highlights his Torah-observance and the Torah-disobedience of others, and he blames the latter for exile.

12. Every word in the above parenthesis occurs in cultic contexts in the LXX (ὁλοκαύτωσις [LXX Lev 6:2]; θυσία [LXX Lev 1:9, 13, 17; 2:1–2, 5–7, 15; 3:1; 5:13; 6:16; Sir 34:18; 35:5; 46:16; 50:13], θυμίαμα [LXX Lev 16:13], and καρπῶσαι [LXX Lev 2:11]).

action to receive his mercy. The prayer of the three friends confirms this when they acknowledge they did not have a place to offer a sacrificial burnt-offering in order to find God's mercy (προσφορὰ οὐδὲ θυμίαμα οὐ τόπος τοῦ καρπῶσαι ἐναντίον σου καὶ εὑρεῖν ἔλεος) (LXX Dan 3:28). This statement alludes to the Levitical cult (cf. LXX Lev 6:2). Thus, the prayer suggests there is no means by which to receive the Lord's forgiveness through cultic action since the temple cult's absence is parallel with the friends' statement that there is no place to offer a sacrifice to find God's mercy. In this context, Azariah asks God to use his death and the deaths of his friends to perform the necessary cultic action to provide national cleansing for the covenant community in the place of the temple cult, which LXX Dan 3:39 communicates with the optative προσδεχθείημεν in the statement ἐν ψυχῇ συντετριμμένῃ καὶ πνεύματι τεταπεινωμένῳ προσδεχθείημεν ὡς ἐν ὁλοκαυτώμασι κριῶν καὶ ταύρων καὶ ὡς ἐν μυριάσιν ἀρνῶν πιόνων (LXX Dan 3:39).

Furthermore, Azariah prays that God would use their deaths to cleanse the nation while in exile as long as the temple cult was ineffective with the prayer "let our sacrifice be in your presence today also to propitiate behind you because there is no shame in those who trust in you so that we would also consecrate behind you" (οὕτω γενέσθω ἡμῶν ἡ θυσία ἐνώπιόν σου σήμερον καὶ ἐξιλάσαι ὄπισθέν σου ὅτι οὐκ ἔστιν αἰσχύνη τοῖς πεποιθόσιν ἐπὶ σοί καὶ τελειῶσαι ὄπισθέν σου) (LXX Th. Dan 3:40).[13] Azariah wanted God to receive (προσδεχθείημεν) their deaths "just as" (ὡς) he received the function of the burnt offerings in the Levitical cult (ὡς ἐν ὁλοκαυτώμασι κριῶν καὶ ταύρων καὶ ὡς ἐν μυριάσιν ἀρνῶν πιόνων). The numerous Levitical cultic terms (ὁλοκαύτωσις, θυσία, προσφορά, θυμίαμα, καρπῶσαι, ὁλοκαυτώμασι, and ἐξιλάσαι) applied to Daniel's three friends and their identification with the Torah-disobedient nation suggest that they function in the narrative of LXX Th. Dan 3 as proper representatives and substitutionary cultic sacrifices to bring to Israel the mercy (ἔλεος) and cleansing (ἐξιλάσαι) traditionally provided by the temple cult and Yom Kippur (LXX Th. Dan 3:38–40).

III. Martyrdom and Reconciliation in 2 and 4 Maccabees

2 and 4 Maccabees present the Jewish martyrs as Israel's representatives, substitutes, and as the nation's Yom Kippur. After killing Eleazar in 2 Macc 6, Antiochus compelled a mother and her seven sons to

---

13. For a discussion of the text-variant in the different Greek versions, see Williams, "Martyr Theology in Hellenistic Judaism," 499 n. 12.

eat unlawful foods (2 Macc 7:1). They were faced with death if they disobeyed. Yet, they rebelled against Antiochus. As a result, each suffered torture and death (2 Macc 7:2–41). While encouraged by his mother to trust God as he faced Antiochus's wrath (2 Macc 7:28–29), the seventh son stated that "we suffer because of our own sins" (ἡμεῖς γὰρ διὰ τὰς ἑαυτῶν ἁμαρτίας πάσχομεν) (2 Macc 7:32; cf. 2 Macc 5:17). His words echo the cry of Daniel's three friends in LXX Dan 3:28–29 and 3:37 (2 Macc 7:32; cf. 2 Macc 5:17).[14] The seventh son's confession is almost exactly the same as his old brother (the sixth son), who was martyred earlier in the narrative, in 2 Macc 7:18 (ἡμεῖς γὰρ δι' ἑαυτοὺς ταῦτα πάσχομεν ἁμαρτόντες εἰς τὸν ἑαυτῶν θεόν ἄξια θαυμασμοῦ γέγονεν). Just as the confession of Daniel's three friends, the confession of both the sixth and the seventh sons acknowledges that sin is the foundational reason that the martyrs suffer in the narrative of 2 Maccabees at the hands of Antiochus and that the martyrs' deaths are the foundational reason why God "will be reconciled again to his servants" (εἰ δὲ χάριν ἐπιπλήξεως καὶ παιδείας ὁ ζῶν κύριος ἡμῶν βραχέως ἐπώργισται καὶ πάλιν καταλλαγήσεται τοῖς ἑαυτοῦ δούλοις) (2 Macc 7:33; cf. 2 Macc 1:5; 7:37–38; 8:29).

References to the Lord's servants, who were Torah-observant Jews, as dying for the soteriological benefit of non-Torah-observant sinners in 2 Macc 7:33 conceptually connect with Isa 53. Isaiah 53 asserts that YHWH's servant will serve as the means by which the nation's sin is forgiven and the means by which YHWH will declare many righteous to be in the right (LXX Isa 53:4–6, 8, 10–12). Although the verb καταλλαγήσεται in 2 Macc 7:33 is absent in LXX Isa 53, the infinitive δικαιῶσαι and the adjective δίκαιον in LXX Isa 53:11 communicate the concept of reconciliation between God and sinners because the soteriological reality communicated with the words δικαιῶσαι and δίκαιον is the result of the servant's death for the sins of others. In other words, the act of YHWH declaring to be in the right those for whom the Servant dies in order to take away their sins results in reconciliation between YHWH and the transgressors for whom the Servant dies. In addition to the Isaianic language, 2 Maccabees appropriates Levitical cultic language.

The seventh son's statements that "we suffer because of our sins" and that "he will again be reconciled to his servants" refer to Israel as

14. Similarly Wolfgang Kraus, *Der Tod Jesu als Heiligtumsweihe: Eine Untersuchung zum Umfeld de Sühnevorstellung im Römer 3:25-26a*, WMANT 66 (Neukirchener-Vluyn: Neukirchener, 1991), 35. However, Kraus argues against a cultic background behind 2 Macc 7:32–38.

a nation, which includes the martyrs.¹⁵ This seems right because of the first person plural ἡμεῖς, the phrase διὰ τὰς ἑαυτῶν ἁμαρτίας, and the first person plural verb πάσχομεν. The need for God to be reconciled again to his servants reveals that enmity exists between God and his people in the narrative due to the apostasy of many Jews away from their God to follow Antiochus's Hellenistic policies (1 Macc 1; 2 Macc 5:18; 6:12–16). However, the martyrs were individually innocent of religious apostasy (cf. 1 Macc 1–2; 2 Macc 7; 4 Macc 6), which is evident by their Torah-observance in the face of death. Their suffering was a corollary of their refusal to embrace Greek culture as many of their kinsmen had begun to embrace it (cf. 2 Macc 5:1–8:5; 4 Macc 6).¹⁶ The reconciliation needed by their martyrdom is the cessation of God's wrath against the people because of the sin of some within the community and a return of friendship between YHWH and the nation. In this respect, the seventh son interprets the situation of the nation and his brothers in light of Deut 32, and he interprets the vindication of YHWH's servants in Deut 32:36 to be accomplished by means of his faithful death and the faithful deaths of his brothers, who are both *representatives of* and *substitutes for* the nation.

In LXX Deut 32:36a, in his final words to Israel, Moses states that the Lord will vindicate his people, and "he will feel compassion for his servants" (καὶ ἐπὶ τοῖς δούλοις αὐτοῦ παρακληθήσεται), whereas 2 Macc 7:33 stresses that the Lord "will be reconciled again by means of his servants" (καὶ πάλιν καταλλαγήσεται τοῖς ἑαυτοῦ δούλοις). The former accentuates *what* God will do for his people (namely, show them mercy) (cf. 2 Macc 7:6), but the seventh son's prayer stresses *the means* by which God will show mercy (namely, through his servants, the faithful martyrs). That the martyrs would be the means by which God would be reconciled to his nation is strengthened by the noun καταλλαγή and the verb καταλλαγήσεται in 2 Maccabees, both of which always concern reconciliation between the Lord and his people in 2 Maccabees (cf. 2 Macc 1:5; 7:33; 8:29).¹⁷

---

15. So van Henten, *Maccabean Martyrs*, 137–8. As van Henten (ibid., 137 n. 51) astutely points out, "the verb ἁμαρτόντες occurs only in 2 Macc. 7:18 and 10:4, where it also refers to the sinning of the people as a body."

16. Angelo P. O'Hagan, "The Martyr in the Fourth Book of the Maccabees," *LA* 24 (1974): 94–120, esp. 108, against Theofried Baumeister, *Die Anfange der Theologie des Martyriums*, MBT 45 (Münster: Aschendorff, 1980), 41–2.

17. For more detailed discussions of reconciliation in 2 Maccabees and for alternative interpretations of the nature of reconciliation in 2 Maccabees, see Cilliers Breytenbach, *Versöhnung: Eine Studie zur paulinischen Soteriologie*, WMANT 60

4. *Representation and Substitution* 141

Before the seventh son utters these words in 2 Macc 7:32–38, the author places a panegyric speech in the mouth of both Eleazar in 2 Macc 6 and in the mouths of the mother and her seven sons in 2 Macc 7. Prior to these speeches, the author lucidly asserts the sin for which the martyrs suffered torturous death was the nation's rebellion against the Torah (2 Macc 5:20–7:32; cf. 1 Macc 1:11–15). The respective texts in 2 and 4 Maccabees do not state anywhere that the martyrs themselves actually violated Torah along with the rest of the nation. Nevertheless, the "we" in "we suffer because of our sins" (2 Macc 7:32) includes the martyrs along with rebellious Israel for the following reasons.

First, the martyrs were members of YHWH's covenant-community for which they suffered (cf. 2 Macc 7:16, 30, 30–32, 38). Second, Antiochus is called the adversary of the Hebrews and not simply the adversary of the martyrs (2 Macc 7:31). Third, the author begins his discussion of the martyrological narratives with a positive statement about the role of suffering in the lives of God's people. (2 Macc 6:12–17).[18] Thus, 2 and 4 Maccabees' presentations of the martyrs' suffering echo Israel's antecedent Deuteronomic history, thereby fulfilling the Deuteronomic curses set forth in Deut 27–28 and 32 against Israel via the nations due to the disobedience of some within the nation (cf. Deut 28:1–14 with 28:15–68). The seventh son's words demonstrate that the principle set forth in Leviticus and reiterated in Deuteronomy (namely, when a few in the covenant-community sinned against God and suffered the consequences of their sin, the entire covenant-community including the martyrs suffered the consequences of this sin) was still alive and well in 2 Maccabees.[19] The martyrs suffered precisely because they refused to yield to an extreme form of Hellenism, contrary to many fellow Jews (cf. 2 Macc 5:1–8:5; 4 Macc 6),[20] and their kinsmen's acceptance of Antiochus's Hellenistic regime resulted in God's judgment of the entire nation through Antiochus (cf. 1 Macc 1), as promised in Deut 28:1–68. Therefore, the martyrological narratives present the seventh son and the other martyrs as representatives of the nation and as substitutes for the nation to pay for Israel's sin, which also became a payment for their

(Neukirchen-Vluyn: Neukirchener, 1989); Stanley E. Porter, καταλλασσω in *Ancient Greek Literature, with Reference to the Pauline Writings*, EFN 5 (Cordoba: Ediciones El Almendro, 1994).

18. So van Henten, *Maccabean Martyrs*, 139.
19. Cf. Num 25:11; Isa 1:1–26; LXX Dan 3:24–90; Wis 3:1–6.
20. O'Hagan, "The Martyr," 94–120, esp. 108. Against Baumeister, *Die Anfange*, 41–2.

sins by virtue of their membership within the covenant-community (cf. 2 Macc 7:32).[21] 2 Maccabees 5:1–7:38 supports this interpretation.

As a result of the nation's rebellion against God's law, the temple and the land were dishonored (2 Macc 5:27–6:6). When Antiochus and Menelaus (a Jewish high priest) entered the temple in Jerusalem, they profaned it (2 Macc 5:15–16). To eradicate God's judgment against the nation, the seven sons voluntarily offer themselves to die for Israel to achieve God's forgiveness (2 Macc 7:32–38).[22] 2 Maccabees 7:32–38 suggests that the seventh son was confident that God would be reconciled again to the nation through the martyrs' deaths because he asserts that God "will be reconciled again to his servants" in 2 Macc 7:33 and because 2 Macc 7:37–38 affirms the seventh son wants God to end his wrath against the nation by means of the deaths of him and his brothers on behalf of the nation (ἐγὼ δέ καθάπερ οἱ ἀδελφοί καὶ σῶμα καὶ ψυχὴν προδίδωμι περὶ τῶν πατρίων νόμων ἐπικαλούμενος τὸν θεὸν ἵλεως ταχὺ τῷ ἔθνει γενέσθαι καὶ σὲ μετὰ ἐτασμῶν καὶ μαστίγων ἐξομολογήσασθαι διότι μόνος αὐτὸς θεός ἐστιν ἐν ἐμοὶ δὲ καὶ τοῖς ἀδελφοῖς μου στῆσαι τὴν τοῦ παντοκράτορος ὀργὴν τὴν ἐπὶ τὸ σύμπαν ἡμῶν γένος δικαίως ἐπηγμένην).[23]

The most important parts of the above prayer in 2 Macc 7:37–38 for my thesis are the seventh son's statements "be merciful quickly to the nation" in 7:37 and "to end the wrath of the almighty in me and in my brothers" in 7:38. The grammatical construction in 2 Macc 7:37 is similar to the one in 4 Macc 6:28. Eleazar asks God in the latter text to provide mercy for the nation through his death (ἵλεως γενοῦ τῷ ἔθνει σου). In 2 Macc 7:37, the seventh son prays that God would "quickly be merciful to the nation" (ἵλεως ταχὺ τῷ ἔθνει γενέσθαι) through his death. In both 4 Macc 6:28 and 2 Macc 7:37, the martyrs urge God to grant mercy to the nation through their deaths for it. They offered themselves to God to pay

---

21. So Marinus de Jonge, *Christology in Context: The Earliest Christian Response to Jesus* (Philadelphia: Westminster, 1988), 181–2; U. Kellermann, "Zum traditionsgeschichtlichen Problem des stellvertretenden Sühnetodes in 2 Makk 7:37," *BN* 13 (1980): 63–83, esp. 69; van Henten, *Maccabean Martyrs*, 137, against Sam K. Williams, *Jesus' Death as Saving Event* (Missoula: Scholars Press, 1975), 79 n. 29; Seeley, *The Noble Death*, 87.

22. Similarly Lohse, *Märtyrer und Gottesknecht*, 67–9; J. Gnilka, "Martyriumsparänese und Sühnetod in synoptischen und jüdischen Traditionen," in *Die Kirche des Anfangs: Für Heinz Schürman* (Leipzig: St. Benno-Verlag, 1977), 223–46; J. Downing, "Jesus and Martyrdom," *JTS* 14 (1963): 279–93, esp. 288–9; van Henten, *Maccabean Martyrs*, 140–4. Against a sacrificial reading of 2 Macc 7:32–38, see Williams, *Jesus' Death*, 82–8; Goldstein, *II Maccabees*, 316.

23. Against Schwartz, *2 Maccabees*, 317.

for the nation's sin, which also became a payment for their sin by virtue of their membership within the community (cf. 2 Macc 7:32). Thus, the function of the martyrs' deaths for Israel parallels the function of Yom Kippur for Israel. That is, the martyrs represent and stand in the place of rebellious Israel, and they are the means by which and the place at which atonement is made for the nation to achieve YHWH's reconciliation, just as the animals stand in the place of Israel (= the sacrificial ritual), represent the people (= the scapegoat ritual), and are the means by which Israel's sins are purified/covered/atoned during Yom Kippur (Lev 16),[24] just as the Servant stands in the place of Israel as the means by which the nations' sins are purified/covered/atoned in Isa 53. As the ensuing narrative of 2 Macc 8:1–5 suggests, the martyrs' deaths are the means by which YHWH's wrath ceases against Israel and the means by which reconciliation is achieved in the narrative of 2 Maccabees.

Scholars debate the meaning of 7:38.[25] The debate pertains to how one should interpret the seventh son's statement that God's wrath would end ἐν ἐμοὶ δὲ καὶ τοῖς ἀδελφοῖς μου (2 Macc 7:38). Sam K. Williams wrote an important monograph on Jesus's death and martyrdom in which he argued in part that the seven sons do not "avert" God's wrath away from the nation by means of their deaths. According to Williams, the phrase ἐν ἐμοὶ δὲ καὶ τοῖς ἀδελφοῖς μου does not suggest the means by which the wrath of God is "averted" away from Israel, but the point at which the wrath of God is "averted."[26] He simply affirms that the wrath of God would end "with" him and "with" his brothers. Williams maintains his view partly because he rejects the idea that 2 Maccabees teaches vicarious atonement.[27] According to him, 2 Maccabees only presents the martyrs' suffering and death as exemplary for their fellow Jews to imitate when they face their own suffering and death.[28]

Williams's analysis is partially correct in two ways. First, the author of 2 Maccabees states that the suffering and deaths of the martyrs were exemplary (2 Macc 6:28, 31; cf. 2 Macc 6:24–31). Eleazar's death was an example of nobility for the entire nation to follow (2 Macc 6:28, 31). Even 4 Maccabees, where martyrdom is glamorized, speaks of the

---

24. Contra Williams, *Jesus' Death*, 79 n. 29; Kellermann, "Zum traditionsgesr chichtlichen Problem," 69; van Henten, *Maccabean Martyrs*, 137.
25. Williams, *Jesus' Death*, 83–8; H. W. Surkau, *Martyrien in jüdischer und frühchristlicher Zeit*, FRLANT 36 (Göttingen: Vandenhoeck & Ruprecht, 1938), 59.
26. Williams, *Jesus' Death*, 83–90.
27. Ibid.
28. Ibid.

martyrs' deaths as exemplary for others (4 Macc 6:18–21; 9:23; 10:3, 16; 11:15; 12:16; 13:8–18; 17:23). Second, Williams is correct to note the preposition ἐν in the phrase ἐν ἐμοὶ δὲ καὶ τοῖς ἀδελφοῖς μου στῆσαι τὴν τοῦ παντοκράτορος ὀργὴν has more meanings than "by means of."

In response to Williams's first observation, 2 Maccabees presents the martyrs as examples to be imitated by Israel (2 Macc 6:24–31). The exemplary nature of the martyrs' deaths in 2 and 4 Maccabees does not preclude their deaths from functioning as representatives of the nation, as substitutes for the nation, and as atoning sacrifices. The authors present the martyrs' deaths as exemplary, representative, and as a substitution (cf. 2 Macc 6:18–7:38; with 4 Macc 9:23; 10:3, 16; 11:15; 12:16; 13:8–18; 17:21–22). In response to Williams's second observation, the preposition ἐν likely conveys instrumentality in 2 Macc 7:38 ("by means of") for multiple reasons. First, the preceding meaning occurs in numerous places in 2 Maccabees (2 Macc 1:28; 5:20; 7:29; 15:11; cf. 4 Macc 9:22; 16:15). Second, the prepositional phrases occur in a context where the seventh son urges God to be reconciled to the nation again (2 Macc 7:33).[29] Three, the term should be translated as "by means of" in 2 Macc 7:29, which is a text in close proximity of 2 Macc 7:38. If the translation "by means of" is correct in 2 Macc 7:38, then the seventh son's prayer would be interpreted to mean that he wanted God to end his wrath "by means of" his death and "by means of" the deaths of his brothers. This interpretation suggests the seventh son wants his death and the deaths of his brothers to satisfy God's wrath against the nation in a substitutionary manner since the martyrs die as representatives of the nation.

2 Maccabees 5:1–8:5 supports that God fulfilled the seventh son's expectation through the martyrs' deaths, for the latter text states that God was reconciled to the nation after the martyrs die (2 Macc 8:1–5).[30] In light of this, one reason God put an end to his wrath against the nation is the martyrs' deaths.[31] For example, 2 Macc 1:5 begins with a prayer

---

29. For additional examples, see A. T. Robertson, *A Grammar of the Greek New Testament in the Light of Historical Research* (Nashville: Broadman, 1934), 589–91; Herbert Smyth, *Greek Grammar*, 21st ed. (Cambridge, MA: Harvard University Press, 2002), 376–7.

30. Schwartz (*2 Maccabees*, 317) observes that 2 Macc 8:4–5 applies 7:38.

31. J. W. van Henten, "The Tradition-Historical Background of Romans 3:25," in *From Jesus to John: Essays on Jesus and New Testament Christology in Honour of Marinus de Jonge*, ed. M. de Jonge and Martinus C. de Boer, JSNTSup 84 (Sheffield: JSOT, 1993), 117–21, esp. 117, against Williams, *Jesus' Death*, 85–9; Seeley, *The Noble Death*, 88. Cf. Kellermann, *Auferstanden in den Himmel*, 54–5. William H. Brown ("From Holy War to Holy Martyrdom," in *The Quest for the Kingdom of God: Studies in Honor of George E. Mendenhall*, ed. H. B. Huffmon,

that God "would be reconciled" to his people and not forsake them during an "evil time" in the first letter in the book prior to the epitome in 2:19–15:37. The "evil time" spoken of in 2 Macc 1:5 probably refers to Hellenization on account of the distress that consequently came upon Torah-zealous Jews when apostate Jews revolted against the holy city and embraced Antiochus's Hellenistic policies (2 Macc 1:7–8; 2:17–18).

Before the epitome, the author reminds his fellow Jews in Egypt (to whom he is writing) that God has saved his people from the Greek tyrant, restored temple worship, and he expresses hope that God would soon show his mercy to all Jews scattered throughout the world by gathering them at his holy temple in Judea (2 Macc 2:17–18). The epitome begins with a recounting of how God showed his mercy to the Jews through Judas and his brothers during the Maccabean crisis (2 Macc 2:19–22), and the author suggests he intends to set forth this story by summarizing Jason of Cyrene's five-volume work (2 Macc 2:23). The epitome ends with the author asserting the Hebrews possessed the city of Judea after Judas and his army cut off Nicanor's (a Gentile king's) head and cut out his tongue (2 Macc 15:32–37). Thus, reconciliation with God in 1:5, God's mercy and salvation in 2:18, and God's mercy and salvation in 15:37 frame the martyrological sections of the epitome in 6:18–7:42. Such an arrangement could suggest the author wants to communicate that the reason by which God's reconciliation, mercy, and salvation came to the covenant-community through Judas and his brothers was the faithful martyrs, which the ensuing narrative of 5:1–8:5 supports.

While Antiochus was finishing his second invasion of Egypt in the narrative of 2 Maccabees, he heard Judea was in revolt (2 Macc 5:1–11). He immediately left Egypt to seize Jerusalem (2 Macc 5:11b–14). Antiochus entered the holy temple and profaned it, for he was oblivious to the fact that God was using him to defile the temple on account of his anger with Israel (2 Macc 5:17–18). Just as the temple suffered pollution and judgment because of the nation's sin, it also experienced God's blessings when he pardoned the nation (2 Macc 5:20a; cf. Lev 16:16, 30). 2 Maccabees 5:20b states that God's wrath ended, and the glory of Israel was restored to the nation "by means of the reconciliation of the Great Lord" (2 Macc 8:5; cf. Lev 9:1–10:2).

After the author describes the reversal of the abominations that Antiochus committed against Israel (2 Macc 5:21–6:11), he discusses

---

F. A. Spina, and A. R. Green [Winona Lake, IN: Eisenbrauns, 1983], 287–8) states that "Judas and his men are asking God to accept the present national suffering as sufficient, not only to atone for the nation's sins, but as sufficient to invoke his wrath upon the Syrian armies."

why the Jews suffered by means of Antiochus. He offers this explanation immediately before he writes about the martyrdoms of Eleazar, the mother, and her seven sons (2 Macc 6:18–8:2). In 2 Macc 6:12–17, the author urges his readers not to be discouraged by the calamities God brought against the nation by asserting that he provided the calamities against the nation for her benefit. The author also states that God would soon judge the Gentile nations when they reach the full measure of their sins, but he would not deal with Israel in this way. Instead, God judged Israel through Antiochus, and the martyrdom of some was representative of his divine judgment against the entire nation. The author explains that God neither withdrew his mercy from his people nor forsook them (2 Macc 6:13–16). The author, then, highlights the deaths of the martyrs in 2 Macc 6:18–8:2 to demonstrate how God's mercy was achieved for the nation (2 Macc 5:20; 8:5–7). 2 Maccabees 6:18–8:5 suggests God reveals his mercy to Israel by his reconciliatory acts toward the nation, because after the seventh son promises God's future judgment of Antiochus (2 Macc 7:33), he states that he (just as his brothers) offers his life to God with the prayer that he would be merciful to the nation through their deaths (2 Macc 7:37). His optimistic prayer in 2 Macc 7:37 follows the seventh son's confident assertion in 2 Macc 7:33 that the "Lord will be reconciled to his own servants." Subsequent to the author's presentations of the martyrdoms of Eleazar, the mother, and her seven sons (2 Macc 6:18–7:42), the author immediately discusses the response of the Torah-zealous Jews to the martyrs' deaths.

In 2 Macc 8, Judas Maccabaeus reappears in the narrative. He and other Torah-zealous Jews ask God to be merciful to the martyrs, the temple, and the city (2 Macc 8:2–3). They also pray the Lord would hear the blood of the martyrs, that he would remember the destruction of the innocent babies, that he would remember the blasphemies against his name, and that he would hate all of the evil committed against Israel (2 Macc 8:4). The reconciliation for which the author prays in 2 Macc 1:5, the mercy of which the author speaks in 2 Macc 2:18; 5:20; 6:12–16, and 15:37, the mercy for which the martyrs die in 2 Macc 7:32–38, and the mercy for which Judas prays in 2 Macc 8:1–4 becomes a reality when God is reconciled again to the nation by reversing his wrath away from the Jews against Antiochus and his army (2 Macc 5:1–8:5).

To the contrary, other scholars have argued that effective prayer was the reason the Lord became reconciled once again to the people and to the nation in 2 Maccabees.[32] Indeed, the reconciliation for which the seventh

---

32. Schwartz, *2 Maccabees*, 329.

son asserts that his death and the deaths of his brothers would achieve for the nation becomes a reality for Israel in the narrative after Judas's prayer, and God's glory was again restored to both the temple and the nation through their deaths after Judas's prayer. However, to make Judas's prayer the primary basis upon which God becomes reconciled to Israel in the narrative is too narrow of a reading of 5:1–8:5, because God's reconciliation does not take place in this section until *after* the martyrs die (cf. 2 Macc 5:20–8:5; 4 Macc 17:21–22).

Judas's prayer was effective. But the exegetical question remains: Why is his prayer effective? The narrative suggests the prayer is efficacious because the martyrs died for the nation. Thus, the efficacy of Judas's prayer does not disprove that the martyrs' deaths functioned as Israel's Yom Kippur. In fact, Philo notes prayers were offered at Yom Kippur, along with fasting, to propitiate God (ἱλασκόμενοι τὸν πατέρα τοῦ παντὸς) as the participants asked him to forgive their old sins and to bring new blessings (*Moses* 2:24).

Therefore, the text of 2 Macc 7:32–38 teaches that the martyrs function in the martyrological narratives as representatives of and as substitutes for Israel's sin and that they function as the nation's Yom Kippur for at least six reasons. First, the temple cult was dysfunctional. Second, the seventh son and his brothers suffered and, eventually, died because of the nation's sin (2 Macc 7:32; cf. Lev 16:3, 5, 6, 9, 21, 25, 34). Third, the martyrs offered their lives to God in death to achieve reconciliation for the nation (2 Macc 7:37; cf. Lev 16:30). Fourth, the seventh son asserted God would again be reconciled to the nation through his death (2 Macc 7:37b; cf. Lev 16:30). Fifth, the seventh son prayed God would deliver the nation from his wrath through his death and through the deaths of his brothers (2 Macc 7:38; cf. Lev 16:30).[33] Sixth, God was reconciled to the nation once again by means of the martyrs' deaths (2 Macc 5:1–8:5; cf. Lev 16:30).

IV. Jewish Martyrdom, God's Mercy, Satisfaction, and Purification in 4 Maccabees

That the martyrs functioned as representatives of, as substitutes for, and in the place of Israel's Yom Kippur in the martyrological narratives is even stronger in 4 Maccabees than in 2 Maccabees because of the explicit cultic language applied to the martyrs' deaths. In 4 Maccabees, the author

---

33. Similarly van Henten, *Maccabean Martyrs*, 143–4. Against Williams, *Jesus' Death*, 83–8.

describes the martyrdom of Eleazar in 4 Macc 6 and offers his concluding interpretation regarding the function of their deaths for the nation in 4 Macc 17:21–22. The author describes Eleazar as a scribe of high rank (2 Macc 6:18), from a priestly family, and an expert in the law (4 Macc 5:4, 35). Antiochus urges him to disobey the Torah and eat swine (2 Macc 6:18; 4 Macc 5:6). Instead, Eleazar voluntarily chooses death. As a result, Antiochus severely tortures him (4 Macc 6:1–8). As he bleeds profusely from the scourges that tore his flesh and from being pierced in his side with a spear (4 Macc 6:6), Eleazar prays God would use his death to achieve three benefits for Israel: (1) mercy (4 Macc 6:28), (2) satisfaction (4 Macc 6:28), and (3) purification (4 Macc 6:29).

1. In the face of death, Eleazar urges God in 4 Macc 6:28 to be merciful to Israel through his death (ἵλεως γενοῦ τῷ ἔθνει σου) (2 Macc 4:1–6:31; 4 Macc 5:4–6:40). Numerous texts throughout 4 Maccabees support the view that Eleazar's request for mercy is a request for deliverance from God's wrath (2 Macc 4:16–17; 6:12–17; 4 Macc 17:21–22), a wrath that he pours out on Israel in the narrative through Antiochus in order to chasten his people (1 Macc 1:1–64; 2 Macc 6:12–17; 7:32). In 4 Macc 4:19–20, Jason, the high priest, changed the nation's way of life from Torah observance to compliance with the Greek way of life so that he both constructed a gymnasium in Judea and abolished the care of the temple (καὶ ἐξεδιήτησεν τὸ ἔθνος καὶ ἐξεπολίτευσεν ἐπὶ πᾶσαν παρανομίαν ὥστε μὴ μόνον ἐπ' αὐτῇ τῇ ἄκρᾳ τῆς πατρίδος ἡμῶν γυμνάσιον κατασκευάσαι ἀλλὰ καὶ καταλῦσαι τὴν τοῦ ἱεροῦ κηδεμονίαν). As a result, the Lord's divine anger caused Antiochus to make war on Israel (ἐφ' οἷς ἀγανακτήσασα ἡ θεία δίκη αὐτὸν αὐτοῖς τὸν Ἀντίοχον ἐπολέμωσεν) (4 Macc 4:21). Hence, Antiochus issued a decree that anyone practicing Judaism would die (δόγμα ἔθετο ὅπως εἴ τινες αὐτῶν φάνοιεν τῷ πατρίῳ πολιτευόμενοι νόμῳ θάνοιεν) (4 Macc 4:23).

4 Maccabees 6:28 supports the view that Eleazar's prayer urges God to use his death to provide salvation for Israel from God's wrath through Antiochus. He asks God to be satisfied with the martyrs' judgment for the nation (ἀρκεσθεὶς τῇ ἡμετέρᾳ ὑπὲρ αὐτῶν δίκῃ).[34] With this request, Eleazar expresses that he offers his life to God as both a representative of and a substitute for Israel to achieve God's mercy, and he hopes that his provision would satisfy God's wrath against the nation. This interpretation

---

34. For other possible substitutionary uses of ὑπὲρ in atonement texts, see LXX Exod 21:20; Lev 26:25; Deut 32:41, 43; Mic 7:9; Wis 1:8; 14:31; 18:11; cf. 1 Macc 5:32; 2 Macc 1:26; 3:32; Rom 5:6–11; 8:32; 1 Cor 1:13; 11:24; 15:3; 2 Cor 5:14–15, 21; Gal 1:4; 2:20–21; 3:13; 1 Thess 5:10.

seems correct for at least three reasons. First, Eleazar offers this petition to God while he faces his judgment for the people and as a representative of the people by means of Antiochus's persecution (4 Macc 6:28; 17:22; cf. 1 Macc 6:60; Ps 68:32; Jer 18:4; Dan 4:2). Second, judgment (δίκη) consistently refers to divine judgment throughout 4 Maccabees (4 Macc 4:13, 21; 8:14, 22; 9:9, 15, 32; 11:3; 12:12; 18:22).[35] Third, the author applies the cultic language of blood to Eleazar in 4 Macc 6:29 to refer to the cleansing power of Eleazar's death for the nation.[36]

Since Eleazar's first request, that God would be merciful to the nation (ἵλεως γενοῦ τῷ ἔθνει σου), is the main clause in the sentence ἵλεως γενοῦ τῷ ἔθνει σου ἀρκεσθεὶς τῇ ἡμετέρᾳ ὑπὲρ αὐτῶν δίκῃ, the adverbial participial clause (ἀρκεσθεὶς τῇ ἡμετέρᾳ ὑπὲρ αὐτῶν δίκῃ) is a continuation of the first request in 4 Macc 6:28a and likewise takes the tone of a prayer of entreaty, as the first part of the prayer. Other uses of the adjective ἵλεως elsewhere in 4 Maccabees support that in 4 Macc 6:28, Eleazar asks God to accept his death as the means through which he would save the nation from his judgment. For example, (1) prior to Antiochus's torture of the seven sons in 4 Macc 8:14, he urges them to provide mercy for themselves by eating unclean meat. Obedience to Antiochus would have ensured their salvation from his judgment. (2) In 4 Macc 9:24, as Antiochus inflicts torture upon one of the seven sons, he exhorts his brothers to follow his example of godliness and he states through his godliness God's mercy would save the nation. (3) After the seventh son refuses to obey Antiochus in 4 Macc 12:4–16, he hurls himself into Antiochus's fire that Antiochus used to threaten him and the other brothers. As he entered the fire, the seventh son prays God would be merciful (ἵλεως) to save the nation through his death (4 Macc 12:17).

2. 4 Maccabees 6:29 states Eleazar asks God to make his blood to be Israel's purification (καθάρσιον αὐτῶν ποίησον τὸ ἐμὸν αἷμα).[37] Since Eleazar has already prayed that God would bring mercy to Israel and end his wrath against Israel through his death, Eleazar's request in 4 Macc 6:29 suggests he urges God to make his death a substitute for the nation's violation of Torah to accomplish national purification and salvation. Eleazar's request likewise urges God to let his death function as Israel's Yom Kippur. The substitutionary nature of Eleazar's request is apparent

35. Cf. 2 Macc 8:11, 13.
36. For other connections in the LXX between God's mercy and deliverance from judgment, see Exod 32:12, 33; Num 14; Deut 21:1–8; 2 Chr 6:25–27, 39; 7:14; Amos 7:2; Jer 5:1, 7; 27:20; 38:34; 43:3.
37. See also 4 Macc 1:11; LXX Dan 3:38–40.

when he asks God to make his αἷμα to be Israel's purification (2 Macc 5:17–18; 6:15; 7:32; 12:42; 4 Macc 5:19; 17:21; cf. Lev 16:16, 30), and the function of his death as the Yom Kippur for the nation is set forth with the words purification and blood and in 17:21–22 when the author states the martyrs died propitiatory deaths to purify the homeland and to save the nation with language and concepts straight from Lev 16.

The blood of the animals in Lev 16 served to purify the nation from all of its sins and to provide salvation from the looming judgment of YHWH if Yom Kippur was not performed in compliance with Torah (cf. Lev 9:1–16:34). Eleazar asks God to use his blood to be Israel's Yom Kippur by granting the nation mercy and satisfaction as a result of his blood (4 Macc 6:28–29). 4 Maccabees 17:21–22 in fact states that the martyrs propitiated God, saved the nation, and accomplished national purification for the homeland.

As I have argued elsewhere,[38] besides 4 Macc 6:29, καθάρσιον occurs nowhere else in the LXX. However, καθάρισμος is a cognate of καθάρσιον. The latter occurs in the LXX and in the New Testament to refer both to the purification of Israel and to Christians. In both testaments, one receives purification through cultic blood (Exod 29:36; 30:10; cf. 2 Pet. 1:9), through ritual cleansing (Lev 14:32; 15:13; cf. Mark 1:44; Luke 2:22; 5:14; John 2:6; 3:25), through God's forgiveness (Num 14:18), through the cleansing of holy utensils (1 Chr 23:28), through the purification of the temple (2 Macc 1:18; 2:16, 19; 10:5), or through one's piety (4 Macc 7:6). The author's presentation of Eleazar as an expert in the law, his priestly status, and his priestly familial heritage in the narratives of 2 and 4 Maccabees (2 Macc 6:18; 4 Macc 5:4, 35) suggests that his comments about his death in 4 Macc 6:28–29 are overtly cultic.[39] Moreover, since the narrative of 4 Maccabees states that Antiochus abolished the sacrificial system, killed anyone who yielded allegiance to the Torah (1 Macc 1:41–64; 2 Macc 5:4, 35), controlled the temple, and prohibited compliance with the Torah (2 Macc 1:5; 7:32–38; 4 Macc 6:28–29; 17:20–21), Eleazar's request likely, then, urges God in 4 Macc 6:28–29 to use his death and the deaths of the other martyrs to substitute for the absence of temple sacrifices, which would have included the Yom Kippur ritual since Antiochus forbade all sacrifices, so that the nation would corporately experience God's cleansing of forgiveness through the martyrs as the Yom Kippur sacrifices.

---

38. Williams, *Maccabean Martyr Traditions*.
39. See also 2 Macc 6:18; 4 Macc 5:4, 35.

3. In the final part of his prayer in 4 Macc 6:29b, Eleazar asks God to receive his death as a ransom for the nation (καὶ ἀντίψυχον αὐτῶν λαβὲ τὴν ἐμὴν ψυχήν). The term ἀντίψυχον ("ransom") in 4 Macc 6:29b likewise occurs in 4 Macc 17:21. There the term suggests the martyrs' deaths purified and saved the nation, because the author connects ἀντίψυχον with both the nation's purification from sin and with its salvation and because the author identifies the nation's death as a propitiatory (καὶ διὰ τοῦ αἵματος τῶν εὐσεβῶν ἐκείνων καὶ τοῦ ἱλαστηρίου τοῦ θανάτου αὐτῶν ἡ θεία πρόνοια τὸν Ἰσραηλ προκακωθέντα διέσωσεν). Furthermore, 4 Macc 6:29b reveals an explicit lexical connection with Yom Kippur with the compound ἀντίψυχον, which occurs as two different words (ἀντὶ τῆς ψυχῆς) in LXX Lev 17:11 in a context where the author discusses Yom Kippur (Lev 16) and the atoning function of blood on behalf of one's life (Lev 17:11).[40]

The restriction not to eat blood in LXX Lev 17:11 due to its redemptive effect for the soul (ἀντὶ τῆς ψυχῆς) includes the blood that atones for sin at Yom Kippur, for in Lev 16–17 YHWH's prohibition not to eat blood emerges to highlight the importance of the function of the animal's blood offered as atonement. This point is supported by YHWH's statement in Lev 16–17 that the blood makes atonement (Lev 16:5–20; 17:12). Similarly, the blood of the martyrs in 4 Macc 6:28–29 and 17:21–22 accomplishes atonement and thereby functions as the nation's Yom Kippur, for the martyrs' blood achieves the same effect as the animals' blood during the Yom Kippur ritual: namely, national purification and salvation (cf. Lev 16:5–34; 4 Macc 17:21–22). The narrator states this in a straightforward way in 4 Macc 17:21–22 with his assertion that the martyrs purified the homeland by means of their deaths (τὴν πατρίδα καθαρισθῆναι ὥσπερ ἀντίψυχον γεγονότας τῆς τοῦ ἔθνους ἁμαρτίας καὶ διὰ τοῦ αἵματος τῶν εὐσεβῶν ἐκείνων καὶ τοῦ ἱλαστηρίου τοῦ θανάτου αὐτῶν ἡ θεία πρόνοια τὸν Ἰσραηλ προκακωθέντα διέσωσεν).

A function of ἀντίψυχον in 4 Macc 6:29 and 17:21, then, is to communicate that the blood of the martyrs was the required price paid to achieve both Israel's purification and salvation (cf. 4 Macc 17:21–22), just as the sacrificial ritual on Yom Kippur required the blood of the animal to cover/ atone for the sins of the people (Lev 16).[41] In fact, 4 Macc 17:21 asserts

---

40. So Douglas A. Campbell, *The Deliverance of God: An Apocalyptic Rereading of Justification in Paul* (Grand Rapids: Eerdmans, 2009), 650–1.

41. For a different emphasis, see Rajak, *The Jewish Dialogue with Rome and Greece*, 109–11. She argues that the primary function of the ἀντίψυχον in 4 Maccabees "was to establish a connection between persecution, in the Diaspora, and

that the homeland was purified "just as" (ὥσπερ) the martyrs became a ransom for the sin of the nation.⁴² Williams, followed by Seeley, argued that the adverb ὥσπερ in 4 Macc 17:21 supports the view that the author of 4 Maccabees "metaphorically" means that God received the martyrs' deaths "just as" (ὥσπερ) he received sacrifices since he deemed their deaths as an act of expiation.⁴³ Williams concludes the adverb does not support expiation.⁴⁴

However, 4 Macc 17:22 speaks against this reading since the author states that "through the blood of these godly ones" (i.e. the martyrs) and "through their propitiatory death," God saved the nation from his wrath (καὶ διὰ τοῦ αἵματος τῶν εὐσεβῶν ἐκείνων καὶ τοῦ ἱλαστηρίου τοῦ θανάτου αὐτῶν ἡ θεία πρόνοια τὸν Ισραηλ προκακωθέντα διέσωσεν). Consequently, the author of 4 Maccabees appears to be echoing Lev 16–17, especially the feast of atonement and the Yom Kippur ritual, when he discusses the martyrs' deaths since he repeatedly uses similar cultic language from Lev 16–17 to describe the function of the martyrs' deaths for the nation in a cultic setting without a functional temple.⁴⁵

4. The author of 4 Maccabees interprets the martyrs' deaths to be both sacrificial in nature and a saving event for the nation in 4 Macc 17:21–22 (καὶ τὸν τύραννον τιμωρηθῆναι καὶ τὴν πατρίδα καθαρισθῆναι ὥσπερ ἀντίψυχον γεγονότας τῆς τοῦ ἔθνους ἁμαρτίας καὶ διὰ τοῦ αἵματος τῶν εὐσεβῶν ἐκείνων καὶ τοῦ ἱλαστηρίου τοῦ θανάτου αὐτῶν ἡ θεία πρόνοια τὸν Ισραηλ προκακωθέντα διέσωσεν). He describes their deaths by using the phrase τοῦ ἱλαστηρίου τοῦ θανάτου.⁴⁶ The term ἱλαστήριον occurs in 4 Macc 17:22 with other cultic vocabulary (e.g. "sin" [ἁμαρτίας], "blood" [διὰ τοῦ αἵματος], and "to purify" [καθαρισθῆναι]), a cultic concept [ἀντίψυχον γεγονότας τῆς τοῦ ἔθνους ἁμαρτίας]), and a soteriological term (διέσωσεν). Additionally, the cultic concept of consecration occurs in

---

victory, in Palestine, and to bridge the awkward geographical disjunction between two locations."

42. Williams, *Jesus' Death*, 177–9.
43. Ibid.
44. Ibid.
45. Against Kraus, *Der Tod Jesu als Heiligtumsweihe*, 38–9. For further evidence, see 4 Macc 6:28–29; 7:8; 17:10, 21–22; 18:4; cf. Exod 33:12–34:9; As. Mos. 9:6–7; 10:2–10; 2 Macc 5:20–7:38.
46. In 4 Macc 17:22, a major textual variant exists pertaining to the function of ἱλαστήριον. For a discussion, see H. J. Klauck, *4 Makkabäerbuch*, JSHRZ 3.6 (Gütersloh: Gerd Mohn, 1989), 753, van Henten, "The Tradition-Historical Background of Rom. 3:25," 101–28, esp. 123, and deSilva, *4 Maccabees*, 250.

4. Representation and Substitution

4 Macc 17:19–20 (καὶ γάρ φησιν ὁ Μωυσῆς καὶ πάντες οἱ ἡγιασμένοι ὑπὸ τὰς χεῖράς σου καὶ οὗτοι οὖν ἁγιασθέντες διὰ θεὸν τετίμηνται οὐ μόνον ταύτῃ τῇ τιμῇ ἀλλὰ καὶ τῷ δι' αὐτοὺς τὸ ἔθνος ἡμῶν τοὺς πολεμίους μὴ ἐπικρατῆσαι). The idea of the consecration of the martyrs in 4 Macc 17:19–20 joins with the other cultic concepts mentioned above to make the context of the martyrs' deaths overtly cultic and similar to Yom Kippur.

4 Maccabees 17:22 and Rom 3:25 are the only places in available literature where an author applies ἱλαστηρίον to the death of Torah-observant Jews in a cultic context for the soteriological benefit of non-Torah-observant sinners. The term ἱλαστηρίον refers to the mercy seat in contexts in the LXX where priests atoned for sin through the sacrifice of blood (Lev 16:14–15). God commands Israel to put the ἱλαστηρίον above the ark of the covenant in the holy of holies, the place where only the high priest could enter (Exod 25:17–20; 37:6). God commands the priest to make atonement on the ἱλαστηρίον to provide cleansing for sin (Exod 25:18–22; 31:7; 35:12; 37:6–8; Lev 16:14–15), and God appears above the ἱλαστηρίον to show his acceptance of atonement (Exod 25:22; Lev 16:2; Num 7:89). The term also occurs in LXX Ezek 43:14–20 in reference to a place at which atonement takes place by the pouring out of blood.[47]

---

47. The occurrence of ἱλαστηρίον in the context of 4 Macc 17:21–22 is certainly cultic for the above reasons, but also since the term itself is part of a semantic family of ἱλας-words that often occur in cultic contexts in the LXX that speak of atoning for sin, since these words often translate from the Hebrew root, which often means "to atone," and since some form of ἱλαστηρίον occurs in Leviticus's prescriptions regarding Yom Kippur (cf. LXX Lev 16:2, 13–15). I am not asserting that the ἱλας words-group always translates from the Hebrew that means "to atone" (cf. LXX Exod 32:14; 2 Kgs 21:3; 1 Chr 6:34; 2 Chr 29:24; Ps 105:30; Ezek 43:14–20; Zech 7:2; 8:22). I am not affirming that the ἱλας word-group always conveys the idea of atoning sacrifice (cf. LXX Exod 32:14; Prov 16:14). For example, ἐξιλάσασθαι is often cultic and often refers to the cleansing that takes place when sins are atoned (LXX Exod 30:10; Lev 1:4; 4:20, 26, 31, 35; 5:6, 10, 13, 16, 18, 26; 6:23; 7:7; 16:29; Num 5:8; 6:11; 8:12, 19, 21; 15:25, 28; 17:11, 12; 28:22, 30; 29:5, 11; 31:50; 1 Kgs 3:14; 2 Kgs 2:13; 1 Chr 6:34; 2 Chr 29:24; 30:18; 2 Esd 20:34; Ps 105:30; Ezek 43:20, 22; 45:17; Sir 3:3, 30; 5:6; 20:28; 28:5; 34:19; 45:16, 23). However, the one occurrence of ἱλάσθη in the LXX is not cultic, and it is altogether void of sacrificial ideas (LXX Exod 32:14). In LXX Exod 32:14, ἐξιλάσασθαι translates from a root that means "to repent" and highlights YHWH's mercy to Israel in spite of the nation's idolatry. Rather, my point is simply that ἱλας words often occur in cultic texts and often speak of sacrificial atonement when this word group occurs with explicit cultic vocabulary, as it does in 4 Macc 17:21–22. Thus, 4 Macc 17:21–22 speaks of the martyrs' deaths

In his unpublished doctoral thesis, focusing on Rom 3:25, Daniel P. Bailey argues that ἱλαστήριον in 4 Macc 17:22 and in Rom 3:25 have distinct meanings.[48] The author of 4 Macc 17:22 uses the term in a way consistent with its occurrence in the Hellenistic world (i.e. propitiatory), but Paul uses the term in a way consistent with its occurrence in the biblical world (i.e. mercy seat). According to Bailey, to argue that ἱλαστήριον refers to sacrificial atonement in 4 Macc 17:22 is a mistake. After reviewing the evidence in the relevant Hellenistic literature that supports reading the term as propitiatory, Bailey argues that various inscriptions in the Hellenistic world affirm that ἱλαστήρια were offered either to propitiate the wrath of offended deities or to gain their favor.[49] He also argues that τηρίον words do not regularly refer to actions, but to places.[50] Bailey concludes that ἱλαστήριον in 4 Macc 17:22 as it relates to the martyrs' deaths should "be sought against a non-sacrificial background."[51] According to Bailey, 4 Maccabees nowhere states that the martyrs died as atoning sacrifices for Israel's sin.

Bailey's doctoral thesis is a careful and thorough contribution to scholarship. To my knowledge, it provides the most extensive lexical analysis of ἱλαστήριον based on ancient texts and ancient inscriptions in English-speaking scholarship. Bailey's concern, though, is exclusively a lexical one. His work seeks to offer a better translation of ἱλαστήριον in Rom 3:25 by analyzing every ancient text and inscription that has lexical affinity to it. I agree with his argument that the occurrence of the same term in different texts (i.e. 4 Macc 17:22 and Rom 3:25) does not necessitate that the term should be translated the same way in both texts. Nevertheless, Bailey's thesis and arguments (if I correctly understand them) seem to pit his lexical analysis against the context within which ἱλαστήριον occurs.

---

with specific sacrificial/cultic language that closely resembles the Old Testament cult and that echoes Yom Kippur, especially since 4 Macc 17:21–22 states that the martyrs brought divine favor to Israel via blood and purification when they died for the nation.

48. Daniel Peter Bailey, "Jesus as the Mercy Seat: The Semantics and Theology of Paul's Use of Hilasterion in Romans 3:25" (PhD diss., University of Cambridge, 1999), 5–12, esp. 11–12. I wish to thank Dr Bailey for e-mailing me a copy of his dissertation.

49. For the above analysis and summary of Bailey's view, see deSilva, *4 Maccabees*, 250–1, who cites Bailey ("Jesus as the Mercy Seat," 31–75).

50. Finlan, *Background and Content*, 200–203, who cites Bailey.

51. The above quote comes from deSilva (*4 Maccabees*, 251), who summarizes Bailey's view.

Therefore, his analysis prevents the term from conveying its contextual theme.[52] In my view, regardless of how one translates ἱλαστήριον in 4 Macc 17:22, since the term occurs in the same context as other atonement vocabulary and concepts found in Lev 16–17 (e.g. judgment, purification of the nation, ransom, vicarious death, sin, and blood), ἱλαστήριον in 4 Macc 17:22 at least alludes to the Yom Kippur ritual; it at least suggests that the martyrs' deaths are functioning as Israel's Yom Kippur, and it at least suggests that the martyrs die in the narratives as representatives of and as substitutes for Israel.[53]

4 Maccabees 6:28–29 speaks of the martyrs' deaths in the context of blood, purification, and ransom. Likewise, 4 Macc 17:21–22 speaks of the martyrs' deaths in the context of purification for the nation, ransom, blood, and salvation.[54] The author's reference to the consecration of the martyrs for God in 4 Macc 17:20 (ἁγιασθέντες διὰ θεὸν) and the participle προκακωθέντα in reference to the mistreatment of the nation in 4 Macc 17:22 recall the imagery of setting apart the animals for atonement and terminology of the afflictions at Yom Kippur (cf. LXX Lev 16:29–32).[55] Therefore, the contextual evidence in 4 Macc 6:28–29 and 17:21–22 challenges the conclusion that ἱλαστήριον in 4 Maccabees should be understood as a pagan reference to a non-cultic/non-sacrificial background. I suggest 4 Macc 6:28–29 and 17:21–22 together affirm that the martyrs offered themselves to God as representatives of the nation, as substitutes for the nation, and the martyrs functioned as Israel's Yom Kippur in the narrative of 4 Maccabees.[56]

---

52. For a similar critique, see also Finlan, *Background and Content*, 200.

53. Similarly, Daniel Stökl Ben Ezra, *The Impact of Yom Kippur on Early Christianity: The Day of Atonement from Second Temple Judaism to the Fifth Century*, WUNT 153 (Tübingen: Mohr Siebeck, 2003), 115. deSilva (*4 Maccabees*, 250–1) argues that the author uses the cultic language from the Yom Kippur ritual to describe the effect of the martyrs' deaths.

54. deSilva, *4 Maccabees*, 249–50.

55. Ben Ezra, *The Impact of Yom Kippur on Early Christianity*, 116.

56. deSilva, *4 Maccabees*, 202–3. Similarly, Marinus de Jonge, "Jesus' Death for Others and the Death of the Maccabean Martyrs," in *Text and Testimony: Essays on New Testament and Apocryphal Literature in Honour of A. F. J. Klijn*, ed. T. Baarda, A. Hilhorst, G. P. Luttikhuizen, and A. S. van der Woude (Kampen: Uitgeversmaatschappij J. H. Kok, 1988), 142–51, esp. 150–1. For comments about the righteous described with similar language as in LXX Lev 16:24, see Wis 2:11–3:6; 14:16; As. Mos. 9.1–10.10.

V. Deuteronomy, Jewish Martyrology, Representation, Substitution, and Galatians 3:13

In this section, I argue Gal 3:10–14 has exegetical points of contact with Jewish martyrology. I attempt to show that both traditions apply Deuteronomy to Torah-observant Jews who became accursed for those under Torah's curse to achieve their soteriological benefit. After Antiochus killed Eleazar in 2 Macc 6, he compelled a mother and her seven sons to eat unlawful foods (2 Macc 7:1). They were faced with tortures and punishment (just as Eleazar) if they disobeyed, but the seven sons and their mother rebelled against Antiochus. As a result, each suffered torture and death (2 Macc 7:2–42). As the mother exhorts her seventh son to trust God and suffer martyrdom (2 Macc 7:28–29), he affirms the Jewish people "suffered because of their own sins" (2 Macc 7:32; cf. 2 Macc 5:17). The seventh son's remarks in 2 Macc 7:32 echo the cry of Daniel's three friends in LXX Dan 3:28–29 and in 3:37, who likewise confess that Israel suffered "because" of its sin of Torah-disobedience (2 Macc 7:32; cf. 2 Macc 5:17; 7:18). The seventh son's confession reveals an important connection with Deut 27 and 28 and Gal 3:10–14. In Gal 3:13, Paul presents Christ as the solution to the problem of the curse of the law for Jews and Gentiles (cf. 3:10) with language that is quite similar to the Jewish martyrological traditions. I begin my analysis in this section with a discussion of Deuteronomy.

1. Deuteronomy 27 and 28 state that if Israel disobeyed Torah in the land, they would be cursed but if they obeyed, they would be blessed. As I discussed earlier, Deut 27:26 summarizes the curse pronouncements of Deut 27:9–25, and the former text reiterates to Israel the importance of their obedience in the land by stating "cursed is the one who will not uphold the words of this Torah to do them." According to Deut 27:15–26 and 28:15–62, these curses would overcome Israel while they lived in the land, and according to 28:64–68, these curses would enslave them to other nations and drive them out of the land that the Lord promised to give to them if they obeyed Torah. Deuteronomy forcefully emphasizes obedience to the stipulations results in long life in the land (Deut 5:33; 8:1; 11:8, 26–32) and that the Lord's curses will stick to Israel "until he destroys" them from entering the land to inherit it (28:21). These curses would come against the entire nation even if some within the community obeyed, as supported by Israel's subsequent exiles from the land.[57]

---

57. Wright's view (*Climax*, 145) that "no Jew who failed to keep Torah, and knew that he or she was failing to keep Torah, needed to languish for long under the

2. The martyrs suffered the Deuteronomic curses of the community's disobedience in 2 Maccabees. The seventh son's assertion in 2 Macc 7:32, that "we suffer because of our sins" and in 7:33 that God "will again be reconciled to his servants," are Deuteronomic statements. They affirm Torah-observant martyrs suffer along with the nation by association with the nation.[58] Neither 2 nor 4 Maccabees states that the martyrs themselves actually violated Torah. The martyrs were members of YHWH's covenant community for which they suffered (cf. 2 Macc 7:16, 30, 30–32, 38). The narrative calls Antiochus the adversary of the Hebrews instead of the adversary of the martyrs (2 Macc 7:31). The seventh son martyred utters these words as a representative of the nation, supported by the fact that he asserts "we" suffer for "our own" sins, even though 2 Maccabees states nowhere the martyrs violated Torah. The martyrological narratives follow statements about the positive role of suffering in the lives of the Lord's covenant-people (2 Macc 6:12–17). 2 Maccabees 7:16 suggests Antiochus believed the death of the seven sons proved God had forsaken the Jewish people. The martyrs suffered with and for the nation by association, although they were Torah observant. In this respect, 2 Maccabees' presentation of the martyrs' suffering and death echoes Israel's antecedent Deuteronomic history, because the narrator presents the martyrs as fulfilling the Deuteronomic curses set forth in Deut 27–28. This is supported by the blessings and curse motif in 2 Maccabees (see my Chapter 3). 2 Maccabees' appeal to Deut 32 in 2 Macc 7:33 supports this interpretation.

Deuteronomy 32 is Moses's song of praise to the Lord for his faithful provision to Israel and a promise of Israel's sure judgment if she disobeys the Lord. In LXX Deut 32:36, the text states the Lord will judge his people and show compassion to his servants (ὅτι κρινεῖ κύριος τὸν λαὸν αὐτοῦ καὶ ἐπὶ τοῖς δούλοις αὐτοῦ παρακληθήσεται εἶδεν γὰρ παραλελυμένους αὐτοὺς καὶ ἐκλελοιπότας ἐν ἐπαγωγῇ καὶ παρειμένους). 2 Maccabees 7:33 applies LXX Deut 32:36 to the martyrs by stating the Lord "will be reconciled again by means of his servants" (καὶ πάλιν καταλλαγήσεται τοῖς ἑαυτοῦ δούλοις). Deuteronomy 32:36 accentuates *what* God will do for his people (namely, show them mercy) (cf. 2 Macc 7:6), but the seventh son's prayer in 2 Macc 7:33 stresses *the means* by which God

---

awful threat of either exclusion from the covenant people or, for that matter, eternal damnation" does not take into account the severity of the threats of exile and death for those who violate any component of Torah.

58. So van Henten, *Maccabean Martyrs*, 137–8. Van Henten (ibid., 137 n. 51) astutely points out the verb translated as "to sin occurs only in 2 Macc. 7:18 and 10:4, where it also refers to the sinning of the people as a body."

will show mercy (namely, through his servants, the faithful martyrs). The book's comments about reconciliation in 2 Macc 1:5 and in 8:29 support the view that 2 Macc 7:33 presents the martyrs as a means by which God would end the Deuteronomic curses and be reconciled again to the nation, for reconciliation in 2 Macc 1:5 and in 8:29 concern reconciliation between the Lord and his people and because reconciliation in these texts frames the seventh son's remarks about reconciliation in 7:33 (cf. 2 Macc 1:5; 7:33; 8:29).

3. Texts in 4 Maccabees likewise apply Deuteronomy to the Jewish martyrs. 4 Maccabees develops the theme of martyrdom to defend the thesis that religious reason has absolute mastery over one's passions (4 Macc 1:1). 4 Maccabees 4:19–21 states that after the high priest led the nation away from Torah, the Lord became angry and used Antiochus to wage war against Israel. The elaborate discussions of the martyrdoms of Eleazar, the mother, and her seven sons in 5:1–12:19 and the narrator's comments regarding the efficacy of the martyrs' deaths in 17:21–22 suggest God displayed the curses of Deuteronomy by means of both Jewish expulsion from and death in the land, both of which Deuteronomy promises to all who disobey Torah (Deut 21:22, 26; 28:21; 30:15–20). LXX Daniel 3 has this same Deuteronomic principle since Daniel and his three friends are in exile precisely because of the failure of some within the covenant community to obey Torah (cf. LXX Dan 3:1–90).

4. In Gal 3:10–14, Paul applies Deuteronomy to Jesus in a way similar to the martyrological narratives to fit his exegetical, theological, and polemical purposes. First, similar to the Jewish martyrological narratives, Paul applies Deuteronomy to a Torah-observant Jew who suffered the curse of Torah for those under Torah's curse when he states "Christ redeemed us from the curse of the law by becoming a curse for us, so that we would receive the blessing of Abraham, so that we would receive the Spirit by faith" (Gal 3:13–14; cf. 2 Macc 7:33; 4 Macc 6:28–29; 17:21–22). Second, Paul appeals to Deut 21:23 and 27:26 in Gal 3:13 by stating "cursed is everyone who hangs upon a tree." This statement is the third time in 3:10–14 that Paul appeals to Deuteronomy. He appeals to Deut 27:26 and 28:58 earlier when he states in Gal 3:10 that a curse comes to all who do not obey Torah. Scholars fiercely debate Paul's use of Deuteronomy in Gal 3:10 and 3:13,[59] but the point I want to emphasize for my thesis is that Paul applies Deuteronomy to Jesus (a Torah-observant

---

59. For example, see Wright, *Climax*, 144–51; de Boer, *Galatians*, 197–216; Moo, *Galatians*, 201–16.

Jew) to support the view that Jesus's death (and no other) ends Torah's curse for all (Jews and Gentiles) under it, just as the Jewish martyrological narratives apply Deuteronomy to the martyrs (Torah-observant Jews) to show that the martyrs' deaths (and no others) end Torah's curse only for Jews under it.

5. Similar to the Jewish martyrological narratives, Paul presents Jesus's death (a Torah-observant Jew) as a representation in Gal 3:13 with Deuteronomic language in order to advance his exegetical, theological, and polemical purposes in Gal 3:10–14. The martyrs suffered the Deuteronomic curses because of the nation's Torah-disobedience, but the martyrological narratives emphasize the martyrs were faithful to Torah even unto death (2 Macc 5:1–8:5; 4 Macc 6:1–17:22). Their suffering was Deuteronomic: that is, judgment by association with those who violated Torah. The sins of some within the nation brought judgment against the martyrs, but the martyrs' steadfast devotion to Torah brought salvation and reconciliation to the nation (2 Macc 5:1–8:5; 4 Macc 6:28–29; 17:21–22).

Likewise, Paul states in Gal 3:10 that Torah brings a curse upon those under Torah, but Gal 3:13 states Jesus (a Torah-observant Jew) suffered the curse of Torah for those under its curse by taking upon himself their curse. Neither the Jewish martyrological narratives nor Paul in Galatians suggest that the martyrs (the Jewish martyrological narratives) or Jesus (Galatians) disobeyed Torah. In the narratives of 2 and 4 Maccabees, the Torah-observant martyrs suffered with the people because they identified with the non-Torah-observant nation (2 Macc 7:32–38; 4 Macc 6:28–29; 17:21–22). Paul asserts that although Jesus was born under the law's domain (Gal 4:4) and cursed by the law (Gal 3:13), he was not a minister of sin (Gal 2:17). Consequently, he was able to deliver those under Torah's jurisdiction from the present evil age (Gal 1:4) and to redeem them from Torah's curse (Gal 3:13; 4:5), because of his death for those under its curse (Gal 1:4; 3:13; 4:5).[60]

The representative function of the martyrs' deaths in the Jewish martyrological narratives is evident by their guilt by association with the Torah-disobedient nation and by their death for the nation's disobedience (instead of a death for their individual transgressions) (cf.

---

60. This point of comparison by no means intends to make an ontological equivalence between the martyrs and Jesus. Rather, the intent here is simply to note that these texts give either the explicit impression that the martyrs (2 and 4 Maccabees) or the implicit impression that Jesus (Galatians) obeyed Torah. Both explicitly state that both died for those who were under the curse of the law.

2 Macc 7:32–38; 4 Macc 6:28–29; 17:21–22; LXX Dan 3:1–90).[61] Paul's interpretation of Jesus's death in Gal 3:13 presents Jesus both as a representative of and a substitute for those under Torah's curse to deliver them from it in that he specifically suggests Jesus's death delivers both Jews and Gentiles from this curse and that it gives to them the Abrahamic blessing of the Spirit by faith.

First, Paul asserts in Gal 3:13 the means by which Christ redeemed the "us" from Torah's curse was "by becoming a curse for us." Paul has already established in Gal 3:10 Torah-subscribers are under Torah's curse in the present age. Paul emphasizes this by his urgent insistence throughout the letter that the Galatians should not turn away from his gospel (Gal 1:6–9; 2:15–5:2). He also emphasizes that those "from works of law" are under a curse because it is part of the present evil age (cf. 1:4), prioritizes human agency (3:12), imprisons all people under sin (3:22) and enslaves them under the elements of the world (4:3), and because they disobey its demands, a point which his citations of Deut 27:26 and 28:58 may imply. In Gal 3:11, he continues by interpreting Hab 2:4 to mean life comes by faith and not by keeping Torah. In Gal 3:12, citing Lev 18:5, he provides the reason for his assertion in 3:11 that the law justifies no one: namely, the law promises life only to the one who obeys its demands. Thus, in Gal 3:11, Paul cites Hab 2:4 to emphasize the importance of faith in Christ and to contrast faith with works of law. In Gal 3:12, he cites Lev 18:5, which promises that the doers of the law receive not its curse but the blessing/promise of life. But, in Gal 3:10, he begins his argument, saying those of works of law are under its curse. In Gal 3:12, Paul's argument against Torah escalates, for he militates against any form of Torah allegiance by saying, "the law is not from faith, but the one who does them will live by them." All people under the law are under a curse, but the reason those under the curse of the law escape its curse is because "Christ died to redeem us from the curse of the law by becoming a curse for us" (3:13). That is, the curse is transferred to Christ to deliver those under it.

Second, to defend his statement about the effect of the death of Christ in 3:13, Paul applies Deut 21:23 to Jesus's crucifixion. Jesus suffered the curse of the law, but Paul seems to affirm in Gal 3:10–13 that Jesus obeyed Torah, because his death for the "us" under Torah's curse achieved

---

61. For example, see 2 Macc 5:17–18; 6:14–15; 7:18, 32; 8:5; 10:45. 2 Maccabees 5:17 specifically states that God's wrath fell upon the nation because of the sins of some within the city, and the seventh son states in 2 Macc 7:32 that the martyrs suffered the wrath of the Almighty because of *their* own sins.

the blessing of life for those for whom he died (Gal 3:13–14). This is supported by Paul's remarks that Jesus's death actually "redeemed" the "us" from Torah's curse in Gal 3:13 and that Jesus's death achieved benefits for those under Torah's curse in Gal 3:14. In Paul's view, Jesus accomplished this redemption for those under Torah's curse because he himself was born under Torah (Gal 4:4–5).

Similar to the Jewish martyrological narratives' presentation of the martyrs' deaths, Paul remarks nowhere that Jesus disobeyed Torah and consequently suffered its curse because of his disobedience. To the contrary, Paul's remarks in Galatians about Jesus's giving up of himself speaks to his faithfulness. He declares Jesus gave himself "for our sins" (1:4), "loved me and gave himself for me" (2:20), "redeemed us from the curse of the law by becoming a curse for us" (3:13), and was "born from a woman and born under the law to redeem those under the law" (4:4–5). Furthermore, Jesus's faithfulness to Torah can be seen by Paul's statements that his death accomplished specific benefits for those for whom he died. He "delivered us from our sins" (1:4), "redeemed us from the curse of the law" (3:13), distributed the life-giving Spirit to Jews and Gentiles by his redemption (3:14, 21; 4:5), and God raised Jesus (i.e. gave him life) from the dead after his death "for us" (1:1). To state the point in the words of Deuteronomy, Jesus's obedience to Torah brought life (i.e. to the one who obeyed and to those for whom he died) (Deut 5:32–33; 8:1; 11:8–9, 18–25, 28; 28:1–14; 30:15–16), but disobedience to Torah results in a curse/death (Deut 4:25–28; 11:28; 28:15–68; 30:17–20). According to Paul, Jesus was accursed, died, but resurrected (i.e. experienced the life promised in Torah for those obedient to Torah) and imparts life to those under its curse because he represented those who were under Torah's curse (Gal 1:1, 4, 15; 3:10–13, 21; 4:5).

6. Similar to the Jewish martyrological narratives' presentation of the martyrs' deaths, Paul presents Jesus's death (a Torah-observant Jew) as a substitute for others in Gal 3:13 with Deuteronomic language in order to advance his exegetical, theological, and polemical purposes in Gal 3:10–14. The substitutionary death of a Torah-observant Jew is another similarity with a Jewish martyrological understanding of Deuteronomy. In 2 Maccabees, the martyrs died for the nation to reconcile the nation to God (2 Macc 7:33). They suffered for the nation's sins (not their own) (2 Macc 5:17; 7:32); they prayed that God would be reconciled again to the nation (not just to themselves) through their deaths (2 Macc 7:37–38), and the narrative states *after* the martyrs died in 8:5 that God's wrath was turned to mercy toward the nation. In 4 Macc 6:28–29, Eleazar asks God to use his blood as a ransom to bring mercy to the nation and to satisfy

God's wrath against it. In 4 Macc 17:21–22, the author summarizes the martyrological narratives affirming their blood actually purified the homeland and saved the nation from the wrath of the Almighty by means of their deaths.

Likewise, Paul suggests in Gal 3:13 that Jesus's death was a substitute for the "us" for whom he died. J. Louis Martyn rejected that Gal 3:13 teaches substitutionary atonement. Instead, he argues Paul's primary concern is God's apocalyptic deliverance in Christ, who delivers enslaved humans from the present evil age and from the slavery of the law. Christ took on the curse in his body and experienced victory over evil via the crucifixion.[62]

However, Martyn's reading of Gal 3:13 seems to minimize Paul's appropriation of the Deuteronomic curses to Jesus's death and the benefits that his death accomplished for those under Torah's curse. Paul states Jesus redeemed us "by becoming a curse" in Gal 3:13. His curse-bearing death provided soteriological benefits for those for whom the death was offered: deliverance from the curse (3:13), justification by faith (2:16; 3:12), eternal life (3:21), the indwelling presence of the Spirit (3:14; 4:5), crucifixion to the world (2:20; 6:14), Christ living in those who are crucified with Christ (2:20), and new creation (6:15).

In an article in 2001 and in a monograph in 2006, David A. Brondos insisted a substitutionary reading of redemption in Gal 3:13 is wrong headed.[63] He argued Paul believed Christ attained redemption for those under Torah's curse when God resurrected him from the dead "in response to his self-giving since from his position at God's right hand he is now certain to make that redemption come to pass," for Paul believed the important point about Jesus's death was that he gave up his life while seeking to redeem "others."[64] Brondos contended that when Paul refers to Jesus's death on the cross, he has in mind his resurrection and exaltation, both of which "make God's promises a reality."[65] Brondos argued Paul was "acquainted with the foundational story as present in the Jesus tradition and primitive [preaching]," which viewed the cross in the context of a story "in which the cross was a result of and an expression of Jesus's willingness" to surrender his life for others, not as an isolated event.[66] The

---

62. Martyn, *Galatians*, 318 n. 110.
63. David A. Brondos, *Paul on the Cross: Reconstructing the Apostle's Story of Redemption* (Minneapolis: Fortress, 2006), 144–9; idem, "The Cross and the Curse: Galatians 3:13 and Paul's Doctrine of Redemption," *JSNT* 81 (2000): 3–32.
64. Brondos, "The Cross and the Curse," 23.
65. Ibid., 25–6.
66. Ibid.

"redemption" promised is the result, says Brondos, of God raising Jesus from the dead and exalting him in response to his self-surrendering death.[67]

According to Brondos, these points can be easily established when Paul speaks of Jesus's crucifixion throughout his ministry and in his writings. Paul emphasizes Jesus's "obedience to the Father's will," as can be seen in Gal 1:4 when he asserts Jesus gave himself according to the Father's will "to deliver us from the present evil age" and in Gal 2:20 when he states Jesus "gave himself for me."[68] As Brondos says, "in obedience to God's will, Jesus was seeking to deliver others from the present evil age, making their redemption and forgiveness a reality."[69] When God, therefore, "responded to Jesus's self-offering by raising him" from the dead and "by exalting him" at his right hand, those who were already part of the Jesus community or would become part of it "were forgiven and justified by God," because "their ultimate acceptance by God became a certainty when he bestowed upon Christ their Lord the power and authority to deliver them from his wrath to be poured out upon sinners and the unrighteous on the day of judgment and salvation; in essence, Jesus' resurrection was God's affirmative response to what his Son had been seeking for them."[70] Humans can be saved now "through Christ" and not by Torah obedience, because submission to Torah does not "lead to life" in the "new age."[71]

Brondos's rejection of substitution in Gal 3:13 seems misguided for the following reasons. First, he assumed the story of redemption on the forefront of Paul's thinking can only be found in Jesus tradition or in primitive Christian preaching. To the contrary, as Stephen Finlan has shown, Paul uses a variety of traditions (martyrological, Hebrew cultic) and metaphors (legal, economic) to present the effect of Jesus's death for others, not just one.[72] Second, Brondos read Paul's remarks in Gal 3:13 in light of 1 Cor 15:3, where Paul associates a tradition handed down to him with Jesus's death and resurrection. He assumed this tradition refers to Jesus tradition and primitive Christian preaching when in fact it could refer to a martyrological tradition. Brondos's method seems unconvincing, because Gal 3:13 was possibly written in the 40s, or at the latest the early 50s, of the first century CE, because 1 Cor 15:3 was probably written in the 50s of the first century CE, and because the tradition in 1 Cor 15:3

---

67. Brondos, *Paul on the Cross*, 149.
68. Brondos, "The Cross and the Curse," 24.
69. Ibid.
70. Ibid., 26–7.
71. Ibid.
72. E.g. Finlan, *Background and Content*.

could be referring to a martyrological tradition reflected in early Christian preaching. Thus, there is no reason to think that Paul's remarks in Gal 3:13 must be the result of his acquaintance with the tradition mentioned in 1 Cor 15:3 or that the tradition therein refers only to Jesus tradition or primitive Christian preaching void of a martyrological influence since Paul could have become acquainted with the specific tradition in 1 Cor 15:3 after he wrote Gal 3:13 or the tradition in 1 Cor 15:3 could have been interpreted along the lines of Jewish martyrology prior to Paul receiving it.

Third, that Paul associates Jesus's death with the Father's will and redemption in Gal 1:4, 2:20, and elsewhere in his writings, does not prove the background behind Paul's remarks in Gal 3:13 is a pure Jesus-tradition or primitive Christian preaching unaffected by antecedent Jewish tradition. Paul nowhere in Galatians explicitly connects his remarks in Gal 3:13 only to Jesus-tradition or primitive Christian preaching as defined by Brondos. But, as I am arguing, Paul seems to apply a martyrological reading of Deuteronomy to the death of Jesus in Gal 3:13 and shapes the martyrological ideas accordingly to make his specific argument about Jesus's unique death for Jews and Gentiles in Gal 3:13.

This latter point can be established from Gal 3:10–14 by observing Paul's remarks regarding the soteriological benefits that Jesus's death achieved for the "us" under Torah's curse and by considering the structure of Paul's argument in 3:10–12. For example, first, Paul establishes that Torah brings a curse upon Torah-breakers (3:10). He also confirms the law will not justify anyone in God's law-court, because the righteous one lives by faith (3:11). He likewise confirms that the law promises life only to those who obey its stipulations (3:11–12). Paul extends the curse in Galatians to those who proclaim a Torah-observant and Gentile-exclusive gospel instead of a Torah-free and Gentile-inclusive gospel (1:6–9; 2:11–14; 6:16). According to Paul, Jesus was not a minister of sin (2:17), but died for those under Torah's curse (1:4; 3:13), was resurrected from the dead (1:1), and imparted the blessing of the Spirit to the "us" whom he redeemed from Torah's curse (3:13–14).

Second, Paul states that Christ redeemed "us" from Torah's curse by receiving a curse for them. The vicarious suffering and death of a Torah-observant Jew, as the means by which those under Torah's curse would be redeemed from its curse, is found nowhere in Deuteronomy.[73] Instead, Deuteronomy states that Torah curses those who disobey its demands (Deut 27–28). According to Deuteronomy, the only sure means by which

---

73. Although arguing for a different point, Finlan (*Background and Content*, 104–5) made me aware of this observation.

one escapes the Deuteronomic curses are obedience to Torah and repentance when Torah has been violated (Deut 28:10–30:20), not the death of a Torah-observant Jew for those under Torah's curse. Thus, this observation suggests that Paul's application of the Deuteronomic curses to Jesus, a Torah-observant Jew, who died for those under Torah's curse, is a martyrological reading of Deuteronomy in that it has similarities with this tradition in what it affirms about the death of a Torah-observant Jew for the soteriological benefits of non-Torah-observant people.

Third, the "us" whom Christ redeems from Torah's curse in Gal 3:13 is a group who is under the curse due to both Torah-allegiance and Torah-disobedience, because Paul remarks in 3:10 by citing Deut 27:26 that "as many are from works of law are under a curse: for it is written that everyone who does not abide in all things written in the book of the law in order to do them is accursed." Deuteronomy 27:26 suggests that the curse comes to those who disobey Torah, not simply to those who are under Torah's domain or to those who simply subscribe to some of its stipulations (e.g. circumcision).[74] However, Paul uses Deut 27:26 in a rather puzzling way: namely, to contend that those who subscribe to the law are accursed.

Deuteronomy 27–28 says disobeying Torah brings one under a curse, whereas Paul asserts that those who subscribe to Torah are under a curse and quotes Deut 27:26 to support his assertion when in fact it seems to make the opposite point in the context of Deuteronomy. Paul seemingly appropriates Deut 27:26 this way since his entire argument in Gal 3:1–14 is the pathway to the Abrahamic blessing is not Torah, but faith in Christ. Christ redeems the "us" from Torah's curse by receiving the curse of the law for them, and the "us" will receive the redemption (Gal 3:13) and the blessing/Spirit (Gal 3:14) purchased by Christ, even though they were formerly under Torah's curse, because Christ died for them. Consequently, herein lies the essence of substitution in Gal 3:13 and this text's connection with a martyrological reading of Deuteronomy: similar to the way the Jewish martyrs took the Deuteronomic curses of Torah upon themselves because of the nation's sin of disobedience to save and purify it from Torah's curse, Paul suggests Jesus took the Deuteronomic curses upon himself for the "us" under Torah's curse to redeem them from the law's curse.

In his 2004 monograph, *The Background and Content of Paul's Cultic Atonement Metaphors*, Finlan maintained Paul's background in Gal 3:13b is Levitical and not Deuteronomic, because the idea of being redeemed

---

74. Against de Boer, *Galatians*, 199–201.

from the curse of the law is beyond the scope of Deuteronomy.[75] However, neither Deuteronomy nor Leviticus alone provide *the* background behind Gal 3:13. Instead, I argue *a* Jewish martyrological reading of Deuteronomy provides a background against which to understand Paul's remarks about substitution in Gal 3:13. Below I offer five reasons.

First, Deuteronomy's provision for the curse is obedience and repentance, not the death of a human for those under Torah's curse (Deut 28:10–30:20). However, Paul appeals to Deuteronomy at least three times in Gal 3:10 (Deut 27:26; 28:58) and Gal 3:13 (Deut 21:23). In Gal 3:13, he specifically cites Deut 21:23 in connection with Jesus's redemption of the "us" from the curse of the law. Second, in Leviticus, priests offer animals to take away sins and to provide ritual purification instead of human sacrifices (Lev 1–5; 16). In the Jewish martyrological narratives and in Gal 1:4 and 3:13, the martyrs (martyrological narratives) and Jesus (Gal 1:4; 3:13–14) reverse the Deuteronomic curse. Third, the sacrificial rituals and the scapegoat ritual have different functions. The priests sacrifice animals as atonement (Lev 16:3–7, 11, 14–20, 30), but the scapegoat was sent away into the wilderness to Azazel to carry away sin (Lev 16:8–10, 21–22). The martyrs and Jesus are the only means by which the curse is dealt with. Fourth, Galatians does not speak of Jesus's death for others with explicit Levitical cultic language. Concepts like blood-atoning sacrifice are not explicitly mentioned in association with Jesus's death. Even when Paul states Jesus died for sins, he explains the purpose for this death was to "deliver us from the present evil age" (1:4).[76]

Fifth, once the penitent identified with the burnt offering and the scapegoat, the animals became defiled, which explains why the burnt offering was sacrificed and why the scapegoat was sent away into the wilderness to carry away the sins of the people (Lev 16:21–22, 30). The Jewish martyrs (humans), on the other hand, like Jesus, were Torah-observant Jews, who suffered the curse of Torah by association with the accursed and who offered themselves to God to achieve the blessing of life for those under Torah's curse by actually becoming accursed for them (2 Macc 7:1–8:5; 4 Macc 6:28–29; 17:21–22; Gal 3:10–14). The latter point is envisaged by their death. Consequently, similar to the Jewish martyrs, Jesus thereby delivered from Torah's curse the "us" under its curse by means of suffering its curse/judgment for them so that they

---

75. For example, see Finlan, *Background and Content*, 110.

76. But Christ's death "for sins" (1:4), the language of redemption (3:13; 4:5), and the reference to Torah throughout the letter (cf. 3:10) could very well evoke sacrificial imagery.

would be emancipated from the curse and so that they would receive the soteriological blessing of the Spirit and all that this blessing entails for all in Christ (cf. 2:16–6:15). But, unlike the Jewish martyrs, Jesus's death provides soteriological blessing for both Jews and Gentiles and is the definitive means by which deliverance from the present evil age comes (1:4), redemption from the curse of the law is realized (3:13), and the new age of the Spirit begins (3:1–14; 4:5, 21–31; 5:16–26; 6:15), both now and in the age to come apart from Torah obedience (Gal 1:8–9; 5:21; 6:15).

VI. Summary

The Jewish martyrological narratives present the martyrs as dying as representatives of and substitutes for non-Torah-observant Jews (LXX Dan 3:1–90; 2 Macc 7:32–38; 4 Macc 6:28–29; 17:21–22). In the face of death, Eleazar urges God in 4 Macc 6:28 to be merciful to Israel through his death (ἵλεως γενοῦ τῷ ἔθνει σου) (2 Macc 4:1–6:31; 4 Macc 5:4–6:40). 4 Maccabees 6:29 states Eleazar asks God to make his blood to be Israel's purification (καθάρσιον αὐτῶν ποίησον τὸ ἐμὸν αἷμα). In the final part of his prayer in 4 Macc 6:29b, Eleazar asks God to receive his death as a ransom for the nation (καὶ ἀντίψυχον αὐτῶν λαβὲ τὴν ἐμὴν ψυχήν). The author of 4 Maccabees interprets the martyrs' deaths to be both sacrificial in nature and a saving event for the nation in 4 Macc 17:21–22 (καὶ τὸν τύραννον τιμωρηθῆναι καὶ τὴν πατρίδα καθαρισθῆναι ὥσπερ ἀντίψυχον γεγονότας τῆς τοῦ ἔθνους ἁμαρτίας καὶ διὰ τοῦ αἵματος τῶν εὐσεβῶν ἐκείνων καὶ τοῦ ἱλαστηρίου τοῦ θανάτου αὐτῶν ἡ θεία πρόνοια τὸν Ισραηλ προκακωθέντα διέσωσεν). Deuteronomy 27 and 28 state that if Israel disobeyed Torah in the land, they would be cursed, but if they obeyed, they would be blessed. The martyrs suffered the Deuteronomic curses of the community's disobedience in 2 Maccabees. Texts in 4 Maccabees likewise apply Deuteronomy to the Jewish martyrs. In Gal 3:10–14, Paul applies Deuteronomy to Jesus in a way similar to the martyrological narratives to fit his exegetical, theological, and polemical purposes. Similar to the Jewish martyrological narratives, Paul presents Jesus's death (a Torah-observant Jew) as a representation in Gal 3:13 with Deuteronomic language in order to advance his exegetical, theological, and polemical purposes in Gal 3:10–14. Similar to the Jewish martyrological narratives' presentation of the martyrs' deaths, Paul also presents Jesus's death (a Torah-observant Jew) as a substitution for others in Gal 3:13 with Deuteronomic language in order to advance his exegetical, theological, and polemical purposes in Gal 3:10–14.

VII. Conclusion

I have argued in a twofold manner that 2 and 4 Maccabees and Paul in Galatians appropriate the Deuteronomic theme of blessing and curse in similar and yet different ways. First, the authors present the Torah-observant Jewish martyrs as dying as representatives of and as substitutes for non-Torah-observant Jews in the Jewish martyrological narratives. Second, in Gal 3:13, Paul presents Jesus as dying as a representative of and a substitute for non-Torah-observant Jews and Gentiles. The martyrs died for the sins of fellow Jews to deliver them from the law's curse. Jesus died for the sins of Jews and Gentiles to redeem both groups from the law's curse to give them the Abrahamic blessing of the Spirit, to make them part of the family of Abraham, and to give both groups the Deuteronomic blessing of life in this age and in the age to come.

5

Lexical, Grammatical, and Additional Conceptual Similarities Between Second Temple Jewish Martyrological Traditions and Galatians

This chapter focuses on lexical, grammatical, and additional conceptual similarities between Second Temple Jewish martyrological traditions and Galatians in order to support the thesis of *a* Jewish martyrological background behind Gal 3:13. I discuss two specific kinds of similarities in this chapter. First, building upon Stephen Anthony Cummins's lexical and grammatical work in his monograph on Gal 1–2,[1] I discuss lexical and grammatical similarities between Second Temple Jewish martyrological traditions and Galatians. I argue Paul's letter to the Galatians has multiple lexical and grammatical similarities and points of contact with Jewish martyrological traditions. This section simply lists and briefly discusses the texts in which these lexical and grammatical connections occur in order to highlight these similarities.

Second, I discuss the additional conceptual similarities between the Jewish martyrological traditions and Gal 3:13 that are important for my thesis, but do not provide enough material to provide their own independent chapter. This part of the analysis argues the Jewish martyrological narratives and Galatians are similar in that they are highly polemical in their efforts to defend Judaism (Jewish martyrological narratives) or the gospel (Galatians). 2 Maccabees seeks to defend the superiority of Judaism over Hellenism and argues against extreme Hellenization in an effort to dissuade Jews from eradicating a Jewish way of life with a turn from

---

1. Cummins, *Paul and the Crucified Christ in Antioch*, 100–135. Cummins's work and my monograph have two entirely different concerns. But his work pointed me to many lexical and grammatical similarities between the Jewish martyrological traditions and Galatians, even though his primary concern is Paul's autobiography in Gal 1–2. I also include lexical and grammatical connections between 2 and 4 Maccabees and Galatians that I discovered independently of Cummins's work.

the law. 4 Maccabees argues religious reasoning (i.e. devotion to Torah) masters the "passions," even in the face of extreme suffering. Paul seeks to defend his Torah-free and Gentile-inclusive gospel against the Torah-observant and Gentile-exclusive gospel of his opponents as he argues against compelling the Gentiles to live a Jewish way of life in an effort to dissuade the Galatians from turning away from his gospel to embrace a Jewish way of life.

I. Lexical and Grammatical Similarities Between the Martyrological Traditions and Galatians

There are numerous lexical and grammatical similarities between Second Temple Jewish martyrological traditions and Galatians. I have not included certain particles and conjunctions since these words occur so frequently in other Second Temple Jewish texts that their appearance in both the Jewish martyrological traditions and Galatians proves nothing. Instead, I list and briefly discuss what I deem to be significant nouns, verbs, and phrases in the Jewish martyrological traditions and Galatians that support the Jewish martyrological narratives are a background in front of which to read Gal 3:13.

1. Ἰουδαϊσμός is an important term in the martyrological narratives and in the argument of Galatians. The first time Ἰουδαϊσμός occurs in any extant ancient source is in 2 Maccabees and again in 4 Maccabees. In 2 and 4 Maccabees, Ἰουδαϊσμός refers to a Torah-observant Jewish way of life resistant to a more comprehensive Greek way of life known as Hellenism (cf. 2 Macc 4:11–17). In 2 Macc 2:21, Ἰουδαϊσμός refers to the Jews who fought bravely for a Jewish way of life with Judas Maccabeus and his brothers to purify the temple, to dedicate the altar, and to wage war against Antiochus Epiphanes IV and Eupator so that they would regain the temple, liberate the city, and reconstitute the Torah as the law of the land (2 Macc 2:19–22).

In 2 Macc 8:1, Ἰουδαϊσμός refers to those Jews committed to a Torah-observant Jewish way of life and who entered into villages with Judas Maccabeus to summon fellow Torah-observant Jews to fight with them to preserve God's law (8:1). These asked the Lord to be merciful to the Jewish people suffering oppression, to be merciful to the temple that the tyrant profaned, to be merciful to the city of Jerusalem that was destroyed, to hear the cries of the spilt blood of the Jewish people, to remember the innocent babies, to remember the blasphemies against his name, and to demonstrate his hatred for the evil committed against him, his people, the temple, the city, and the land (8:2–4). In 14:38, Ἰουδαϊσμός refers to Razis, an elder of Jerusalem, who was accused of living a Jewish way of life. Razis loved his fellow-citizens, had a good reputation, and was recognized by name as a "father of the Jews" (14:37). He was brought forth in judgment for Ἰουδαϊσμός (living a Jewish way of life) (14:38). He also earnestly risked both body and soul for Ἰουδαϊσμός. In each case in 2 Maccabees, the term Ἰουδαϊσμός and those committed to Ἰουδαϊσμός function in the narrative as Jewish resistance against a comprehensive and extreme form of Ἑλληνισμος (ἦν δ' οὕτως ἀκμή τις Ἑλληνισμοῦ καὶ πρόσβασις ἀλλοφυλισμοῦ διὰ τὴν τοῦ ἀσεβοῦς καὶ οὐκ ἀρχιερέως Ἰάσωνος ὑπερβάλλουσαν ἀναγνείαν) (4:13; cf. also 4:11–17).

In 4 Macc 4:26, Ἰουδαϊσμός occurs in the context of Antiochus's severe persecution of the Jews. The author identifies Antiochus as a terrible man, who removed Onias from the priesthood and appointed his brother Jason in his place (4:15–16). Jason converted the nation into a Greek city, altering its government, building gymnasiums, and abolishing the temple in violation of Torah (4:19–20). These acts provoked the Lord's anger against Israel (4:21). Consequently, Antiochus made war against them (4:21). Antiochus sacked Jerusalem and forbade them from following their ancestral laws (4:22–23). However, when many of the people refused to comply with Antiochus's decree to abandon their Jewish way of life, he used torture and other tactics to compel them to deny Ἰουδαϊσμός.

In Galatians, Paul uses the term Ἰουδαϊσμός twice. In both contexts, he refers to his prior manner of life before he became a follower of Christ (Gal 1:13–14). He associates his previous manner of life in Ἰουδαϊσμός with violent persecution of the church (1:13). He connects his violence in Ἰουδαϊσμός with resistance to the Christ-following community, a resistance that he identifies as surpassing great zeal for the traditions of his fathers (1:14). To clarify, this does not mean that all forms of Ἰουδαϊσμός were violent. However, Paul's form of Ἰουδαϊσμός was violent. His violent resistance in Ἰουδαϊσμός to the Christ-following community is similar to the resistant zeal of Ἰουδαϊσμός in 2 and 4 Maccabees. The major difference between the two violent forms of Ἰουδαϊσμός is that one zealously fought to preserve Ἰουδαϊσμός from Hellenismos, and the other fought to preserve Ἰουδαϊσμός from a Jewish, Gentile-inclusive Jesus-following movement that proclaimed a crucified Jewish man as the Messiah of Jews and Gentiles without requiring Gentiles to conform to a Jewish way of life.

2. *The Jewish martyrological traditions and Galatians use the term* ζηλωτής *to refer to those zealously devoted to* Ἰουδαϊσμός. In 2 Macc 4:2, ζηλωτής refers to Onias. Simon slandered Onias, saying he had been the cause of the calamity that had befallen the nation (4:1). He accused him of plotting against the government (4:2), although he protected his fellow citizens and was a ζηλωτής for Torah (4:2). In 4 Macc 18:12, the author uses the term to refer to the ζηλωτής of Phinehas, who murdered an Israelite man and a Gentile woman for transgressing the covenant to remove the wrath of the Lord away from the people (cf. LXX Num 25:7–13).

In Gal 1:13–14, Paul refers to his previous life in a violent form of Judaism, a life he lived prior to his Damascus Road experience. In Gal 1:14, he specifically links his life of Ἰουδαϊσμός with a life of violent ζηλωτής for the ancestral traditions similar to the Jewish martyrological traditions.

3. *A form of the phrase* τὸ ἔθνος *occurs in the Jewish martyrological traditions and Galatians.* In 2 Maccabees, τὸ ἔθνος occurs in the plural form to refer to non-Jewish (i.e. Gentile) communities who do not obey Torah and who attack Jews (2 Macc 1:27; 4:35; 6:4, 14; 8:16; 10:4; 11:3; 12:13; 13:11; 14:14–15; 15:8, 10). In 2 Macc 8:9, τὸ ἔθνος in the plural specifically refers to Gentile efforts to exterminate Jews.

In Galatians, Paul uses a plural form of τὸ ἔθνος to refer to non-Torah-observant Gentile communities. In Gal 1:16, he states God revealed his son in order to announce him as good news amongst the Gentiles (ἐν τοῖς ἔθνεσιν). In 2:2, he states that he went up to Jerusalem with Titus (a Greek) and Barnabas (a Jew) to present to the Jewish pillars of the church the gospel he preaches among the Gentiles (ἐν τοῖς ἔθνεσιν). In 2:8–9, Paul affirms the Jewish pillars of the Jerusalem church acknowledged the validity of his ministry to the Gentiles (εἰς τὰ ἔθνη) and Peter's to the Jews. In 2:12, he says Peter ate with Gentiles until some came from James. In 2:14–15, he challenges Peter in the presence of Jews and Gentiles for compelling the Gentiles to live like Jews. He reminds Peter that Jews are Jews by nature and not sinners by association with the Gentiles (2:15). In 3:8, Paul says God promised to Abraham the justification of the Gentiles, and in 3:14 he declares that the blessing of Abraham comes to Gentiles by faith because Jesus died to redeem "us" from the curse of the law (3:14).

4. *A form of the verb* ἀναγκάζω *("to compel") occurs in the Jewish martyrological traditions and Galatians.* In 2 Macc 6:1, Antiochus sent an Athenian senator to "compel the Jews" to forsake Torah (cf. 2 Macc 11:11). In 2 Macc 6:18–21, the king compelled Eleazar with threats of

torture and death to eat unclean food. In 2 Macc 6:21–22, those charged to enforce this compulsion pulled Eleazar aside and compelled him with the promise of salvation to pretend to eat unlawful meat so that he would escape the king's judgment. In 4 Macc 15:7, the author states the mother of the seven sons, whom she watched become martyrs, was compelled to have sympathy for them because of the many sufferings she experienced with them (καὶ διὰ πολλὰς τὰς καθ' ἕκαστον αὐτῶν ὠδῖνας ἠναγκασμένη τὴν εἰς αὐτοὺς ἔχειν συμπάθειαν).

In Gal 2:3, Paul says the Jewish pillars of the church did not compel Titus, the Greek, to be circumcised when he went up to Jerusalem to present his gospel to them. In Gal 2:14, Paul asked Peter why he was compelling the Gentiles to live a Jewish way of life. In Gal 6:12, Paul states that the opponents in Galatia are compelling the Galatians to be circumcised only so that they would not be persecuted by the cross of Christ and so that they would boast in the Galatians' circumcised flesh (6:13).

5. The Jewish martyrological traditions and Galatians speak of δικαιοσύνη. In 4 Maccabees, the author uses δικαιοσύνη to refer to virtue (justice/ righteousness) (cf. 4 Macc 1:18). In Galatians, Paul uses δικαιοσύνη as a forensic term to refer to God's saving righteousness or justification by faith. In 2:21, Paul says that if δικαιοσύνη comes by means of law, then Christ died in vain. In 2:16 and 2:17, he uses a verbal cognate (δικαιόω) to refer to justification by faith. In 3:6, he says righteousness (δικαιοσύνη) was reckoned to Abraham by faith. In 3:21, he says that if the law gives life, then righteousness (δικαιοσύνη) would come by means of law. In 3:24, he uses a verbal cognate (δικαιόω) of δικαιοσύνη to talk about justification by faith. In 5:5, Paul says we await by faith the hope of righteousness (δικαιοσύνη).

6. A form of the πίστις *word group or cognate terms occur in the Jewish martyrological traditions and in Galatians.* In 2 Macc 3:12, the author refers to the Jews who were faithful to the temple (τοὺς πεπιστευκότας τῇ τοῦ τόπου ἁγιωσύνῃ). In 2 Macc 3:22, the author refers to the things which were entrusted to those who faithfully guarded the temple (τὰ πεπιστευμένα τοῖς πεπιστευκόσιν), while those at the temple pleaded with the Lord to protect the temple.[2] In 4 Macc 7:19, the author refers to those

---

2. In 2 Macc 1:2, in the first letter to the Jews in Egypt, the author prays that God would remember his covenant with Abraham and his offspring, his faithful servants (τῶν δούλων αὐτοῦ τῶν πιστῶν). Cf. also 2 Macc 3:22; 7:24.

who believe in immortality. In 4 Macc 7:21, he refers to believing or trusting in God. In 4 Macc 15:24, the author refers to the mother's faith in God as she watched the torture and execution of her seven sons. In 4 Macc 16:22, the author exhorts his audience to have the "same faith in God" as the afflicted mother.

In Galatians, Paul uses the πίστις word group or cognate terms to refer to faith in Christ. In Gal 1:23, Paul says the churches of Judea heard about his preaching of the faith. In 2:7, Paul says he was entrusted (πεπίστευμαι) with the gospel for the uncircumcision. In 2:16, he refers to believing (ἐπιστεύσαμεν) in Christ and faith in Christ (διὰ πίστεως Ἰησοῦ Χριστοῦ). He restates justification by faith in 3:11–12. In 2:20, Paul declares he lives by faith in the son of God. In 3:2 and 3:5–9, with a series of questions, he reminds the Galatians they experienced the Spirit by faith, not by works of law. 3:14 says we receive the Spirit by faith. 3:22–26 mentions believing and faith multiple times. The promise was given by faith to those who believe (3:22). Those under the law were held in custody under the law before faith came (3:23), because they were imprisoned to the faith later to be revealed (3:23). The law was a pedagogue until Christ so that we would be justified by faith (3:24). After faith came, we were no longer under the pedagogue of the law (3:25). In Christ, all are God's sons through faith (3:26). We await by the Spirit by faith the hope of righteousness (5:5). Faith works through love (5:6). Faithfulness (πίστις) is a fruit of the Spirit (5:22). Paul exhorts the Galatians to work the good toward all people, especially toward those of households of faith (6:10).

7. *The Jewish martyrological traditions and Galatians use the adverb* εὐθέως. In obedience to the Gentile king, Heliodorus immediately set out for Jerusalem to confiscate funds from the temple treasury (2 Macc 3:8). Jason "immediately" turned the citizens of Jerusalem over to the Greek way of life once he became high priest (4:10). In his paranetic section in 2 Macc 6:13–17, the author(s) asserts it is good to punish immediately the ungodly (6:13). After the aged Eleazar told the tyrant he refused to eat the meat, he "immediately" went to the rack to be tortured (6:28). Nicanor "immediately" tried to capture and sell Jewish slaves to obtain tribute owed to the Romans (8:10–11). The king "immediately" appointed Nicanor as governor and commissioned him to kill Judas (14:12). The Jews listened to their leader and "immediately" pursued battle with Nicanor and his army (14:15–16). In 4 Macc 10:8, they "immediately" brought the third son to the wheel of torture. In Gal 1:16, when recounting

his autobiography, Paul informs the Galatians he did not "immediately" go up to Jerusalem to those who were apostles before him after God revealed his son to him that he might announce his as good news to the Gentiles.

8. The Jewish martyrological traditions and Galatians use the term ἐπαγγελία. Thinking the seventh son would give into the tyrant after he witnessed the torture and executions of his six siblings, Antiochus released him (4 Macc 12:1–8). After the mother exhorted him to endure sufferings for the sake of God's law just as his brothers (12:7), the seventh son requested to be released to address the king and his friends (12:8). They were pleased because of the boy's "promise" (12:9).

In Galatians, Paul uses a form of ἐπαγγελία more than once. The "promises" were spoken to Abraham and to his offspring (3:16). The law, given 430 years after the "promise," does not nullify the "promise" (3:17). If the inheritance comes by means of the law, then it does not come by means of "promise" (3:18). The law is not contrary to the "promises" of God (3:21). The Scripture shut up all things under sin so that the "promise" would be given by faith in Jesus to every believer (3:22). If you belong to Christ, then you are the offspring of Abraham, namely, heirs with respect to the "promise" (3:29). The covenant of the slave woman represents the flesh, whereas the covenant of the free woman represents the "promise" (4:23). The children from the free woman of the promise are children of the "promise" (4:28).

9. The Jewish martyrological traditions and Galatians use the term κληρονομία. 2 Maccabees 2:4 asserts that Moses saw the "inheritance of God." 2 Maccabees 2:17 affirms that God saved his people and gave the "inheritance" to all through the law (cf. 2:18). In Gal 3:18, Paul affirms that the "inheritance" does not come by means of the law, but by faith in Jesus Christ (2:16–4:31).

10. The Jewish martyrological traditions and Galatians use the phrase κατ' ἰδίαν to refer to a private meeting. Onias's concern for his people moved him to appeal "privately" (κατ' ἰδίαν) to the king (2 Macc 4:5). The men responsible for the unlawful sacrifice compelled Eleazar "privately" (κατ' ἰδίαν) to provide his own meat and to pretend to eat the unlawful sacrifice (6:21; cf. 9:26; 14:21). Paul refers to a private visit (κατ' ἰδίαν) with the pillars of the church in Jerusalem (Gal 2:2).

11. The Jewish martyrological traditions and Galatians use the term ἀναστροφη *to refer to one's conduct.* 2 Maccabees 6:23 uses the term to refer to Eleazar's noble conduct. Paul uses the term to refer to his previous manner of life in Judaism (Gal 1:13).

12. The Jewish martyrological traditions and Galatians use a form of the verb μετατίθημι *to refer to the idea of turning from something.* Ptolemy took the king aside to change (μετέθηκεν) his mind (2 Macc 4:46). Antiochus promised to make the seventh son rich if he would turn away from his fathers' Torah-observant ways (μεταθέμενον ἀπὸ τῶν πατρίων) (7:24). 4 Maccabees 2:18 asserts the wise mind (δυνατὸς γὰρ ὁ σώφρων νοῦς) is able to turn (τὰ μὲν αὐτῶν μεταθεῖναι) the sinful passions (κατὰ τῶν παθῶν). In Gal 1:16, Paul laments he is shocked the Galatians were turning so quickly to another gospel (οὕτως ταχέως μετατίθεσθε εἰς ἕτερον εὐαγγέλιον) from the one who called them into the grace of Christ.

13. The Jewish martyrological traditions and Galatians use a form of the verb πείθω. Menelaus urged Andronicus to kill Onias. Andronicus persuaded (πεισθεὶς) him by deceit to approach him, and he murdered him (2 Macc 4:34). Ptolemy attempted to bribe (τὸ πεῖσαι) the king (2 Macc 4:45).[3] Paul seeks to please (πείθω) God with his gospel proclamation (Gal 1:10). The Galatians were running well until someone hindered them not to be persuaded (πείθεσθαι) by the truth (5:7). Paul is confident (ἐγὼ πέποιθα) in the Lord that the Galatian assemblies would not turn away from his gospel (5:10).

14. The Jewish martyrological traditions and Galatians use a combination of a form of the verb δίδωμι *and the adjective* δεξιά *to refer to one party forming an alliance with another.* Andronicus gave the right hand of fellowship (δοὺς δεξιάν) to Onias before he killed him (2 Macc 4:34). In 2 Macc 11:26, the author(s) refer(s) to someone giving "pledges of friendship" (δοὺς δεξιάς). The king negotiated a pledge (δεξιὰν ἔδωκεν) with the people in Beth-zur (13:22). After hearing about the victory of Judas over his army (14:18), Nicanor sent three ambassadors to form pledges of friendship (δοῦναι καὶ λαβεῖν δεξιάς) with Judas (14:19). When Peter, James, and John discerned the grace given to Paul (τὴν χάριν τὴν δοθεῖσάν μοι) to preach the gospel, the pillars gave to him and his missionary colleagues the right hand (δεξιὰς ἔδωκαν) of fellowship (κοινωνίας) (Gal 2:9).

---

3. Cf. also 2 Macc 7:26, 40; 8:18; 9:27; 10:20, 34; 11:14; 12:14; 15:7; 4 Macc 2:6; 4:25; 5:16; 6:4; 8:12, 17, 26; 9:18; 10:13; 12:4–5; 15:10; 16:24; 18:1.

15. The Jewish martyrological traditions and Galatians use a form of the noun ἐπιθυμία *to refer to desire or lust.* In 4 Maccabees, reason dominates the emotions that prevent self-control, and one of those emotions is "lust" (ἐπιθυμίας) (1:3). Reason that hinders "desire" (ἐπιθυμία) is before pleasure (1:22). Moderation is self-control "over the passions" (τῶν ἐπιθυμιῶν) (1:31), and reason rules over both fleshly and physical desires (τῶν ἐπιθυμιῶν) (1:32). The desires (αἱ ἐπιθυμίαι) of the mind are invalidated because of communion with beauty (2:1).[4] In an argument about the Spirit's power to overcome the flesh, Paul exhorts the Galatians to walk in the Spirit with the promise they would by no means walk in the "lust of the flesh" (ἐπιθυμίαν σαρκὸς) if they heeded his command (5:16). In the same argument later in the section, Paul exclaims those who belong to Christ have crucified the flesh "with the passions and the lusts" (σὺν τοῖς παθήμασιν καὶ ταῖς ἐπιθυμίαις) (5:24).

16. The Jewish martyrological traditions and Galatians use a form of the verb πορθέω *to talk about the destruction of or the abolishment of the law (4 Maccabees) or the destruction of the faith/church of God (Galatians).* Antiochus plundered (καὶ ὡς ἐπόρθησεν αὐτούς) his enemies (4 Macc 4:23). As one of the martyrs suffered torture, he asked Antiochus the reason he was attempting to destroy him and his family (πορθεῖς) (11:4). Paul says that he was himself attempting to destroy the church of God (ἐδίωκον τὴν ἐκκλησίαν τοῦ θεοῦ καὶ ἐπόρθουν αὐτήν) and that the assemblies of Judea in Christ heard that he was attempting to destroy the faith in his previous manner of life in Judaism (μόνον δὲ ἀκούοντες ἦσαν ὅτι ὁ διώκων ἡμᾶς ποτε νῦν εὐαγγελίζεται τὴν πίστιν ἥν ποτε ἐπόρθει) (Gal 1:13, 23).

17. The Jewish martyrological traditions and Galatians use a form of the verb καταλύω *to refer to destruction.* 2 Maccabees and 4 Maccabees refer to the abolishment of the law (2 Macc 2:22; 4:11; 4 Macc 1:6, 11; 4:16, 20, 24; 5:33; 7:9; 8:15; 11:24; 14:8; 17:2, 9). In Gal 2:18, Paul asserts that he would be a transgressor of the law if he rebuilds the law by referring to rebuilding the things that he destroyed (Gal 1:13).

18. The Jewish martyrological traditions and Galatians use a form of the verb Ἰουδαῖος *to refer to a Jew/Judean.* In 2 Macc 1:7, the author uses a plural form of Ἰουδαῖος to write to the Jews in Egypt in the first letter attached to the book.[5] In 4 Macc 5:7, the author uses a plural form

---

4. Cf. also 4 Macc 2:4, 6; 3:2, 11–12, 16; 5:23.
5. Cf. also 2 Macc 1:10; 3:32; 4:11, 35–36; 5:23, 25; 6:1, 6, 8; 8:10–11, 32, 34, 36; 9:4, 7, 15, 17–19; 10:8, 12, 14–15, 24, 29; 11:2, 15–16, 24, 27, 31, 34; 12:1, 3, 8, 17, 30, 34, 40; 13:9, 18–19, 23; 14:5–6, 14, 37, 39; 15:2, 12.

of Ἰουδαῖος to refer to pursuing the worship of the Jews (φιλοσοφεῖν τῇ Ἰουδαίων θρησκείᾳ). In Gal 2:13, when Peter withdrew from table-fellowship with the Gentiles in Antioch, the rest of the Jews followed his hypocrisy (καὶ συνυπεκρίθησαν αὐτῷ [καὶ] οἱ λοιποὶ Ἰουδαῖοι). In Gal 2:14, Paul reminds Peter that although he was a Jew (Ἰουδαῖος ὑπάρχων), he was living a Gentile manner of life until those from James came down from Jerusalem. In Gal 2:15, he reminds Peter that Jews are "Jews by birth" (Ἡμεῖς φύσει Ἰουδαῖοι). In Gal 3:28, Paul says that in Christ Jesus there is neither "Jew" (οὐκ ἔνι Ἰουδαῖος) nor Greek (οὐδὲ Ἕλλην).

19. The Jewish martyrological traditions and Galatians use a form of the noun φύσις to refer to something that is natural, originates from nature, or to one's natural birth or descent. In 4 Maccabees, the author refers to the emotions of pleasure and pain as naturally concerned with the soul and body (παθῶν δὲ φύσεις εἰσὶν αἱ περιεκτικώταται δύο ἡδονή τε καὶ πόνος τούτων δὲ ἑκάτερον καὶ περὶ τὸ σῶμα καὶ περὶ τὴν ψυχὴν πέφυκεν) (1:20).[6] In Gal 2:15, Paul reminds Peter they were Jews "by birth" (φύσει). In 4:8, as he appeals to the Galatians not to abandon his gospel, he asserts they served idols that were not naturally gods prior to their faith in Christ (Ἀλλὰ τότε μὲν οὐκ εἰδότες θεὸν ἐδουλεύσατε τοῖς φύσει μὴ οὖσιν θεοῖς).

20. The Jewish martyrological traditions and Galatians use a form of the noun ἀλήθεια to refer to truth. In 2 Maccabees, ἀλήθεια refers to true/accurate information (3:9; 7:6). In 4 Maccabees, ἀλήθεια is used in relation to an appeal to Eleazar to do what is beneficial for him in order to deliver himself from torture and martyrdom (5:11). The author also employs ἀλήθεια to refer to the law as truly divine (6:18). In Gal 2:5 (ἡ ἀλήθεια τοῦ εὐαγγελίου), 2:14 (τὴν ἀλήθειαν τοῦ εὐαγγελίου), and 5:7 (ἀληθείᾳ), Paul uses ἀλήθεια to refer to the gospel.

21. The Jewish martyrological traditions and Galatians use a form of the ὀρθο word group. 4 Maccabees uses the adjective ὀρθος to refer to sound reason (4 Macc 1:15; 6:7). Paul uses the verb ὀρθοποδέω to refer to walking in step with the gospel (Gal 2:14).

22. The Jewish martyrological traditions and Galatians use a form of the verb θέλω. 2 and 4 Maccabees use the verb to talk about one's desire or one's will to do something (2 Macc 2:24; 12:16; 4 Macc 17:9). In Galatians, Paul uses the verb to refer to one's desire to distort the gospel

---

6. Cf. also 4 Macc 5:8–9, 25; 13:27; 15:13, 25; 16:3.

of Christ (1:7) or to refer to his desire or willingness to know something (3:2). In 4:9, he speaks of the Galatians' willingness to enslave themselves again to idols as they contemplate a turn away from his gospel. In 4:17, the verb refers to Paul's opponents' desire to shut out the Galatians from the people of God. In 4:20, the verb refers to Paul's desire to be with the Galatians so that he could change his tone with them. In 4:21, the verb refers to the Galatians' desire to be under the law. In 5:17, the verb refers to the Galatians incapacity to do whatever they want as their desires pertain to the flesh and Spirit. In Gal 6:12–13, the verb refers to the opponents' desires to boast in the flesh because they, who desire the Galatians to receive circumcision, do not even keep the law themselves.

23. The Jewish martyrological traditions and Galatians use the term στύλος. In 4 Macc 17:9, στύλος refers to the mother of the seven sons, who both watched her sons become tortured and murdered and who also suffered torture and martyrdom. She is identified as the στύλος of her children. In Gal 2:9, Paul identifies Peter, James, and John as the pillars of the church with the noun στύλος.

24. The Jewish martyrological traditions and Galatians use a form of the noun σάρξ. 4 Maccabees uses σάρξ to refer to the martyrs' bodies (6:6).[7] Paul uses the term σάρξ to refer to one's bodily/human existence (Gal 2:20; 4:14, 23; 6:12–13), to circumcision (3:3), to sickness (4:13), to the old age and the realm dominated by sin (5:13, 16–17, 19), and to one's sinful desires dominated by the realm of the old age (6:8).

25. The Jewish martyrological traditions and Galatians use a form of the verb ἐξουθενέω *to refer to a group or to a person becoming despised.* 2 Maccabees 1:27 identifies exilic Jews as those who were despised by the Gentiles. In Gal 4:14, Paul reminds the Galatians that they did not despise their temptation in his flesh when he was sick.

26. The Jewish martyrological traditions and Galatians use a form of the verb ταράσσω. In 2 Macc 15:19, the verb refers to Jews who were emotionally troubled or anxious because of fear for their physical well-being due to war. In Gal 1:7 and 5:10, Paul uses the verb to refer to those who disturb the Galatians' faith by tempting them to turn away from his gospel to another gospel.

---

7. Cf. also 4 Macc 7:13, 18; 9:17, 20, 28; 10:8; 15:15, 20.

27. The Jewish martyrological traditions and Galatians use a form of the verb πάσχω *to refer to suffering.* In 2 and 4 Maccabees, the verb refers to suffering at the hands of Gentiles (2 Macc 6:30; 7:18, 32; 9:28; 4 Macc 9:8; 10:10; 14:9). In Gal 3:4, the verb refers to suffering because of one's faith in Christ.[8]

28. The Jewish martyrological traditions and Galatians use a form of the verb διώκω *to refer to the pursuit of someone or persecution.* In 2 Maccabees, the verb refers to pursuing someone with the intent of physically harming them (2:21; 5:8). In Galatians, the verb refers to pursuing someone with the intent of harming them physically (1:13, 23; 4:29; 5:11; 6:12).

29. The Jewish martyrological traditions and Galatians use a form of the προκοπ *word group.* In 2 Macc 8:8, εἰς προκοπὴν refers to the advancement of a military adversary. In Gal 1:14, the verb προέκοπτον refers to Paul's advancement in Judaism as he was persecuting the church of God (1:13).

30. The Jewish martyrological traditions and Galatians use a form of the noun πατήρ. In 2 Maccabees and 4 Maccabees, the noun refers to an earthly father or an ancestral father (2 Macc 9:23; 4 Macc 2:19; 7:1, 5, 11; 10:2; 16:20; 18:9). In Galatians, πατὴρ refers to God (1:1, 3–4; 4:6) and an earthly father (4:2).

31. The Jewish martyrological traditions and Galatians use the prepositional phrase ἐν ἐμοί. In 2 Macc 7:38, the seventh son prays that God's wrath would cease to be ἐν ἐμοὶ ("by means of me") and his brothers. In Galatians, Paul uses ἐν ἐμοὶ to refer to God revealing his Son in him to announce him as good news to the Gentiles, to say the Galatians were glorifying God in him when they heard about his conversation (1:24), and to affirm that Christ lives in him (2:20).

32. The Jewish martyrological traditions and Galatians use a form of the verb ζηλόω *to refer to living in a zealous way.* In 2 Macc 4:16, a form of the verb ζηλόω refers to having zeal for the ways of one's enemies. In Gal 4:17–18, Paul uses the verb to refer to his opponents seeking the Galatians with inappropriate zeal so that they would seek them.

---

8. For a discussion of suffering in Galatians, see Dunne, *Persecution and Participation in Galatians*.

33. The Jewish martyrological traditions and Galatians use a form of the verb ἀνατίθημι. In 2 Macc 5:16, ἀνατεθέντα refers to the vessels which were set forth by other kings. In Gal 2:2, ἀνεθέμην refers to Paul setting forth his gospel to the pillars in Jerusalem.

34. The Jewish martyrological traditions and Galatians use a form of the noun δόξα. In 2 Maccabees (2:8) and 4 Maccabees (1:12) the noun refers to the Lord's honor or splendor.[9] In Galatians, δόξα likewise refers to God's glory/splendor/honor (1:5).

35. The Jewish martyrological traditions and Galatians use a form of the noun ἁμαρτία. In 2 and 4 Maccabees, ἁμαρτία refers to sin as disobedience to Torah (2 Macc 2:11; 5:17; 6:14–15; 7:32; 12:42–43, 45; 4 Macc 5:19; 17:21). In Galatians, ἁμαρτία refers to individual acts of disobedience (1:4), to Torah disobedience (2:17), and to a power that enslaves (3:22).

36. The Jewish martyrological traditions and Galatians use a form of the verb τρέχω. In 2 and 4 Maccabees, forms of τρέχω refer to running or charging toward something (2 Macc 5:2; 4 Macc 12:10; 14:5). In Gal 2:2, Paul says he went up to Jerusalem to present his gospel to the pillars so that he would not run his race of the gospel in vain. In 5:7, Paul says the Galatians were running the race of the gospel well before the opponents hindered them from obeying the truth.

37. The Jewish martyrological traditions and Galatians use a form of the verb ἀθετέω. The verb refers to nullifying contracts (2 Macc 13:25; 14:28). In Gal 2:21, Paul says he does not nullify God's grace by preaching that righteousness comes through the law. In 3:15, the verb refers to nullifying a covenant.

38. The Jewish martyrological traditions and Galatians use a form of the noun διαθήκη. In 2 Maccabees, διαθήκη refers to God's covenant with Abraham and his offspring (1:2; 7:36). In 8:15, διαθήκη refers to the covenant of the martyrs' ancestors. In Gal 3:15 and 3:17, Paul uses διαθήκη to refer to the Abrahamic covenant continuing after the Mosaic law entered into the present evil age.

---

9. Cf. 2 Macc 3:26; 4:15; 5:16, 20; 6:11; 14:7; 15:2, 13; 4 Macc. 5:18; 6:18; 7:9; 18:24.

39. The Jewish martyrological traditions and Galatians use a form of the noun βασιλεία. In 2 and 4 Maccabees, the term refers to an earthly kingdom (2 Macc 4:7; 9:25; 10:11; 11:23; 14:6, 26; 4 Macc 15:13; 17:10). In Gal 5:21, βασιλεία refers to the kingdom of God.

40. The Jewish martyrological traditions and Galatians use a form of the noun γένος. In 2 and 4 Maccabees, γένος refers to family, descent, or a member of a group (2 Macc 1:10; 4 Macc 15:13).[10] In Gal 1:14, γένος refers to fellow Jews within Judaism.

41. The Jewish martyrological traditions and Galatians use a form of the term ἀνάθεμα. In 2 Maccabees, ἀνάθεμα refers to some kind of offering (2 Macc 2:13; 9:16). In Gal 1:8–9, ἀνάθεμα refers to an apostolic curse upon anyone who preaches another gospel besides the one preached by Paul.

42. The Jewish martyrological traditions and Galatians use the adjective ἐπικατάρατος *to refer to a curse.* In 4 Macc 2:19, ἐπικατάρατος refers to the curse of the Shechemites. In Gal 3:10 and 3:13, ἐπικατάρατος refers to the curse of the law (3:10) and Jesus's deliverance of "us" from the curse of the law (3:13).[11]

II. Polemical Similarities Between the Jewish Martyrological Traditions and Galatians

In addition to the lexical and grammatical similarities between the Jewish martyrological traditions and Galatians, there are also polemical similarities between these traditions and Galatians. I begin with a discussion of 2 and 4 Maccabees. Then, I discuss Galatians. Finally, I offer a summary.

1. 2 and 4 Maccabees defend the superiority of Judaism. In 2 Macc 6:18–7:42, the author(s) and final redactor present the martyrdoms of Eleazar, the mother, and her seven sons as conquering the Greek tyrant, Antiochus, and his gods by their steadfast devotion to their God, his law, and their religion, even in the face intense suffering and death. Eleazar

---

10. Cf. also 2 Macc 5:22; 6:12; 7:16, 28, 38; 8:9; 12:31; 14:8–9; 4 Macc 17:10.
11. The noun ὑπόκρισιν occurs in 2 Macc 6:25 to refer to Eleazar's refusal to be complicit in hypocrisy to spare himself from torture and death. The verb συνυπεκρίθησαν occurs in Gal 2:13 to refer to Christ-following Jews playing the role of the hypocrite by imitating Peter's actions to withdraw from table fellowship with Christ-following Jews.

welcomed death with honor rather than pollute his life and religion when Antiochus commanded him to eat swine (6:18–31). One of the seven sons, acting as the spokesperson for his mother and his brothers, vociferated in the Hebrew tongue that they were ready to die for their religion rather than transgress the laws of their ancestors (7:2). 2 Maccabees discourages Jewish assimilation into Hellenism via its presentation of the resilience of the faithful martyrs in the martyrological sections of 7:1–42 and by the discussion of the efficacy of the martyrs' deaths (8:1–5).

In 4 Maccabees, the martyrological sections of 6:1–12:19 and the author's commentary in 17:21–22 about the effect of the martyrs' deaths defend the veracity and superiority of Judaism against Hellenism.[12] The martyrs remain steadfast to Judaism and to their God. Consequently, the author asserts that their deaths purified and saved the nation (17:21–22).

In 4 Macc 1:1, the author states his thesis that religious reasoning masters the passions. He reiterates this thesis throughout 4 Maccabees (1:17; 2:23; 13:1–18:24) and defends it through the steadfast devotion of Eleazar, the mother, and her seven sons to God's law. Additionally, the author's encomium of the martyrs and the mother's speech, after watching the execution of her seven sons, serves as the proof of the thesis. Religious reasoning comes from obedience to Torah (1:1–6:30). The author argues Judaism is invincible (9:18), and Torah obedience leads to participation in the immortality of the soul (5:37; 7:16–19; 13:17). Thus, both 2 and 4 Maccabees seek to defend the veracity of and superiority of Judaism over Hellenism for the purpose of persuading them to remain faithful to Torah.

2. In Galatians, Paul similarly defends his gospel with anti-Torah polemics. In Gal 3:13, Paul refers to the death of the cursed Christ to defend the superiority and veracity of his gospel, which (by the time he wrote Galatians) was becoming more popular with Gentiles. He presents the cursed Christ as an argument against his agitators' gospel (cf. 1:7).

Paul states from the outset of the letter that those who turn away from his gospel distort the gospel and are under a curse (1:6–9; 2:11–14). He presents Jesus's death, not the law, as the solution for those under the Deuteronomic curse (3:10–13) and as the pathway through which both the Abrahamic blessing and the Mosaic covenant find their fulfillment (3:1–4:31).

Paul's argumentative tone begins the letter. With a curse-pronouncement in 1:6–9 and a conditional blessing pronouncement in 6:16, Paul frames 3:1–6:10 with both expressions of shock and exhortations not to turn away

---

12. More than one scholar has pointed out that 2 Maccabees defends the superiority of Judaism.

from his Torah-free Gentile-inclusive gospel to the non-Torah-observant Gentile-exclusive gospel of the opponents. In 1:6–9, Paul expresses shock that the Galatians were turning so quickly from his gospel to another gospel. He also anathematizes those who either believe or preach another gospel besides his. In Gal 1:10, he asserts that he pleases God and not men, giving the impression that the Torah-observant preachers seek to please men. In Gal 1:11–2:10, Paul argues his gospel is superior to the other gospel because he asserts he received it from Jesus Christ and God, the Father, who raised him from the dead (1:1).

In 2:11–14, Paul argues his gospel is superior to the Torah-observant gospel when he rebukes Peter for requiring the Gentiles to live a Jewish way of life in Antioch. He names his life in Judaism as a former way of life after God revealed his son in him to preach him as good news to the Gentiles (1:13, 15, 16). In Gal 2:15–21, he reminds Peter that Jews and Gentiles are justified by faith in Christ and not by works of the law. In Gal 5:1–6:10, Paul urges the Galatians to live in the freedom of the gospel and in the power of the Spirit rather than embrace another gospel.

In Gal 6:11–16, Paul ends the letter by accusing those who preach circumcision of being afraid of being persecuted for the cross of Christ (6:12). He accuses them of not keeping the law themselves (6:13). In 6:14–16, Paul concludes the letter by saying he boasts only in the cross of Jesus Christ and not in circumcision.

Thus, the Jewish martyrological traditions and Galatians are polemical. The former polemically argue for the veracity and the superiority of Judaism over Hellenism and to persuade Jews not Hellenize. Paul's entire argument in Galatians is polemical. He defends his gospel against his opponents, who preach circumcision and Torah, in order to dissuade the Galatians from turning away from his gospel to the other so that they would inherit the kingdom of God.

III. Additional Theological and Conceptual Similarities Between the Jewish Martyrological Traditions and Galatians

The Jewish martyrological traditions and Galatians have additional theological and conceptual points of contact. Both refer to zeal for the law (4 Macc. 16:16; Gal 1:14). Both refer to Jew–Gentile relations (2 Macc 5:1–8:5; Gal 2:11–14). Both refer to the importance of a covenant (2 Macc 1:2; 7:36; 8:15; Gal 3:15, 17). Both refer to the curse of disobeying Torah and the blessing of obeying Torah (2 Macc 7:32–38; Gal 3:10–12).[13] Both refer to the Abrahamic covenant (2 Macc 1:2; Gal

---

13. For other texts of curse and blessing, see Gal 1:6–9; 2:11–14; 6:16.

3:15–18). Both refer to an angel from heaven in the context of a divine curse or judgment (2 Macc 11:6; 15:21–23; 4 Macc 4:10; Gal 1:8). Both refer to retributive judgment (2 Macc 5:17; 6:12–17; 7:28–32; 4 Macc 6:28–29; Gal 3:10–13). Both refer to suffering and persecution (2 Macc 5:1–7:42; 4 Macc 5:1–17:16; Gal 1:13, 23; 3:4; 4:13–29; 5:11; 6:12–17). Both have parenetic sections that appeal to their respective audiences to be faithful to God in the context of suffering (2 Macc 6:12–17; Gal 4:12–6:10). Both refer to eternal life (2 Macc 7:9, 23, 29; 4 Macc 5:37; 7:18–19; 13:13; Gal 1:1; 2:19–3:29).

IV. Conclusion

This chapter focused on lexical, grammatical, and additional theological and conceptual similarities between Second Temple Jewish martyrological traditions and Galatians in order to support the thesis of *a* martyrological background behind Gal 3:13. I discussed two specific kinds of similarities in this chapter. First, building upon Stephen Anthony Cummins's lexical and grammatical work in his monograph on Gal 1–2,[14] I discussed lexical and grammatical similarities between Second Temple Jewish martyrological traditions and Galatians. I argued Paul's letter to the Galatians has multiple lexical and grammatical similarities and points of contact with Jewish martyrological traditions. This section simply listed and briefly discussed the texts in which these lexical and grammatical connections occur in order to highlight these similarities.

Second, I discussed the additional conceptual similarities between the Jewish martyrological traditions and Gal 3:13 that are important for my thesis, but do not provide enough material to provide their own independent chapter. This part of the analysis argued the Jewish martyrological narratives and Galatians are similar in that they are highly polemical in their efforts to defend Judaism (Jewish martyrological narratives) or the gospel (Galatians). 2 Maccabees seeks to defend the superiority of Judaism over Hellenism and argues against extreme Hellenization in an effort to dissuade Jews from eradicating a Jewish way of life with a turn from the law. 4 Maccabees argues religious reasoning (i.e. devotion to Torah) masters the "passions," even in the face of extreme suffering. Paul seeks to defend his Torah-free and Gentile-inclusive gospel against the Torah-observant and Gentile-exclusive gospel of his opponents and argues against compelling the Gentiles to live a Jewish way of life in an effort to dissuade the Galatians from turning away from his gospel to embrace a Jewish way of life.

14. Cummins, *Paul and the Crucified Christ in Antioch*, 100–35.

6

CONCLUSION:
A JEWISH MARTYROLOGICAL READING
OF GALATIANS 3:13

This concluding chapter applies the analysis from Chapters 2–5 to support a Jewish martyrological reading of Gal 3:13. Based on the analysis, this chapter concludes there are similarities and dissimilarities between the Jewish martyrological traditions and Galatians. A discussion of these similarities and dissimilarities attempts to strengthen the thesis that the Jewish martyrological traditions are *a* background (not *the* background) against which we should read Gal 3:13 and that Paul has discontinuities with these traditions to fit his own exegetical, theological, and polemical purposes in his argument in Galatians. While acknowledging that there are areas of discontinuity between Jewish martyrology and Paul's presentation of the cursed Christ in Gal 3:13, this chapter also discusses the reason a Jewish martyrological reading of Gal 3:13 provides fresh insights into the death of the cursed Christ "for us" in Paul's soteriology in Galatians.

I. Deuteronomic Blessings and Curses in Second Temple Jewish Martyrological Traditions

In Chapter 2, I analyzed the Deuteronomic blessings and curses motif in the Jewish martyrological traditions for the purpose of providing data for a comparative reading of the Deuteronomic blessing and curse motif in Galatians in Chapter 3. I made six specific arguments in that chapter. First, the Jewish martyrological traditions conflate the Abrahamic blessing and Deuteronomic blessings to show the pathway to the Abrahamic blessing is obedience to Torah. Second, the Jewish martyrological traditions appropriate Deuteronomic blessings to Torah-observant Jews. Third, the Jewish martyrological traditions appropriate the Deuteronomic curses to non-Torah-observant Jews. Fourth, the Jewish martyrological traditions posit Torah-observant Jewish martyrs as the means by which non-Torah-observant Jews would receive the life promised in Torah. Fifth, the Jewish martyrological traditions interpret the promise of temporal life in the land as eternal life in the age to come through faithful Torah observance. Sixth, the Jewish martyrological traditions suggest Torah-observant Jews would experience eternal life in the age to come by Torah observance. I supported these arguments with an analysis of selected texts from LXX Dan 3 and 2 and 4 Maccabees

2 Maccabees' presentation of martyrdom supports conceptual connections with the Deuteronomic blessings and curses. (1) The Torah-observant martyrs suffered with non-Torah-observant Jews (7:32). The martyrs represent the nation (7:32). They were members of YHWH's covenant community for which they suffered (7:16, 30, 30–32, 38). The author of 2 Maccabees calls Antiochus the adversary of the Hebrews, not simply the adversary of the martyrs (7:31). (2) The martyrological narratives follow statements about the positive role of suffering in the lives of God's covenant people (6:12–17). The author suggests Antiochus believed the deaths of the seven sons proved the Lord had forsaken his people (7:16). But blessing comes to the nation because of the martyrs' Torah-observant and faithful deaths (7:28–32), while suffering because of non-Torah observance (6:18–8:5).

The martyrs suffered and died with and for the nation, although they were Torah-observant. 2 Maccabees' presentation of the martyrs' suffering and death echoes Israel's antecedent Deuteronomic history, thereby personifying the Deuteronomic blessings and curses set forth in Deut 27–28 in a new context in the deaths of the martyrs. The author's appeal to Deut 32 supports this conclusion.

Deuteronomy 32 is Moses's song of praise to the Lord for his faithful provision to Israel. The chapter also promises the certainty of judgment if the nation disobeys Torah. In LXX Deut 32:36, the text states the Lord will vindicate his people, and he will show compassion to his servants. 2 Maccabees 7:33 applies this text to martyrdom by stating that the Lord will be reconciled again to his servants. The martyrs brought reconciliation (peace and blessing) to the land by means of their deaths (1:5; 7:33; 8:29). Curse comes to the nation because of non-Torah observance; curse comes upon the martyrs because of the nation's non-Torah observance, and Deuteronomic blessing comes upon the nation because of the martyrs' faithful deaths, Judas's military action, and effective prayer.

The analysis of texts in 4 Maccabees supported the following. 4 Maccabees 4:19–21 states that after Jason, the high priest, led the nation astray from Torah, the Lord became angry and used Antiochus to wage war against Israel. The elaborate discussions of the martyrdoms of Eleazar, the mother, and her seven sons in 5:1–12:19, and the narrator's comments regarding the efficacy of the martyrs' deaths in 17:21–22 suggest the Lord displayed the curses of Deuteronomy by means of both Jewish exile from the land and death in the land, both of which Deuteronomy connects to Torah-observance and non-Torah-observance (Deut 21:22, 26; 28:21; 30:15–20). The Lord also distributes the Deuteronomic blessing of peace in the land through the martyrs' deaths (6:28–29; 17:21–22). The author of 4 Maccabees emphasizes the martyrs' loyalty to the law by asserting more than once that they were eager to die for it (5:16, 33–34; 6:21, 27, 30; 7:7–8; 9:2, 15; 11:12, 27; 13:9, 13; 15:9, 29; 16:16; 17:16). He also alludes to commandments in Torah (1:34; 2:5–6, 8–10, 14). Thus, since death in the land was in fact one of those curses pronounced in Deuteronomy against those who disobey Torah (e.g. 8:1), 4 Maccabees applies the Deuteronomic curses to the non-Torah-observant nation and to the Torah-observant martyrs. Blessings came to the nation in the narrative through the deaths of the Torah-observant martyrs for the law, but disobedience to the law of Moses brought a curse.

II. Deuteronomic Blessings and Curses in Galatians

In Chapter 3, I argued that in a way similar to, and yet different from, the Jewish martyrological traditions, Paul presents both Jews and Gentiles as recipients of the Deuteronomic blessings and curses in Galatians. He contends that Jesus, the Torah-observant (but cursed) Christ, suffered the Deuteronomic curses for others, experienced the blessing of life (i.e. resurrection), and delivered those for whom he died from the curse of the law. Jesus's death for Jews and Gentiles delivers them from the present evil age so that they would participate by faith in the Deuteronomic blessing of life in this age and in the age to come and so that they would be delivered from the law's curse. But those without faith in Christ are currently under the Deuteronomic curses and are devoted to destruction if they preach another gospel contrary to the one preached by Paul. The purpose of the analysis in this chapter was to support the view that Galatians has both continuities with and discontinuities with the blessing and curse motif in the Jewish martyrological traditions in order to add further support for the position that the Jewish martyrological traditions are *a* background behind Paul's remarks about the cursed Christ in Gal 3:13. However, Paul modifies the martyrological ideas in these traditions to fit his polemical purposes in Galatians. The chapter endeavored to support the following arguments about Paul's appropriation of the Deuteronomic blessings and curses in Galatians.

First, Paul appropriates the Deuteronomic blessings and curses to Jews and Gentiles without ethnic restriction. That is, he maintains both Jews and Gentiles are under the curse of the law because both groups are under the present evil age (Gal 1:4), under a curse (3:10), under sin (3:22), under slavery (3:23; 4:21–25), and under the elements of the world (4:8–9). Second, Paul appropriates Deuteronomic blessings to those who identify with Jesus Christ, the seed of Abraham, apart from works of the law, and he applies the Deuteronomic curses to those who identify with works of Torah apart from or in addition to faith in Christ without ethnic restriction. Third, Paul conflates the Abrahamic and Deuteronomic blessings and curses in Galatians to emphasize that both the Abrahamic blessing and the Deuteronomic blessing pertain to the distribution of the Spirit and justification by faith, extended to Jews and Gentiles by faith in the Messiah, and that both are realized in the death (and resurrection) of the Messiah, Jesus, apart from Torah. The Deuteronomic curses come to those under works of law.

In the Jewish martyrological traditions, the Deuteronomic blessings are conferred to the Jewish martyrs in order to deliver the nation from the curse of the Torah because of the nation's disobedience to it. The Jewish martyrological narratives suggest the covenant with Abraham is fulfilled for Jews by means of their Torah-observance and the noble deaths of the Jewish martyrs for Israel (2 and 4 Maccabees), by means of military action (2 Maccabees), and by means of effective prayer (2 and 4 Maccabees). Paul, however, suggests the Deuteronomic curses are realized in Torah-observant Jews and Gentiles who remain under the curse of the law outside of faith in Jesus, the Messiah, in Galatians. But Jesus, the Jewish Messiah, personified the Deuteronomic curse (death) and blessing (resurrection/life) on behalf of Jews and Gentiles under the Deuteronomic curse to confer the Abrahamic blessing, namely, a universal outpouring of the Spirit (and all of the Spirit's benefits) upon Jewish and Gentile followers of Christ, so that the life, promised in the law, would be realized by Jews and Gentiles by faith in Christ apart from Torah-observance (Gal 3:1–5:26). Fourth, Paul understands the promise in Lev 18:5 and Deut 27–30, that Torah observance leads to long life in the land, as eternal life. This eternal life is experienced in this age and in the age to come apart from the works of the law by Jews and Gentiles who place faith in Jesus because he died (and resurrected) to deliver them from the present evil age and from the curse of the law. Fifth, Jesus received the Deuteronomic curse so that Jews and Gentiles would receive both the Abrahamic blessing of the Spirit and the Deuteronomic blessing of life.

Sixth, the Abrahamic blessing of the Spirit and the Deuteronomic blessing of life are realized in the universal distribution of the Spirit to Jews and Gentiles by faith because of the death of the Christ who delivers Jews and Gentiles from the curse of the law. Paul conflates the Abrahamic and Deuteronomic blessings and curses in Galatians to emphasize that both the Abrahamic blessing and the Deuteronomic blessing are extended to Jews and Gentiles by faith in the Messiah and realized in the death (and resurrection) of the Messiah, Jesus, apart from Torah, whereas the Jewish martyrological narratives suggest the covenant with Abraham is fulfilled for Jews by means of Torah observance and the noble deaths of the Jewish martyrs for Israel (2 and 4 Maccabees), by means of military action (2 Maccabees), and by means of effective prayer (2 and 4 Maccabees).

According to Paul, both the Abrahamic curse and the Deuteronomic curse are realized in Torah-observant Jews and Gentiles who remain under the curse of the law outside of faith in Jesus, the Messiah, in Galatians. But Jesus, the Jewish Messiah, received the Deuteronomic curse on behalf of Jews and Gentiles under the Deuteronomic curse so that the Abrahamic blessing, namely, a universal outpouring of the Spirit upon Jewish and Gentile followers of Christ, would be distributed to Jews and Gentiles by faith in Christ apart from Torah observance.

III. Representation and Substitution in Second Temple Jewish Martyrological Traditions and in Galatians 3:13

Relying upon the definition of J. W. van Henten, in Chapter 4, I defined a Jewish martyrology as a story about a Torah-observant Jew who dies as a martyr at the hands of an antagonist Gentile tyrant instead of yielding to the threat of the pagan authorities, when the Tyrant presents the Torah-observant Jew with the choice of renouncing obedience to Torah or suffering death as a result of his obedience to Torah.[1] The Jewish martyr dies to accomplish soteriological benefits for those in the covenant community whose disobedience to Torah provides the reason in the narrative as to why those Torah observant in the community suffer martyrdom at the hands of a Gentile tyrant. The Second Temple texts discussed in this chapter fit within this definition.

In Chapter 4, I argued the Jewish martyrological narratives present the martyrs as dying as representatives of and substitutes for non-Torah-observant Jews (LXX Dan 3:1–90; 2 Macc 7:32–38; 4 Macc 6:28–29; 17:21–22). In the face of death, Eleazar urges God in 4 Macc 6:28 to be merciful to Israel through his death (ἵλεως γενοῦ τῷ ἔθνει σου) (2 Macc

---

1. For a definition of Jewish martyrology, see the sources cited in Chapter 4.

4:1–6:31; 4 Macc 5:4–6:40). 4 Maccabees 6:29 states Eleazar asks God to make his blood to be Israel's purification (καθάρσιον αὐτῶν ποίησον τὸ ἐμὸν αἷμα). In the final part of his prayer in 4 Macc 6:29b, Eleazar asks God to receive his death as a ransom for the nation (καὶ ἀντίψυχον αὐτῶν λαβὲ τὴν ἐμὴν ψυχήν). The author of 4 Maccabees interprets the martyrs' deaths to be both sacrificial in nature and a saving event for the nation in 4 Macc 17:21–22 (καὶ τὸν τύραννον τιμωρηθῆναι καὶ τὴν πατρίδα καθαρισθῆναι ὥσπερ ἀντίψυχον γεγονότας τῆς τοῦ ἔθνους ἁμαρτίας καὶ διὰ τοῦ αἵματος τῶν εὐσεβῶν ἐκείνων καὶ τοῦ ἱλαστηρίου τοῦ θανάτου αὐτῶν ἡ θεία πρόνοια τὸν Ισραηλ προκακωθέντα διέσωσεν). Deuteronomy 27 and 28 state that if Israel disobeyed Torah in the land, they would be cursed, but if they obeyed, they would be blessed. The martyrs suffered the Deuteronomic curses of the community's disobedience in 2 Maccabees. Texts in 4 Maccabees likewise apply Deuteronomy to the Jewish martyrs.

In Gal 3:10–14, Paul applies Deuteronomy to Jesus in a way similar to the martyrological narratives to fit his exegetical, theological, and polemical purposes. Similar to the Jewish martyrological narratives, Paul presents Jesus's death (a Torah-observant Jew) as a representation in Gal 3:13 with Deuteronomic language in order to advance his exegetical, theological, and polemical purposes in Gal 3:10–14. Paul presents Jesus's death (a Torah-observant Jew) as a substitution for others in Gal 3:13 with Deuteronomic language in order to advance his exegetical, theological, and polemical purposes in Gal 3:10–14.

IV. Lexical, Grammatical, and Additional Conceptual Similarities Between Second Temple Jewish Martyrological Traditions and Galatians

In Chapter 5, I discussed lexical, grammatical, and additional conceptual similarities between Second Temple Jewish martyrological traditions and Galatians in order to support the thesis of a Jewish martyrological background behind Gal 3:13. I discussed two specific kinds of similarities in this chapter. First, building upon Stephen Anthony Cummins's lexical and grammatical work in his monograph on Gal 1–2,[2] I discussed several lexical and grammatical similarities between Second Temple Jewish martyrological traditions and Galatians. I argued that Paul's letter to the Galatians has multiple lexical and grammatical similarities and points of contact with Jewish martyrological traditions. This section simply listed and briefly analyzed the texts in which these lexical and grammatical connections occur in order to highlight these similarities.

2. Cummins, *Paul and the Crucified Christ in Antioch*, 100–135.

Second, I pointed out additional conceptual similarities between the Jewish martyrological traditions and Gal 3:13 that are important for my thesis, but that do not provide enough material to provide their own independent chapter. This part of the analysis argued the Jewish martyrological narratives and Galatians are similar in that they are highly polemical in their efforts to defend Judaism (Jewish martyrological narratives) or the gospel (Galatians). 2 Maccabees seeks to defend the superiority of Judaism over Hellenism and argues against extreme Hellenization in an effort to dissuade Jews from eradicating a Jewish way of life by turning from the law. 4 Maccabees argues religious reasoning (i.e. devotion to Torah) masters the "passions," even in the face of extreme suffering. Paul, however, seeks to defend his Torah-free and Gentile-inclusive gospel against the Torah-observant and Gentile-exclusive gospel of his opponents. He further argues against compelling the Gentiles to live a Jewish way of life in an effort to dissuade the Galatians from turning away from his gospel to embrace a Jewish way of life.

V. The Contribution of a Jewish Martyrological Background Behind the Death of the Cursed Christ in Galatians 3:13

To my knowledge, no book-length monograph has been written to compare and contrast Jewish martyrological traditions with Gal 3:13 with the intent of arguing they provide *a* background against which to understand Paul's remarks about the cursed Christ in Gal 3:13. This monograph has argued Jewish martyrological traditions are *a* background behind Gal 3:13, but they are not saying exactly the same thing about the martyrs' deaths for Israel (Jewish martyrological traditions) and Christ's "redemption of us from the curse of the law by becoming a curse for us" (Gal 3:13). This monograph contributes to the conversation regarding the representative versus the substitutionary nature of Jesus's death in Galatians by arguing a Jewish martyrological background behind Gal 3:13 allows for both ideas to be present in Paul's conception and presentation of the Christ's death in Galatians since the Jewish martyrological narratives provide the earliest examples of Torah-observant Jews dying as representatives of and as substitutes for others.

A comparative reading of Gal 3:13 with Jewish martyrological traditions provides another historical context (amongst others) to help readers understand that in Christ, Paul now claims the heirs of the Abrahamic blessing and the heirs of the life promised in Torah are Jews and Gentiles by faith in Christ apart from works of the law in light of the revelation of God about the cursed/crucified Christ. The Jewish martyrological traditions make it clear that Torah leads to life. The teachers in Galatia likewise taught that law leads to life. The Jewish martyrological traditions further demonstrate that even when Jews died for the sins of the nation for disobeying Torah, a goal of Jewish resilience is to provoke others to be faithful to Torah and to motivate the nation to return to Torah observance. The teachers in Galatia appear to be zealous for the Galatians to embrace Torah and attempt to win converts to Torah observance.

Paul, on the other hand, suggests the death of the cursed Christ put an end to Torah once and for all because Torah is part of the present evil age. In Paul's re-conceptualization of Torah in light of God's revelation of the cursed (and resurrected) Christ to him and in light of a Jewish martyrological background behind the death of the cursed Christ, Paul suggests the law only leads to a curse and to a dead end with respect to eschatological life in this age and in the age to come. Since the law cursed the Christ, Paul suggests all under its jurisdiction in this present evil age are certainly under its curse. The cursed Christ became cursed by the law even though he was Torah-observant, whereas the martyrs were promised life in this age and in the age to come because of their obedience to Torah.

Paul suggests Jesus suffered the curse of the law, but distributed the life promised in it by means of a universal distribution of the Spirit to Jews and Gentiles who have faith in Jesus. Paul uses Jewish martyrological ideas to show that the cursed Christ did for Jews and for Gentiles what the law could not do: namely, distribute the universal promise of the Abrahamic blessing, which is the Spirit and the soteriological blessings realized by the indwelling presence of the Spirit in the hearts of Jews and Gentiles. Thus, when Paul says "Christ redeemed us from the curse of the law," he presents Jesus's death, the death of the cursed Christ, as the most significant death in Jewish history that finally by faith redeems everyone (Jews and Gentiles) under the law's jurisdiction from its universal curse. The death of the cursed Christ was both similar to and different from the Jewish martyrs before him, whose deaths both delivered Jews from the curse of the law and whose obedience to the law led them (the martyred) to the life that Torah promised. Paul contends that the death of the cursed Christ was similar to but different from the deaths of the Jewish martyrs since the cursed Christ represented those under the curse and since he became a curse for them so that Jews and Gentiles would receive the life promised in Torah. The life promised in Lev 18:5 and elsewhere is only realized by faith in the cursed Christ, who redeemed Jews and Gentiles from the curse of the law by becoming a curse for them, so that they would receive the Abrahamic blessing of life in the Spirit by faith in this age, a life that leads them to life in the age to come.

Bibliography

Abel, Felix Marie. *Les Livres des Maccabées*. Paris: J. Gabalda, 1949.
Arenhoevel, Diego. *Die Theokratie nach dem 1. und 2. Makkabäerbuch.* Walberger Studien der Albertus-Magnus-Akademie Theologische Reihe 3. Mainz: Matthias-Grünewald-Verlag, 1967.
Attridge, Harold. "2nd Maccabees." Pages 176–83 in *Jewish Writings of the Second Temple Period: Apocrypha, Pseudepigrapha, Qumran, Sectarian Writings, Philo, Josephus*, edited by Michael E. Stone. Compendia Rerum Iudaicarum Ad Novum Testamentum 2. Philadelphia: Fortress, 1984.
Augustine. *Augustine's Commentary on Galatians*. Translated by Eric Antone Plumer. Oxford Early Christian Studies 5. New York: Oxford University Press, 2003.
Bailey, Daniel Peter. "Jesus as the Mercy Seat: The Semantics and Theology of Paul's Use of Hilasterion in Romans 3:25." PhD, University of Cambridge, 1999.
Baumeister, Theofried. *Die Anfänge der Theologie des Martyriums*. MBT 45. Münster: Aschendorff, 1980.
Baumgarten, Joseph M. "Does *TLH* in the Temple Scroll Refer to Crucifixion?" *JBL* 91 (1972): 472–81.
———. "Hanging and Treason in Qumran and Roman Law." *Erets-Yisrael* 16 (1982): 7–8.
Betz, Hans Dieter. *Galatians*. Hermeneia. Philadelphia: Fortress, 1979.
Betz, Otto. *Jesus, der Herr der Kirche: Aufsätze zur Biblischen Theologie II*. WUNT 52. Tübingen: Mohr Siebeck, 1990.
Bickermann, Elias. "Ein jüdischer Festbrief vom Jahre 124 v. Chr. (II Macc. 1.1–9)." *ZNW* 32 (1933): 233–53.
Bird, Michael F. *An Anomalous Jew: Paul among Jews, Greeks, and Romans*. Grand Rapids: Eerdmans, 2016.
Bird, Michael F., and Preston M. Sprinkle, eds. *The Pistis Christou Debate, The Faith of Jesus Christ: Exegetical, Biblical, and Theological Studies*. Peabody, MA: Hendrickson, 2009.
Blank, Josef. *Paulus und Jesus: Eine Theologische Grundlegung*. Studien zum Alten und Neuen Testament 18. Munich: Kösel-Verlag, 1968.
Boer, M. C. de. *Galatians: A Commentary*. NTL. Louisville: Westminster John Knox, 2011.
Bolyki, János. "As Soon as the Signal Was Given (2 Macc. 4.14): Gymnasia in the Service of Hellenism." Pages 131–9 in *The Books of the Maccabees: History, Theology, Ideology: Papers of the Second International Conference on the Deuterocanonical Books, Pápa, Hungary, 9-11 June, 2005*, edited by Géza G. Xeravits and József Zsengellér. JSJSup 118. Leiden: Brill, 2007.
Bowersock, G. W. *Martyrdom and Rome*. Cambridge: Cambridge University Press, 1995.
Breytenbach, Cilliers. *Versöhnung: Eine Studie zur Paulinischen Soteriologie*. WMANT 60. Neukirchen-Vluyn: Neukirchener, 1989.
Brondos, David A. "The Cross and the Curse: Galatians 3.13 and Paul's Doctrine of Redemption." *JSNT* 81 (2001): 3–32.
———. *Paul on the Cross: Reconstructing the Apostle's Story of Redemption*. Minneapolis: Fortress, 2006.

Brownlee, William H. "From Holy War to Holy Martyrdom." Pages 281–92 in *The Quest for the Kingdom of God: Studies in Honor of George E. Mendenhall*, edited by H. B. Huffmon, F. A. Spina, and A. R. Green. Winona Lake, IN: Eisenbrauns, 1983.

Bruce, F. F. *The Epistle to the Galatians: A Commentary on the Greek Text*. New International Greek Testament Commentary. Grand Rapids: Eerdmans, 1982.

Bunge, Jochen Gabriel. "Untersuchungen zum zweiten Makkabäerbuch: Quellenkritische, literarische, chronologische und historische Untersuchungen zum zweiten Makkabäerbuch als Quelle syrisch-palästinensischer Geschichte im 2. Jh. v. Chr." PhD diss., Rheinische Friedrich-Wilhelms-Universität, 1971.

———. "Theos Epiphanes: Zu den ersten fünf Regierungsjahren des Antiochos IV Epiphanes." *Historia* 23 (1974): 57–85.

Campbell, Douglas A. *The Deliverance of God: An Apocalyptic Rereading of Justification in Paul*. Grand Rapids: Eerdmans, 2009.

Chapman, David W. *Ancient Jewish and Christian Perceptions of Crucifixion*. Grand Rapids: Eerdmans, 2010.

Ciampa, Roy E. *The Presence and Function of Scripture in Galatians 1 and 2*. WUNT 2/102. Tübingen: Mohr Siebeck, 1998.

Cohen, Shaye J. D. *The Beginnings of Jewishness: Boundaries, Varieties, Uncertainties*. Hellenistic Culture and Society 31. Berkeley: University of California Press, 1999.

Collins, John J. *Jewish Cult and Hellenistic Culture: Essays on the Jewish Encounter with Hellenism and Roman Rule*. JSJSup 100. Leiden: Brill, 2005.

———. *The Invention of Judaism: Torah and Jewish Identity from Deuteronomy to Paul*. Oakland, CA: University of California Press, 2017.

Cook, John Granger. *Crucifixion in the Mediterranean World*. WUNT 327. Mohr Siebeck, 2014.

Cosgrove, Charles H. *The Cross and the Spirit: A Study in the Argument and Theology of Galatians*. Macon, GA: Mercer University Press, 1988.

Cummins, Stephen Anthony. *Paul and the Crucified Christ in Antioch: Maccabean Martyrdom and Galatians 1 and 2*. SNTSMS 114. Cambridge: Cambridge University Press, 2001.

Cunliffe, Barry W., and Tomlin Roger, eds. *The Temple of Sulis Minerva at Bath*. Vol. 2. 2 vols. Committee for Archaeology 16. Oxford: Oxford University Committee for Archaeology., 1988.

Dahl, Nils. "The Atonement: An Adequate Reward for the Akedah? (Rom. 8.32)." Pages 15–29 in *Neotestamentica et Semitica: Studies in Honour of Matthew Black*, edited by E. Earle Ellis and Max E. Wilcox. Edinburgh: T. & T. Clark, 1969.

Daly, Robert J. *Christian Sacrifice: The Judaeo-Christian Background before Origen*. SCA. Washington, DC: The Catholic University of America Press, 1978.

———. "Soteriological Significance of the Sacrifice of Isaac." *CBQ* 39 (1977): 45–75.

Das, A. Andrew. *Galatians*. Concordia Commentary: A Theological Exposition of Sacred Scripture. St. Louis: Concordia, 2014.

———. *Paul and the Jews*. LPS. Peabody, MA: Hendrickson, 2003.

———. *Paul and the Stories of Israel: Grand Thematic Narratives in Galatians*. Minneapolis: Fortress, 2016.

———. *Paul, the Law, and the Covenant*. Peabody, MA: Hendrickson, 2001.

Davis, Basil S. *Christ as Devotio: The Argument of Galatians 3:1–14*. Lanham, MD: University Press of America, 2002.

deSilva, David A. *4 Maccabees: Introduction and Commentary on the Greek Text in Codex Sinaiticus*. SCS. Leiden: Brill, 2006.

———. *The Letter to the Galatians*. NICNT. Grand Rapids: Eerdmans, 2018.

Donaldson, T. L. "The 'Curse of the Law' and the Inclusion of the Gentiles: Galatians 3.13-14." *NTS* 32 (1986): 94–112.

Doran, Robert. *2 Maccabees: A Critical Commentary*. Minneapolis: Fortress, 2012.

———. "The Second Book of Maccabees." In *The New Interpreter's Bible*, Vol. 4. Abingdon, 1996.

———. *Temple Propaganda: The Purpose and Character of 2 Maccabees*. CBQMS 12. Washington, DC: Catholic Biblical Association of America, 1981.

Downing, John. "Jesus and Martyrdom." *JTS* 14 (1963): 279–93.

Duncan, George Simpson. *The Epistle of Paul to the Galatians*. London: Hodder & Stoughton, 1934.

Dunn, James D. G. *The Epistle to the Galatians*. Black's New Testament Commentaries. Peabody, MA: Hendrickson, 1993.

———. *Jesus, Paul, and the Law: Studies in Mark and Galatians*. Louisville: Westminster John Knox, 1990.

———. *The Theology of Paul the Apostle*. Grand Rapids: Eerdmans, 1998.

Dunne, John Anthony. *Persecution and Participation in Galatians*. WUNT 2/454. Tübingen: Mohr Siebeck, 2017.

Ego, Beate. "God's Justice: The 'Measure for Measure' Principle in 2 Maccabees." Pages 151–54 in *The Books of the Maccabees: History, Theology, Ideology: Papers of the Second International Conference on the Deuterocanonical Books, Pápa, Hungary, 9-11 June, 2005*, edited by Géza G. Xeravits and József Zsengellér. JSJSup 118. Leiden: Brill, 2007.

Finlan, Stephen. *The Background and Content of Paul's Cultic Atonement Metaphors*. Atlanta: SBL, 2004.

Fitzmyer, Joseph A. "Crucifixion in Ancient Palestine, Qumran Literature, and the New Testament." *CBQ* 40 (1978): 493–513.

Fung, Ronald Y. K. *The Epistle to the Galatians*. Grand Rapids: Eerdmans, 1988.

Gager, John G. *Curse Tablets and Binding Spells from the Ancient World*. New York: Oxford University Press, 1992.

Gathercole, Simon J. *Where Is Boasting: Early Jewish Soteriology and Paul's Response in Romans 1-5*. Grand Rapids: Eerdmans, 2001.

Gnilka, J. "Martyriumsparänese und Sühnetod in synoptischen und jüdischen Traditionen." Pages 223–46 in *Die Kirche des Anfangs: Für Heinz Schürmann*, edited by Rudolf Schnackenberg, Josef Ernst, and Joachim Wanke. Erfurter Theologische Studien 38. Leipzig: St Benno-Verlag, 1977.

Goldstein, Jonathan A. *II Maccabees*. AB 41A. Garden City, NY: Doubleday, 1983.

Grimm, Carl L. W. "Das zweite, dritte, und vierte Buch der Maccabäer, vierte Lieferung." In *Kurzgefasstes Exegetisches Handbuch zu den Apokryphen des Alten Testamentes*, edited by Otto Fridolin Fritzsche. Leipzig: S. Herzel, 1857.

Gruen, E. S. "The Origins and Objectives of Onias' Temple." *SCI* 16 (1997): 47–70.

Habicht, Christian. *Gottmenschentum und griechische Städte*. Zetemata 14. Munich: Beck, 1956.

———. "Hellenismus und Judentum in der Zeit des Judaas Makkabäus." Pages 97–104 in *Jahrbuch der Heidelberger Akademie der Wissenschaften für das Jahr 1974*. Heidelberg: Carl Winter, 1975.

———. *Makkabäerbuch 2*. JSHRZ, 3.1. Gütersloh: Gerd Mohn, 1979.

Hamerton-Kelly, R. B. "Sacred Violence and the Curse of the Law (Galatians 3.13): The Death of Christ as Sacrificial Travesty." *NTS* 36 (1990): 98–118.

Hanson, Anthony Tyrrell. *Studies in Paul's Technique and Theology*. Grand Rapids: Eerdmans, 1974.

Hardin, J. K. *Galatians and the Imperial Cult.* WUNT 2/237. Tübingen: Mohr Siebeck, 2008.
Harmon, Matthew S. *She Must and Shall Go Free: Paul's Isaianic Gospel in Galatians.* Beihefte zur Zeitschrift für die Neutestamentliche Wissenschaft und die Kunde der Älteren Kirche 168. Berlin: de Gruyter, 2010.
Hays, Richard B. *Echoes of Scripture in the Letters of Paul.* New Haven: Yale University Press, 1989.
———. *The Faith of Jesus Christ: The Narrative Substructure of Galatians 3:1—4:11.* 2nd ed. Grand Rapids: Eerdmans, 2002.
———. "Galatians." In *The New Interpreter's Bible*, Vol. 12. Nashville: Abingdon, 2000.
Hengel, Martin. *Judaism and Hellenism.* Trans. John Bowden. London: SPCK, 1974.
Hengel, Martin, and Anna Maria Schwemer. *Paulus zwischen Damaskus und Antiochien: Die Unbekannten Jahre des Apostels.* WUNT 108. Tübingen: Mohr Siebeck, 1998.
———. *Paul Between Damascus and Antioch.* Trans. John Bowden. London: SCM, 1997.
Henten, J. W. van. "Das jüdische Selbstverständnis in den ältesten Martyrien." Pages 127–61 in *Die Entstehung der jüdischen Martyrologie*, edited by J. W. van Henten, Boudewijn Dehandschutter, and H. J. W. van der Klaauw. Studia Post-Biblica 38. Leiden: Brill, 1989.
———. *The Maccabean Martyrs as Saviours of the Jewish People: A Study of 2 and 4 Maccabees.* JSJSup 57. Leiden: Brill, 1997.
———. "Maccabees, Fourth Book of." In *The Eerdmans Dictionary of Early Judaism*, edited by J. J. Collins and Daniel Harlow. Grand Rapids: Eerdmans, 2010.
———. "The Tradition-Historical Background of Rom. 3.25." Pages 101–28 in *From Jesus to John: Essays on Jesus and New Testament Christology in Honour of Marinus de Jonge*, edited by M. de Jonge and Martinus C. De Boer. JSNTSup 84. Sheffield: JSOT, 1993.
Henze, Matthias. "Additions to Daniel." Pages 122–39 in *Outside the Bible: Ancient Jewish Writings Related to Scripture*, edited by Louis H. Feldman, James L. Kugel, and Lawrence H. Schiffman. Lincoln: University of Nebraska Press, 2013.
———. "The Prayer of Azariah and the Song of the Three Jews." Page 129 in *Outside the Bible: Ancient Jewish Writings Related to Scripture*, edited by Louis H. Feldman, James L. Kugel, and Lawrence H. Schiffman. Lincoln: University of Nebraska Press, 2013.
Himmelfarb, Martha. *Between Temple and Torah: Essays on Priests, Scribes, and Visionaries in the Second Temple Period and Beyond.* Texte und Studien zum Antiken Judentum. Tübingen: Mohr Siebeck, 2013.
Howard, George. *Paul: Crisis in Galatia. A Study in Early Christian Theology.* SNTSMS 35. New York: Cambridge University Press, 1979.
Janssen, L. H. "Some Unexplored Aspects of Devotio Deciana." *Mnemosyne* 34 (1981): 357–81.
Jonge, M. de. *Christology in Context: The Earliest Christian Response to Jesus.* Philadelphia: Westminster, 1988.
———. "Jesus' Death for Others and the Death of the Maccabean Martyrs." Pages 142–51 in *Text and Testimony: Essays on New Testament and Apocryphal Literature in Honour of A. F. J. Klijn*, edited by A. S. van der Woude, Tjitze Baarda, G. P. Luttikhuizen, and A. Hilhort. Kampen: Uitgeversmaatschappij J. H. Kok, 1988.
Kahl, Brigitte. *Galatians Re-Imagined: Reading with the Eyes of the Vanquished.* Minneapolis: Fortress, 2010.
Keim, Paul Arden. "When Sanctions Fail: The Social Function of Curse in Ancient Israel: A Thesis." PhD diss., Harvard University, 1992.

Kellermann, Ulrich. *Auferstanden in den Himmel: 2 Makkabäer 7 und die Auferstehung der Märtyrer.* Stuttgart Bibelstudien 95. Stuttgart: Verlag Katholisches Bibelwerk, 1979.

———. "Zum traditionsgeschichtlichen Problem des stellvertretenden Sühnetodes in 2 Makk 7, 37f." *BN* 13 (1980): 63–83.

Kim, Seyoon. *The Origin of Paul's Gospel.* WUNT 2/4. Tübingen: Mohr, 1981.

Klauck, Hans-Josef. *4. Makkabäerbuch.* JSHRZ 3.6. Gütersloh: Gerd Mohn, 1989.

Kraus, Wolfgang. *Der Tod Jesu als Heiligtumsweihe: Eine Untersuchung zum Umfeld der Sühnevorstellung in Römer 3,25-26a.* WMANT 66. Neukirchen-Vluyn: Neukirchener, 1991.

Kuhn, Heinz W. "Die Bedeutung der Qumrantexte für das Verständnis des Galaterbriefs aus dem Münchener Projekt: Qumran und das Neue Testament." Pages 169–221 in *New Qumran Texts and Studies: Proceedings of the First Meeting of the International Organization for Qumran Studies, Paris, 1992,* edited by George J. Brooke and Florentino García Martínez. STDJ 15. Leiden: E. J. Brill, 1994.

Lagrange, Marie-Joseph. *Saint Paul: Épître aux Galates.* Paris: Lecoffre, 1942.

Lane, Eugene. *Corpus Monumentorum Religionis Dei Menis.* 4 vols. Leiden: Brill, 1971.

Lee, Sang Meyng. *The Cosmic Drama of Salvation: A Study of Paul's Undisputed Writings from Anthropological and Cosmological Perspectives.* WUNT 2/276. Tübingen: Mohr Siebeck, 2010.

Lightfoot, J. B. *The Epistle of St. Paul to the Galatians: With Introductions, Notes and Dissertations.* Reprint. Grand Rapids: Zondervan, 1957.

Lincicum, David. *Paul and the Early Jewish Encounter with Deuteronomy.* Grand Rapids: Eerdmans, 2010.

Lindars, Barnabas. *New Testament Apologetic.* Philadelphia: Westminster, 1961.

Lohse, Eduard. *Märtyrer und Gottesknecht.* FRLANT 46. Göttingen: Vandenhoeck & Ruprecht, 1955; 2nd ed., 1963.

Longenecker, Bruce W. *The Triumph of Abraham's God: The Transformation of Identity in Galatians.* Nashville: Abingdon, 1998.

Longenecker, Richard N. *Galatians.* WBC 41. Thomas Nelson, 1990.

Martyn, J. L. *Galatians: A New Translation with Introduction and Commentary.* AB 33A. New York: Doubleday, 1997.

Matera, Frank J. *Galatians.* Sacra Pagina 9. Collegeville, MN: Liturgical Press, 1992.

McLean, Bradley H. "The Absence of an Atoning Sacrifice in Paul's Soteriology." *NTS* 38 (1992): 531–53.

———. "Christ as a Pharmakos in Pauline Soteriology." *SBLSP* 30 (1991): 187–206.

———. *The Cursed Christ: Mediterranean Expulsion Rituals and Pauline Soteriology.* JSNTSup 126. Sheffield: Sheffield Academic, 1996.

Merklein, Helmut. "Die Bedeutung des Kreuzestodes Christi für die Paulinische Gerechtigkeits und Gesetzesthematik." Pages 1–106 in *Studien zu Jesus und Paulus.* WUNT 43. Tübingen: Mohr Siebeck, 1987.

Momigliano, Arnaldo. *Prime line di storia della tradizione Maccabaica.* Reprint. Amsterdam: Hakkert, 1968 (1930).

———. "The Second Book of Maccabees." *CP* 70 (1975): 81–88.

Moo, Douglas J. *Galatians.* BECNT. Grand Rapids: Baker Academic, 2013.

Morkholm, Otto. "The Accession of Antiochus IV of Syria: A Numismatic Comment." *American Numismatic Society Museum Notes* 11 (1964): 63–73.

Morland, Kjell Arne. *The Rhetoric of Curse in Galatians: Paul Confronts Another Gospel.* ESEC 5. Atlanta: Scholars Press, 1995.

Nickelsburg, George W. E. *Jewish Literature Between the Bible and the Mishnah: A Historical and Literary Introduction*. Philadelphia: Fortress, 1981.

Niese, Benedikt. "Kritik der beiden Makkabäerbücher nebst Beiträgen zur Geschichte der makkabäischen Erhebung." *Hermes* 35 (1900): 268–307.

Novenson, Matthew V. *Christ Among the Messiahs: Christ Language in Paul and Messiah Language in Ancient Judaism*. New York: Oxford University Press, 2012.

O'Brien, Kelli S. "The Curse of the Law (Galatians 3.13): Crucifixion, Persecution, and Deuteronomy 21.22-23." *JSNT* 29 (2006): 55–76.

Oepke, Albrecht. *Der Brief des Paulus an die Galater*. Berlin: Evangelische Verlagsanstalt, 1960.

O'Hagan, Angelo P. "The Martyr in the Fourth Book of Maccabees." *Liber Annuus* 24 (1974): 94–120.

Pate, C. Marvin. *The Reverse of the Curse: Paul, Wisdom, and the Law*. WUNT 2/114. Tübingen: Mohr Siebeck, 2000.

Porter, Stanley E. Καταλλασσω *in Ancient Greek Literature: With Reference to the Pauline Writings*. Estudios de Filología Neotestamentaria 5. Cordoba: Ediciones el Almendro, 1994.

Räisänen, Heikki. *Paul and the Law*. Philadelphia: Fortress, 1986.

Rajak, Tessa. *The Jewish Dialogue with Greece and Rome: Studies in Cultural and Social Interaction*. Arbeiten zur Geschichte des Antiken Judentums und des Urchristentums 48. Leiden: Brill, 2001.

Redditt, Paul L. "The Concept of Nomos in Fourth Maccabees." *CBQ* 45 (1983): 249–70.

Richardson, Peter. *Israel in the Apostolic Church*. SNTSMS 10. Cambridge: Cambridge University Press, 1969.

Riches, John. *Galatians through the Centuries*. Oxford: Wiley-Blackwell, 2013.

Richnow, W. "Untersuchungen zu Sprache und Stil des 2. Makkabäerbuches: Ein Beitrag zur hellenistischen Historiographie." PhD diss., Georg-August-Universität zu Göttingen, 1967.

Robertson, A. T. *A Grammar of the Greek New Testament in the Light of Historical Research*. Nashville: Broadman, 1934.

Roo, J. C. R. *Works of the Law at Qumran and in Paul*. NTM 13. Sheffield: Sheffield Phoenix, 2007.

Sanders, E. P. *Paul and Palestinian Judaism: A Comparison of Patterns of Religion*. Minneapolis: Fortress, 1977.

———. *Paul, the Law, and the Jewish People*. Philadelphia: Fortress, 1983.

Schams, Christine. *Jewish Scribes in the Second-Temple Period*. JSOTSup 291. Sheffield: Sheffield Academic, 1998.

Schreiner, Thomas R. "'Works of the Law' in Paul." *NovT* 33 (1991): 217–44.

Schuppe, E. "Petasos." *PW*, 1938.

Schwartz, Daniel R. *2 Maccabees*. CEJL. Berlin: de Gruyter, 2008.

———. "Judean or Jew? How Should We Translate Ιουδαῖος in Josephus?" Pages 3–27 in *Jewish Identity in the Greco-Roman World*, edited by Jörg Frey, Daniel R. Schwartz, and Stephanie Gripentrog. Ancient Judaism and Early Christianity 71. Leiden: Brill, 2007.

———. "Maccabees, Second Book of." Pages 905–7 in *The Eerdmans Dictionary of Early Judaism*, edited by John J. Collins and Daniel C. Harlow. Grand Rapids: Eerdmans, 2010.

———. "The Two Pauline Allusions to the Redemptive Mechanism of the Crucifixion." *JBL* 102 (1983): 259.

Schweitzer, Albert. *The Mysticism of Paul the Apostle*. New York: Seabury, 1931.

Scott, James M. "For as Many as Are of Works of the Law Are Under a Curse (Galatians 3.10)." Pages 187–221 in *Paul and the Scriptures of Israel*, edited by Craig A. Evans and James A. Sanders. JSNTSup 85. Sheffield: JSOT, 1993.

———. "Paul's Use of Deuteronomic Tradition." *JBL* 112 (1993): 645–65.

———. "Restoration of Israel." Pages 796–805 in *Dictionary of Paul and His Letters*, edited by G. F. Hawthorne and R. P. Martin. Downers Grove, IL: InterVarsity, 1993.

Scurlock, JoAnn. "167 BCE: Hellenism or Reform?" *JSJ* 31 (2000): 125–61.

Sechrest, Love L. *A Former Jew: Paul and the Dialectics of Race*. LNTS 410. New York: T&T Clark International, 2009.

Seeley, David. *The Noble Death: Graeco-Roman Martyrology and Paul's Conception of Salvation*. JSNTSup 28. Sheffield: Sheffield Academic, 1990.

Sherwin-White, Susan M., and Amélie Kuhrt. *From Samarkhand to Sardis: A New Approach to the Seleucid Empire*. Berkeley: University of California Press, 1993.

Sievers, Joseph. *The Hasmoneans and Their Supporters: From Mattathias to the Death of John Hyrcanus I*. South Florida Studies in the History of Judaism 6. Atlanta: Scholars Press, 1990.

Silva, Moisés. "Galatians." Pages 785–812 in *Commentary on the New Testament Use of the Old Testament*, edited by G. K. Beale and D. A. Carson. Grand Rapids: Baker Academic, 2007.

———. "Ἀνάθεμα." In *New International Dictionary of New Testament Theology and Exegesis*. Grand Rapids: Eerdmans, 2014.

Simkovich, Malka Zeiger. "Greek Influence on the Composition of 2 Maccabees." *JSJ* 42 (2011): 293–310.

Smyth, Herbert Weir. *Greek Grammar*. 21st ed. Cambridge, MA: Harvard University Press, 2002.

Sprinkle, Preston M. *Law and Life: The Interpretation of Leviticus 18:5 in Early Judaism and in Paul*. WUNT 2/241. Tübingen: Mohr Siebeck, 2007.

Stanley, Christopher D. "'Under a Curse': A Fresh Reading of Galatians 3.10–14." *NTS* 36 (1990): 481–511.

Stökl Ben Ezra, Daniel. *The Impact of Yom Kippur on Early Christianity: The Day of Atonement from Second Temple Judaism to the Fifth Century*. WMANT 163. Tübingen: Mohr Siebeck, 2003.

Surkau, Hans Werner. *Martyrien in jüdischer und frühchristlicher Zeit*. FRLANT 36. Göttingen: Vandenhoeck & Ruprecht, 1938.

Tcherikover, Victor. *Hellenistic Civilization and the Jews*. Philadelphia: Jewish Publication Society of America, 1959.

Thielman, Frank. *Paul & the Law: A Contextual Approach*. Downers Grove, IL: InterVarsity, 1994.

Trafton, Joseph. "4 Maccabees." In *The New Interpreter's Study Bible: New Revised Standard Version with the Apocrypha*, edited by Walter J. Harrelson. Nashville: Abingdon, 2003.

VanderKam, James C. "High Priests." Pages 739–42 in *The Eerdmans Dictionary of Early Judaism*, edited by Daniel C. Harlow and John J. Collins. Grand Rapids: Eerdmans, 2010.

Versnel, Henk S. "Beyond Cursing: The Appeal to Justice in Judicial Prayers." Pages 60–106 in *Magika Hiera: Ancient Greek Magic and Religion*, edited by Christopher A. Faraone and Dirk Obbink. Oxford: Oxford University Press, 1997.

———. "Making Sense of Jesus' Death: The Pagan Contribution." Pages 213–94 in *Deutungen des Todes Jesu im Neuen Testament*, edited by Jörg Frey and Jens Schröter. WUNT 181. Tübingen: Mohr Siebeck, 2005.

———. "Two Types of Roman Devotio." *Mnemosyne* 29 (1976): 365–410.
Wakefield, Andrew Hollis. *Where to Live: The Hermeneutical Significance of Paul's Citations from Scripture in Galatians 3:1-14*. Academia Biblica 14. Leiden: Brill, 2003.
Waters, Guy Prentiss. *The End of Deuteronomy in the Epistles of Paul*. WUNT 2/221. Tübingen: Mohr Siebeck, 2006.
Watson, Francis. *Paul and the Hermeneutics of Faith*. London: T&T Clark International, 2004.
———. *Paul and the Hermeneutics of Faith*. 2nd ed. New York: Bloomsbury T&T Clark, 2015.
Watson, Lindsay. *Arae: The Curse Poetry of Antiquity*. Leeds: Cairns, 1991.
Westerholm, Stephen. *Israel's Law and the Church's Faith: Paul and His Recent Interpreters*. Grand Rapids: Eerdmans, 1988.
Wet, Chris L. de. "Between Power and Priestcraft: The Politics of Prayer in 2 Maccabees." *Religion & Theology* 16 (2009): 150–61.
Wilcox, Max. "Upon the Tree—Deut 21:22–23 in the New Testament." *JBL* 96 (1977): 85–99.
Wilhelm, Adolf. "Zu einigen Stellen der Bücher der Makkabäer." *Akademie der Wissenschaften in Wien, Philosophisch-Historische Klasse: Anzeiger* 74 (1937): 15–30.
Williams, David S. "Recent Research in 2 Maccabees." *CBR* 2 (2003): 69–83.
Williams, Jarvis J. *Christ Died for Our Sins: Representation and Substitution in Romans and Their Jewish Martyrological Background*. Eugene, OR: Pickwick, 2015.
———. *A Commentary on Galatians*. NCCS. Eugene, OR: Wipf & Stock, forthcoming.
———. "Cultic Action and Cultic Function in Second Temple Jewish Martyrologies: The Jewish Martyrs as Israel's Yom Kippur." Pages 233–63 in *Sacrifice, Cult, and Atonement in Early Judaism and Christianity: Constituents and Critique*, edited by Henrietta L. Wiley and Christian A. Eberhart. Atlanta: SBL, 2017.
———. *Maccabean Martyr Traditions in Paul's Theology of Atonement: Did Martyr Theology Shape Paul's Conception of Jesus's Death?* Eugene, OR: Wipf & Stock Publishers, 2010.
———. "Martyr Theology in Hellenistic Judaism and Paul's Conception of Jesus's Death in Romans 3.21–26." Pages 493–521 in *Christian Origins and Hellenistic Judaism: Social and Literary Contexts for the New Testament*, edited by Stanley E. Porter and Andrew W. Pitts. Leiden: Brill, 2012.
Williams, Sam K. *Jesus' Death as Saving Event*. Missoula: Scholars Press, 1975.
Wilson, Todd A. *The Curse of the Law and the Crisis in Galatia: Reassessing the Purpose of Galatians*. WUNT 2/225. Tübingen: Mohr Siebeck, 2007.
Winkler, K. and K. Stuiber. "Devotio." *RAC* 3 (1972): 849–62.
Witherington, Ben. *Grace in Galatia: A Commentary on St. Paul's Letter to the Galatians*. Grand Rapids: Eerdmans, 1998.
Wolff, Hans Julius. *Das Recht der griechischen Papyri Ägyptens in der Zeit der Ptolemäer und des Prinzipats*. 2 vols. HA 10/5. Munich: Beck, 1978.
Wright, N. T. *The Climax of the Covenant: Christ and the Law in Pauline Theology*. Minneapolis: Fortress, 1991.
———. *Paul and the Faithfulness of God*. 2 vols. Christian Origins and the Question of God. Minneapolis: Fortress, 2013.
———. *What Saint Paul Really Said: Was Paul of Tarsus the Real Founder of Christianity?* Grand Rapids: Eerdmans, 1997.
Young, N. H. "Who's Cursed — and Why? (Galatians 3:10-14)." *JBL* 117 (1998): 79–92.

Index of References

Old Testament / Hebrew Bible

Genesis
3:16–19	12, 126
3:23–24	12, 126
4:14	12, 126
12	39
12–50	103
12:1–50:26	82
12:1–3	54, 55, 61, 62
12:1–3 LXX	128
12:3	28, 38, 39, 129
12:3 LXX	128
15	29
15:1–6	54
15:1–5	62
15:6	54, 55
15:6 LXX	128
15:16 LXX	69
18:18 LXX	128
18:19	38
22:1–24	54
22:18 LXX	39
26:5 LXX	39

Exodus
2:24–25	74
18:16 LXX	60
18:20 LXX	60
20:1	54, 55
20:2–6	55
20:3–6	66
20:17 MT	87
22:6–7 LXX	63
22:7–9	63
22:22–24 LXX	64
22:28	89
24:1–8	54
32:1–35	55

Leviticus
1–6	137
1–5	166
1:4	153
1:9 LXX	137
1:13 LXX	137
1:17 LXX	137
2:1–2 LXX	137
2:5–7 LXX	137
2:11 LXX	137
2:15 LXX	137
3:1 LXX	137
4–5	36
4:20	153
4:26	153
4:31	153
4:35	153
5:6	153
5:10	153
5:13	153
5:13 LXX	137
5:16	153
5:18	153
5:26	153
6:2 LXX	137, 138
6:16 LXX	137
6:23	153
7:7	153
9:1–16:34	150
9:1–10:2	145
11:1–47	72, 92
11:1–47 MT	137
11:1–31	87
11:7–8	70
14:32	150
15:13	150
16–17	36, 151, 152, 155
16	36, 137, 143, 150, 151, 166
16:2	153
16:2 LXX	153
16:3–7	166
16:3	147
16:5–34	151
16:5–20	151
16:5	147
16:6	147
16:8–10	166
16:9	147
16:11	166
16:13 LXX	137
16:13–15 LXX	153
16:14–20	166
16:14–15	153
16:16	145, 150
16:21–22	166
16:21	147
16:24 LXX	155
16:25	147
16:29–32 LXX	155
16:29	153
16:30	145, 147, 150, 166
16:34	147
17–26	113
17	114
17:5 LXX	113
17:10–16	70, 92
17:11	151
17:11 LXX	151
17:12	151
18	114
18	112
18–20	114
18:1–26:46	112
18:1–5	114
18:2 LXX	114
18:3 LXX	114
18:4 LXX	114

18:5	6, 35, 50, 72, 76, 80, 81, 95, 97, 103, 108, 109, 131, 137, 160, 189, 193	8:12	153	4:31–39	56
		8:19	153	4:31	60
		8:21	153	4:40	56, 57
		14	149	4:44–11:32	56
		14:18	150	4:45	57
		15:25	153	5:1–21	56
		15:28	153	5:1	57
		17:11	153	5:2	56
18:5 LXX	110–13, 115, 121, 127	17:12	153	5:7–10	66
		20:10–13	55	5:10	56
		21:3 LXX	99	5:22–23	56
		25:1–5	55	5:31	57
18:6–30 LXX	114	25:7–13 LXX	172	5:32–33	137, 161
18:6–23	114	25:11	141	5:33	83, 111, 156
18:24–30	114	28:22	153		
18:28	114	28:30	153	6:1–25	56
19	114	29:5	153	6:1	57
20	114	29:11	153	6:5	66
20:10–20	114	31:50	153	6:13–15	66
20:22–24	114			6:17	57
20:26	113	*Deuteronomy*		6:20	57
21:20 LXX	148	1:5	57	6:24	57
25:17–20	153	1:6–4:43	53	7:1–26	56
25:22	153	1:6	54	7:1–11	55
26:25	148	1:8	54	7:9–26	54
26:42	60	3:27	55	7:11	57
27:28 LXX	99	4:1–26:19	83, 111	8:1–20	56
28:18–22	153	4:1–43	55	8:1	83, 111, 137, 161
29:36	150	4:1–40	66		
30:10	150	4:1	55, 57	8:5 LXX	69
30:10 LXX	153	4:2	55	8:11	57
31:7	153	4:3	55	9:1–10:11	56
32:12	149	4:4	55	10:12–11:32	56
32:14	153	4:5–6	57	10:18	64
32:14 LXX	153	4:6	55	11:8–9	137, 161
32:33	149	4:8	57	11:8	83, 111, 156
33:12–34:9	152	4:9–10	55		
35:12	153	4:9	55	11:18–25	137, 161
37:6–8	153	4:10	55	11:24	38
37:6	153	4:13	55	11:26–32	83, 111, 156
		4:14	55, 57		
Numbers		4:21–22	55	11:26–29 LXX	100
5:8	153	4:23	55	11:26–28	72
5:21–27	38	4:25–28	137, 161	11:28	137, 161
5:27 LXX	37, 119	4:25–26	55	11:28 LXX	100
6:11	153	4:27–29	56	11:32	57
7:89	153				

Deuteronomy (cont.)		27–29	42	28:1–14	83, 91,
12:1–26:19	56	27–28	57, 72,		111, 137,
12:1–31	66		83, 84,		141, 161
12:1	57		89, 111,	28:1	56
12:16	57		113, 141,	28:10–30:20	165, 166
13:1–19 LXX	100		157, 164,	28:14 LXX	71
13:12–16 LXX	100		165, 187	28:15–68	56, 83,
13:18 LXX	99, 100	27	33, 57,		111, 137,
13:18–19 LXX	100		83, 107,		141, 161
13:19 LXX	100		111, 156,	28:15–62	83, 111,
14:1–21	70		167, 191		156
14:1–2	92	27:1–28:68	56, 83,	28:15	56
17:11	57		111	28:15 LXX	100
17:18–19	57	27:1–28:59 LXX	129	28:16	99
17:20 LXX	71	27:1	56, 83,	28:16 LXX	100
19:15–21	90		111	28:19	99
21:1–8	149	27:3	57	28:21	83, 96,
21:22	96, 158	27:8	57		111, 156,
21:22 LXX	123	27:9–26	56, 83,		158, 188
21:22–23 LXX	123		111, 156	28:22	43
21:22–23	124	27:9–25	83	28:27–28	43
21:23	11, 24,	27:9–10	83, 111	28:35	43
	28, 35,	27:13 LXX	100	28:45 LXX	100
	40, 43,	27:15–26	83, 99,	28:46	43
	44, 119,		111, 156	28:58–61	43
	158, 160,	27:15–26 LXX	100	28:58	6, 34, 43,
	166	27:15–25	34, 107		56, 57,
21:23 LXX	37, 117,	27:26	6, 24, 26,		107, 110,
	121,		30, 34,		118, 158,
	123–8		35, 43,		160, 166
21:26	96, 158		46, 57,	28:58 LXX	111, 114,
23:6 LXX	100		72, 83,		117
24:19–21	87		107, 108,	28:59	43
27–32	42		110, 111,	28:61	57
27–30	24, 26,		115, 116,	28:64–68	83, 111
	27, 30,		118, 156,	28:64	43
	34, 36–9,		158, 160,	29	29, 56
	50, 54,		165, 166	29:1–30:20	56
	61, 62,	27:26 LXX	34, 107,	29:1	56
	69, 76,		111, 112,	29:2–3	56
	80, 81,		114, 117,	29:4	56
	95, 97,		129	29:9	56
	103, 107,	28–30	34, 107	29:15	43
	108, 115,	28	57, 156,	29:18	12, 126
	118, 119,		167, 191	29:19–29 LXX	37
	129, 132,	28:1–68	141	29:19	43
	189			29:20	57

29:25	12, 126	*Joshua*		*Psalms*	
29:26–27	43	6:17–18 LXX	99	21:7 LXX	38
29:26 LXX	100	6:18 LXX	99	37:26 LXX	38
29:27–28 Eng.	43	7:1 LXX	99	68:32	149
29:27–28	12, 126	7:11 LXX	99	72:8	38
29:28	57	7:12–13 LXX	99	72:18	38
30	27, 56	22:20 LXX	99	93:12–13 LXX	69
30:1–10	40			105:8–10	60
30:1–5	56	*Judges*		105:30	153
30:1 LXX	100	1:17 LXX	99	118:18 LXX	69
30:2	38				
30:6–8	56	*1 Kings*		*Proverbs*	
30:6	43	3:14	153	10:7	38
30:9–10	56			16:14	153
30:10	6, 34, 57, 107	*2 Kings*			
		2:13	153	*Isaiah*	
30:11	56	16:1–17:23	72	1:1–26	141
30:14	57	17:22–23	137	19:24 LXX	38
30:15–68	161	19:35–36	75	24–25	39
30:15–20	54, 96, 158, 188	21:1–18	72	24:5	60
		22:19 LXX	37, 119	40–55	42
30:15–16	137, 161	23:26–25:11	137	53	24, 41–44, 143
30:20	55	23:31–24:17	72		
30:20 LXX	39			53 LXX	139
30:17–20	137, 161	*1 Chronicles*		53:4–6 LXX	139
31:1–34:12	57	2:7 LXX	99	53:4–5	43
31:2	55	6:34	153	53:4	43
31:9	57	28:9 LXX	60	53:5	41
31:11–12	57			53:8–9	43
31:24	57	*2 Chronicles*		53:8	43
31:26	57	6:25–27	149	53:8 LXX	139
32	26, 43, 76, 84, 140, 141, 157	6:39	149	53:10–12	43
		7:14	149	53:10–12 LXX	139
		29:24	153	53:11 LXX	139
		30:18	153	54:4	43
32:6	76	31:21	60	65	36
32:36	43, 71	34:24–28	37	65:4	70
32:36 LXX	73, 140, 157, 187	36:19–20	137	65:17–25	104
				66:17	70
32:41	148	*Ezra*			
32:43	43, 148	2:2	60	*Jeremiah*	
32:46	57			4:1 LXX	38
32:48–52	55	*Nehemiah*		4:2	38
32:49	61	1:1	60	5:1	149
34:1–4	61	2:1–7:3	60	5:7	149
34:5	61	12:27–43	60	11:5 LXX	39
				17	36

Jeremiah (cont.)		3:28–37	135	Zechariah	
17:5–6	12, 126	3:28–29 LXX	82, 156	7:2	153
18:4	149	3:28–29 LXX	156	8:13	38, 119
24	36	3:28–29	139	8:13 LXX	37
24:9	119	3:28	135, 136, 138	8:20–23 LXX	39
24:9 LXX	37			8:22	153
27:20	149	3:29	135	14:11 LXX	99
38:34	149	3:30–31	135		
43:3	149	3:32	135, 136	Malachi	
49:18	119	3:33–36	136	1:20–23	37
49:18 LXX	37	3:34–35	136		
51:8	119	3:36–37	136	NEW TESTAMENT	
51:8 LXX	37	3:36	136	Mark	
51:12	119	3:37	136, 139	1:44	150
51:12 LXX	37	3:37 LXX	82		
		3:38–40 LXX Th	138	Luke	
Ezekiel		3:38–40 LXX	149	2:22	150
17	39	3:38–40	137	5:14	150
23:36–49	68	3:38	137		
34:26	38	3:39	138	John	
42:17	153	3:40 LXX Th	138	2:6	150
43:14–20 LXX	153	4:2	149	3:25	150
43:14–20	153	6 MT	134		
43:20	153	8:23	69	Acts	
43:22	153	9:11	34, 37	7:58	125
				21:27	137
Daniel		Amos		23:5	89
1–6 MT	134	2:4	60		
1:1–2:49	136	7:2	149	Romans	
1:4	136			3:25–26	41
1:8–19	136	Micah		3:25	153, 154
1:8–9	136	7:9	148	4	42
1:12–19	136			4:25	42
3	133, 134, 136, 138	Habakkuk		5:6–11	148
		1:1–11 LXX	112	8:3	41
3 LXX	2, 3, 158, 187	1:1–4 LXX	112	8:32	148
		1:6 LXX	112	9:3	12
3 LXX Th	138	1:12 LXX	112	10:4	46
3:1–90 LXX	158, 160, 167, 190	1:12–2:1 LXX	112	11:1	120
		1:13 LXX	112		
3:23	135	2:3 LXX	112	1 Corinthians	
3:24–97	134	2:4	6, 35, 160	1:13	148
3:24–90	134, 141	2:4 LXX	110–13, 115, 121, 127	11:24	148
3:24–40	134			15	105
3:24–25	135			15:3	148, 163, 164
3:27–28	136				
3:27	135			16:22	12, 126

2 Corinthians
5:4–5　12, 126
5:14–15　148
5:21　41, 45, 148

Galatians
1–2　47, 48, 51, 169, 185, 191
1　113
1:1　98, 104, 105, 109, 113, 116, 161, 164, 180, 184, 185
1:3　42, 104
1:3–4　11, 120, 180
1:4　2, 3, 29, 40–2, 44, 45, 98, 104–6, 108, 109, 113, 115, 116, 119–22, 125–8, 130, 148, 159–61, 163, 164, 166, 181, 189
1:6–3:14　98
1:6–9　108, 160, 164, 183, 184
1:6　99, 126
1:7　179, 183
1:8–9　14, 99, 100, 104, 167, 182
1:8　12, 126, 185
1:10　100, 176, 184
1:11–2:10　184
1:11–17　11, 120
1:13–14　103, 171, 172
1:13　171, 176, 177, 180, 184, 185
1:14　171, 172, 180, 182, 184
1:15–16　105, 109, 113, 116, 120
1:15　105, 114, 161, 184
1:16　172, 174, 176, 184
1:23　174, 177, 180, 185
1:24　180
2–3　113
2:11–21　47
2:11–14　103, 106, 109, 120, 164, 183, 184
2:12　172
2:13　178, 182
2:14–15　172
2:14　103, 173, 178
2:15–5:2　160
2:15–21　184
2:15　172, 178
2:16–6:15　167
2:16–4:31　175
2:16　10, 98, 104, 110, 113, 115, 116, 120, 122, 127, 162, 173, 174
2:17–21　21
2:17　130, 159, 164, 173, 181
2:18　110, 177
2:19–3:29　185
2:19–21　104, 105, 116
2:19–20　32, 46, 105, 106, 110
2:19　2
2:20–21　98, 109, 148
2:20　2, 41, 44, 45, 113, 128, 161–4, 179, 180
2:21　2, 9, 34, 110, 116, 181
2:2　172, 175, 181
2:3　103, 173
2:5　178
2:7　103, 174
2:8–9　172
2:9　179
3–4　101, 107
3　29, 30, 32, 38, 39, 41, 100, 106
3:1–6:15　127
3:1–6:10　183
3:1–5:26　189
3:1–5:1　106, 120
3:1–4:31　62, 99, 183
3:1–29　99, 106, 113, 116
3:1–14　3, 13, 99, 165, 167
3:1–9　116
3:1–5　10, 127
3:1　2, 98, 105, 109, 116, 126, 128
3:2–14　116, 129

Galatians (cont.)

3:2–5	101, 113, 128		161, 183, 185		24, 25, 27–9, 32, 33, 35–7, 39–42, 44, 46–52, 89, 97–9, 103, 105, 106, 109, 113–26, 128–33, 148, 156, 158–70, 182, 183, 185, 186, 188, 190–2
3:2–4	127	3:10–12	3, 101–3, 110, 116, 118, 164		
3:2	35, 174, 179	3:10	11, 13, 14, 17, 25, 30, 33, 35–9, 43, 46, 89, 98–102, 104–11, 113–22, 125–7, 129, 156, 158–60, 164–6, 182, 189		
3:3	179				
3:4	180, 185				
3:5–9	174				
3:6–4:7	107				
3:6–9	30, 35, 100, 103, 118, 128, 129				
3:6–8	116				
3:6	101, 127, 128, 173				
3:7	101, 128				
3:8–14	36, 37				
3:8–10	40	3:11–14	116	3:14	3, 12, 25, 31, 44, 99–101, 103–6, 116, 119, 126–8, 165, 172, 174
3:8	38–40, 101, 103, 115, 116, 127, 128, 172	3:11–12	17, 35, 109, 115, 116, 118, 121, 164, 174		
3:9–14	101	3:11	110, 111, 114, 115, 121, 160, 164	3:15–5:1	109
3:9	30, 101, 112, 118, 128, 129			3:15–29	103
				3:15–25	35
				3:15–18	185
3:10–14	1–4, 6, 27, 29–32, 35, 36, 44, 46, 48, 101, 103, 106, 107, 117, 119, 127, 129, 156, 158, 159, 161, 164, 166, 167, 191	3:12–13	104	3:15	103, 181, 184
		3:12	102, 103, 108, 110, 111, 113–16, 119–21, 160, 162	3:16	101, 103, 104, 129, 168, 175
				3:17–18	103
		3:13–14	3, 5, 28, 36, 40, 99, 104–6, 109, 116, 117, 127, 129, 158, 161, 164, 166	3:17	103, 110, 175, 181, 184
				3:18	175
				3:19–4:7	104
				3:19–3:1	116
				3:19–25	10
				3:19	9, 105, 110
3:10–13	15, 16, 20, 27, 100, 160,	3:13	1–9, 11–15, 20,	3:21	9, 99, 103, 105, 109, 110,

	116, 121, 161, 162, 173, 175	4:4	45, 109, 122, 130, 159	5:2–4 5:2	127 99, 105, 110
3:22–4:7	109, 110	4:5–6	106, 117, 119, 121, 127, 129	5:3–4 5:3	109 101, 103, 108
3:22–26	174				
3:22–23	122				
3:22	9, 103, 105, 106, 109, 119, 122, 126, 127, 160, 174, 175, 181, 189	4:5	40, 45, 103, 105, 106, 109, 119, 126, 130, 159, 161, 167	5:4 5:5–6 5:5	99, 110, 115, 126 104 115, 116, 173, 174
		4:6	104, 127, 180	5:6 5:7	10, 46, 174 176, 178, 181
3:23–4:31	115, 119, 121	4:8–11	11, 98		
3:23–4:7	126	4:8–10	10	5:10	176, 179
3:23–4:4	120	4:8–9	189	5:11	3, 180, 185
3:23–25	120	4:8	178		
3:23–24	103	4:9	45, 105, 109, 122, 126, 127, 179	5:13–26 5:13–16 5:13–14 5:13	116 104 106 109, 119, 179
3:23	126, 174, 189				
3:24–4:2	122				
3:24	116, 120, 173, 174	4:12–6:10 4:13–29	185 185	5:16–26	105, 106, 110, 116, 120, 127, 167
3:25	46, 174	4:13	179		
3:26–29	45	4:14	179		
3:26	174	4:17–18	180		
3:28	105, 120	4:17	179	5:16–21	104
3:29	101, 103, 129, 168, 175	4:20 4:21–5:1	179 104, 110, 116	5:16–17 5:16	179 99, 104, 105, 116
4:1–11	32, 120	4:21–31	45, 105, 107, 109, 127, 167	5:17 5:19 5:21	179 179 116, 167, 182
4:1–7	45				
4:1–3	10				
4:1–2	126	4:21–27	106		
4:2	180	4:21–25	189	5:22–23	105
4:3–10	110	4:21	179	5:22	104, 106, 174
4:3	45, 105, 106, 109, 121, 122, 126, 127, 160	4:23 4:28 4:29 4:30	175, 179 175 180 126	5:24 5:25	106 3, 101, 104, 105, 116
		5:1–6:10	184		
4:4–7	127	5:1–6	10	6:2	106
4:4–6	105, 122	5:1	11, 105, 106, 119, 120	6:8 6:10 6:11–16 6:12–17	104, 179 174 184 185
4:4–5	45, 106, 119, 125, 128, 161	5:2–6:15	105		

Galatians (cont.)		*Tobit*		*1 Maccabees*	
6:12–13	103, 118, 179	4:5	71	1–7	58
		13:3–5	39	1–2	140
6:12	105, 106, 173, 180, 184	13:5–10	39	1	62, 140, 141
		13:9–18	38		
		13:11–18	39	1:1–64	148
6:13	173, 184	14:9	60	1:11–15	137, 141
6:14–16	184			1:41–64	150
6:14–15	11, 116, 120	*Judith*		1:41–45	137
		4:6	89	3:58–59	137
6:14	3, 10, 98, 105, 106, 162	4:8	89	4:54–60	137
		4:14	89	5:32	148
		11:11–15	70	6:1–16	62
6:15–16	120	15:8	89	6:60	149
6:15	46, 104, 106, 110, 116, 118, 120, 122, 162, 167			7:14	79
		Wisdom of Solomon		7:26–30	79
		1:8	148	8:17	65
		2:11–3:6	155	12:20–23	89
		3:1–6	141		
6:16	108, 110, 118, 164, 183, 184	14:31	148	*2 Maccabees*	
		18:11	148	1:1–2:18	58
6:17	2, 3, 105	*Ecclesiasticus*		1:1–9	59
		3:3	153	1:2	60, 61, 82, 173, 181, 184
Ephesians		3:30	153		
5:16	40	5:6	153	1:2–15:37	62
		10:19	71	1:3	60, 82
Philippians		19:24	71	1:4	60, 62, 82
3:6	10	20:28	153	1:5	74, 84, 139, 140, 145, 146, 150, 158, 187
		28:5	153		
Colossians		34:18	137		
4:5	40	34:19	153		
		35:5	137		
1 Thessalonians		44:20	39	1:7–8	145
5:10	148	44:21	38	1:7	58, 82, 177
		45:16	153		
2 Peter		45:23	153	1:8–9	82
1:9	150	46:16	137	1:9	59
		50:1–21	89	1:10–2:18	59, 60, 82
APOCRYPHA		50:13	137	1:10	177, 182
1 Esdras				1:11	62
1:46	71	*Baruch*		1:11–12	60
		1:20	37	1:11–16	62
2 Esdras		2:34	39	1:11–17	60
20:34	153	3:8	37, 119	1:12	62
		3:9	102	1:17	62
		4:1	60	1:18–36	60

1:18	150	4:1–6:31	148, 167, 190	4:46	176
1:26	148			4:48	62
1:27	172	4:1–6	64	5:1–8:5	129, 130, 140, 141, 144–7, 159, 184
1:28	144	4:1	64, 172		
2:1	61	4:2	64, 65, 80, 172		
2:2	61				
2:3	61	4:3	64	5:1–7:42	185
2:4	61, 175	4:5–7	64	5:1–7:38	142
2:8	181	4:5	175	5:1–11	145
2:11	62, 181	4:7	64, 182	5:2	181
2:13	182	4:8	64	5:4	150
2:16	150	4:9–11	62	5:6	62
2:17–18	61, 145	4:9	64	5:8	65, 180
2:17	175	4:10	65	5:11–6:17	66
2:18	145, 146, 175, 176	4:11–17	170, 171	5:11–14	145
		4:11–15	65	5:15–21	68
2:19–15:37	145	4:11	65, 177	5:15–20	137
2:19–15:37	58	4:12	65, 66	5:15–16	142
2:19–32	58, 61	4:13–6:31	74	5:15	65, 68
2:19–22	61, 145, 170	4:13	66, 171	5:16	181
		4:14	66	5:17–20	69
2:19	150	4:15	66, 181	5:17–19	68
2:21	80, 87, 170, 180	4:16–17	67, 69, 148	5:17–18	145, 150, 160
2:22	65, 80, 177	4:16	66, 180	5:17	82, 139, 156, 160, 161, 181
		4:17–15:37	66		
2:23	58, 145	4:17	65, 80		
2:24	178	4:19–20	67	5:18	140
3:1–15:37	59	4:19	66	5:20–8:5	147
3:1	61, 62, 64, 65, 67	4:20	71	5:20–7:38	152
		4:21–23	67	5:20–7:32	141
3:4–6	64, 67	4:24	67	5:20	68, 144–6, 181
3:4	63, 67	4:25	67		
3:5–6	63	4:26	67	5:21–6:11	145
3:6	63	4:27	67	5:21	68
3:7–28	64	4:30	67	5:22–23	68
3:8	174	4:31	67	5:22	75, 182
3:9	178	4:32	67	5:23–24	68
3:10	63	4:33–34	67	5:23	177
3:12	173	4:33	67	5:25–26	68
3:15	63, 64	4:34	67, 176	5:25	71, 177
3:22	173	4:35–36	177	5:26	68
3:24	68	4:35	67, 172	5:27–6:6	142
3:26	181	4:37	67	5:27	74
3:29–34	64, 67	4:38	67	5:35	150
3:29–33	62	4:39–5:10	68	6	138, 141, 156
3:32	148, 177	4:45	176		

2 Maccabees (cont.)	6:21	71, 175	7:28–29	82, 139, 156
6:1–7:42 80	6:23–31	71		
6:1–2 68	6:23	176	7:28	182
6:1 62, 65,	6:24–31	143	7:29	81, 144,
68, 172,	6:24	71		185
177	6:25	182	7:30–8:5	61
6:31 143	6:28	65, 71,	7:30–38	3, 68
6:3–4 69		143, 174	7:30–32	84, 141,
6:3 68	6:30	180		157, 187
6:4 68, 172	7	71, 73,	7:30	72, 84,
6:5 65		140, 141		141, 157,
6:6 69, 177	7:1–8:5	166		187
6:7 68, 69	7:1–42	183	7:31	84, 141,
6:8 69, 177	7:1	68, 71,		157, 187
6:9 69		139, 156	7:32–38	73, 130,
6:10 69	7:2–41	139		141, 142,
6:11 69, 181	7:2–42	82, 156		146, 150,
6:12–17 69, 84,	7:2	65, 71,		159, 167,
141, 146,		183		184, 190
148, 157,	7:3–4	71	7:32–33	69
185, 187	7:3	71	7:32	72, 82,
6:12–16 140, 146	7:5–6	71		83, 139,
6:12 69, 182	7:5	71		141–3,
6:13–17 174	7:6	75, 140,		147, 148,
6:13–16 146		157, 178		150, 156,
6:13–14 69	7:7–42	72		157, 160,
6:13 174	7:7	71		161, 180,
6:14–15 160, 181	7:9–10	72		181, 187
6:14 172	7:9	65, 80,	7:33–38	73
6:15–16 69		81, 185	7:33	73, 74,
6:15 69, 150	7:11	65		84, 139,
6:16 70	7:16	84, 141,		140, 142,
6:18–8:5 70, 84,		157, 182,		144, 146,
146, 187		187		157, 158,
6:18–8:2 146	7:18	72, 82,		161, 187
6:18–7:42 74, 82,		139, 140,	7:36	73, 181,
145, 146,		156, 157,		184
182		160, 180	7:37–38	73, 139,
6:18–7:41 74	7:20–29	72		142, 161
6:18–7:38 144	7:23	65, 72,	7:37	65, 73,
6:18–31 70, 183		81, 185		74, 142,
6:18–21 172	7:24	173, 176		146, 147
6:18 68, 70,	7:26	176	7:38	72, 74,
148, 150	7:28–32	84, 128,		84, 141,
6:19 70		130, 185,		142, 144,
6:21–22 71		187		157, 180,
				182, 187

7:40	176	8:36	62, 65, 76, 177	10:45	160
8	146			11:1–2	77
8:1–10:9	74	9:1–29	62, 74	11:2–3	62, 77
8:1–5	143, 144, 183	9:1	76	11:2	177
		9:2	76	11:3	172
8:1–4	146	9:3	76	11:4	77
8:1	74, 170	9:4–15	62	11:5	77
8:2–4	74, 171	9:4	62, 76, 177	11:6	77, 185
8:2–3	62, 146			11:7	77
8:2	80	9:5–6	76	11:8–12	77
8:4	146	9:5	76	11:10	77
8:4–5	144	9:7–11	76	11:11	172
8:5–36	74	9:7	76, 177	11:13–37	77
8:5–7	146	9:13–28	76	11:13	77
8:5	74, 75, 80, 145, 160, 161	9:14	62	11:14	176
		9:15	177	11:15–16	177
		9:16	182	11:23	182
8:6	75	9:17–19	177	11:24	177
8:7	75	9:23	180	11:26	176
8:8	180	9:25	182	11:27	177
8:9	75, 172, 182	9:26	175	11:30–31	70
		9:27	176	11:31	65, 177
8:10–11	75, 177	9:28	180	11:34	177
8:10	75	10	76	12:1	177
8:11	149, 174	10:1–8	74	12:2	77
8:12–13	75	10:1–3	76	12:3–4	77
8:13	149	10:3–8	76	12:3	177
8:14–15	75	10:4	72, 76, 140, 157, 172	12:5–6	77
8:15	181, 184			12:7–9	78
8:16–17	75			12:9	177
8:16	172	10:5	150	12:10–11	78
8:17	62	10:8	177	12:11–12	78
8:18	176	10:10–13:26	77	12:13	78, 172
8:19	75	10:10	77	12:14	78, 176
8:20	75	10:11	182	12:15	78
8:21–22	75	10:12	177	12:16	78, 178
8:21	65, 75	10:14–15	177	12:17	177
8:23	76	10:14	77	12:26–28	78
8:24	76	10:15–16	77	12:30	177
8:29	74, 76, 84, 139, 140, 158, 187	10:18–23	77	12:31	62, 182
		10:20	176	12:34	177
		10:24	77, 177	12:38	78
		10:25–38	77	12:39–45	80
8:30–33	76, 77	10:27	62	12:39	78
8:32	177	10:29	177	12:40–44	74
8:34–36	76	10:34	176	12:40	78, 177
8:34	177	10:35	67	12:41–42	78

2 Maccabees (cont.)		14:31	79	Pseudepigrapha	
12:42–43	181	14:32	79	*1 Enoch*	
12:42	78, 150	14:33	62, 79	5	37
12:43	62, 78	14:35–36	79, 81	5:6	37, 119
12:44–46	81	14:37–46	81	10:21	39
12:45	181	14:37	62, 80,	81:4	101
13:1–7	77		171, 177	82:4	101
13:3–8	68	14:38	80, 87,	93	40
13:8	77		171	102	37
13:9–12	77	14:39–40	80		
13:9	77, 177	14:39	177	*3 Baruch*	
13:10	74	14:41–42	80	4	39
13:11	172	14:43	80		
13:13–14	62	14:44–45	80	*4 Maccabees*	
13:13	77	14:45	67, 80	1:1–6:30	183
13:14	65, 77	14:46	80	1:1–3:18	85, 87
13:15–16	77	15:2	75, 177,	1:1–12	86
13:16–17	79		181	1:1	84–6,
13:18–26	79	15:6–16	81		158, 183
13:18–19	177	15:6–8	81	1:2–4	86
13:22	176	15:7	176	1:2	86, 94
13:23	177	15:8–10	74	1:3–7	86
13:25	181	15:8	172	1:3	177
14:1–13	79	15:9	81	1:6	177
14:3–4	79	15:10	172	1:8	94
14:5–6	177	15:11	144	1:9	86
14:6	182	15:12	177	1:11	149, 177
14:6–14	79	15:13	181	1:12	181
14:7	181	15:14	63	1:13–18	86
14:8–9	182	15:17–20	81	1:13–14	86
14:12–13	79	15:17	62	1:14	85
14:12	174	15:19	179	1:15	178
14:14–15	172	15:20–37	81	1:17	86, 94,
14:14	79, 177	15:21–27	81		183
14:15–16	174	15:21–23	185	1:19–21	86
14:15	79	15:22–24	81	1:19	86
14:18–25	79	15:28–34	81	1:20	178
14:18	176	15:28	81	1:22	177
14:19	176	15:29	81	1:25	86
14:21	175	15:30–33	80	1:29–30	86
14:26–37	81	15:32–37	145	1:30–35	86
14:26	79, 182	15:33	62	1:30	94
14:27	79	15:36	59	1:31	177
14:28–29	79	15:37	62, 145,	1:32	177
14:28	181		146	1:34	87, 94,
14:30	79	15:38–39	59		96, 188

2:1	177	4:5	89	5:11	178	
2:3	86	4:6–26	90	5:13	92	
2:4	177	4:7	90	5:14–38	92	
2:5–6	86, 87, 94, 96, 188	4:8	90	5:14	92	
		4:9	90	5:16	88, 92, 94, 96, 176, 188	
		4:10	90, 185			
2:6–7	86	4:11	90			
2:6	176, 177	4:12	90	5:17–21	88	
2:7–9	86	4:13–14	90	5:17	92	
2:8–11	94	4:13	149	5:18–21	87	
2:8–10	96, 188	4:15	87, 91, 171	5:18–19	92	
2:8	86			5:18	94, 181	
2:9	86, 87	4:16	91, 177	5:19	150	
2:10–23	87	4:17–18	91	5:20–21	94	
2:10	86, 87, 94	4:18	91	5:20	92	
2:11	86	4:19–21	95, 158, 187	5:21	92	
2:12	86			5:22	92	
2:13	86	4:19–20	148, 171	5:23–24	92	
2:14	86, 94, 96, 188	4:19	91, 94	5:23	177	
		4:20	91, 177	5:24	92	
2:15	86	4:21–26	91	5:25–29	92	
2:18	86, 176	4:21	91, 148, 149, 171	5:25	88, 92, 94, 178	
2:19	180, 182					
2:23	86, 87, 94, 183	4:22–23	91, 171	5:27–38	92	
		4:23–24	94	5:27	94	
2:24	86	4:23	91, 148, 177	5:29	88, 94	
3:1–16	87			5:33–35	94	
3:1	86	4:24–25	91	5:33–34	96, 188	
3:2	177	4:24	88, 177	5:33	177	
3:5	86	4:25	176	5:35	148, 150	
3:11–12	177	4:26	88, 91, 171	5:37	183, 185	
3:16	177			6	140, 141, 148	
3:17–18	86	5:1–17:24	87			
3:19–4:26	85, 89	5:1–17:16	185	6:1–17:22	129, 159	
3:20–4:26	89	5:1–12:19	95, 158, 188	6:1–12:19	183	
3:20–4:5	89			6:1–8	148	
3:20–21	89	5:1–7:23	85, 92	6:1	93	
3:20	87, 94	5:2	92	6:3	93	
3:21	89	5:3	92	6:4–8	93	
4:1–7	90	5:4–6:40	148, 167, 191	6:4	176	
4:1–2	89			6:6	148, 179	
4:1	89, 90	5:4	92, 94, 148, 150	6:7	178	
4:2–3	89			6:8–11	93	
4:3	89	5:5–13	92	6:15–27	61	
4:4	89	5:6	148	6:18–7:42	85	
4:5–6	90	5:8–9	178	6:18–21	144	

4 Maccabees (cont.)

6:18	94, 178, 181	7:22	94	10:8	174, 179		
		8:1–15:13	93	10:10	94, 180		
6:21	94, 96, 188	8:1–14:10	85	10:11	95		
		8:1	93, 96, 188	10:13	176		
6:27	88, 93, 94, 96, 188	8:7	93	10:15	95		
		8:8	93	10:16	144		
		8:9–14	93	10:20	71		
6:28–30	128	8:12–13	93	11:2	94		
6:28–29	3, 94, 96, 130, 150, 152, 155, 158, 159, 161, 166, 167, 185, 188, 190	8:12	176	11:3	95, 149		
		8:14	149	11:4	94, 177		
		8:15–9:9	93	11:5	88, 94		
		8:15	177	11:12	88, 94, 96, 188		
		8:17	176	11:15	144		
		8:22	149	11:23	95		
		8:25	87, 94	11:24	177		
6:28	93, 142, 143, 148, 149, 190	8:26	176	11:27	94, 96, 188		
		8:28	86				
		9:1–25	61	12:1–8	175		
6:29	93, 94, 148–51, 167, 191	9:1	61, 94	12:4–16	149		
		9:2	87, 94, 96, 188	12:4–5	176		
				12:7	175		
6:30	88, 93, 94, 96, 188	9:3–9	94	12:8	175		
		9:4	94	12:9	175		
		9:8	94, 180	12:10	181		
6:31	86	9:9	61, 95, 149	12:12	149		
7:1	86, 180			12:14	94		
7:5	86, 180	9:10–17:24	94	12:16	144		
7:6–7	88	9:15	94, 96, 149, 188	12:17	149		
7:6	150			12:18	95		
7:7–19	61	9:17	179	13:1–18:24	183		
7:7–9	94	9:18	94, 176, 183	13:1	86		
7:7–8	96, 188			13:3	86		
7:8	88, 152	9:20	179	13:7	86		
7:9	88, 177, 181	9:21	61	13:8–18	144		
		9:22	144	13:9	94, 96, 188		
7:10	86	9:23	144				
7:11	180	9:24	149	13:13	61, 94, 96, 185, 188		
7:13	179	9:28	179				
7:16–19	183	9:29	95				
7:16–18	86	9:31	94	13:15	61, 71		
7:18–19	185	9:32	95, 149	13:17	61, 183		
7:18	179	10:2	180	13:22	94		
7:19	173	10:3	144	13:24	94		
7:21	174	10:4	95	13:27	178		
7:22–23	86	10:7	71	14:1	86		

14:5	181		150–2,	25:12–22	39
14:5–6	95		154, 155,	25:21–22	38
14:8	177		158, 159,	27:17	101
14:9	180		162, 166,	31:15–20	39
14:11–17:1	85		167, 183,	31:20	38
14:20	61		188, 190,		
15:1	86		191	*Liber Antiquitatum*	
15:3	94	17:21	150–2	*Biblicarum*	
15:4	86	17:22	149,	18	39
15:9	94, 96,		152–5	23:10	102
	188	17:23	94, 144	26:13	69
15:10	176	18:1	61, 84,		
15:13	178, 182		94, 176	*Prayer of Manasseh*	
15:14–32	93	18:2	86	8	101
15:15	179	18:3–24	85		
15:20	179	18:3	85, 88, 95	*Psalms of Solomon*	
15:24	174	18:4	85, 88,	2:2	137
15:25	178		94, 95,	14:2–3	102
15:28	61		152		
15:29	94, 96,	18:5	85, 95	*Testament of Asher*	
	188	18:6–24	85	7:3	39
15:32	86, 94	18:9	180		
16:1–2	86	18:10	94	*Testament of Judah*	
16:3	178	18:12	172	24:3–6	39
16:15	144	18:22	149		
16:16	94, 96,	18:23–24	95	*Testament of Levi*	
	184, 188	18:23	61, 95	4:6	38
16:20	61, 180	18:24	181	10:4	37, 119
16:22	174			16:5	37, 119
16:24	176	*Assumption of Moses*		18:9–10	39
16:25	61, 95	9:1–10:10	155		
17:2–18:2	85	9:6–7	152	*Testament of Naphtali*	
17:2	177	10:2–10	152	8:3	39
17:6–22	61				
17:9	177–9	*Jubilees*		*Testament of Zebulun*	
17:10	95, 152,	1:16	37, 119	9:8	39
	182	5:10	101		
17:12	94, 95	10:3	101	DEAD SEA SCROLLS	
17:16	96, 188	20:6–10	39	*4QpNah*	
17:18	95	20:9	38	frgs. 3–4,	
17:19–20	153	20:10	39	col: 1, ll: 7–8	123, 124
17:20–21	150	21:21–24	39		
17:20	155	22:11–23	39	*1QH*	
17:21–22	3, 94–6,	22:16–18	137	11:15–16	60
	128, 130,	23:10	101	13:32–33	60
	144, 147,	23:16–25	39	22 [frg. 4:]12	60
	148,				

1QS	
II	37
II:16	37
V:12	37

11QTemple	
45:11–12	63
45:16–17	63
47:7–18	63
64:10–11	124
64:7–8	124
64:6–13	123

CD	
I	37
I:5–8	29
I:17	37
III:18	40
IV:4	39
IV:9	39
XII:1	63
XV:2–3	37

PHILO
De migratione Abrahami
118–26	38
120–22	39

De praemiis et poenis
126–72	37
171–72	39

De vita Mosis
1.291	38
2.24	147

JOSEPHUS
Antiquities
2.137	88
3.218	71
4.302–307	37
8.229	71
11.317–19	89
12.138–46	65
12.146	63
15.5.417	137
17.339	89
18.34–35	89
20.224–51	89

CLASSICAL AND ANCIENT
CHRISTIAN LITERATURE
Appian
The Syrian Wars
11.66	62

Aristotle
Athēnaīn politeia
51.1	63

Diogenes Laertius
Vita
7.110	86

Euripides
Electra
1323–24	14

Herodotus
Historiae
4.64–65	71

Homer
Iliad
9.456	14

Justin
Dialogus cum Tryphone
89.1–2	43
89.3	44
95.1–2	44

Juvenal
Satire
14.98–99	88

Livy
Histories
10.28.12–18	19
10.29.5	19
30.20.7	14

Plato
Laws
6:764B	63
871b	14
931b–c	14

Pliny
Natural History
28.10–21	14

Plutarch
Crassus
16	14

Polybius
Histories
31.9	62

Seneca
Epistulae Morales
94.53	14

Strabo
5.4.7	65

Tacitus
2.69	14
5.4.3	88

Virgil
Aeneid
4.607–29	14
1412.845	19

INDEX OF AUTHORS

Abel, F. M. 52
Arenhoevel, D. 53
Attridge, H. 52

Bailey, D. P. 154
Baumeister, T. 140, 141
Baumgarten, J. M. 124
Betz, H. D. 44, 45, 103, 108, 117
Betz, O. 41
Bickermann, E. 59
Bird, M. F. 101, 113, 121
Blank, J. 46
Boer, M. C. de 46, 112, 127, 159, 165
Bolyki, J. 66
Bowersock, G. W. 71
Breytenbach, C. 140
Brondos, D. A. 4, 162, 163
Brown, W. H. 144
Bruce, F. F. 5
Bunge, J. G. 52, 53, 59

Campbell, D. A. 151
Chapman, D. W. 123, 124
Ciampa, R. E. 100
Cohen, S. D. 61
Collins, J. J. 61, 65, 102
Cook, J. G. 124
Cosgrove, C. H. 127
Cummins, S. A. 47, 48, 169, 185, 191

Dahl, N. 6
Daly, R. J. 6
Das, A. A. 6, 101, 108, 117, 118, 129
Davis, B. S. 5, 13–19, 20, 120
deSilva, D. A. 84, 86, 88, 91, 117, 152, 154, 155
Donaldson, T. L. 5, 118
Doran, R. 53, 58–60, 62–64, 66–69, 71, 74, 75
Downing, J. 142
Duncan, G. S. 31
Dunn, J. D. G. 31, 46, 47, 102, 115, 118
Dunne, J. A. 122, 180

Ego, B. 62

Finlan, S. 5, 25, 154, 163, 164, 166
Fitzmyer, J. A. 124
Fung, R. Y. K. 5

Gager, J. G. 15
Gathercole, S. J. 102
Gnilka, J. 142
Goldstein, J. A. 53, 59, 142
Grimm, C. L. W. 52
Gruen, E. S. 62

Habicht, C. 53, 57, 59, 69, 71
Hamerton-Kelly, R. B. 6
Hanson, A. T. 6
Hardin, J. K. 21
Harmon, M. S. 3, 4, 41–3
Hays, R. B. 1, 46, 110, 113
Hengel, M. 68, 91, 123
Henten, J. W. van 59, 63, 64, 69–73, 80, 84, 85, 96, 133, 140–4, 147, 152, 157
Henze, M. 134, 135
Himmelfarb, M. 57, 64, 65, 71
Howard, G. 112

Janssen, L. H. 18
Jonge, M. de 142, 155

Kahl, B. 21–4
Keim, P. A. 36
Kellermann, U. 71, 142–4
Kim, S. 31
Klauck, H.-J. 152
Kraus, W. 139, 152
Kuhn, H. W. 123
Kuhrt, A. 65

Lagrange, M.-J. 12
Lane, E. 18
Lee, S. M. 24, 25, 109
Lightfoot, J. B. 5
Lincicum, D. 33–5, 57, 107

Lindars, B. 44
Lohse, E. 48, 142
Longenecker, B. W. 101
Longenecker, R. N. 5, 46

Martyn, J. L. 5, 6, 46, 113, 118, 162
Matera, F. J. 112
McLean, B. H. 1, 5, 7–12, 121, 126
Merklein, H. 36
Momigliano, A. 52, 59
Moo, D. J. 102, 103, 113, 117, 159
Morgan, W. 36
Morkholm, O. 64
Morland, K. A. 5, 36–41, 108, 119

Nickelsburg, G. W. E. 52, 60
Niese, B. 58, 59, 71
Novenson, M. V. 117

O'Brien, K. S. 123–25
O'Hagan, A. P. 140, 141
Oepke, A. 999

Pate, C. M. 25, 26, 119
Porter, S. E. 141

Räisänen, H. 32
Rajak, T. 133, 151
Redditt, P. L. 87
Richardson, P. 118
Riches, J. 5
Richnow, W. 58
Robertson, A. T. 144
Roo, J. C. R. 113

Sanders, E. P. 101, 102
Sanders, J. A. 31
Schams, C. 70
Schreiner, T. R. 102
Schuppe, E. 66
Schwartz, D. R. 36, 58, 59, 62–65, 76, 130, 142, 144, 146
Schweitzer, A. 10

Schwemer, A. M. 123
Scott, J. M. 34, 107
Scurlock, J. 68
Sechrest, L. L. 120
Seeley, D. 6, 7, 142, 144
Sherwin-White, S. M. 65
Sievers, J. 52
Silva, M. 99, 107
Simkovich, M. Z. 75
Smyth, H. W. 144
Sprinkle, P. M. 113–16
Stanley, C. D. 118
Stökl Ben Ezra, D. 155
Stuiber, K. 18
Surkau, H. W. 143

Tcherikover, V. 65
Thielman, F. 109
Tomlin, S. O. 15
Trafton, J. 87

VanderKam, J. C. 89
Versnel, H. S. 12, 15, 16, 18

Wakefield, A. H. 5, 109, 122
Waters, G. P. 26, 27, 41
Watson, F. 27, 28, 129
Westerholm, S. 32
Wet, C. L. de 62
Wilcox, M. 6
Wilhelm, A. 68
Williams, D. S. 53, 58, 60
Williams, J. J. 85, 106, 133, 134, 138, 147, 150
Williams, S. K. 142–4, 152
Wilson, T. A. 108
Winkler, K. 18
Witherington, B. 5, 118
Wolff, H. W. 63
Wright, N. T. 1, 29–33, 102, 107, 118, 129, 156, 159

Young, N. H. 1, 109